BURLINGAME PUBLIC
LIBRARY
480 PRIMROSE ROAD
BURLINGAME, CA 94010

D0992254

REDEEMING DEMOCRACY
IN AMERICA

AMERICAN POLITICAL THOUGHT
Wilson Carey McWilliams and Lance Banning
Founding Editors

REDEEMING DEMOCRACY IN AMERICA

Wilson Carey McWilliams

Edited with an introduction by
Patrick J. Deneen and Susan J. McWilliams

University Press of Kansas

320.973
M258r

© 2011 by the University Press of Kansas
All rights reserved

Published by the University Press of Kansas (Lawrence, Kansas 66045),
which was organized by the Kansas Board of Regents and is operated
and funded by Emporia State University, Fort Hays State University,
Kansas State University, Pittsburg State University, the University of
Kansas, and Wichita State University

Library of Congress Cataloging-in-Publication Data
McWilliams, Wilson C.
Redeeming democracy in America / Wilson Carey McWilliams ;
edited, with an introduction, by Patrick J. Deneen and Susan J. McWilliams.
p. cm. — (American political thought)
Includes bibliographical references and index.
ISBN 978-0-7006-1785-2 (cloth : alk. paper)
1. Democracy—United States. 2. Political participation—United States.
3. United States—Politics and government—Philosophy. I. Deneen, Patrick J., 1964–
II. McWilliams, Susan Jane, 1977– III. Title.
JK1764.M395 2011
320′973—dc22
2011002811
British Library Cataloguing-in-Publication Data is available.

Printed in the United States of America
10 9 8 7 6 5 4 3 2 1

The paper used in this publication is recycled and contains
30 percent postconsumer waste. It is acid free and meets the minimum
requirements of the American National Standard for Permanence of
Paper for Printed Library Materials Z39.48-1992.

CONTENTS

ACKNOWLEDGMENTS

Throughout his work, Wilson Carey McWilliams returned again and again to the fact of our mutual insufficiency and thus the inescapable reality that we are associational creatures who require others of our kind to live and certainly to flourish. In keeping with that truth, we have depended on numerous people to compile this volume of Carey's writing, and we offer them our heartfelt thanks.

Considerable thanks are owed to several colleagues at Rutgers University who began the process of indexing Carey's considerable writings shortly after his death. Carey's longtime friend, Dennis Bathory, with the assistance of Alina Vamanu, photocopied stacks of Carey's publications and assiduously indexed what they found. Their great efforts served as the basis of this volume's bibliography.

Sean Beienburg, under the auspices of a Mellon Post-baccalaureate Fellowship awarded him by Pomona College, tracked down and transcribed many of the essays that appear in this volume (and many that did not make its final cut). He was both a meticulous copy editor and a thoughtful participant in conversations about how to organize this book. At Georgetown University, Rachel Blum Spencer completed the Herculean task of tracking down the permissions necessary to reprint the essays that are collected here. Such is not the easiest task in the best of situations, but this was not the best of situations; many of the rights for these essays proved especially hard to find, and Rachel is to be credited for the months of good humor and patience this job required.

We also offer our deepest thanks to Fred Woodward, Susan Schott, and the rest of the staff at the University Press of Kansas. Carey was a longtime friend to both Fred in particular and this press in general, serving with the historian Lance Banning as the founding coeditors of its renowned series of books in American political thought. We have no doubt that he would have been both deeply pleased and honored that a collection of his own essays on American political thought was to be published by Fred and would appear in the University Press of Kansas catalog.

Russell Muirhead and Harvey Mansfield offered excellent and incisive suggestions for improving the original book manuscript. We thank them both for their counsel and for their early enthusiasm about this project.

We also thank Nancy Riley McWilliams, Carey's wife of thirty-seven years, for supporting the idea of this collection from the beginning.

Finally, and most deeply, we offer our thanks to Wilson Carey McWilliams. Our gratitude for his presence in our lives as a friend, father, teacher, and fellow citizen can never be exhausted. Thinking of Carey, we are always reminded of what might be William Penn's most memorable lines:

They that love beyond the World, cannot be separated by it.
Death cannot kill, what never dies.
Nor can Spirits ever be divided that love and live in the same Divine
    Principle; the root and record of their Friendship.
If Absence be not death, neither is theirs.
Death is but Crossing the World, as Friends do the seas; They live in
    one another still.
For they must needs be present, that love and live in that which is
    Omnipresent.
In this Divine Glass, they see Face to Face; and their Converse is Free,
    as well as Pure.
This is the Comfort of Friends, that though they may be said to Die,
    yet their Friendship and Society are, in the best Sense, ever present,
    because Immortal.

(Penn, *Fruits of Solitude*)

Introduction

by Patrick J. Deneen and
Susan J. McWilliams

WILSON CAREY MCWILLIAMS WAS A CHILD of the West—born on September 2, 1933, in Santa Monica, California—who grew up surrounded by the cowboy fantasies of individual liberation and the futuristic dreams of technological progress for which that region of the country is still known. At the same time, he grew up hearing the refrains of what he would call the older, alternative American political tradition. As he mentions in chapter 9, his father, the historian and journalist Carey McWilliams, was a great moralist known for his uncompromising and "radical" stands, stands often taken on behalf of the connection between self-governance and human dignity. And his mother, Dorothy Hedrick McWilliams, was an educator from a large clan of educators who stressed the importance of association, family, and religion (especially in its Presbyterian form).

McWilliams attended the University of California at Berkeley both as an undergraduate and a graduate student, receiving his B.A. in 1955 and his Ph.D. several years later. At Berkeley, McWilliams was active in student politics, involved particularly in the civil rights movement and calls for more inclusive government at the university. He also spent much of this time as a part of the armed forces, first as a student in the Reserve Officers' Training Corps (ROTC) program and then as an enlisted member of the U.S. Army, in the Eleventh Airborne Division. Of course, that combination of commitments—left-wing politics and military service—would come to seem quite unusual to Americans in subsequent decades. But for McWilliams, there was no inherent contradiction between the two; at the most basic level, he viewed his activism and his military service merely as variant forms of fulfilling public duties and civic obligations. For that reason, even though he was often identified as one of the first voices of the New Left, he would become uncomfortable with the student politics of the 1960s and 1970s, which moved away from the language of civic responsibility and became subsumed in talk of individual liberation and freedom from government at large. Such a vision could never square with McWilliams's understanding, spelled out in chapter 7, of freedom as a discipline, inseparable from the fulfillment of civic obligations.

He taught at Oberlin College for a number of years before moving to the East Coast, where he taught briefly at Brooklyn College before going to Rutgers University. McWilliams spent the last thirty-five years of his career at Rutgers, where he published most of the work for which he would become known. His first book, *The Idea of Fraternity in America* (which won the National Historical Society prize in 1974), explored the "alternative tradition" of American political thought throughout the nation's history, notably in its literary figures. He also wrote an astonishing number of essays, many of which developed and refined his central theses about the "two voices" of the American political inheritance—that official voice of its liberal founding and the more informal but vital voice that was especially the inheritance of an older, even ancient pedigree. The most important and representative of those essays—especially about his beloved if imperfect America—are collected in this volume.

Carey—as most friends called him—was fond of telling stories about his great-aunt Willie and her voting habits. Great-aunt Willie was a woman of formidable religious devotion, an instructor at the Bible Institute of Los Angeles who was fond of invoking Isaiah 53, with its story of the suffering servant, in everyday conversation. In accordance with the dictates of her piety, Great-aunt Willie wanted her vote to represent God's wishes. She told people she wanted God himself to direct her hand at the voting booth. In order to help make that happen, she avoided all talk about candidates and issues before election day, to ensure that nothing would interfere with the divine vibrations that God might send to communicate his preferences to her. And God surely did speak to Great-aunt Willie, McWilliams would reflect, "because she always voted the straight Democratic ticket!"

That story, a version of which appears in chapter 11 of this volume, was a staple of McWilliams's repertoire, hinting at many of the central "ambiguities and ironies" that he brings to the fore in his teachings about American politics. They are the ambiguities and ironies that come to light in this volume, which we will briefly outline here.

For one thing, Great-aunt Willie's behavior captures some of what McWilliams calls, also in chapter 11, the "sanctity around the shrouded voting booth" and the habits of veneration that have always been present in American political life. The American political inheritance is significantly religious in its nature, born in biblical language and Puritan understandings. The Bible is an "indispensable key to our language, meanings, and thought," as McWilliams writes in chapter 2, so that the study of American politics requires at least some degree of familiarity with biblical text and attention to the place of religion in American political life. This means more

than approaching religion as a historical artifact or curiosity; it means seeing the critical role that religion plays in the American experiment. In particular, McWilliams follows Alexis de Tocqueville's teaching that "the spirit
of religion" has long been the counterweight to the national "spirit of liberty," the communal and sacred nature of the former tempering the excesses
of the latter, with its tendency to tempt us into lives that are dominated by
private concerns and that are inattentive to the common good. Great-aunt
Willie was motivated, in no small measure, by that kind of spirit—what
McWilliams often calls the critical "second voice" of American politics.
Her behavior reflects an ancient belief in the virtue of government by soul,
as opposed to government by the body and its more immediate demands.
Moreover, it encapsulates the kind of reverence that McWilliams thinks we
all owe politics itself. As he often told his students, citizenship rests on what
is most mysterious about us, the peculiar human nature that allows us to
see outside and judge the laws even as we stand within them. We should
regard merely our *capacity* for citizenship with a kind of reverence and awe,
sensing the whole that embraces us as parts. Our Declaration of Independence rests on what Robert Frost rightly called a "mystery," the radical
moral proposition that human equality is "self-evident."

And yet, as McWilliams knew, we latter-day Americans are likely to look
upon Great-aunt Willie's method of electoral information-gathering as naive or misguided. More and more, Americans are raised with the voice of
only one parent in their ears, reared in the language of liberalism, with its
roots in the modern social contract tradition of Thomas Hobbes and John
Locke. The "spirit of liberty" drowns out the "spirit of religion" a little
more every day. This pattern dates back to the Federalists' victory at the
founding, a victory that privileged the atomizing logic of liberalism over
more ancient emphases on the mutual dependence and obligations of human beings. Americans now live in a nation in which increasingly "extreme
individualisms" have become not only evident but mainstream, so much
so that our conventional political distinctions between "conservative" and
"liberal," as McWilliams discusses in chapter 9, mask the prevailing liberal
strains that dominate the entire political spectrum. They also mask the anguished tensions within both so-called conservative and liberal thought, as
Americans across the board struggle to articulate those convictions—such
as an opposition to abortion or a commitment to progressive taxation—
that are not easily expressed within the limits of a liberal lexicon.

That kind of anguish only points toward a deeper anguish in American
culture. The terrible paradox of the American political tradition is that, for
all its emphasis on individual rights and liberation, its means of "liberating"

individuals ultimately rob individuals of their dignity. The large scale of American life teaches Americans that they do not matter, not as voters or workers or members of a public. High rates of mobility make it difficult for Americans to form long-term attachments, and they weaken those private institutions—such as families, churches, and local communities—that not only offer informal avenues for civic association but also, as McWilliams says in chapter 10, teach "an older creed which speaks more easily of the public as a whole, appealing to patriotism, duty, and the common good." For McWilliams, President George W. Bush's advice to Americans in the wake of the September 11, 2001, terrorist attacks—to "get on with your lives, hug your kids, and go to the mall"—bespeaks a nation in which citizenship and citizens are treated as dispensable. Even in moments of widespread patriotic desire, Americans learn that they are not needed as citizens, not needed for public service, but needed only as private individuals and consumers. In other words, as McWilliams puts it in the first chapter of this volume, even though Americans often talk as if the country has grown "more democratic" over time, the truth is the opposite.

For significant periods of American history, McWilliams writes, political parties have been the one more or less formal mechanism working against this trend. Parties offer the opportunity for Americans to have a civic identity and "[urge] their followers to set aside lesser differences in order to defeat the greater enemy," as McWilliams says in chapter 10. And often, they have been instrumental in helping to create or solidify local communities. McWilliams—an avowed and proud partisan, as the punch line to the story of Great-aunt Willie suggests—worries that the weakening of party organizations, particularly at the local and regional levels, is another crack in the levee that weakens the democratic character of the United States and enervates what he calls, in chapter 12, the "national soul."

With their origins in private associations and affiliations, parties embody a substantial irony of American politics: our public institutions speak in the language of private right whereas our private associations have been more inclined to speak in the language of public connection and duty. Moreover, political parties point to the deeper, seemingly paradoxical truth that the United States has been a nation at its singular best when it has been most double-voiced: animated by *both* the "spirit of liberty" and the "spirit of religion" and the broader teachings that each term represents. The most beautiful harmonies in the American song emerge when the dissonance is strongest. Thus, McWilliams might say, particularly given the current state of things, the American project stands its truest chance of moving forward by moving, to some degree, back.

As befits a person who put so much emphasis on the ambiguities and ironies in American politics and who sought to see the nation in terms of its whole rather than its parts, McWilliams resisted the many attempts that were made to place him in limited or specific "schools" of American political thought. He was sometimes called a "communitarian"—and indeed, late in his life, he edited a volume celebrating the twenty-fifth anniversary of the publication of Amitai Etzioni's *Active Society*—and he was sometimes called a "Straussian"—and indeed, he spoke and wrote admiringly of Leo Strauss's work. But McWilliams never referred to himself in terms of either of those labels or others, nor did he restrict his professional associations to a single, self-identified group of people. The scholars he most admired came from both the political Left (such as his teachers Norman Jacobson, John Schaar, and Sheldon Wolin) and the Right (such as Allan Bloom and Harvey Mansfield), and not a few were finally unclassifiable (such as Christopher Lasch). And though he did maintain a lifelong allegiance to the Democratic Party, he was not afraid to criticize the party from within, especially on those matters in which he thought his fellow partisans had lost their sense of the whole.

By all who knew him, McWilliams—who died suddenly on March 29, 2005—was known for his generous sense of humor. He told stories, among them the story of Great-aunt Willie, with a grand comic flair, and he rarely spoke or wrote without including a few well-placed jokes. This inclination, perhaps more than any explicitly "political" attachment, reveals the spirit that lies at the heart of his outlook on American politics. Comedy turns on the exposure of our human pretensions and the fact of our human incompletion. The comic mocks the pretense of individual mastery, which is precisely the kind of pretense that, in McWilliams's telling, runs wild in the contemporary American regime. Comedy thus reveals what, in chapter 6, McWilliams calls our "pathetic" nature. That is, in pointing to our shared incompletion, the comic's art subtly reminds us that we are each part of a whole, bound to each other in soul as well as body. In doing so, comedy speaks in America's "second voice" and returns us to the ancient teachings that our public life increasingly neglects.

To be sure, comedy and tragedy are not far removed, and it is possible to read McWilliams's analysis of American political life as a tragic story, told through a veil of tears. In large measure, his story of the American republic reads as a story of decline. But McWilliams is never without hope; "while the practical problem of revitalizing citizenship is enormous," he writes, "it is challenging rather than insuperable." In America, the second voice of our tradition may be soft, but it has not been silenced. Its truths still find ways to be heard: sometimes in our history, sometimes in our churches and families and schools, sometimes in our literature. And it is the voice—the voice in which McWilliams, perhaps better than any other American political thinker, speaks—that resounds through these essays, loud and clear.

McWilliams was among the twentieth century's most profound and learned students of the American political tradition. This is true in spite of the fact that he produced only one sustained work on the American tradition at the beginning of his career. Yet over the course of his career, he wrote a vast quantity of essays, reviews, and articles on nearly every aspect of the American tradition, much of which escaped the attention of mainstream political scientists and much of which was undiscovered even by his friends and admirers. Without the publication of this volume, just how incisive an interpreter of American political thought he proved to be throughout his long career may have remained unknown to many, including those who knew him as well as members of a new generation who never encountered him in person. This volume—published five years after his death—will solidify his reputation and will generate a hunger for more among readers who may wonder how such gems of scholarship and insight escaped the notice of so many. For those we suspect will crave more McWilliams—not only for the depth of his insights but also for the sheer pleasure of his prose—a bibliography of his extensive work is included at the end of this volume.

PART I
American Foundations

1

Democracy and the Citizen: Community, Dignity, and the Crisis of Contemporary Politics in America

MOST AMERICANS WOULD AGREE that the Constitution has become more democratic with time.[1] We know the evidence for this view. The vote has been extended to racial minorities, women, and eighteen-year-olds. We elect senators directly, property qualifications have virtually disappeared, the poll tax is unconstitutional, and all of us are entitled to equal protection of the laws. As these examples suggest, one person one vote is the measure by which most Americans assess degrees of democracy. Most of us, in other words, see voting by majority rule as the defining characteristic of a democratic regime.

This view is correct as far as it goes, but it rests on a fragmentary idea of democracy. I rely on an older, more comprehensive understanding that makes citizenship, rather than voting, the defining quality of democracy.[2] Common sense tells us that speaking and listening precede voting and give it form. Democracy is inseparable from democratic ways of framing and arguing for political choices. Almost all agree, for example, that elections in so-called people's democracies are shams. At a deeper level, moreover, democracy depends on those things that affect our ability to speak, hear, or be silent. In this sense, I will argue that democracy requires community, civic dignity, and religion. Similarly, I will argue that in certain important

Originally published as "Democracy and the Citizen: Community, Dignity, and the Crisis of Contemporary Politics in America," in *How Democratic Is the Constitution?* ed. Robert A. Goldwin and William A. Schambra (Washington, D.C.: AEI Books, 1980), 79–101. Reprinted with the permission of the American Enterprise Institute for Public Policy Research, Washington, D.C. Part of a book series devoted to the Constitution, *How Democratic Is the Constitution?* featured essays by a number of scholars, several of whom are mentioned by McWilliams in the course of his essay. This article is considered by many of McWilliams's admirers to be among his best—arguably the most forceful, mature, and focused statement of his view of the American founding and the flawed regime it established.

9

respects, the Constitution, contrary to the prevailing view, was more democratic in the past than it is today, especially in providing greater dignity for
the citizen and greater protection against "tyranny of the majority."

My argument, obviously, extends beyond what established opinion understands by democracy, especially since my notion of democracy includes
things not considered "political" by most Americans. In order to combat
such deeply entrenched ways of thinking, I will have to turn to the foundations of our political thought.

The Ancient Idea of Democracy

To ancient political science, citizenship came first in the ordering of democracies. Aristotle established the first principle of democracy as political liberty, "ruling and being ruled" in turn, sharing the responsibilities of rule as
well as the duty to obey.[3] In a democratic regime, each citizen must be able
to share in defining the public's alternatives and have "an equal say in what
is chosen and for what end."[4] Since the equality of all citizens is a democratic tenet, democracies make decisions according to number, but Aristotle
took care to show that majority rule is derived from the principle of equal
citizenship and shared rule.

Majority rule is, after all, a difficult precept. Why should a minority accept the rule of a majority it considers wrongheaded? According to John
Locke, the authority of the majority rests on a combination of force and
consent.

> It is necessary that the body should move that way whither the greater
> force carries it, which is the consent of the majority, or else it is impos-
> sible it should act or continue one body, one community, which the
> consent of every individual that united into it agreed that it should.[5]

At first blush, Locke's case for majority rule rests on the minority's agreement to form a political community, but that consent as readily obliges the
minority to accept *any* system of rule in preference to political dissolution
or civil war. The majority's specific title derives from its "greater force"—
implicitly, the impossibility, under natural conditions, of coercing the many
and the ease of coercing the few. Locke, however, limited his argument to
the state of nature and conditions akin to it. In civil society, as Locke knew
well, majorities cannot be equated with greater force; a minority may easily
comprise citizens who are wealthier and more skilled in military matters.[6]

If the wealthy and strong accept the rule of the poor and unskilled, it cannot be because they are forced. It is often observed that the minority must believe that the majority will respect its "rights," ensuring its essential minimum without which it would fight. Certainly, a minority must have such confidence, but is that trust *enough*? Why would a strong minority settle for so little when force might give it so much more? The strong minority bends to majority rule only when it accepts the principle—the political equality of all citizens—from which that rule derives. I can believe that all citizens have an equal share of justice without believing that the majority is always right. You and I can be equal and ignorant when it comes to astrophysics, yet I can insist that my opinion is correct no matter how many equally ignorant people share yours.

Similarly, a strong majority refrains from oppressing the minority because it too accepts the principle of equal citizenship and political participation. Members of the minority, as equals, must be allowed their say. (In fact, to give the minority equal time, as we do, gives it more than an equal share, since fewer citizens are allowed the same time.) As Delba Winthrop comments, a democrat who takes equal political liberty seriously "does not intend a tyranny of the majority."[7]

Both the majority and the minority must regard the principle of civic equality and equal participation more strongly than their partisan creeds and their private interests. In a democracy, citizenship rules partisanship and public principles govern private interests. Citizens of all factions must, to that extent, prefer the good of the whole to that of the part.

Civic virtue is reemphasized by the consequences of political liberty. Aristotle observed that the democratic stress on political liberty—freedom to participate in public life as part of the whole—suggests a second form, individual liberty—"living as one likes" as though one *were* a whole. Democrats "say," Aristotle commented, that liberty must involve "living as you like" because slaves do not live as they like.[8] This argument by democrats is evidently fallacious: "That which is not slave" is not an adequate definition of "a free person." A child who is not a slave, for example, has not come into "man's estate." This is, however, the sort of error that citizens unfamiliar with philosophy might be expected to make.

There is a second error in the democratic argument. In ordinary terms, no one lives as he "likes." The slave is not defined by living under a rule but by having no say about that rule. Voicelessness, not restraint, is the mark of a slave. This second mistake is possible only because the good citizen, in being ruled, feels he is *doing* as he likes. So he may be. The public-spirited citizen, ruling, acts for the common good, and being ruled is liberating in part since it allows a greater attention to one's own good. This is especially true if my rulers are no worse than I am, and I expect them to be guided by common principles.[9] Aristotle's argument suggests that patriotic and law-abiding but unphilosophic citizens come to believe that freedom is "living as one likes," an error that does little damage so far as they are concerned. Aristotle pointed out, however, that this idea leads to the claim of freedom from any government or, indeed, from any restraint at all. The children of public-spirited citizens, taught the mistaken "second principle" of democracy, become private-regarding individualists.[10] They may accept democracy as a second-best substitute (especially since democracy does not ask us to be ruled by anyone in particular), but it will be only that. "In this way," Aristotle observed guardedly, the second principle "contributes" to a "system of liberty based on equality."[11] Preferring to be free from all rule, the individualist supports democracy from weakness and lack of spirit, but he is not a democrat. His attitudes will be partisan or even more narrowly concerned with his own interests. If he obtains office, he will not subordinate his private will or interest to the good of the community, since to do so, in his eyes, would be slavish. Democracy can survive a few such citizens but not many. If they become predominant, majority rule will become tyrannical, with civil conflict the least danger facing the regime. The second principle, individual liberty, must be kept subordinate to the democratic first principle, political liberty and equal citizenship, if democracy is to stave off decay.

Whatever democrats "say," democracy does not promise "living as one likes." Its aim is self-rule. Autonomy is possible for human beings only as parts of wholes, in which our "partiality" and the things to which we are "partial" are recognized as secondary, though important. In essential ways, politics frees us. In the world of the tribe, most citizens do similar work; in the city, we work at what we do best. In the clan, custom and blood-law regulate life. As a child, I am hopelessly dependent, and I value the rules of custom and kinship, which tell my parents that they must care for me. As I approach adulthood, however, this choiceless automation comes to seem impersonal, if not oppressive. The polis allows me to find friends who choose me (as I choose them) because they like me, not my genealogy.[12] In this sense, the polis is naturally "prior" to the individual because the human being as an end presumes the polis as a means.[13]

The excellent or complete human being is the end for which the city exists; for him, if for anyone, it might be said that freedom is "doing as one likes." Such a human being, however, would recognize his debt to the city and know that his freedom involves obligations. Moreover, the fully self-ruled men realize that the thing they rule, the self, is not something they make. My nature sets the limits to my rule. If I command myself to be young forever, my orders are hostile to self-rule because they seek to subject the self that I am to another, imagined self. To be self-ruled, I must be ruled by my nature as a human being and by the nature of which humanity is a part. In that higher sense, self-rule does imply "doing as one likes," for it requires that I do what I truly like, according to nature, or, to put it another way, I must do what is "liked" by nature, "the one" of which I am only a part.[14]

Self-rule requires, then, that I be free to do what is according to nature. No barrier in my environment or in me must stand in the way. To help me toward self-rule, democracy must provide me with an environment that has resources enough to permit me to live in a fully human way. It must also educate me so that my soul will be free to follow nature. For its own health, democracy must try to teach me that human freedom is possible only when I act as a part of a whole and that my good, the good of a part, depends on that of the whole.

This lesson can never be learned perfectly. My body reminds me constantly that I am separate; my senses are my own and no one else's. The body and the senses take us beyond mere survival and pleasure; as we know, powerful feelings and passions may move us to sacrifice our lives and liberties. My body and my senses move me to such sacrifice only on behalf of things they take to be my own. The perimeter of the senses is narrow and makes me the center of the world.

When governments and law urge me to support the common good, they may find an ally in my reason or my soul, but they must expect resistance from my body and senses conducted in the name of my dignity. If, for example, reason assures me that government has consulted people like me in making policy, my emotions will answer that it has not consulted *me*.[15] Civic virtue requires that we govern some of our strongest feelings and desires. In that sense, as Aristotle argued, to rule free men—and hence, to be a citizen of a democracy—one must first learn how to be ruled.[16]

If government is radically at odds with my senses, my dignity, and my private interests, however, I will feel it as a kind of tyranny. I will resist it, retreating into private refuges if it is strong and defying it if it is weak. I may be compelled to obey, but I will not learn to be ruled.

Classical political philosophy argued in favor of the small state in part because the polis was within the periphery of the senses, reducing the distance and the conflict between public good and private interest. In a small community, if my taxes help to build a reservoir, I will be drinking the water it provides, and my sense will testify to the benefits of civic duty. In a large state, by contrast, any benefit I derive from a dam in Idaho is indirect, as distant from my senses as Idaho itself.[17]

Similarly, the small state lets me know my fellow citizens and my rulers.[18] More important, they know *me*. This is especially true in stable communities, for people I have known only a short time are people I know only superficially. Moreover, if people move frequently, I will not feel confident that we share a common destiny or a common good. Rather, I am likely to suspect that they may desert me in a time of trouble; I may feel compelled to protect myself by deserting them first. The common good reigns weakly in a hobo jungle or a trailer park. Small and relatively stable communities, by contrast, encourage confidence and fidelity.

Finally, the small state is suited to democracy. In a small state, it is possible for me to have my say. In a large state, only a few can be heard beyond private circles. Small communities give a larger proportion of citizens the chance not only to speak but to speak adequately. Too, relations of trust encourage speech; we need not be silenced for fear of "giving offense" or by the suspicion that our community is too fragile to bear disagreement. Of course, a much larger percentage of the citizens of a small community can hold office. To put it another way, in the small state I matter and my choices are visibly important. A small state comports with my dignity.[19] In this respect, it is less important that I speak or hold office than that I be able to do so. If I listen or obey, it then must be presumed that I chose to do so. Silence and law-abidingness are dignified forms of conduct. The large state, however, tends to rob obedience and silence of their dignity, making them matters of necessity. In modern America, for example, we do not really respect the respectable.

The small state is the natural home of democracy. It makes possible "ruling and being ruled in turn," and it helps to strengthen public spirit. The small state, however, demands that we restrain our ambitions for power and for wealth. Similarly, democracy presumes some restraint on the extremes of wealth and poverty. Democracy does not require economic equality, but it does require a sense of commonality and equal dignity. The sense of the common good is weakened where the impoverishment of some does not affect, or even contribute to, the wealth of others. The wealthy are tempted to believe that they do not need the many and to behave with arrogance; the poor become desperate if they see their poverty as a badge of indignity and shame.[20] The desire for wealth must be restrained in all classes. Economic gain must be subordinated to stability and civility in democratic life.

In summary, democracy claims to be a regime characterized by liberty, but it depends on restraint. It requires citizens who are willing to sacrifice for the common good and, correspondingly, a restraint of the passions. Even those concepts that educate the passions gently, like the small state and relative economic equality, require restraint on private desires. Democracy depends on some knowledge of the limits of personal liberty and human nature. It hopes that citizens will see the law and nature not as confining prisons in which the self is trapped but as boundaries that delineate the self. Put another way, democracy aims at the governance of body by soul. That aim is audacious. In the best of us, the body's obedience is imperfect; democracy is not a government by the best. Citizens cannot be assumed to have the faith of saints or the reason of philosophers. Democracies rely on true opinion, rather than knowledge, and on piety, rather than revelation. These lesser excellences, nevertheless, depend on the greater. Ordinary citizens need the example of the best human beings in order to imitate, as part of the exacting regimen of civic education, the reverence for law and nature that, in the best, emanates from the freedom of spirit.

The Framers' Rejection of the Ancients

Ideas like these, especially as glossed by Christian theologians, were a major part of the cultural inheritance of Americans at the birth of the Republic. Custom and controversy made many such teachings familiar to Americans who had little notion of their origins. Those who rejected classical political philosophy as a whole clung to one part or another. The framers, however, were self-conscious modern men who rejected the tradition. They felt themselves the vanguard of an intellectual revolution as well as political founders. The struggle over the form and spirit of the Constitution was, in many ways, a battle between the old science of politics and the new.

Although the framers appealed to "republican" ideals, they meant "republic" in a special, modern sense. Their real concern was liberty, not republican government, and they set as the "first object of government" the protection of the "diversity in the faculties of men." Their aim was private rather than public freedom; they elevated Aristotle's second principle to the first place in political life.[21]

Human beings, in the framers' creed, are by nature free, morally independent without obligations to nature or to their fellows. For the framers, the separateness of the body—if not the body itself—was the defining fact of human nature (hence the tendency, in ordinary speech, to separate "nature" and "nurture," equating natural conduct with what springs spontaneously from the body). By nature, our desires are free, and we seek to do as we like. Above all, we desire self-preservation, a "great principle" worthy to be ranked with "absolute necessity" and "the transcendent law of nature and of nature's God."[22]

Nature will not let us preserve ourselves. In the end, nature will kill us. The naturally free individuals of the framers' theory find themselves obstructed, at almost every point, by nature and their fellows. By nature, we strive to acquire the power to do as we will and, ultimately, to master nature itself.

By the familiar locutions of social contract theory, people discover that their unaided efforts leave them too exposed to attacks by others and too weak to trouble nature seriously. Reason suggests to the individual that he would do better in combination with others; governments are created "by the consent of the governed," since morally independent beings can be bound only by their consent. If our consent *creates* obligation, then nothing can evaluate our consent: whatever we consent to will be "right."[23] The theory presumes, of course, that we will never truly consent to give up our rights to "life, liberty and the pursuit of happiness"; this only emphasizes that our consent (and hence government) can only be self-limited. As Walter Berns demonstrates, the governed can consent, according to the Declaration of Independence, to regimes other than democracy. Civic education in an established polity does all that it need or should do when it persuades us to consent. Political participation is quite needless if we are persuaded that government protects our private rights and interests; public spirit, in any strict sense of that term, is *undesirable.* Government is always to some degree oppressive, since we give up to it some of the liberty that is ours by natural right. We ought to surrender such liberty grudgingly and watchfully; whatever civic duties our consent entails, we should perform with an eye to our private liberties. The "consent of the governed" does not require democracy, and it discourages citizenship.

For human beings as the framers understood them, the really desirable regime is not democracy but a tyranny in which I am the tyrant, able to command the bodies and resources of others to "live as I like." Failing that, I prefer not to be ruled at all. Tyranny is unlikely and insecure, and anarchy is impractical because of the "inconveniences" of the state of nature, but these prudential objections do not affect the basic argument. Human nature strains against the law, our passions resisting the necessity to which reason gives its consent. "Why has government been instituted at all? Because the passions of men will not conform to the dictates of reason and justice without constraint." In Madison's famous rhetoric, "What is government itself but the greatest of all reflections on human nature? If men were angels, no government would be necessary," and consequently, "in framing a government . . . [y]ou must first enable the government to control the governed."[24]

In controlling the governed, majority rule—"the republican principle"—is invaluable. In the first place, all other things being equal, the majority will possess "greater force" than the minority, as in Locke's argument; its support will provide the power to constrain. Since other things are not equal, as Madison knew, and the majority is likely to be relatively poor and discontented, its consent removes one probable source of disorder.

The consent of the majority, of course, is impermanent. Having given our consent, we regret the constraint it entails, especially since under the government's protection, we forget the dangers that moved us to consent. The Revolutionary War, Madison wrote, encouraged an excessive reliance on the "virtue and intelligence" of the people, since it "repressed the passions most unfriendly to order and concord," producing a patriotism not to be expected in more tranquil times. Periodic elections are needed to renew consent or, at least, to provide the government with the support of a current majority; such elections should not be so frequent as to undermine the public's "veneration" for a regime.[25] The fundamentally unpolitical nature of human beings makes majority rules and periodic elections prudent, though not strictly necessary. Democracy in the modern sense derives from our supposed indisposition to all forms of rule, including democracy. The case for modern democracy rests in part on the undemocratic nature of humankind.

However, majority rule and periodic elections do not oblige the government to "control itself," the second concern in framing free government. In the normal course of events, the majority will be partisan, moved by private motives, and disposed to oppression. "Neither moral nor religious motives can be relied on" to restrain it, and in any case, it is not the business of government to educate the soul. If man has a soul, it is free by nature; legitimate government is obliged to leave it so.[26]

It is no surprise then that the framers rejected the classical case for the small state. Madison was hostile to the "spirit of locality" in general, not only in the states. Small communities afford the individual less power, less mastery, and hence less liberty than do large states. Moreover, the small community lays hold of the affections of the individual and leads him to accept the very restraints on his interest and liberty that are inherent in smallness.[27] The classics urged the small state in part because it might encourage the individual to limit and rule his private passions. Madison rejected such states because he rejected that sort of restraint. Small communities limit opportunities and meddle with the soul. At best, they are outdated associations that once advanced individual interests but now fetter the new science of politics.

All "face-to-face" communities are suspect. In very small districts, Madison warned, representatives are likely to be "unduly attached" to their constituents. The affections are too intense, the bonds of community too strong. "Great and national objects," on one hand, and individual liberty, on the other, are necessarily endangered. In a large assembly, especially if it is "changeable," the individual is not attached *enough*. In the crowd, the individual is too anonymous for a "sensible degree of praise or blame for public measures" to attach to him. His private passions are loosed because he is freed from the consequences of his acts. At the same time, by the face-to-face quality of the assembly, the individual is enabled to discover those who share his ambitions, resentments, and desires. "A common passion or interest will, in almost every case, be felt by a majority of the whole; a communication and concert results from the form of government itself."[28]

In one context, Madison seemed to suggest that the problem results from our unequal capacities for reason.

> In a nation of philosophers . . . [a] reverence for the laws would be sufficiently inculcated by the voice of an enlightened reason. But a nation of philosophers is as little to be expected as the philosophical race of kings wished for by Plato.[29]

In fact, however, a nation of philosophers would make no difference if it were a polis: "Had every Athenian citizen been a Socrates, every Athenian assembly would still have been a mob."[30] This is a striking, even shocking assertion although it follows from the framers' theory. Madison argued that the passions can never be educated, even in the best and wisest human beings; they can only be repressed and controlled. In the assembly, each citizen-Socrates would sense his anonymity. He would no longer fear the shame of visibly pursuing private interests or oppressive designs, and he would join others in carrying these designs into effect. Socrates is not king, "the epitome of a free man who participates in politics for the common good" and a model for democratic citizens, but a craven tyrant who fears being found out.[31]

If this is true of Socrates, it is even more true of the rest of us. There are no citizens in the classical sense of the term, just as there are no kings. There are only tyrants, more or less strong. Liberty requires that we be kept weak. The small state, however, makes us feel strong or at least that we matter. That very virtue, in the framers' eyes, becomes a damning vice.

Madison and Hamilton argued that the control of the majority lies in the "enlargement of the orbit" of republican rule, creating a large state in which a majority must be composed of diverse factions, unlikely to agree about much for long. The number of such factions, however, is no more important than the distance between the bodies of the individuals composing the factions. That distance guarantees that a common sentiment cannot be felt, except in so diffuse a form as to be unimportant. The ideal regime is "dispassionate" even more than "disinterested." Interest, at least, is calculable and easily channeled by institutions and laws. The passions must be "controlled and regulated" by government.[32]

Free government aims to minimize coercion, but the passions can be disciplined without much direct force. Human beings will be fearful enough when they are weak and alone.

> The reason of man, like man himself, is timid and cautious when left alone; and acquires firmness and confidence in proportion to the number with which it is associated.[33]

Individuals in the large state, unable to "communicate and concert" easily, are likely to feel "timid and cautious." The states and local communities, however, are barriers to this salutary isolation. In them, individuals are too intimately associated with others who are close to their affections; citizens are encouraged to be rash and turbulent in relation to the general government, whereas local regimes deprive them of private liberty. Consequently, the federal government must gain access to the individual, breaking the locality's monopoly on his affections and attracting to the central regime "those passions which have the strongest influence upon the human heart."[34] At least somewhat freed from local regimes, the individual will also be more timid, cautious, and alone.

This has a benefit beyond fearful obedience. Since human reason "acquires firmness and confidence in proportion to the number with which it is associated," those opinions shared by the majority of Americans will be held with overwhelming force. There will not be many such opinions—no more, perhaps, than the general principles of the Declaration of Independence— but they will be all but unquestioned. In the large state, weak individuals hesitate to advance eccentric views and adopt with confidence ideas shared by the many. It is a strange result for a theory that began with a concern for the freedom of the soul.

The Anti-Federalists and the Old Science of Politics

However, as Alfred F. Young reminds us, the framers did not have it all their own way.[35] We tend, in fact, to underestimate the strength of Anti-Federalist views, since many who shared Anti-Federalist beliefs and apprehensions joined Jefferson in accepting the Constitution as a working document, hoping to shape it by interpretation, practice, and amendment.[36] The federalism of the Constitution resulted from politics, not from the framers' wishes. Both Madison and Hamilton desired a far more centralized regime than that framed in the Constitution.[37]

Although the Anti-Federalists, as Berns comments, spoke in the language of rights and contracts then current among educated men, their position derived from the older science of politics.[38] The language of individual rights did not really suit the Anti-Federalists. They were far more likely than their antagonists to refer to government and society as "natural." Civic virtue was a central concern of their political argument, and they were zealous to defend true opinion and small states as the foundations of civic education. Centinel scorned governments that were "republican" in form only, insisting that the "reality" required a virtuous people. As Berns observes, Anti-Federalists sometimes supported religious tests and, even more often, legislation to promote public morals. A free people, Melancton Smith argued, is necessarily exposed by its very freedom to a "fickle and inconstant" spirit. Government must be vulnerable to this inconstancy. Free government requires the foundation provided by a stable private order, the "old communities" settled in "time and habit" to which Samuel Bryan appealed. Such communities should be rooted in the people's affections. They require an ordered life and a rough equality, protecting community against the conflicts engendered by luxury, competition, and anxiety. A democracy, George Clinton said in a nice turn of phrase, should be "well-digested."[39]

Only in small states, Richard Henry Lee contended, can the laws possess the "confidence" of the people. Confidence, we should remember, is a much more active and embracing term than "consent." It suggests speaking one's mind, as in "confiding" to another. It also implies that citizens "confide"— give or entrust—themselves to the laws, yielding private interest and opinion to public rule. Such a spirit required, Lee observed, a government within the emotional, sensory range of the individual, one limited like man himself, Agrippa wrote, to a "narrow space."[40]

A federal regime could acquire confidence only if representatives, who make the laws, are able to convey it. In the first place, the citizen must know his representative and be known by him, establishing a tie between the "natural aristocracy" and the "democracy." No "government of strangers" is acceptable.[41] For Madison, it was enough that the representative know the "local circumstances and lesser interests" of the electors. George Mason argued, by contrast, that the representative should "mix with the people, think as they think, feel as they feel, ought to be perfectly amenable to them and thoroughly acquainted with their interest and condition."[42] Mason included Madison's demand for an intellectual knowledge of the "interest and condition" of the people, but he put it last, giving precedence to the requirement of emotional comprehension and personal relationship, considerations Madison put aside.

Moreover, if the representative is to convey confidence, he must represent the minority as well as the majority. For this to be possible, majorities and minorities, like the citizens Aristotle described, must prefer the public good to their partisan interests. The district must be a community, convinced that its likenesses outweigh its differences.

To Madison's objection—that very small districts tie representatives to parochial interests—the Anti-Federalists responded that only such districts can give the representative the authority (confidence) to *sacrifice* private interests. Of course, representatives from small districts may be mean- or private-spirited. Unless the electors are ensured their say, however, they will not consider themselves represented, and resenting the indignity, they will stand on the defensive. In a large district, we may trust our representative to defend the district's interests; we are unlikely to trust his decision to sacrifice them.[43]

Madison's argument illustrates his differences with the Anti-Federalists. The district must be large enough to avoid "undue attachment" but small enough for the representative to know the district's interest. This latter limit, however, is not a strict one. A shrewd representative can master the interests of a large district. Congressmen today, who represent close to a half million people, prove the point. In fact, if a district is large, according to Madison's principles, it should be very large, since in all face-to-face meetings, passion prevails. On the other hand, a "numerous and changeable" body cannot be moved by a sense of the common good.[44] This comment, in relation to the Senate, illuminates Madison's intent. Congressional districts, intended to be large if not especially changeable, are not *meant* to be moved by the common good. The refusal of a minority within such districts to be "represented" merely adds another faction to the multiplicity that protects liberty, and it may help to fragment locality. Madison rejected a system of representation intended to convey confident, public-spirited support for the common good, in favor of representatives who can provide the consent of a "numerous and changeable" multifactional majority.

Madison also maintained that large districts would be more likely to contain "fit characters" than small ones. Since candidates would be less able, in large districts, to practice the "vicious arts" of electioneering, "fit characters" would be more likely to win office. Madison, of course, knew well that demagogy is easier when addressing a large audience than a small one; that is not the sort of "vicious art" he had in mind. He referred to "cabals" that organized (and often bribed) local electorates. Organizing or bribing a large electorate is undeniably more difficult; hence, the "suffrages of the people" would be more "free." As a result, well-known and celebrated persons would be more likely to win election.[45]

This argument, however, illustrates what John Lansing meant when he observed that elections can be only the "form" of freedom.[46] All elections require some organization; the selection of contending candidates and the identification of "serious" contenders in a large field are obvious examples. Large electorates favor those with established advantages—the wealthy, the famous, and urbanites, who "live compact" with "constant connection and intercourse."[47] The Anti-Federalists, on the whole, were partisans of direct election, but, unlike later and less wise enthusiasts, they recognized that mass electorates are to the advantage of *elites.* Martin Van Buren observed thirty-five years later that nonpartisan elections benefit the upper classes and the celebrated and consequently undermine respect for institutions by inspiring belief that elections are a fraud, concealing "real" decisions made elsewhere.[48] To the Anti-Federalists, democratic elections were tied to the local polls, closer to a caucus than to the secret ballot and relatively open to the candidacy of ordinary citizens. The Anti-Federalists retained the idea of a citizen as someone who shares in rule, hence their support for annual elections and rotation in office. All citizens, George Clinton declared, should have the chance to win public office and honor, for the "desire of rendering themselves worthy" of office nurtures patriotism and civic virtue.[49] In this too, the Anti-Federalists defended the older science of politics against the new.

Trained in a rhetoric that exaggerated dangers in order to anticipate them, the Anti-Federalists overstated the immediacy of the threat posed by the Constitution.[50] They were sometimes wrong altogether about specific provisions. In the main, however, they understood the Constitution correctly.

"Consolidation," the Pennsylvania Anti-Federalists observed, "pervades the whole document."[51] The states, close to the people, possessed their confidence and affection and were safe against direct assault. The shrewd reader, however, would discern a certain "studied ambiguity" in the language of the Constitution, made more ominous with all "essential" powers given to the central government.[52] Anti-Federalists were not mollified by reassurances: "It is a mere fallacy, invented by the deceptive powers of Mr. Wilson, that what rights are not given are reserved."[53] In the combination of power and ambiguity, the Anti-Federalists detected a desire to reduce the states, "slowly and imperceptibly," to a "shadow of power," forms without functions.[54] It would be hard, in any event, to argue that the Anti-Federalists did not read the Constitution properly.

Established opinion, especially attachment to states and localities, imposed on the framers. By its influence on politics and political men, the older idea of democracy voiced by the Anti-Federalists profoundly affected the use and interpretation of the Constitution and its powers. In many ways, American political history can be read as a conflict between the institutional design of the Constitution, reflecting the framers' "new science," and public mores, habit, and beliefs. Alexis de Tocqueville gave his opinion that the "manners of the Americans" were the "real cause" of our ability to maintain democratic government.[55] However, George Clinton was correct: "Opinion and manners are mutable," especially given the "progress of commercial society"; in the long run, the government "assimilates the manners and opinions of the community to it."[56] Clinton's observation suggests an amendment to Tocqueville: the manners of the Americans are more important than the laws, but in the end, the laws transform manners in their own image.

Certainly, that is what the framers hoped. Thwarted of his centralizing ambitions, Madison became, with years, more tolerant of the states. He had not changed his aims. He simply became more convinced that indirect means, especially from the power of commerce, would achieve his goal. The railroads, he told George Bancroft, would "dovetail" the states. (Justice Johnson, concurring in *Gibbons v. Ogden,* similarly observed that with the "advancement of society," commerce necessarily comes to include more and more spheres of life.)[57] The new science of politics was too subtle to attempt frontal attacks; the older traditions, lacking the clarity and coherence of the classical science of politics from which they derived, were too easily confused to do more than fight a stubborn delaying action. The older idea of democracy now faces final defeat, and its defenders seem reduced to garbled romanticism. The triumph of the new democracy over the old, however, is a bleak enough prospect to alarm any surviving citizens into wakefulness.

The Framers' Triumph and the Tyranny of the Majority

Fifty years after the ratification of the Constitution, Tocqueville refined and restated the Anti-Federalist case. In large states, Tocqueville argued, democracy was especially exposed to "tyranny of the majority." Equality denies the authority of one individual over another but suggests the authority of the many over the authority of the few. When society is small enough so that the majority may be perceived as *individuals,* equality permits and encourages me to discount it. Consequently, "small nations have therefore ever been the cradle of political liberty." Tocqueville, in fact, seemed to reverse the framers' argument. The instability and turbulence of small states are marks of their freedom, the proof that local tyrannies, however intrusive, can be overthrown. Tocqueville referred to political, not individual, liberty. The small state's limited resources check individual ambition and direct the citizen to the cultivation of the "internal benefit of the community," including a nurturing of civic virtue. Large states are better suited to great projects and the pursuit of power, particularly because, unlike localities, they are rarely governed by custom.[58] Large states, then, may suit private liberty, but large *democracies* are a particular case.

Given the weight of numbers, the idea of equality makes it hard for me, even in spirit, to oppose the majority. The majority becomes overwhelming, impersonal, and imponderable. I cannot perceive it as so many faces, since it has become faceless. In the small state, I may hope to change enough votes by my eloquence or my skill at electioneering to transform a minority into a majority. In large states, such a result is improbable at best. The "tyranny of the majority" was not like the coherent majority factions that Madison feared, nor was it like the tyrannies of the past. It was an "affair of the mind," crushing the spirit as it left the body free. Later in the century, James Bryce referred to the "fatalism of the multitude," contending that most Americans, taking their impotence for granted, regarded prevailing opinions as "facts of nature" to which they could only adapt. In such circumstances, public criticism of dominant ideas would be rare, hesitant, probably ignored, and in the end likely to be forgotten.[59]

Along with this tendency to public conformity, Tocqueville observed, went an inclination to private self-seeking and "individualism." Making the citizen feel insignificant, mass democracy affronts his dignity, losing most of its chance to nurture civic virtue. Public life injures the citizen's self-esteem, and he retreats into private life, especially when established opinion speaks of the right to, and the rightness of, private liberty. As the public sphere grows larger and more powerful, the private sphere shrinks, the individual breaking his ties to his fellows one after another, a "freedom" that "threatens in the end to confine him entirely within the solitude of his own heart."[60]

This combination of public freedom and private weakness, with its attendant consequence, nearly uniform adherence to those ideas supported by large majorities, is precisely what Madison had urged and sought to establish. Seeking to avoid the despotism of a visible majority, the framers had encouraged the tyranny of an invisible one. Freeing the body, they had made it too easy to enslave the soul.

Tocqueville saw several barriers to tyranny of the majority. Religion taught Americans a law beyond the will of the majority and a code of morals at odds with calculations of utility. It commanded love and sacrifice, the moral signs of nobility. Divine monarchy restrained and elevated secular democracy, especially since the loneliest American could seek asylum from the tyranny of the majority at the feet of the king.[61]

Second, local regimes appealed to the citizen's dignity and "engendered and nurtured" his civic spirit. "The public spirit of the Union is . . . nothing more than an abstract of the patriotic zeal of the provinces."[62] Finally, local regimes enabled the citizen to learn the "arts of association" through participation, making him stronger and more confident in relation to national majorities. Public life became a source of dignity rather than humiliation. Without politics, an American "would be robbed of one half of his existence. He would feel an immense void in the life which he was accustomed to lead, and his wretchedness would be unbearable."[63]

Tocqueville did not highly value American political parties, but clearly they belong in his case. Many a Republican is able to defy majority opinions because he can identify them as Democratic heresies. Rooted in local ward and precinct allegiances, traditional parties—by a hierarchy of personal relationships and partisan fraternities—connected the "right opinion" of localities to the national regime. Similarly, parties appealed to private motives (the desire for jobs and honors, loyalty to one's friends, and hatred for one's enemies), hoping to woo them to the support of public principles and honor. Traditional parties were, in crucial ways, the schools for civic education, inculcating the middling sort of civic virtues possible in a vast state.[64]

Today, however, all these institutions are in disarray. Religion is in retreat; the evangelical exceptions to the rule, far from denying the general tendency, proclaim it fervently. Increasingly, states and localities lack the resources needed to address public problems. Ignore the effects of war; commerce alone has devoured the local community and reduced local regimes to near impotence. The Supreme Court conceded long ago that commerce, "the plainest facts of our national life," must take precedence over federalism in defining the constitutional order.[65] The Court's decision was probably prudent, but the ascendancy of economic life over locality implies the supremacy of private motives, pursued in accord with presumed "necessities," over deliberation and choice. That, obviously, is not good news for democracy.

The states and localities have lost more than material power; their influence on our characters and their hold on our affections are rapidly declining. Localities are decreasingly stable (approximately a quarter of the population moves every year); trust is necessarily limited and superficial.[66] More and more, we live in neighborhoods and social circles that are not political bodies combining all or most of the things necessary for the good life but associations formed on the basis of highly specialized similarities of private pursuit and fortune.[67] Too much of what we need and are is left out of such "communities" for us to confide much of ourselves to them. We live increasingly private lives, as Tocqueville warned; instability and weakness erode our capacities for intimacy, life beyond the moment, and mutual dependence. Even the family is embattled, rivaled by the impermanent relationships it is coming to resemble. The "culture of narcissism" bespeaks the fall of the great barriers to tyranny of the majority.[68]

In public and economic life, the citizen is dwarfed by titanic organization and confused by change. Inequalities of wealth and position are only a part of the problem, though such inequalities undoubtedly restrict access to office or to the rostrum. Those social critics who suggest that capitalism and private wealth are the root of all the ills of American democracy are guilty of making our problems appear less severe than they are. Wealth *can* be limited or equalized, although assembling a majority to support such policies would be difficult. Inequalities of organizational power are less tractable. Large-scale organizations are an artifact of the size and complexity of our regime. Any organization large enough to affect the market or the government's policy is almost certain to be so large as to offend the dignity of its members. We can regulate these private regimes but only by increasing *public* bureaucracy and large-scale organization.[69]

The mass media are prototypic of such "private governments." In one sense, the media control who is allowed to address the public and on what terms. Private, often self-selected, leaders in the media chair our public forum, able to set the terms of deliberation.[70] Sponsors, at least in television, have little control over content; a program with a strong following finds a seller's market. *Both* sponsors and media leaders are dominated by their eagerness for programs that score well in the "ratings." Our choice of programs, however, is no democratic decision. When we turn the dial, we do not make a decision that consciously involves *public* standards. (This matters. Not long ago, a majority endorsed the idea of "family time" as public policy while expressing distaste for the programs that filled such slots.) We certainly do not deliberate. The "ratings" aggregate our private choices, and those choices, in turn, tyrannize the media's "men of power." At the same time, a host of specialized journals and radio stations appeals to narrowing private circles. The public sphere expands, the private sphere contracts. Neither speaks the language of citizenship or democracy.

The citizen finds little in public life to elevate his spirit or support his dignity; he finds much that damages both. Political parties, which sought to connect private feelings with public life, are waning along with the communities that were their foundation.[71] Increasingly, the citizen retreats into the "solitude of his own heart," denying the country the allegiance it needs to address looming crises and himself those possibilities that still exist for friendship and freedom.

Democracy has few footholds in modern America. Strengthening democratic life is a difficult, even daunting, task requiring sacrifice and patience more than dazzling exploits. Foreign policy alone forbids dismantling the mass state. We could equalize wealth but not power. Wealth—to the extent that it differs from organizational power—at least complicates the lives of our organizational oligarchs. Even if, by some miracle, we *could* equalize power and make all Americans equal in all things, we would still face the stubborn problem of dignity. In the mass state, indignity is inherent. In such a state, equality would imply that *no one* matters. I have no desire to minimize the grievances of the poor, but it seems to me that indignity, not inequality, is our real complaint. A great many Americans would forgo material gains if they felt they were listened to or even that their *listening* mattered. A great many more would make greater sacrifices if they felt they would be known and remembered.

Democratic citizenship requires dignity. Neither dignity nor citizenship is at home in an unstable society or a large state. Whatever possibilities we have for democratic life require us to turn government's resources to the task of protecting and reconstructing community and private order. We can, at least, repeal laws that place families at a disadvantage in taxation, that weaken local communities, and that are designed to shatter political parties. We can seek laws and policies that enhance and support stability in our relationships, our expectations, and our laws themselves. A "transformation" is required only in a very special sense; we need a movement away from the transformations that have regularly weakened the democratic aspects of our life.

Democracy requires, I think, an end to the moral dominion of the great modern project that set humankind in pursuit of the mastery of nature. Democracy is for friends and citizens, not masters and slaves. The ultimate ground for democratic ideas of equality and the highest limitation on democracy's excesses both derive from a universe in which humanity is at home, my dignity is guaranteed by the majesty of the law I obey, and perhaps even "those who have no memorial" do not pass from memory.

2

The Bible in the American Political Tradition

THE BIBLE IS THE GREAT GATE to Western culture, an indispensable key
to our language, meanings, and thought.[1] Scripture, moreover, has a special importance in American political thought and history. The Bible, I will
be arguing, has been the second voice in the grand dialogue of American
political culture, an alternative to the "liberal tradition" set in the deepest
foundations of American life.[2]

I will also be contending, consequently, that increasing unfamiliarity with
the Bible makes it harder and harder for Americans to understand their origins and their mores or to put words to their experiences. More and more,
Americans speak a language shaped by liberalism and by the more extreme
individualisms that are liberalism's contemporary heirs.[3] Lacking knowledge of the Bible, Americans are likely to be literally inarticulate, unable to
relate themselves to American life and culture as a whole and locked a little
more securely in Tocqueville's prison of the self.[4]

In the first place, my concern here is with the Bible, not religion. People
who are not religious in any orthodox sense may revere or be deeply influenced by the Bible; in American thought, Melville is an obvious example.[5]
At the same time, there are numberless people who are deeply religious but
who have only a limited or superficial knowledge of the Bible and its doctrines. It is also worth remembering, especially in contemporary America,
that there is no shortage of nonbiblical, or even antibiblical, religions.[6]

Before turning to America, I will try to spell out the main lines of the
Bible's teaching about politics. Like Georges Dumezil, I will be speaking
of the "structures of thought" rather than the "reconstitution of events."[7]
Consequently, I will make only passing reference to the history *of* the Bible
or to the Bible *as* history.[8] My purpose here is with a text and a doctrine,

Originally published as "The Bible in the American Political Tradition," in *Religion and Politics,* ed. Myron J. Aronoff, Political Anthropology series, vol. 3 (New
Brunswick, N.J.: Transaction, 1984), 11–45. This republication has been edited for
length. Reprinted by permission of the publisher. Copyright © 1984 by Transaction
Publishers.

and as with all didactics, the way in which the Bible teaches is inseparable from what is taught.

At the outset, it is important to distinguish sacred writing from other forms of religious communication. In Revelation, God addresses specific persons. His presence is felt with overwhelming force and verifies itself, at least for the moment, although lapses and doubts may set in later on.[9] Preaching also speaks to specific audiences and is likely to be tailored to the immediate needs and concerns of the hearers. Scripture, however, is "proclaimed to the whole world" or at least to all literate persons. Its audience is radically unspecific. The Bible can be read by base and evil people: at the same time, it speaks of high and extraordinary things, beyond the reach of custom and law. Scripture is patently dangerous: Charles Manson, to take only one recent example, found a warrant for mass murder in Revelation.

Yet the risk of scripture is linked to its egalitarian character. Preaching makes the teacher the focus of attention and authority: it relies on the teacher's eloquence and cannot be separated from the impact of his or her person. This is especially true because preachings ordinarily cannot be reexamined. Audiences listen more or less passively, and they hear the preacher's message from the outside. The Puritan congregation of Hawthorne's *Scarlet Letter* mistook Arthur Dimmesdale's spiritual anguish for a kind of holiness, and its reverence only made matters worse. Preaching, consequently, has to be judged on the same principle that makes Jesus's words preferable to his works: we owe greater respect to whatever takes us closer to the heart of things.[10]

Scripture, in contrast to preaching, is relatively impersonal. It persuades by words and images, arguments and testimonies. It can also be put to the question repeatedly. Moreover, the reader is a far more active participant than the hearer. Scripture is silent. Consequently, even if I sincerely intend to be guided by the author, I can never be certain that my reading corresponds to the author's meaning.[11] This blurs the line between the author and the reader: I cannot be certain what is the author's and what is mine. Scripture thus reduces the ambivalence of the taught, the human resistance to being instructed offered in the name of dignity. Israel, the Bible tells us, is "stiff-necked" because the people resist being "fed."[12] Moses must "make an end of speaking" before Israel can really be asked to "set your hearts on all the words which I testify."[13]

The Bible is democratic in another sense. It is a single text and can be common ground for a people. Differences in understanding arise from differences in the depth of one's reading without losing that dimension of commonality. Hence, patterning themselves on the scripture, the Puritans sought a "plain style" that could speak to the "common auditory" and "direct the apprehensions of the meanest."[14]

Nevertheless, the Bible does teach different things to different levels of understanding. Moses tells parents that they must *command* their children to follow the law as the "life" of the people.[15] But a parent cannot order a child to set his or her "heart" on the law. Parents can only demand that the child observe and study the law, hoping that through practice and reading the child will learn what cannot be commanded.[16]

Similarly, Paul wrote, "From a child thou hast known the holy scriptures which are able to make thee wise unto salvation through faith in Christ Jesus." Paul's comment presumes that there is a distinction between knowing the scriptures with a child's mastery and being made wise by scripture. Paul also follows tradition in regarding wisdom as the highest reward of scripture.[17] Salvation is not the distinctive gift of the Bible because God can and does save souls without scriptural learning. Yet scripture must convey its wisdom in the same words with which it teaches fools.

The more seriously one takes scripture, the more one is compelled to assume that the words, order, and relationship of biblical texts reflect that complex educational task. The Bible includes folk stories and familiar songs, and it is full of borrowings. All of these elements, however, have been edited for a purpose.[18] In fact, Lévi-Strauss (following Wellhausen) regards scripture as "deformed" because its editors made it intellective, without the "spontaneous" quality of folk culture.[19] That criticism, of course, only emphasizes the design of scripture. "This is not mere compilation," Martin Buber wrote, "but a composition of the greatest kind."[20]

Conflicts and ambiguities in the text were permitted to remain there, which raises the possibility that they are intended. The Bible, for example, contains two accounts of the death of Saul. According to the first, Saul fell on his own sword when no one in his entourage would slay him; in the second story, Saul was slain by an Amalekite who seems to have had some vague connection to David's court. The Bible places these stories in adjoining chapters but in different books. A sporadic reader might miss the discrepancy, but any serious student is bound to notice it.[21] The text, in other words, leaves its attentive readers with a mystery. Complexities and incoherencies of this sort pose questions and invite—even *drive*—reflective readers to seek answers to their riddles.[22]

Similarly, scripture is allusive, and allusion suggests comparison to the material to which it refers. Only those who recognize the allusion, of course, can begin to think about its meaning. Cross-references and concordances are helpful, but allusion is often subtler than such mechanical devices comprehend. Calum Carmichael points out, for example, that Deuteronomy is a farewell speech of Moses to Israel, modeled on the farewell speech of Jacob to his sons. As such, it encourages reflection on the relation between the new, Deuteronomy's explicit law, and the old, the order of custom and clan right. It calls attention, in other words, to the distinction between tribal and political society, to the different mode of speech appropriate to each, and to the change from the Assembly of Israel to the Assembly of the Lord.[23]

"The ancient classics and Bibles," Thoreau wrote, are ordinarily read "as the multitude read the stars, astrologically, not astronomically." Thoreau's prescription for reading such scriptures is to the point: "We must laboriously seek the meaning of each word and line, conjecturing a larger sense than common use permits out of what wisdom and valor and generosity we have."[24] This approach to the Bible is, in any case, especially important in the American context because the most biblical of classical American writers (Melville and Hawthorne, for example) took a similar position.[25]

Any higher understanding of scripture, however, must grow out of reflection on the text as commonly understood. Allegorical interpretations, for instance, ought to be distrusted because they tell us to ignore or slight the apparent meaning.[26] At the highest level, the Song of Solomon may refer to the relation between God and his people or between Christ and the church. The Song speaks, however, about love in the ordinary, fleshly sense. Any exalted meaning, then, must derive from the proposition that profane love points toward sacred love. In these terms, learning about incarnate love and its limitations—being wise about love—is a step, possibly an essential one, to knowledge of higher love.[27]

So understood, scripture can help to answer a democratic mystery. Democracy grows out of the claim of the many to share in the highest things, a leveling up that aims to raise all citizens to the highest possible human stature. This democratic aspiration, however, is at odds with democratic practice. Democratic politics gives commonplace human beings the authority to decide the highest questions of human and political life. Inevitably, democratic practice tends to associate the *norm* with the *average,* leveling down where democratic aspiration raises up. For much of American history, I will argue, the Bible provided the common term between equality and excellence in American political life. If this is true, the declining biblicality of American culture debases our political life.[28] That conclusion is doubly alarming because our times may prove to demand great sacrifice and, hence, a democratic kind of political nobility. That high excellence is a central goal of the Bible's teaching; in the biblical view, all human things are subject to sacrifice.

Biblical religion proclaims that God made man in his own image, but human beings can frame no likeness of God. Nothing in the created world is worthy of worship; no earthly institution is sacred; all this-worldly devotion must be qualified and conditional.[29] The Bible is thus at odds with myth, for myths support and justify the existing patterns and perceptions—the "being and structure"—of society.[30] Myths justify established orders; the Bible demands that established orders justify themselves. As this suggests, biblical religion is never civil religion: it claims the right to judge cities, and it asks that the city serve what is divine.[31]

Like all human societies, ancient Israel developed mythic justifications for its institutions. These lesser and greater idolatries, however, never became as deeply rooted and stable as the mythologies of other nations. The Bible demanded and legitimated a critical stance toward the polity and its life, most visibly reflected in the repeated prophetic assaults on the complacencies of custom, material power, and law.[32]

Nevertheless, Henri Frankfort and his associates exaggerate when they assert that in ancient Hebrew thought "man and nature are necessarily *valueless* before God."[33] Idolatry is disproportionate in placing the creature at the center of creation, but a just correction requires acknowledgment of the creature's real worth. All created things have a value derived from creation and its author: "And God saw everything that He had made, and behold, it was very good."[34] This goodness, however, pertains to human beings (and to all created things) only as parts of the whole.[35]

The Bible confronts us with the fact that human things are vulnerable, contingent, and doomed to oblivion:

As for man, his days are as grass.
As a flower of the field, so he flourisheth.
For the wind passeth over it, and it is gone;
And the place thereof shall know it no more.[36]

Human achievements and excellences are transient and imperfect.[37] But this desolating reminder of human partiality is intended to help in enlisting human allegiance for the whole, the Word that endures.[38] Similarly, the Bible seeks to free human beings from idolatrous polities and societies in order to establish political regimes that, recognizing their own partiality, are more truly just. Politics, like humankind, needs to be born again.[39]

The Bible's teaching about politics begins with the story of Cain and Abel. According to that story, God has "respect" for Abel's offering of the firstlings of his flock but not for Cain's fruit. God's preference is not explained, and this silence is willful: the Bible pointedly does *not* assert that

Abel was preferred because the pastoral life is better than that of agricul-
ture, although that notion was common folklore. The Bible confronts us
with an act that seems arbitrary, like such manifestations of divine favor as
beauty or good birth. God surely has a reason for favoring Abel, but that
reason is not apparent. The story is not concerned with God's reasons but
with Cain's reactions.

Cain regards God's "respect" as a private benefice, not as a common benefit. Hence, Abel's receipt of God's respect reflects on Cain's dignity. Yet the
family as a group is blessed by Abel's good fortune. Similarly, to the extent
that my brother is "mine," his successes are also mine and enhance, rather
than detract from, my dignity. Cain's sense of commonality, however, is too
weak to outweigh his private resentments. To that extent, it matters that
Cain is a farmer and Abel is a shepherd. Whatever the respective merits of
these forms of work, the fact that they are different shows a family beginning to specialize, losing the common work, way of life, and fortune that
are the material basis of simple community.[40] But specialization does not
excuse Cain; it *tempts* him to be blind to the less palpable aspects of community, but such temptations, God tells Cain, can and must be mastered.[41]
Cain's spirit, however, does not govern; it submits to and rationalizes the
demand for private dignity that is rooted in the body and its senses.

Cain's later reaction to his punishment shows, in fact, how individualistic he really is. God makes Cain a "fugitive and a wanderer," and Cain, in
response, gives three reasons that his punishment is unbearable: (1) God
will hide his face from Cain, (2) Cain will be a fugitive and a stranger, and
(3) he will be subject to be slain by whoever finds him. God protects Cain
against only the last of these dangers, but that evidently makes the sentence
bearable. Cain cannot endure the threat of violent death, but he finds it
supportable to be alienated from God and man.[42] Cain is destined to a life
among strangers, all more or less hostile, who stop short of killing him. It
is, consequently, appropriate for Cain to found a city, since that condition
describes urban life, at least in its corrupt form.[43]

There is an undeniable suspicion of the city in this story because the city
is a human problem. The city, as compared with the village, accentuates
the tendency of specialization to call community into question. Social, economic, and emotional distance increases, and the sense of the city as a whole
is lost.[44] Commercial life, moreover, means that the need of one person is
another's chance for gain, and money economies remove the limits to avarice.[45] It was common in the ancient Middle East to see a city disintegrate
into estranged interests and expel or crowd out debtors or losing political
factions.[46] Any city founded by Cainlike individualists is doomed to decay.

Because a city of individualists lacks internal unity, it can acquire the *appearance* of unity only through external goals, the desire to defeat enemies or to gain wealth. But if the common enemy is defeated, he is no longer a reason for unity, and wealth, once acquired, becomes only so many private possessions. The individualistic city, consequently, must seek out new and ever-greater projects—it depends on "growth," as we say today. Hence Babel's reason for building its tower to heaven: "lest we be scattered upon the face of the whole earth."[47] Because such cities are compelled to attempt more and more ambitious projects, however, they will inevitably attempt the impossible. When that occurs, it is not really necessary for God to confuse a city's speech; the citizens of Babel never really spoke the same language.

Yet that story, with all its contemporary echoes, suggests another kind of city, one that would cultivate common speech and internal justice, eschewing expansion and the quest for mastery.[48] In Deuteronomy, the term "city" refers to the city seen from the outside, the city as defined by its externalities and appearances. A city so self-defined would necessarily be hollow. By contrast, the term "gates" refers to the city seen from within or in its inward life, especially in the dispensing of justice.[49] Hence the peculiar appropriateness of the spiritual "Twelve Gates to the City." A polis is unjust and corrupt, in the biblical view, unless it sees its gates as avenues leading in, not superhighways leading out. A city's gates, in this sense, are the mark of its political covenant.[50]

Law and ritual may be the signs of a covenant, but they do not create it. A covenant is based on a perceived likeness of spirit, a common idea of justice, and a deeply felt sense of being one despite the differences of private interest. The good city depends on the psychological willingness and ability to covenant. The heart of political wisdom, then, is knowledge about the spiritual pilgrimage that prepares and educates the soul.

The political education of the soul is a task of intimidating difficulty. Idolatry of self is the most pervasive and ineradicable of all idolatries. Original sin involves the effort to make the self the center of creation or, failing that, to enable the self to be separate and independent. In either case, the effect is to deny one's human status as part of the whole.[51]

The manifestation of self-idolatry is a desire to control and enhance "my own," my body and the things connected to it, most notably my family (and, especially, the "heirs of my body") and my property.[52] All human beings follow these impulses to some degree. Yet implicitly, the desire to preserve and advance my own implies a rejection of all limits on my will, the most remarkable being my mortality. Self-idolatry entails a struggle to master nature.

This, scripture teaches, is an unhappy condition, haunted by anxieties, because it is based on illusions and a flight from humanity's true nature. Paradoxically, self-centeredness is really self-denial.[53] Human beings need to be brought to justice—to the recognition that they are dependent parts of a good whole—in order to be reconciled to themselves. It is not enough for law and nature to restrain us; we need to perceive God's creation as a good in order to value our own finite status.[54]

God teaches this lesson to his chosen by a combination of desolation and mercy.[55] Abraham, surrounded by the carcasses of sacrificed animals, feels a "horror, of great darkness"; Jacob is forced to humble himself before Esau and loses his son Joseph; Joseph is cast into a pit and sold into exile. Devastating experience shatters the defenses of the self, leaving the individual—for the moment at least—with an overwhelming sense of finitude. But Abraham is then promised that his line will be a great nation, and he is given a son in his old age; Esau welcomes Jacob generously, and Israel lives to be reunited with Joseph; Joseph becomes first in Egypt after Pharaoh and recovers his family. These are extraordinary blessings that most human beings will not share. Nevertheless, they afford their recipients a glimpse of God's design, a conviction that the whole is lovely as well as irresistible: "You meant evil against me, but God meant it for good."[56]

Abraham and his descendants gradually develop a sense of participation in wider social and political wholes. Beginning as a family, narrowly distrustful of the world around it and able to adjust internal conflicts only by dissolving into separate patriarchal households, Israel becomes first a tribal society and then a people. After the fall of the false city, Babel, God leads Israel to a new sort of political knowledge.[57]

God's instruction of Israel furnishes a model for political society, for a rightly constructed polity aims to produce public-spirited citizens who also accept their place within God's order. Political society needs to limit and constrain its citizens, demanding sacrifice and punishing them when needed. In so doing, it imitates—in a small, relatively ineffective way—God's desolation of pride. At the same time, a good political order nurtures, educates, and improves its citizens: its chastenings are intended to help teach the lesson that the whole is a good order. The duty to care for the poor is an example of both constraint and nurturance. Good citizens are openhearted to their fellows, but those who will not be openhearted can, and should, be compelled to be openhanded.[58] Covetousness is the only *feeling* forbidden by the Decalogue because community is wounded by envy and avarice alike.[59] The liberal heresy that denies the need for constraint and punishment abandons the means; conservative acceptance of hard-heartedness rejects the end.

In no way does scripture teach that "moral men" are involved in "immoral society."[60] Reinhold Niebuhr's argument, that individuals have moral faculties and political societies do not, is founded in the liberal, individualistic notion that societies and polities are artificial, existing by convention only. The Bible regards peoples as wholes, not merely as collections of individuals, and hence, publics are rightly judged as collectivities.

Abraham's argument against God at Sodom—that it is unjust to destroy the righteous with the wicked—seems to point to the conclusion that God cannot rightfully destroy Sodom if there is even one just person in the city. The Lord breaks off the argument, but the question remains: because Lot is a decent man, how can God rightly destroy Sodom? In fact, Abraham's case is defective because Abraham speaks of righteousness solely in relation to individuals. Lot does not actively participate in Sodom's evil, but he lives in the city and shares its fortunes. He intended to marry his daughters to Sodomites; even when warned of the city's doom, he lingers and has to be seized and led out. Dependent on the city, Lot cannot live without urban life. He is a part of the whole, and despite his private virtues, he bears a share of the city's guilt. God spares Lot out of mercy, not justice.[61]

Nevertheless, the Bible teaches that public spirit will always be opposed by private interest. Education out of self-idolatry is always imperfect. The body continues to make claims against the spirit. Bonds based on righteousness, covenants among the kindred of spirit, must compete with blood kinship, property, and pride. Abraham, called out of his father's house, has been taught repeatedly that blood kinship is less important than righteousness. Yet at the end of his life, Abraham sends his servant to seek a wife for Isaac in Abraham's old country from among Abraham's blood kin. The servant, with a better sense of priorities, chooses Rebekah because she is hospitable to servants and even to animals. Wiser in the ways of human dependence, the servant knows that a generous spirit is more important than bloodline.[62] Yet the servant does not choose Rebekah because he believes her to be the best possible wife for Isaac; he selects her because she is the best within the terms set by Abraham. Servants—public or private—must recognize that the spirit is compelled to make concessions to the limitations of the flesh.

Similarly, Joseph rises out of slavery because he understands the mutability of political favor and fortune and, hence, can profit from the false optimism of others.[63] Yet Joseph brings his people into Egypt and gives them a privileged and resented position in a regime that depends on the life and favor of one man. Joseph's pride in his own statecraft and the regime it has created overrides his more fundamental wisdom. Elevated by Joseph, all Israel is cast into slavery, a collective desolation, and subsequently receives from God the blessing of liberation. The instruction of this shared experience transforms the children of Israel into a people.[64] Even on this grand scale, however, political education is imperfect. Israel's collective wisdom, even more than that of its founders, is sporadic and uncertain.

Given human shortcomings, even the best political regime is twice limited. In the first place, a political society cannot rely simply on the virtue of its people. A covenantal polity requires a unity of institutions to protect the political society when human beings forget or fail. The second constraint is only a little less obvious. The larger the political society, the greater the tension between body and spirit, private feelings and public duties. The increased resistance of the body means, in turn, that large states must rely more on force or appeals to private interest and less on patriotism and public spirit. Political order is likely to be little more than external conformity. In a large state, covenants are fragile if they exist at all; megalopolis, like the idols, rests on feet of clay. The body's parochiality, consequently, imposes a limitation on the size of good political regimes. A world regime, logically, indicated by the common nature of humankind is not suited to fallen humanity. The politics of covenant presumes a world of cities and nations.[65]

Even the best political society, however, is only part of the whole. The nations are subject to the kingdom of God, and all are liable to sacrifice and judgment.[66] Even chosen Israel is only a part—though a uniquely important one—of the order of things. All regimes can become idols, and Israel's often does; only the fortunate have true prophets to attempt to set them right.[67] In fact, false prophets are moved, more often than not, by a kind of patriotism, perverting "the conditional promise to an Israel that would accomplish its tasks into unconditional security for all time."[68]

Jonah sought to evade God's call to prophesy in Nineveh because he foresaw that Nineveh would repent and be forgiven.[69] Jonah presumably wanted Nineveh, Israel's ancient enemy, to be destroyed. Moreover, Jonah's pride was involved: because he had prophesied doom, God's clemency made him look the fool. Nineveh's repentance, however, improves God's creation because the whole is benefited by the excellence of its parts.[70] Pride of state and pride of word must yield, consequently, to the hope that all human beings, becoming more just, may be reconciled to each other and to God.

Let me summarize the Bible's teaching about politics as I have presented it here. (1) Human beings are not born "free and independent." They are subject to limits and are assigned a place in the order of creation; they depend on God, on their fellow humans, and on nature. (2) Human beings begin with a desire for independence and a yearning to do as they will, but this is the result of sin, not the true nature of humanity. (3) Society and polity exist to educate human beings out of self-concern to the greatest extent possible. (4) The good political society is founded on a covenant, a spiritual and moral union, and cultivates justice and fraternity rather than material power, preferring inner excellence to external expansion. (5) Such a regime, given human frailties, must be limited in size and governed by law. (6) The polity is itself a part of the whole, limited and ruled by a higher law. There are, of course, other interpretations of scripture. These propositions are at least a reasonable approximation of the biblical view as Americans originally understood it, and they provide a foundation for examining the place of the Bible in American political thought.

Biblical doctrine played a special role in the founding of America. The Bible was the only common text for white Americans; it soon became almost the only positive bond between blacks and whites. If biblicism was a Protestant predisposition, the Bible was not. Scripture was a common point of reference for groups with differing and often hostile pasts and a stable beacon for peoples who had broken their ties to custom. In the absence of established institutions, the Bible often served as a law book, one far more popular than the already "mysterious," lawyerly science of common law.[71]

The most familiar appeal to scripture, of course, is the Puritan effort to found a Bible polity based on covenant, a concern for fraternity rather than "great things," and the hope of subjecting commerce to moral and legal regulation.[72] Puritan teachings have been studied too often and too well to need exposition here.[73] It does matter, however, that Puritan doctrines, though more intellectual and probably more coherent than comparable teachings, were part of a broadly similar body of teaching pervading colonial America.

Yet despite the centrality of the Bible in early American culture, the founding generation rejected or de-emphasized the Bible and biblical rhetoric. It was, as Alan Heimert comments, a kind of interlude in which gentlemanly conventions and Roman cadences dominated public speech.[74] There were exceptions, like Patrick Henry, but the rule was clear. The Bible, moreover, was even less evident in the framers' political thought.

Against this thesis, Robert Bellah and Phillip E. Hammond contend that the Creator of the Declaration of Independence is a "distinctly biblical God . . . who creates individual human beings and endows them with equality and fundamental rights."[75] This argument, however, is wrong on two counts. In the first place, it misstates the Declaration: human beings are "created equal," not endowed with equality. They are endowed with equal *rights*, a rather different idea.[76] Second, although the "biblical God" undeniably creates human beings, it is far from clear that he endows them with individual rights. The Declaration's language is designed to be acceptable to deists and orthodox believers alike, but this prudential ambiguity is not enough to make the Creator of the Declaration, "Nature's God," the "distinctly biblical God" who is beyond nature and Lord over it.

Even the Declaration's equivocal religiosity is absent from the Constitution and the theory on which it is based. There is no reference to the Bible, as far as I know, in all of the *Federalist*. Madison does refer to divine beings in *Federalist* 51, but his rhetorical allusion itself indicates the difference between Madison's view and the Bible's teaching. Madison asserts that men and angels differ politically because angels need no government. In the Bible, of course, angels are not only governed, they are capable of rebellion.[77] And the most famous biblical reference to men and angels, 1 Corinthians 13:1, suggests that men and angels, in one decisive respect, are comparable in speech, the most political of all faculties: "If I speak with the tongues of men and of angels, and have not charity, I am become as a sounding brass or a tinkling crystal." In the biblical view, politicality is characteristic of both the human and the divine; for Madison, politics—"the greatest of all reflections on human nature"—is unworthy of the divine.

The framers' doctrine speaks of the rights of individuals who are free in the state of nature, rather than referring to their duties within the order of nature. In the political science of the framers, political society is a convenience meant to serve private rights. Politics is intended to protect liberty, the "diversity in the faculties of men," rather than regulating that diversity for the good of the public as a whole. In the strict sense, there is no public and no whole: there are only individual rights, on one hand, and "permanent and aggregate interests," on the other. In this new science of politics, institutions and an extensive republic are to substitute for the covenant as a means of controlling factions.[78] Moreover, human beings—in the framers' teaching—are at war with nature, seeking the mastery that will force nature to yield to their desires. The political regime, their creature, is consequently dedicated to the pursuit of power, which is another argument for a large, commercial republic. In all these respects, the framers' theories are at odds with the Bible's teaching.[79]

The framers recognized that opposition and even welcomed it because they associated the political claims of religion with persecution and with the murderous strife of religious war. Accordingly, the framers were concerned to make religion harmless, rendering it safely subject to political society without even the hope of rule. Madison regarded freedom of religion as an absolute right because he considered religion to be radically private and subjective. It is not much more difficult, Madison wrote Jefferson, to devise a religious creed than to frame a political one, but the public has some claim to do the second and none to do the first.[80] Religion lacks any objective, public, or rational foundation; it belongs wholly to the world of "opinions."

In the framers' design, religion is presumably limited, like other "factions," because—according to the familiar argument of *Federalist* 10—a multitude of sects will be unable to "concert and execute their plans of oppression." In the case of religion, however, Madison was not content to leave it at that: the original Constitution rules out any form of religious test, and Madison shaped the language of the First Amendment to rule out religious establishment at the federal level. (Madison held identical views about the place of religion in the states.)[81] As this indicates, Madison regarded religion as uniquely dangerous, less rational than other factions, less subject to the moderating effects of interest, and more capable of mobilizing majority opinion on its behalf.

Paine's *Common Sense* is almost alone among the great works of the founders in making an explicit appeal to the Bible. Clearly, however, Paine invoked scripture because he aimed to reach a wider public that revered the Bible and knew virtually no other book.[82] Paine's own view that the Bible is "absurd" and a "book of fables" was not openly expressed until much later, in *The Age of Reason*. Yet Paine's rejection of the Bible is only a little less evident in *Common Sense*.

Paine begins his comments on scripture with the assertion that "the quiet and rural lives of the first patriarchs" have a "happy something" lacking in the history of Jewish monarchy. This is an outrageous statement on its face: the lives of the patriarchs are anything but quiet. Moreover, Paine is purposefully vague about the "happy something" that the patriarchal world allegedly possessed.[83]

He goes on to make the correct observation that Israel copied kingship from the heathen, and he offers two examples of the godlessness of monarchy. The first (Judges 8:22–23) cites Gideon's rejection of a crown in favor of rule by the Lord. But immediately after declaring that "the Lord shall rule over you," Gideon asks for gold loot, which he makes into an ephod, "and all Israel went thither a whoring after it, which thing became a great snare to Gideon and to his house" (Judges 8:27). Because a golden ephod was a high priest's vestment, Gideon seems to have assumed a self-consecrated high priesthood.[84] Did Gideon proclaim the Lord's rule only to claim the right to speak for the Lord as a sort of covert king concealed by a mantle of divine authority? There is good evidence for such an interpretation: the name of Gideon's son, Abimelech, means "my father is king."[85]

Like Gideon, Paine wraps himself in a divine disguise. Later in *Common*

Sense, Paine imitates Gideon by declaring that the king of America "reigns above." For secular purposes, Paine goes on, Americans ought to place their Constitution on the "divine law, the word of God." Then, crowning the Constitution, they should proclaim that "the law is king." The rule of law, consequently, rests on divine foundations and seems to derive its authority from God's higher law. Paine goes on to argue, however, that the law's crown ought to be broken up and "scattered among the people, whose right it is."[86] The real sovereign is not the king above but the people below. Moreover, if the people have the right to rule over secular law but secular law rests on divine law, popular sovereignty entails the right to rule over divine law as well.

Paine's second example from scripture seems more straightforward because he cites Samuel's enumeration of the dangers of monarchy (1 Samuel 8:5–20). But Paine stops with verse 20; he omits Samuel's report to the Lord and the Lord's command, "hearken unto their voice and make them a king" (8:22). In fact, Paine then skips to 1 Samuel 12:17–19, although he conceals the omission ("Samuel continued to reason with them . . . and seeing them bent on their folly, he cried out"). Paine ends by announcing that "these portions of Scripture" demonstrate God's opposition to monarchical government. Consequently, Paine argues, there was "as much of kingcraft as priestcraft in withholding the scripture from the people in popish countries."[87] This appeal to Protestant prejudice takes on special significance because *Paine* has just withheld several portions of scripture. In the omitted passages, God has chosen Saul to be king (1 Samuel 9:17) and Samuel has anointed him. Moreover, before Samuel's protest against kinship, cited by Paine (12:17), Samuel has remarked that the Lord will punish his people, as he did their kingless ancestors, only if they do not follow his commandments and obey his voice. It is explicitly possible (although it may be unlikely) to combine kingly government and obedience to God (12:14). God does not favor kingship, and monarchy is not the best regime—in that, Paine is true to the text—but he does regard it as a legitimate form of rule.

A bit later, Paine refers to Saul as chosen "by lot"; scripture claims that he was chosen by God. Paine is asserting that, in reality, God's providences and interventions, as claimed by scripture, are chance occurrences when they are not "priestcraft." This argument comes closer to Paine's real aim. Paine contends that "original sin and hereditary succession are parallels." Does that imply that republican rule can overthrow *both?* So it seems because Paine explicitly claims that America has the power to begin the world again.[88] In fact, Paine sees a clear parallel between overcoming British monarchy and overthrowing God's authority. Arguing against any reconciliation with Britain, Paine cites an idea that Milton "wisely expresses." (Paine is too honest to attribute the notion to Milton himself.) "Never can true reconcilement grow where wounds of deadly hate have pierced so deep." Paine is citing, approvingly, Satan's rejection of any reconciliation with God.[89] This was a familiar text with ministers who supported the American Revolution, but they used it in the orthodox sense. Nathaniel Whitaker, for example, used Satan as the epitome of the "carnal mind" in arguing that the Tories would never be reconciled to America.[90] Whitaker praises the love that can overcome the deepest hate; Paine rejects it. In Paine's view, in other words, the Revolution offers the opportunity to reject Christian forgiveness and humility in favor of a truly national self-assertion (the "happy something" of patriarchal days?) and the human claim to mastery. *Novus Ordo Secolorum,* in these terms, implies that the birth of the American republic amounts to the end of the Christian era.[91]

Very few of the framers went as far as Paine; almost all believed that "religion," vaguely defined, was valuable to civil society. This support for religion, however, did not amount to an endorsement of the Bible or its teachings. Washington invoked religion, for example, because "refined education" is insufficient to establish morality and respect for oaths. Religion, in this view, is reduced to mythology: it *supports* but does not *define* the moral and civil order.[92]

Jefferson accepted Washington's argument—he wondered, for example, whether an atheist's testimony was reliable enough to be accepted at law—but he also went beyond it. Religion, in Jefferson's view, is needed to correct the narrow calculations of self-interest. Slavery is contrary to natural right, and ending slavery is in the interest of humanity as a whole because it removes a temptation to arrogance and a danger to liberty. But the abolition of slavery is not clearly in the interest of *slaveholders*; indeed, it seems likely that it is not. Because religion helps give human beings a more extended sense of their duties to humanity, it is invaluable as an ally of the "Heart" in addressing problems like slavery.[93] But Jefferson's deity speaks the language of natural right, not that of the Bible.

In what he meant to be a private letter, Jefferson made his own view explicit. He found the Hebrew scriptures "degrading and injurious" in their ideas of God and their ethics "not only imperfect, but often irreconcilable with the sound dictates of reason and morality." He revered Jesus. Nevertheless, Jefferson found the New Testament's account of Jesus's teachings to be "mutilated, misstated and often unintelligible," doubtless because Jesus's life was recorded by "unlettered and ignorant men" relying on their memories after a lapse of years. Even with all these apologies, he considered

Jesus's doctrine to be "defective as a whole." It is hardly surprising, then, that Jefferson thought that the Bible should not be put into the hands of children until their minds had been shaped for "religious inquiries" by other sources.[94]

Jefferson was among the most religious of the framers, and his views were broadly characteristic of the founders. The Bible, in this way of thinking, is sometimes wise and useful, but it is often false, fabulous, and perverse. It needs to be subordinated to the enlightened doctrine in which the first political principle is not God's kingdom but human freedom.

For the moment, the framers had their way. Yet as Gordon Wood observes, within a generation the American public—aided by a major increase in literacy and in publishing—intruded on and contended with the enlightened culture of the gentry.[95] The public brought with it a political culture heavily influenced by the Bible to rival the liberalism of the framers. That evangelical Christians made common cause with leaders like Jefferson should not obscure their very different modes of thought.[96]

Fear for the dissenting churches led Isaac Backus to support the ban on religious establishment, but Backus explicitly rejected the idea of "natural right," correctly recognizing that it contradicted the Bible's teaching.[97] Although Backus opposed state aid to any *one* church, he denied that religion was a private matter. The public, Backus argued, has a legitimate interest in supporting religion through Sabbath laws, censorial legislation, and even required public worship.[98] Backus aimed at a distinctly Christian state, one very similar to the "Christian Sparta" for which Sam Adams hoped.[99]

Because the Bible was the high culture of the many, it should not be surprising that even very radical democrats often strove for some form of religious test, such as a profession of faith or a declaration of belief in the Bible.[100] The central political idea of the "awakened," however, was not some form of religious establishment; it was the biblical idea of covenant, the conviction that a political society rests on a civic bond and a unity of spirit. Political institutions are important, but they are only the letter, empty forms that are given life and meaning by the spirit behind them. The Constitution and the laws, in this view, are only superficial indications of the nature of American political society. Public and private spheres intertwine; "the state" can never be separated from "society."[101]

Evangelical religion also maintained the biblical hostility to acquisitiveness and competitive ethics. This was not necessarily an ascetic view. In fact, the critics of "the emerging capitalist ethic" often observed that the limitless desire for riches is itself a form of asceticism. Rather, the critique of acquisitiveness emphasized the danger of self-seeking to the covenant and the threat of the "aristocratic spirit" to republican life.[102] Even a "Turk's paradise" of luxury, Gilbert Tennent declared, is a less serious temptation and moral peril than the desire to be "a sort of independent Being."[103]

As Heimert notes, the liberal-rationalists among the clergy were torn between the traditional view that human beings are political and social by nature and the newer, more individualistic doctrine of natural right. Evangelical leaders, by contrast, were far more likely to defend the biblical teachings that true freedom is found in obedience to the law of nature and in public-spirited citizenship.[104] Yet after the American Revolution, the evangelical clergy largely withdrew from political life, abandoning the field in the critical years of the founding. Disenchantment with the secularity of American politics helped to bring about this retreat, as Heimert observes, but a good deal of the explanation lies within evangelical doctrine itself.[105]

In the first place, the evangelical emphasis on the *insufficiency* of political and social institutions could and did slide over into a denial of the *value* of institutions, virtually rejecting any role for political and social life in the education of the spirit. This was particularly likely because the evangelical method, the appeal to the "gracious affections" of individuals, ran counter to the common good and the idea of the covenant, which were so prominent in the content of the evangelical message. The evangelical movement, in other words, tilted—despite the intentions of its founder—in the direction of political quietism and a fixation on the private conscience.[106]

The argument against institutions carried over into the evangelical view of the Bible. Jonathan Edwards observed that human beings will be blind to the beauties and truth of scripture without inward affection; interpretation is no better than the spirit behind it.[107] This orthodox proposition, however, led the evangelicals to slight the Bible as a *teacher* of the spirit. The evangelical clergy took less care than their Puritan predecessors to be faithful to the text. Instead, they used scripture as a "storehouse of metaphor" in the hope of reaching and rousing the spirits of their listeners. In doing so, they abandoned the public text in favor of private experience, and the quest for lively images and stories often resulted in the loss of context and depth.[108]

The appeal to the reborn heart and to the "gracious affections" also weakened the Bible's recognition of the limitations imposed by the body on the spirit. This, in turn, led evangelical preachers to slight the necessary imperfections and boundaries of covenant and spiritual unity. The Bible envisages a world of nations; Paul denies that these distinctions matter "in Christ," but he does not ignore the reality of national differences in the secular world. Souls may unite, but the flesh divides, and fleshly human beings need the support of those to whom they are close and to whom they matter.[109]

The human needs for nurturance and dignity demand small states and societies, and with them, narrower allegiances never fully identical with our larger duties. By contrast, the Awakening sometimes promised or seemed to promise that it could set the spirit free from the body, attaining a more than biblical felicity. In doing so, it pledged more than it could deliver, understating the barriers to public spirit in America and contributing, consequently, to disillusionment with political life.

Disenchantment with achieving the millennium by transforming spirits encouraged many evangelicals to identify the approach of the kingdom with the historical process. In this view, the advance of science and technology was the herald of a future "spiritual advance."[110] Hawthorne detested this doctrine, satirizing its later versions in "The Celestial Railroad," and his hostility was appropriate. The spiritualization of progress established a common ground with the liberal tradition and weakened religion's critique of modern, secular society.[111]

Nevertheless, evangelical religion at its best remembered the biblical teaching on the limitations of the spirit. It did not promise, consequently, an imminent end of private spirit and partiality. Yet this more biblical evangelism also preserved the idea of the covenant. Madison made individual liberty his first principle and sought, on the model of mechanics, to balance the parts. The wiser evangelists took the common good for their standard and urged, on the model of music, that the parts harmonized to the whole.[112] In so doing, they helped preserve the old teaching for a new time.

In the nineteenth century, the relationship between democracy and the Bible was unmistakable. Religion and citizenship were intertwined popular "romances."[113] The quest for community was the great theme of revivalism, and it found a parallel in the Jacksonian ideal of the Union and the hope for a new covenant, "inward and spiritual," to vivify the formal unity of the laws.[114] The language and stories of the Bible were the most meaningful forms of public speech, pervading oratory and establishing many of the terms and limits of civic deliberation and political life.[115]

Mass democracy made the Bible uniquely valuable as a check on the psychological tyranny of the majority. Religion, as Tocqueville observed, taught a law and a right superior to the will of the majority. It provided a basis for defying the majority—divine monarchy invoked against secular democracy—and it urged the public to limit itself.[116] Scripture, in fact, was an even more specific barrier to the tyranny of the majority because the ancient strictures against syncretism emphasized a duty to resist fashion and opinion in the service of a truth that is more than one among many.[117]

There was another side to religion, of course. Too many of the churches were persuaded to moralize competitive individualism, material success, and historical progress and to elide, if not deny, the limits to human mastery and perfectibility. America may even have strengthened the perennial temptation to reduce religion to mythology, turning the sacred to the service of the profane. Yet, as Peter Berger observes, the Bible was always some sort of obstacle to the "spiritual mobilization" of the church in support of liberal, commercial, and political society. The very existence of the text, with its all-too-different message, was a standing reminder of moral compromises and betrayals of the faith.[118]

Civil religion could be far more comfortable with churches that limited the authority of the Bible or abandoned it altogether, freeing religion—as Channing put it—from the "low views" of "darker ages."[119] This was most evident in Transcendentalism, which exaggerated the faults of the Awakening into a kind of caricature. The scriptures, Emerson declared, "have no epical integrity; are fragmentary; are not shown in their order to the intellect." At best, the words of the Bible are forms that imprison the spirit. Transcendentalism preferred to appeal to intuition, the Word written on the heart. It accentuated the individualism of evangelical religion, jettisoning all public standards for the discipline of the spirit, and it relied in a millennialistic way on the course of history to produce moral order out of the chaos of individual impulse. Men suffer, Emerson wrote, "under evils whose end they cannot see," and they need to be assured that the good is "that which really is being done."[120]

It was a teaching that revolted Hawthorne and Melville, those two great voices of the biblical tradition. Repeatedly, they taught that individualism and the faith in technology were founded on the illusory attempt to deny or escape from the dependence and the capacity for evil that were ineradicable parts of the human soul. Creeds like Emerson's allowed and encouraged Americans to moralize indifference and impoverished political life, and they slighted the human need for the support of friends.[121]

In Melville's *Israel Potter*, Benjamin Franklin is portrayed as the epitome of individualistic rationalism and, hence, the true voice of the tradition of the framers. It was an advised choice: Franklin was already enshrined as a secular saint of the American Enlightenment. Melville began his description of Franklin with apparent respect, likening him to Jacob, especially in the "unselfish devotion which we are bound to ascribe to him"—bound by piety, perhaps; the Bible, as Melville knew very well, depicts Jacob as a cunning competitor and a successful swindler. Melville went on to note the "worldly wisdom and polished Italian tact" under Franklin's air of "Arcadian unaffectedness." His final description was devastating: Franklin is a "Machiavelli in tents," a combination of ancient and modern duplicity and self-seeking. Melville grouped Franklin with Jacob and Hobbes, a trinity suggesting Jacob's temperamental egotism, Hobbes's scientific individualism, and Franklin's extraordinary ability to disguise both these qualities with moralistic cant.[122]

In the event, Franklin deceives and defrauds Israel Potter in any number of ways. In Melville's imagery, *Jacob* (Franklin) thus robs and defeats *Israel* (Potter), reversing the order of scripture. The Bible uses the two names to refer to the qualities warring in Israel's soul, contrasting the competitive Jacob's bitterness toward nature with Israel's acceptance and Jacob's concern for the things of the body with Israel's "inner sight" and attention to the spirit.[123] In the King James translation, Israel even dies before Jacob, but it is Israel who prevails.[124] American individualism, Melville was suggesting, had improved on Jacob's egotism because it had a talent for moralization, which Jacob lacked, donning—as Franklin had—the masks of benevolence and science when either suited his purpose. In modern America, as Melville saw it, moral self-deception was deceiving and overcoming the spirit.[125]

In American philosophy, Caleb Sprague Henry shared Melville's dark vision. In his essay on progress, published in 1861, Henry treated history as a conflict between *civilization,* and with it the "faculty of adopting means to ends," and *Christianity and reason,* which were able to set worthy ends. By nature, civilization is intended to be subordinate to the moral faculties. Left to itself, civilization pursues trivial or base ends—the enhancement of technique and, implicitly, the gratification of every desire. What modern theory regards as "progress," Henry argued, is only the progressive development of civilization, to which modern thought has given the ascendancy. Civilization will not—its admirers aside—add a moral and spiritual dimension: it will *weaken* moral influences with the passing of time, accenting civilization's own irrationalities, its tendency to encourage fraud, the degrading of the poor, and the pursuit of luxury. Commerce and "enlightened self love" will restrain war, as liberal theory hopes, but they are insufficient to bring peace. The constraints of civilization on war are, consequently, certain to fail. Civilization is set on a disaster course and humanity with it; only the possibility that God will intervene offers any hope to his children.[126]

Henry's vision was, in many ways, a model prophecy, and his arguments seem chillingly realistic in the light of our experience.[127] His own contemporaries, however, discounted or ignored Henry's case. Americans had their doubts about liberal political theory and commercial civilization, but—in public, at least—the naysayers were a minority. In any case, the crisis of slavery and the Union shouldered aside, for a time, American anxieties about the direction of modern life.

The Bible, of course, was cited on both sides of the slavery controversy. Its authority was too great for either side to surrender its claim on scripture. Nevertheless, the biblical case for slavery was decisively the weaker of the arguments. The stronger element of the proslavery case is found in New Testament citations adjuring slaves to obey their masters. But those urgings barely tolerate slavery; they do not make it right. Paul tells a slave not to mind being a servant, but he goes on to tell him to accept freedom if he can get it, for the real condition of those who are called by God is to be free of men.[128] Christians, if not all human beings, are free by nature; slavery is only one of many conditions that must be tolerated in a corrupt, less-than-natural world.

Defenders of slavery also appealed to the curse on Canaan, but that argument is simply ludicrous. It *is* Canaan who is doomed to be a "servant of servants," and however we interpret this passage, applying it to Africans is spectacularly bad geography. The real authority for arguments based on supposed racial "inferiorities" lay in science, not scripture.[129]

The antislavery forces, by contrast, pointed to the fact that the God of the Decalogue identifies himself as a liberator, and they also observed that the fugitive slave law was directly contrary to scripture.[130] Moreover, the spiritual freedom attributed to Christians also seems to make liberty a higher law.

The doctrine of natural right contributed at least as much to the argument against slavery. Nevertheless, when Theodore Parker, the Transcendentalist preacher, armed a fugitive slave, he gave him a sword for his body and a Bible for his soul.[131] There was an important truth in Parker's gesture. The doctrine of natural right implied that it was enough to restore a slave to his or her natural freedom. Even a Christian thinker like Theodore Dwight Weld was tempted by the argument that ending slavery would itself redeem America. Scripture, by contrast, argued that it is futile to free the body and neglect the soul. Emancipation calls for more than striking off shackles; it demands nurturance and education in social and political life. Moreover, as Charles Grandison Finney proclaimed, any emancipation was bound to be superficial without repentance and rebirth in white America.[132] A change in the laws is empty, mere form, unless it is preceded by or leads to a change in the covenant.

Lincoln recognized that the slavery issue pointed to a deeper spiritual crisis in the Union. His reference to the "house divided," for example, reaches

beyond slavery to the nature of political freedom itself.[133] The most familiar version of the "house divided" story is found in Mark 3:21–27.[134] The
scribes assert that Jesus drives out demons with power derived from the
prince of demons. Good works, the scribes are contending, may conceal
an evil or hostile intent.[135] A cunning antagonist may surrender or destroy
something of his own in order to insinuate himself into our good graces,
calculating that a small sacrifice now will lead to greater gains later on.

Jesus's response seems to deny that this tactic can succeed. Satan can only
drive out Satan by being "divided against himself." But, like kingdoms and
houses divided against themselves, Jesus asserts, if Satan is so divided, he
"cannot stand, but hath an end." This apparently naive answer reminds us
of a simple truth. Satan's sacrifice of his minions does weaken his army. The
satanic tactic can succeed only if we mistake the real value of things, so that
we give him something of great worth in return for something less valuable,
as in the folk stories in which Satan offers wealth and beauty in return for
the soul. Left to itself, Satan's tactic is self-defeating; only our ignorance and
confusion give it a chance of success.

Jesus goes on to make a subtler point, observing that no one can enter a
strong man's house without first binding him. This is a pointed reference to
the Israel of Jesus's time. In the Christian view, the Pharisees were so fearful that Israel, in the interest of accommodation with Roman and Hellenic
civilization, would give up something essential to its existence as a distinct
people that they insisted on the rigid observance of all rules and customs.[136]
It was Jesus's violation of that code that had led the Pharisees to take counsel against him. But Pharisaism, Jesus argues, far from protecting Israel,
leaves it bound and vulnerable to plunder. It makes error *certain* by raising
means to the level of ends and by confusing the accidental with the essential. A society that cannot vary its means, given the mutability of human
affairs, makes its ends the prisoners of means, subordinating the greater to
the less.[137] That, in fact, virtually defines a "house divided against itself." A
house is not divided against itself because its members differ or have private
interests; that variety is to be assumed. A house becomes divided "against
itself" when what is *unlike* is regarded as more important than what is *akin*.
Hence the ending of the third chapter of Mark: Jesus teaches that those who
do God's will are "my brother and my sister and my mother," to be preferred, in case of conflict, to his blood kin. Private allegiances and interests
must yield to public and higher goods.[138]

Political regimes and social orders—kingdoms and houses—need a measure of liberty, an element of private variation that leaves room for new
ways. Yet, in Jesus's teachings, this liberty itself is only a means to the

common life. It seems to me that Lincoln, reflecting on that text, saw in it the very meaning of *civil* liberty.

American institutions, as the framers designed them, violate Jesus's teaching because they make liberty an end. Liberty is a common principle only in form; its content is radically private. What is like—the public order—is subordinated to what is unlike—the diverse and private interests of individual Americans. Consequently, America is a "house divided" *apart* from its differences about slavery, from the very first principle of its institutions. When Lincoln declared in his first inaugural that "the Union is older than the Constitution," he was appealing to the Declaration of Independence. At Gettysburg, however, his doctrine is more mature, sharper, and more radical. The Declaration asserts that men are created equal but aim to secure their rights. At Gettysburg, Lincoln reversed that order: "conceived" in liberty, America must be "dedicated" to equality. It amounted to the proclamation of a new covenant.[139]

Lincoln was not alone in this sort of reflection. The calamity of the Civil War shook American confidence in the framers' science and evoked a number of attempts to apply biblical traditions to the task of reconstruction. Theorists as different as Horace Bushnell, Orestes Brownson, and Elisha Mulford, for example, agreed in rejecting individualistic ideas of natural right, in contending that human beings are naturally political, and in seeking some way to bring community into national political life.

Bushnell looked to the "little democracies of our towns . . . and legislatures" but found no institutional way to relate these small, vanishing democracies and weakened republics to the Union in the industrial era. Instead, Bushnell appealed to the argument that right rule is morally binding on us with or without our consent, a proposition that, whatever its merits, puts community in intellectual rather than affective terms.[140]

Brownson, relying on Catholic sources, found a legal formula to connect locality and nationality, asserting that sovereignty rests in the states but in the states collectively, as parts of a whole. As Brownson knew, however, constitutional abstractions mean very little without the support of "moral qualities" rooted in political community.[141]

In Mulford's Hegelian version of the covenant, institutions are only the formalized expression of the nation, a "relationship" characterized by continuity and by a conscious, organic "moral personality." The "origins and unity" of the nation are found in the Bible, Mulford maintained. In fact, the Bible is the "book of the life of the nations" and reveals that the nations are involved in an invisible order as well as the relationships of day-to-day life. The true nation has a place in the whole of human life and history. A nation conscious of itself must be aware of the whole; this, Mulford was confident, means that self-conscious nationhood—the nation in its highest form—is necessarily Christian. The Bible, consequently, has an essential role in civic education, and Mulford lamented its absence from university curricula and its decline, in the pulpit, into so many "isolated proof texts."[142] Yet Mulford's reverence for the Bible and his belief that the accumulation of material wealth is a goal suited only to "false civilization" were insufficient to overcome his faith in history. The highest historical forces, Mulford believed, involve sacrifice, not self-assertion; history will lead the nation to its natural end in God.[143]

As arguments like these suggest, Lincoln's new covenant did not prevail. The American crisis of confidence was overridden by the end of the war and the advent of industrial expansion. The desolation of the Civil War passed, but what revived America was not *public* rebirth but *private* well-being. Even those, like Bushnell, Brownson, and Mulford, who criticized the modern and liberal foundations of American political culture were unwilling to criticize seriously, let alone to abandon, modern political and economic institutions. They spoke of a new spirit; they retained the old form. Yet such ideas were not without effect: Lincoln's ideal did survive, and it coexists, warringly, with the liberal creed within American political culture. In the nineteenth century, as Mulford's optimism suggests, such conflicts were easier to sustain than they are today because so many Americans trusted that progress would bring things right.

It was, in any case, a difficult time for biblical doctrine, as the Bible was buffeted by historical criticism and evolutionary theory. There were plenty of theologians, like Lyman Abbott, Henry Drummond, or Theodore Munger, willing to define the Bible in evolutionary terms. The Bible, Munger wrote, is an "unfolding revelation" whose laws and teachings are "evolving their truth and reality in the process of history."[144] Formulations of that sort, obviously, made it easy to dispense with biblical teaching whenever it proved inconvenient, most frequently in the conflict between biblical precepts and the ethics of industrial capitalism.

The moral roots of protest, by contrast, were planted in scripture. Leaders like William Jennings Bryan or Walter Rauschenbusch explicitly appealed to biblical religion, but even humanists like Henry George and Henry Demarest Lloyd, who disclaimed their Christian beginnings, reveal the influence of biblical morality and imagery on every page. Yet even in the Social Gospel, a good deal of the Bible's teaching has been adulterated or lost. There is almost none of the Bible's sense of the limits to human possibility and very little of the Bible's recognition of the moral multidimensionality of human nature. Human meanness and destructiveness tend to be explained away, and the stronger human loyalties are harmonized too easily with broader obligations. The biblical tradition, in other words, showed unmistakable signs of degeneration into sentimentalism.[145]

The Reform Darwinism of Progressive theory drew its metaphors from the fashionable evolutionism of the time. Yet, as Eric Goldman demonstrated, its real lodestar was the ideal of fraternal union, an implicit absolute of political morality.[146] In addition to its own sentimentalism, Progressive teaching turned on a relativism that left its morality without foundation. Over time, the argument disintegrated into the position that values and virtues are "all relative," private in principle, lacking any public dimension. Moreover, Progressives were beguiled by the notion that technology, including the "social sciences" that Progressives did so much to develop, could be shorn of its destructiveness and used to realize good ends. They rejected that most empirical of biblical teachings, the observation that human beings are imperfect creatures, in whose hands power for good always involves power for evil.

Yet more orthodox believers have little to boast of. Embattled by the currents of social change and secularity, they have grown increasingly desperate, and they often seem more concerned to defend the Bible than they are to read it.[147] Moreover, contemporary evangelical Christianity seems inclined to forget, as its predecessors rarely did, that capitalism and technological change are agents of social disintegration and moral decay. Given that error, it is not surprising that self-proclaimed leaders of biblical orthodoxy pass over the fact that, in scripture, the support of the poor is a public duty.[148]

It is undeniable, however, that the influence of biblical teaching has grown less and less powerful and articulate with the passing of time. Biblical ideas and images remain planted in American culture and surface from time to time—in the writings of Steinbeck and Faulkner, for example—but fewer and fewer Americans recognize their source.[149] Even explicit references to the Bible do not prompt many readers to reflect on the text. Nevertheless, the civil rights movement demonstrated, even to the obtuse, the continuing political power of the biblical tradition.

Contemporary America is a house divided, ruled by a Babel of private goals and armed with a technology of unparalleled potential for destruction and domination. Even very secular theorists, impressed with the "contradictions" of our life, now call for "religion," although they ordinarily intend a creed to support the established order, not biblical faith.[150] More orthodox voices are not always better advised. Today, militant believers are inclined to struggle for "nondenominational" prayer in the public schools, a policy that is possibly unconstitutional and certainly vacuous. It would make a good deal more sense to demand "nonreligious" instruction in the Bible as literature, a policy almost certainly constitutional and one with genuine content. Secular instruction in the Bible is better than none, and the Bible, as I have been arguing here, has considerable ability to take care of itself.

In any event, the articulate and silent desperation of our times is great enough that Americans may be willing to abandon some of the illusions of individualism and the quest for mastery, bringing Lincoln's new covenant closer to reality. It is also possible, of course, that America is doomed. That would be a reason for sorrow, but even so, the Bible reminds us that all regimes and peoples wither like the grass and only the Lord endures.

3

Protestant Prudence and Natural Rights

As usual, Alexis de Tocqueville got it right: from the beginning of the Republic, American political culture has been incoherent, an unresolved argument—ordinarily implicit and more or less civil—between the "spirit of liberty" and the "spirit of religion."[1]

Over the years, just as Tocqueville expected, the "spirit of liberty," entrenched in the laws, has gained ground at the expense of its rival, so that today, the languages of individualism dominate moral discourse.[2] In contemporary society, the prevailing norms seem to be an almost universal tolerance and a respect for private liberty, while the biblical voice in American culture is increasingly marginalized or inarticulate.[3] Nevertheless, that the old quarrel persists is clear from the headlines: devoted to material well-being, Americans are also prone to militant and bizarre faiths, unquestioning in their belief in equality yet apparently inclined to accept inequalities greater than those in any other industrial country. And it is only a little less evident that the old contest is still being waged in and for American souls.

Michael Zuckert is right, on the whole, in emphasizing the Lockean secularity of the American founding, the framers' devotion to natural right. I

Originally published as "Protestant Prudence and the Natural Rights Republic," in *Protestantism and the American Founding*, ed. Thomas S. Engeman and Michael P. Zuckert (Notre Dame, Ind.: University of Notre Dame Press, 2004), 143–164. Reprinted by permission of the Notre Dame University Press. *Protestantism and the American Founding* was organized as a series of responses to the lead essay by Michael Zuckert, entitled "Natural Rights and Protestant Politics." Drawn from his book *The Natural Rights Republic*, Zuckert's essay argues that the American founding period is an "amalgam" of various strands of thought and belief, including Lockeanism, liberalism, Republicanism, and Protestantism. In this response, McWilliams agrees in part that the founding was composed of these various strands of thought, but he argues against the view that this "amalgam" constituted an easy "bedfellowship." Further, he seeks to contest Zuckert's view that the Declaration of Independence can be read strictly as an expression of Lockean political philosophy, instead pointing to aspects of the document that show it to be more internally complex and, hence, riven by internal tension—like America itself.

will be arguing, however, that he understates the peculiar harmonics of the American tradition. G. K. Chesterton argued that America is a "nation with the soul of a church," its creed stated in the Declaration of Independence, and up to that point, his view of America's civil theology parallels Zuckert's.[4] But in Chesterton's reading, equality, not natural rights, is the foundation of the American tradition, a teaching that follows Lincoln in seeing a nation "conceived in liberty" but "dedicated to the proposition that all men are created equal."

Linked with Gettysburg in our memory, the battle hymn of our "natural rights republic" is a distinctly Protestant counterpoint, and even in these later days, one can hear that sound, as I suspect Lincoln did, in the silences even more than the tumults of national life.

People of Paradox

In the founding era, Americans were already a "people of paradox," easily convinced of their rights and attracted by Lockean teaching yet, in their various ways, attached to Christianity.[5] In practice, consequently, political speech was necessarily a kind of compromise, its idiom shaped by the ambivalences of publics—and speakers, for that matter—and by the demands of coalition-building (especially, of course, if one hoped to address thirteen colonies, diverse in faith and politics). This ambiguity was partly a rhetorical stratagem, adopted to beguile or persuade, but it was also a defining characteristic, even a fundamental principle, of the American founding itself: an agreement not to agree or to insist on intellectual rigor, a decision to leave disagreements on ultimate issues to a later time and to the subsequent politics of the Republic.[6]

In any case, Americans shared considerable common ground, especially where politics was concerned. Virtually all of them were the products of British experience, more or less accustomed to English institutions and law. They were, almost without exception, devoted to the freedom of conscience (although a great many held that liberty to be compatible with religious establishments). And with some exceptions—Quakers, for example, or High Tory Anglicans—they held at least similar views on the propriety of resistance to oppressive governments.

Zuckert regards this commonality as the result of Lockean influences on Protestant thinking, pointing to the gap between Martin Luther's interpretation of Romans 13 as a demand for passive submission to civil authority and Samuel West's reading of the same text as justifying resistance to unjust government. Certainly, West (and similar thinkers, like Jonathan

Mayhew) reflected Locke's influence, especially in his enthusiasm for the right to rebel. But Zuckert slights the extent to which West's treatment of Romans 13 is truer to the text and has its own thoroughly Protestant provenance. If rulers, as Paul declares, are "not a terror to good works, but to the evil," divinely appointed "to execute wrath on him that doeth evil," then a ruler who commands or even condones evil has violated the terms of his commission—what Calvin called the "true and natural duty of the magistrate"—and is essentially no ruler at all: "dictatorships and unjust authorities," Calvin wrote, "are not ordained governments."[7] The power of magistrates, in these terms, is not unbridled: they are "responsible to God *and to men* in the exercise of their rule" (my italics).[8] Calvin held that even tyranny protects human society and hence has some claim on us, but his argument also indicated that human beings have some title to hold government accountable. Luther, as Zuckert indicates, followed much of the Christian tradition in prescribing nonviolent resistance to illegitimate authority; Calvin famously opened the door, on secular grounds, to resistance of a more active sort.[9]

Still, Zuckert's distinction is pointed: even when they supported armed resistance to Great Britain, the orthodox Protestant clergy ordinarily spoke of reconciliation as desirable, if it could be had without violation of the rights of the colonies. Seeing human beings as naturally social and so many parts of a created whole, they tended to see just dependence as the proper human standard. That view, obviously, is one of the targets of Tom Paine's case for independence in *Common Sense*, an argument that proceeds from a thoroughgoing understanding of the proposition that human beings are naturally free.[10]

The leading spirits of the founding generation were rarely as extreme—and even less frequently as indiscreet—as Paine. Nevertheless, they spoke a decisively secular political language, deriving civil government from natural rights and essentially private purposes, and most were at least skeptical about revealed religion.[11] Yet even those not given to piety had at least three reasons to conciliate and speak respectfully of religion.

In the first place, they were bound to acknowledge the power of religion, its hold on the allegiance of the broader American public: in *Common Sense*, even Paine appealed, albeit deviously, to biblical authority. Second, they saw religion, properly limited, as an invaluable support for secular, civil morality.

In their theorizing, for example, contract was the foundation of civil society, and it was easy to lay out a compelling argument for making the promises necessary to bring society and government into being. But though society and government are clearly useful, the case for keeping promises in civil society is less certain, since for a self-regarding person, the truly desirable state would be the freedom to break one's promises while others keep theirs. The response that it is in my interest to keep my promises (including obedience to the laws) because violators are likely to be detected and punished is too unreliable for civil comfort. The possible gains may easily seem to outweigh the risks where desires are strong, where the prize is very great, or where those who are tempted to break the rules are—like the poor or slaves or women—people on the margins of society who have little or nothing to lose. The more insecure the society, moreover, the more impossible it is to limit the role of government: a free society, consequently, must treat the obligation of contracts as holy, beyond question or calculation. Hence, Locke, defending toleration, excluded atheists: "The taking away of God, but even in thought, dissolves all."[12] The American framers did not go so far, but they treated religion in the private sphere as a crucial ally of the laws.

Third, religion made sovereign claims, if only subtly, on the moral reasoning of the founders. Reason, Locke had argued, indicates that human beings have some responsibility to and for what they have begotten. But reason is not enough, Locke observed in *The Reasonableness of Christianity*, to forbid parents to kill their children by exposing them, as the undeniably civilized ancients had done.[13] That prohibition, Locke conceded, depends on revelation.

The moral rule protecting infants is one Americans still accept, even in these days when "reproductive rights" receive the support of considerable majorities. In fact, both Locke's argument and American civil morals go beyond negative rights and the obligations of contract: they assert that we owe a duty to nurture children once born, that children have a positive right to be cared for that is clearly not "contractual," since children, as they often remind us, did not ask to be born.

In the founding era and since, many Americans have linked such moral propositions to an evolving moral "sense" or "instinct," giving a secular turn to the argument.[14] Even such thinkers, however, are obliged to concede that American culture—and with it, American ideas of what is rational or self-evident—incorporates teachings historically, if not necessarily, rooted in revelation.[15]

Zuckert's analysis, though shrewd, underrates the multivocality of the Declaration of Independence. He is right, of course, to reject Wilmoore Kendall and George Carey's reading of the Declaration as an effort "to make clear above all else" the founders' "commitment to the will of God."[16] But the Declaration's artful ambiguities were designed to allow such interpretations, even if the Declaration's authors were thinking, inwardly, in very different terms. Moreover, Zuckert's claim that the duties of rulers, as envisioned by the Declaration, solely "derive from the original rights" is not entirely accurate—or not unambiguously accurate. Those rights, an endowment or trust, are explicitly unalienable, an entail *on* natural rights that must derive from the Creator's dowering, since it is not evident from the rights themselves.[17]

Similarly, Zuckert to the contrary, the Declaration does not say that there is no authority prior to government; it does not refer to a "state of nature" or even to a "social contract." Rather, Jefferson used a term with grand, Calvinist associations, saying that "to secure these rights, governments are *instituted*" (my italics).

This usage was at least open to the theory on which the Puritans (and most Calvinists) relied, that although it is unnatural for human beings to be without government, God leaves it to them to "institute" it, allowing a certain latitude for human framing and naming. Hence, as Zuckert indicates, John Winthrop held that whereas magistrates are "called" to office by the people, their authority and duty derive from God.[18] In the same way, although Samuel Langdon's 1775 sermon, "Government Corrupted by Vice," adopts the language of natural rights, as Zuckert observes, and is broadly agnostic about the forms of government, Langdon also refers to the human condition without government as "the vilest of slavery and worse than death." Notably, Langdon does not call this "dreadful" situation a state of nature, since he thinks of it as profoundly unnatural, just as he does not think of it as a state of unlimited liberty but of slavery. For Langdon, in fact, the crucial natural right is that of forming "order and government." The rights that matter to Langdon are collective; he does not speak of individual rights at all, and unlike Jefferson, he is tolerably specific about the forms and ways—principally majority rule—by which a "people" can be said to act.[19] Yet Langdon's political doctrine, with some squeezing here and there, can be fitted into the frame of the Declaration, as Jefferson and his committee almost certainly intended.

Most important, beyond bare assertion, the Declaration is silent about the meaning of its first principle of human right, the proposition that human beings are "created equal." It is hard to imagine that this vagueness is not designed, since on its face, the doctrine of equality is contrary to common sense, a mystery calling for explanation.[20]

Up to a point, the "spirit of liberty" and the "spirit of religion" agree about equality. Both John Winthrop and John Locke—and the Declaration, for that matter—treat equality as compatible with differences of wealth and rank, a moral principle not everywhere applied in practice. But at a fundamental level, the two views are at odds. Locke begins with an equality of rights, the "equal right that every man hath to his natural freedom" that effectively gives first place to liberty.[21] Government may rest on equality before the law, but its purpose is to allow inequalities to emerge from the indistinction of the state of nature: the "first object of government," Madison declares, is to protect the "diversity in the faculties of men."[22] Following that view, Zuckert uncharacteristically departs from the text of the Declaration to argue that the Declaration's implicit view of history begins with human beings who are "free and equal," hence naturally independent. Yet even though Jefferson's drafts assert this view, the Declaration's text makes liberty a separate endowment and one that yields precedence to equality.

In so doing, the Declaration conciliates the "spirit of religion." John Winthrop argued, in his "Model of Christian Charity," that God made human beings different in ability so that they would be forced by need to recognize communality and prodded toward equality. Human beings vary only as parts of a whole: "Noe man is made more honourable than another, or more wealthy etc., out of any particuler and singuler respect to himselfe but for the glory of his Creator and the Common Good of the Creature, Man."[23] Where Locke treats equal rights as a means to differentiation, Winthrop makes difference a means to equality.

Moreover, like his text in 1 Corinthians, Winthrop goes on to maintain that human beings need charity in order to warm mere interdependence into cherished and hallowed community.[24] The echoes carry to Gettysburg and beyond: a political society can be dedicated to equality, Winthrop holds, only to the extent that its members are linked in civic fraternity. As Zuckert indicates, the Declaration and the Constitution accept a lower standard, a more diffuse and diverse communion, its union relying on cooler sentiments and calculations of interest. Yet even in that diminished sense, it is still true that any political community affords benefits that are undeserved, most obviously through birthright but also through the civil rights indiscriminately granted to all citizens—a kind of grace, Winthrop would remind us, the mirror of the love God feels for humankind.[25] Democratic citizenship requires that we love our fellows enough to sacrifice for them, when necessary abridging our natural rights to liberty, life, and property out of a sense of civic obligation.[26]

Nevertheless, for all their silences and ambiguities, the Declaration and the Constitution do change the terms of the debate between two visions of equality and political community, giving the "spirit of liberty" a comfort in the laws that is denied to the "spirit of religion." Even so, in the founding era and since, the "spirit of religion" has offered its own rebuttal, sometimes in tumults but more often—and perhaps most tellingly—in a voice that is soft or still.

Strange Bedfellows

Itself beset by disagreements and resentments and necessarily multivocal, eighteenth-century American religion had its own motives for civic accommodation and, hence, the emollients of its varieties of politic discourse.[27]

Protestantism included many ministers and believers who, for all the reasons Zuckert indicates, had come to adopt Locke's teaching, at least in politics and often in religion.[28] The leading congregations in Massachusetts were already sliding toward Unitarianism, and Natural Religion was intellectually voguish almost everywhere. Even among the more or less orthodox, as Zuckert points out, a growing number of Protestants, like Elisha Williams, had taken an important step in the direction of the "natural rights republic." Older Calvinist doctrine treated salvation as highest among the goods of the soul, a list that also included political community and life according to "rules of holiness, integrity and sobriety," a schooling in the "duties of humanity and civility."[29] By contrast, Williams identified the "good of the soul" with salvation, separating the soul from politics in a way that is compatible with secular liberalism.[30] And in the long term, just as Zuckert suggests, teachings like Williams's have tended to become stronger in American religion.[31] In the eighteenth century, however, such thinking was at best radically controversial: Williams's doctrine was so offensive to his fellow Protestants, "Old Light" and "New Light" alike, that he was denied reelection to the Connecticut Supreme Court.[32]

Protestant orthodoxy was still American religion's dominant voice, though hearing its subtleties requires a trained ear. In the first place, its teaching was profoundly rationalistic—despite the "New Light" emphasis on an appeal to the affections—although it held that faith is necessary to reason's full realization. In principle, reason can discern the created whole and can even catch a hint of its Creator: the universe is full of "lamps."[33] But the Fall distorts reason: self-centered human beings resent and resist the truth, that witness to our finitude and mortality. Revelation, by contrast, can liberate us to follow reason, acting in a way analogous to the effect of "spectacles" on natural vision, helping to mediate our quarrel with our own nature.[34] And even though unaided reason falls short of reason informed by revelation, the two overlap: reason marks out a common ground, a public space in which the logic of discourse leads us beyond simple self-preoccupation and in which, up to a point, political deliberation is possible.

Partly as a necessary concession to the speech of that public sphere, the spokesmen of orthodox religion often felt compelled to adapt their teaching to the new intellectual climate, recognizing that "the language of modern heresy would not adequately be refuted by old-fashioned dogmatism."[35] It was common, consequently, for champions of the older understanding to adopt the terms of the newer theorizing as starting points, aiming to turn modern teaching right side up by a combination of dialectic and guile. As Perry Miller wrote of John Wise, who drew on Pufendorf and referred to Locke, "he would use what he had found, but his tongue was in his cheek," and his rhetoric, shaped to the demands of practice, was full of "tricks to catch the unwary."[36]

This tendency to make concessions to prevailing public language, moreover, was more than a design for persuasion. In the political sphere, Protestant doctrine supported a special prudence and restraint in speech as a matter of duty. Christians, Luther argues, are inwardly free, raised by their link to Jesus above all earthly conventions, able to discern the essential equality of human beings. Consequently, they are bound to disdain—in spirit—the distinctions of nation, class, and gender that are indispensable to secular life, including the law, which for a Christian should be needless.[37]

However, Luther goes on to contend that in practice, in a world that includes unbelievers as well as believers—where, in fact, believers come in all degrees of faith, and no faith is perfect—"we cannot live our lives without ceremonies and works." The ordering of secular life demands forms, distinctions, and laws, their boundaries marked by natural reason as opposed to faith.[38]

A Christian's freedom makes him inwardly aware of the inadequacy of such forms, but a believer feels no need for that liberty to be "witnessed by men."[39] Free thought does not entail free expression. Quite the contrary, exercising liberty in the highest sense, a Christian freely limits his speech and conduct in a way suited to the moral and spiritual upbuilding of his fellows, observing and respecting laws made for the sake of the weaker and less edified: as a Christian, Luther wrote, I am to "give myself as a Christ to my neighbor."[40] And for eighteenth-century Calvinists, Alan Heimert observed, it was almost axiomatic that one should not "neglect the spiritual needs of the many in order to titillate the few."[41]

It must be emphasized that this concession to secular practice is not simply a matter of going along with established authorities or prevailing opinions.[42] It is intended to be artful, speaking such truth as circumstance can bear, an educational stratagem in a grand struggle fought for spiritual and moral stakes.[43] "I am made all things to all men," Paul had declared, "that I might by all means save some."[44] This Christian prudence, in its own way, can rival Machiavelli's; Jesus told his disciples that, sent "as sheep among wolves," they should not only be "as harmless as doves" but also be "as wise as serpents," the subtlest of the beasts.[45]

Consider only one example, the first of Nathaniel Niles's remarkable *Two Discourses on Liberty*, originally delivered at Newburyport in 1774.[46] Beyond the inherent force of his argument, Niles spoke with formidable Protestant credentials, in the pulpit or in practical politics: his sermon, as Heimert wrote, affords "an entrance to the mind of Revolutionary Calvinism" and not the least to its rhetoric.[47]

Certainly, Niles ranks among the sharpest critics of liberal theorizing, in politics or religion.[48] He upheld the traditional view that community is magisterial, concerned with the education of the soul—if only because civil liberty depends on liberty in spirit—so that religion and politics are inextricably linked. And as will become clear, Niles was no champion of natural rights, at least in the ordinary sense of that term.

At the same time, however, Niles's proximate political aim in 1774 was to support the colonies in their quarrel with Great Britain. That purpose, obviously, ranged Niles on the side of thinkers who departed from or flatly rejected Christian orthodoxy, especially in its political claims. Pragmatically interested in the working unity of that coalition, Niles—on other occasions a grand controversialist—hoped to avoid giving needless offense to his allies.[49]

Yet Niles also wanted to remind his shrewdest readers of the fundamental antagonism that divided them from secular liberals and partisans of natural religion.[50] Any cooperation was necessarily tentative and transient; those who stood with Niles had to be kept on their guard, alert for the signs of that fundamental conflict. His discourse is accordingly artful, furnished with clues and hints, silently affirming what politic speech seemed to forbid.[51]

Niles made this tolerably clear in the "Advertisement" that preceded the printed version of his discourses.[52] He cannot provide an "exact copy" of the sermon, Niles claims, because he spoke extemporaneously, for the most part. But he has "carefully preserved" those things of which a copy might be desired, retaining the "ideas" and adding "several new thoughts" to replace some now-forgotten "expressions." This indicates a design, a teaching that preserves its essentials but has also been changed, adapted to a new and presumably broader audience. Yet Niles claims to be hurried, calling attention to "imperfections" in "stile and manner" that, he says, doubtless will be observed. Still, he goes on, "every means, however imperfect" is needed to advance the spirit of "true liberty."[53] Lacking complete knowledge of the various "branches of civil liberty," Niles says that he attends only to the "main ideas"—an apparent humility that also asserts Niles's command of liberty's first principles. And he concludes with the observation that "the inquisitive mind will be able to draw a number of important consequences." Niles's "inquisitive" readers, in other words, are invited to look beyond the text and to see through its "imperfections" to the purpose that inspired them.

Niles's aim, he says, is to "awaken" proper sentiments regarding spiritual and religious liberty and, specifically, to argue that civil liberty without spiritual liberty is like "a body without a soul." (In Niles's sense, of course, liberty of spirit does not refer to freedom of conscience from external control but to a spirit that is free inwardly, unensnared by the world's temptations and undaunted by its powers.) This purpose assumes that some of Niles's countrymen deny this and that others have been lulled by them: Niles, in other words, is contending against an insinuating secularism, all too successful in his America.

His text is 1 Corinthians 7:21, a classic statement of the doctrine of Christian liberty: "Art thou called, being a servant? Care not for it. But if thou mayest be free, use it rather." Paul assures believers, in other words, that their spirits can be free despite this-worldly necessities and restraints but also—Niles points out—that it is preferable to be at liberty.[54] And if freedom is a good when enjoyed by one, Niles argues, it must be a greater good when enjoyed by many: hence, he concludes emphatically: "CIVIL LIBERTY IS A GREAT GOOD."[55]

Like Paul, Niles teaches that human beings, though ordinarily blind to the truth, are already emancipated, "bought for a price" by Jesus's sacrifice of himself—of his life, of course, but also of his very divinity.[56] To the discerning, the incarnation shows that the highest sort of freedom, beyond fears and ambitions, beyond the control of "principalities and powers," is the limitation or sacrifice of self out of love for others.[57] Our freedom, consequently, is measured by our capacity to love and our civil liberty by our dedication to the common good. If we are to "perfect" freedom, Niles contends, "everyone must be required to do all that he can that tends to the highest good of the state."[58]

"Originally," Niles declares, "there were no private interests" and, one presumes, no private rights.[59] Even Niles's first audience was probably a little startled, and it would take some considerable agility to make his assertion even minimally compatible with natural rights doctrine.[60] Niles's argument is implicitly Aristotelian: our individuality is developed in and through the polis.[61] Our private rights and interests are "constructed," as we might say nowadays, by the public, "distributed among . . . individuals according as they appear in the eyes of the body politic, to be qualified to use them for the good of the whole."[62] In that sense, what we conventionally call the "particular properties of each individual member" are actually "the public interest deposited in the hands of individuals."[63]

For Niles, as for his Puritan ancestors, political society is a moral and educational enterprise, of which liberty is a part. "Good government is essential to the very being of liberty. . . . Their rise and fall is exactly uniform." Civil liberty demands a regime of laws—for the inclinations and opinions of sinful humanity are no adequate foundation—but law itself aims at edification. It should see that bad citizens are punished but also that good ones are rewarded, hoping to turn even low passions to decent behavior: rightly ordered liberty, Niles comments, "renders political virtue fashionable" and, promoting industry, frugality, "decent conversation and courteous behaviour" prompts "even pride and avarice to mimic humanity, and every generous sentiment."[64]

The goal of civic education is the free spirit, "a spirit that is consonant to a free constitution—a spirit that seeks the highest good of the community, in its proper place," capable of self-government and linked to its fellows by fraternal affection, the old Puritan utopia.[65]

Niles concedes that "there never has been, nor ever will be such a general state of mind" (even contending, in his second discourse, that given the necessary imperfections of politics, the "degree of liberty that can reasonably be expected of earthly states is very low" and tainted with bitterness and blood), but he rejects the implied Machiavellian critique.[66] In fact, Niles argues, the seen points to the unseen: we infer the nature of liberty from "the small degree of liberty, with which we are acquainted." And, implicit in practice, the ideal is the standard by which we properly judge and measure the excellence of the politically possible, just as truly free spirits, though rare, are like "spices" scattered through a society, capable of giving it flavor.[67]

Every good regime, Niles observes, needs an element of free-spiritedness. Even very secular thinkers, as noted earlier, recognized that self-interest is an inadequate support for contracts: breaking one's faith is detestable precisely because contracts are "sacred things." (And if sacred, Niles goes on, addressing his immediate political concern, then binding on kings: anyone who teaches otherwise "dethrones the King, and subverts the constitution of nature itself.")[68]

Moreover, liberty requires watchfulness, the vigilance that comes from seeing freedom as a "sacred loan" from God, to be guarded not only so far as it agrees with our interest or comfort but as a duty.[69] Even government by majority—the safest form of rule, Niles emphasizes, and also the best—may become inattentive or tyrannical, and to oppose or unsettle it is likely to prove at least unpopular and perhaps mortally perilous.[70] Democratic self-government requires an element of nobility, the recognition that "it is great, it is glorious, to espouse a good cause, and it is still more great and glorious to stand alone."[71]

Finally, the free spirit—aware of liberty as a gift from God—discerns that freedom for some is incompatible spiritually with the slavery of others. To enslave another is to pander to the slavishness in ourselves, our desire to avoid labor, our dependence on what gratifies, our itch for dominion. Americans, Niles observes, have been guilty of "a tyrannical spirit in a free country," and as such, they have no consistent moral case against would-be oppressors: "Let us either cease to enslave our fellow-men, or else let us cease to complain of those that would enslave us. Let us either wash our hands from blood, or never hope to escape the avenger."[72]

And for the end immediately in view, Niles urges his hearers to return to "the plain manner of our fore-fathers" and unite, with "piety and economy," in advancing the case of the colonies against Great Britain. In that controversy, Niles argues for defending colonial rights while upholding the authority of the king, the nominally constitutional "personal union" favored by many of those, especially in the clergy, who hoped for some sort of reconciliation. But he also leaves no doubt that Americans should treat the right as "inexpressibly dear."

In the body of his sermon, in other words, Niles presents a communitarian Protestant's political polemic, including the obligatory invocation of the danger of "popery" as well as military despotism, directed largely to practice and conduct, with only incidental reference to the intellectual combats of the day.[73]

Against Locke

Niles's footnotes are a different matter. His first—a very long one—extends his rejection of the idea of natural private rights, beginning with a theological reflection on God's ownership of all things. Locke had argued that God, as maker of heaven and earth, has "given the world to men in common" or "the best advantage of life and convenience," although even in this original state of commonality, "every man has a property in his person."[74] Niles contends that God gave the world to Adam and his posterity "in certain respects" and "to be managed for the grand company" (i.e., God, angels and humans). Thus, in Niles's telling, the original gift is limited—in some ways, angels have management of the world—and for the common good, not simply for self-preservation. And against Locke, Niles argues that in a state of nature, human beings "have nothing that they can call their own" to the exclusion of God, angels or their fellow men. Even our persons, in other words, naturally belong to the whole.[75]

Earthly states, Niles argues, turning to politics, were formed either (1) by the predominance of one individual, who acquired despotic power to rule, preempting the claims of the public in the service of his own interests or passions, or (2) by the compact of the few or the many to secure their own private interests. But both of these regimes, Niles contends, are based on usurpation, the subordination of what is common to the service of private claims. A greater number of private interests checking each other may moderate the worst effects of despotism; it does not change the thing itself. "It matters not whether men who build their notions of government on self-interest, call themselves whigs or tories, friends to prerogative, or to the liberties of the people." And when Niles goes on that "they cannot blame their neighbour for commencing tory when it will be most conducive to his private interest," he makes it reasonably clear that his real animus is directed against Whigs.[76]

Niles is both more pointed and more cryptic at the end of his second footnote, which speaks of that sanctity of contracts that binds both subjects and kings. He refers "truce breakers and traitors" to 2 Timothy 3:1–4, "if they know where to find it," so that they may see "with whom they are ranked by their Maker."[77] The slighting aside, "if they know where to find it" evidently indicates Niles is speaking of people who, if religious at all, are not inclined to dote on scripture. Just as clearly, it is an invitation to consult the passage Niles has cited, in which Paul speaks of covetous "self-lovers" who pursue pleasure without "natural affection." In other words, self-seeking individualism, even when allied with a deist's faith in a "Maker" (though not the revealed word), inherently works to undermine the contracts that are the basis of individualistic social theory.[78]

Even more striking, however, is the subtext that underlies Niles's plea for unity—and the willingness to endure austerity—in the colonial quarrel with Britain. If salvation has not come from King George, Niles comments, "we cannot expect it from the hills. We must look still higher."[79] This is an obvious reference to the 121st Psalm—"I will lift up mine eyes unto the hills, from whence cometh my help"—but Niles's comment is odd, apparently contrary to the psalmist's, since Niles argues that Americans cannot expect help from the hills. Looking "still higher" might refer to the Lord, but the Lord, according to the psalmist, is the source of the help he expects from the hills.[80] Since it not likely that Niles is disdaining the divine aid to which he repeatedly appeals, it seems plausible that Niles's "higher" involves a double entendre, "above" as in a text, referring to Psalm 120.

In that psalm, the singer says that he has lived "with him, that hateth peace," and asks to be delivered "from lying lips and a false tongue." And the psalm concludes, "I am for peace (or, I am a man of peace), but when I speak, they are for war."[81] The psalmist indicates, in other words, that conflict is concealed beneath fair words and the appearance of unity, a combat that will become evident if the psalmist speaks openly. But that, it immediately becomes clear, Niles has no intention of doing.

He advises Americans not to rail against man, preferring the example of Michael, "who railed not against the Devil himself."[82] Niles refers to the ninth chapter of Jude, in which Michael is said not to have dared to rail against Satan, leaving it to the Lord to rebuke him: some criticism is, in the order of things, best left to God. Yet the appeal to Jude is apposite in another way: Jude denounces men who "crept in unawares," corrupting faith and conduct: "These speak evil of those things which they know not, but what they know naturally, as the brute beasts" and who "separate themselves sensual, having not the spirit."[83] This sounds rather like Lockeans or, at least, like advocates of natural religion, so apt to reject spiritual knowledge along with revelation in favor of the instinctive, passional knowledge shared with the beasts or that knowledge derived from the senses. A number of these had surely "crept" into pulpits or positions of influence, if not entirely "unawares": even so, Niles hints, it is not the time to attack them directly.

"David said of Shimei," Niles goes on, "let him curse, for the Lord hath bidden him." In Niles's account, David accepted Shimei's cursing as a punishment from God, "while he was not insensible to the wickedness of Shimei."[84] In this great story in 2 Samuel, David says pretty much what Niles attributes to him, noting sadly that his son Absalom is also in rebellion against him. But he does so from calculation: seeing him bear this affliction, David says, God "will requite me good for his cursing."[85]

Moreover, the story does not end there. When Absalom is defeated, Shimei comes seeking pardon. The "sons of Zeruiah," presumably including the formidable Joab, again urge David to have him killed. David, however, rejects this counsel in the interests of reconciliation, promising to spare Shimei's life.[86] Finally, however, in 1 Kings, a dying David advises Solomon to have Shimei (and Joab, for that matter) put to death.[87] For Solomon to execute Shimei—like Don Corleone's posthumous retaliation through his son, Michael—does not violate David's promise.[88] And as David recognizes, Shimei is too treacherous and too dangerous to be left alive, given the uncertain hand and authority of a new king.

Directing his attentive readers to that story, Niles was teaching that there are times when forbearance is prudent, especially in the interest of avoiding civil conflict. But there are also times, at moments of crisis, and particularly in founding a new regime, when fundamental animosities must be confronted and ultimate loyalties addressed.

Muting denunciations of those enemies in theory who are, for the moment, allies in practice—"there's no evil in the city which the Lord hath not done"—Niles suggests that, like Daniel, he and his fellows should "pour out our hearts before God."[89] This presumably refers to the ninth chapter of Daniel, where the prophet prays for forgiveness and for Jerusalem and receives assurance that the Messianic kingdom will eventually arrive but is warned that "unto the end of the war, desolations are determined."[90] Daniel himself is rendered dumb, having seen the glory of the coming of the Lord: in relation to theoretical disagreements—especially in relation to the City upon the Hill—silence or civil debate should be the political rule, at least until the end of the struggle and possibly until the last days. Niles designed his two discourses as the mirrors of Protestantism's two modes of speech. In the first place, the "laudable" effort to secure civil liberty demands tactical accommodations to secular circumstance and rhetoric tailored to the shape of political practice.[91] But it is the quest for spiritual liberty that sets the measure, weighing tactical choices and defining principles that cannot be compromised and confrontations that cannot be avoided.[92] And it reminds Christians that they speak a language—and seek a city—alien to even the best secular politics, seeing only idols where others see sacred laws. In this world, Niles reminded his hearers, Christians are like Israel, a formerly "enslaved people" passing through "barbarous nations" on their way to liberty: servitude in Egypt yields only to a politics in which all are at least moderately slavish. Consequently, Christians must always be spiritually armed and on guard. They live in a state of "steady warfare, a constant skirmish."[93] Conflict is never overcome, only suppressed; any "cessation of arms," whether from "fear of one another" or from love and hope, leaves

Christians in the "precincts of battle."[94] And in such situations, if it needs saying, one guards one's tongue, partly in order to preserve the Word.

Persistent Divisions

And yet, there are times and seasons when the moral stakes in secular politics call for religion to speak in something more like its own voice, discarding old alliances and institutions in favor of renovation or renewal.[95]

At "the end of the war," as Daniel had been counseled, the founding of a new regime brought the differences between Americans into the political foreground, divisions that—like Solomon and Shimei—often seemed matters of life and death.[96] And religion has won its victories, sometimes great ones, in those early battles and in the Republic's succeeding moments of decision—slavery and the "crisis of the house divided," for example, or the grand combats of the age of reform or in the civil rights movement—providing a critical voice, a vocabulary of protest, and, especially, an egalitarianism warmed into a conviction of fraternity.[97]

That, nevertheless, individualism has gained the upper hand in American life and thought or that acquisitiveness and increasing inequality are defining characteristics in contemporary American society would not have surprised Niles and his fellow Calvinists. Edwards had taught that, short of the end, fallen nature sets the general direction of history, only checked or deflected periodically by divine interventions, which themselves soon give way to resurgent nature.[98]

Believers persist despite these chronic disappointments, Niles and his school argued, because they are confident in final victory. The frustrating delay of that triumph is a test of faith and perseverance: waiting for the end is also an opportunity for witness. It is also a reflection of divine artistry: God chose to give scope to wickedness, Joseph Bellamy contended, because against the background of its apparent success, God's glory would seem even more luminous and beautiful.[99] The sanctified, Niles wrote, expect to see the universe "rising in perfection forever and ever."[100]

Even a smaller degree of that assurance, lightening despair, also moderates any felt need for desperate measures. It encourages a willingness to accept, for this time, the second-rate decencies of civil liberty, to endure the flawed coalitions and abide by the armed truce of republican life.

For that matter, a secular faith in progress can make liberals more willing to conciliate religion, making a place for it at the table of public life—readier, in other words, to trust democratic politics, without insisting, as a precondition, on a distinctively liberal code of rights and neutralities.

If contemporary America is racked by "culture wars," it may be because both sides of the combat have less faith in the end and are hence more eager for signs and proximate victories.[101] A "spirit of liberty" confident that it speaks for nature and a "spirit of religion" that reaches beyond tragedy might find their way back to civility, to serious and reasoned discourse about what is human. And that, if it needs saying, is something we urgently need.[102]

4

The Anti-Federalists, Representation, and Party

BOTH ANTI-FEDERALISTS AND FEDERALISTS claimed to champion representation, but, as was often true in the founding debate, the two sides set similar words to very different music. The Anti-Federalists contended, somewhat derisively, that representation was an ancient idea, a concept "as old as the history of mankind."[1] The Federalists, in contrast, maintained that "the great principle of representation," first developed in "modern Europe," had reached fruition only in the eighteenth-century American idea of "unmixed and extensive republics."[2] Anti-Federalists regarded representation as a second-best substitute for local self-government—a potentially dangerous attenuation of personal responsibility and assent. Their vision of representation would have required representatives to know and like their constituents, share in the community's deliberations, and appreciate local opinions and feelings.[3] The Federalists, on the other hand, valued representation precisely because it permitted an escape from the politics of small communities; they believed that citizens were adequately represented when they elected others to defend their interests.[4]

The Federalists ultimately won the argument, if we judge by the Constitution. Examination of the Bill of Rights—the Anti-Federalist citadel—reveals no indication of a more personalized representation either. History suggests, in fact, that the Federalist model has survived every incursion. The first Congress, for example, submitted to the states an Anti-Federalist-spurred amendment intended to guarantee a numerous representation, but it fell short of ratification.[5] Nevertheless, Anti-Federalist ideas of representation are more than interesting anachronisms. Their concern with and ideas about representation are partially reflected in the American political party system—a kind of representation in itself. In that and in other ways, the Anti-Federalist legacy continues to enrich American political life and thought.

Originally published as "The Anti-Federalists, Representation, and Party," in the *Northwestern University Law Review* 84, no. 1 (Fall 1989): 12–38. Reprinted by special permission of the Northwestern University School of Law.

The Federalist View of Representation

The framers of the Constitution of the United States were informed by the teaching, now familiar to most Americans, that human beings are by nature free, independent, and engrossed in private aims, especially the desire for self-preservation.[6] They believed that in creating government, individuals yield some of their natural freedom in order to pursue their inherent ends more safely and more effectively. Government, consequently, is legitimate only to the extent that it "represents" these private rights, interests, and goals.[7] The only common interest, then, might seem to be the "aggregate" of subjectively perceived private interests. The Federalists were emphatic, however, in holding that there exists an objective, collective interest that, factoring out subjectivities, forms the true standard for representative rule.[8] In this sense, as Locke noted, representative government need not even be elected government; majority rule may give government greater strength, but, in theory, government is representative whenever it furthers our interests, objectively understood.[9]

In practice, however, human nature makes a powerful case for electing representatives. Government is only necessary, Federalist writers argued, because human beings are apt to be narrowly self-interested, parochial, and shortsighted. Often blind to their true interests and always inclined to partiality, they cannot be trusted to judge their own cases;[10] government, therefore, requires that human beings surrender their natural right to judge and punish. In order to safely sacrifice this power, self-interested human beings require that their representatives be selected by objective rules and procedures, independent of subjective, partisan opinion.[11] And once a rule of suffrage has been agreed to, elections have the decisive advantage of settling representation on a quantitative basis—the candidate with the most votes wins. Social peace, as well as natural equality, points toward representatives chosen by vote.[12]

Without too much strain, the Federalist doctrine of representative government can be reduced to a single, concise principle: objective interests, objectively arrived at. This view underlies the Federalist argument in defense of a large republic. Large republics—possible only because of representation—are better suited to defend our natural, objective interests. They combine power with the possibility of a greater division of labor and a broader scope for private liberty than is possible in any small regime. These considerations were virtually decisive for the Federalists. The private advantages of large and diverse states outweighed the supposed public virtues of small and relatively homogeneous ones.[13]

Moreover, the Federalists argued that a large republic permits an enhanced objectivity in the conduct of rule. The ideal representative, they believed, reflects the interests of his constituents but not their subjective feelings and parochial opinions. In a small republic, like the classical city-state, popular assemblies are always at hand even where representative institutions exist, and the regime is forever exposed to partisan passion and discord.[14] For the Federalists, representative government reflected an improvement on the small community and achieved perfection only in a large republic. With a scattered and distant citizenry, "the people in their collective capacity" could be excluded from any direct role in government.[15]

The "republican principle" (majority rule), which limits the danger of minority tyranny, inevitably increases the threat posed by a majority faction.[16] In his celebrated argument in *Federalist* 10, however, James Madison contended that a large republic may embrace so great a variety of interests and factions that any majority will be incoherent and unable to agree on more than a limited number of goals and measures.[17] Republican moderation, in these terms, does not rest on the self-restraint of public-spirited citizens but on the diversity of a large republic, channeled through rightly ordered laws.[18]

The same principle applies to specifically representative institutions. The number of representatives who can deliberate effectively is finite.[19] In any very numerous assembly, only a small fraction will be able to speak on any measure, and leaders must decide who will speak and on what terms.[20] Given this limit on the number of representatives, a larger republic implies larger legislative districts, with a corresponding increase in the variety of interests within each district. Larger legislative districts, in other words, possess a scaled-down version of the advantages Federalists saw in an extensive republic. Because large districts are less apt to be controlled by any one group or faction and are more likely to be relatively free from the parochialities and subjectivities of any one locality, the Federalists concluded that representatives would find it easier to devote themselves to the broader interests of their constituents.[21]

Madison and James Wilson urged, moreover, that large districts would ensure the most desirable representation. "Unworthy candidates," Madison wrote, would have difficulty in large districts practicing "the vicious arts, by which elections are too often carried."[22] Local political organizations and factions would find intrigue and intimidation more difficult. The "suffrages of the people" would be freer and, in general, afforded a wider, better choice of candidates.[23] "Little demagogues," able to rouse popular passions in small communities (especially in the "remote corners of government"), would likewise have less chance of success. Representatives would thus need more than local celebrity to be elected in large districts; as Wilson noted, "It is of more consequence to be able to know the true interest of the candidates, than their faces."[24]

Hamilton recognized the other side of this argument. Assuming, as Madison hypothesized, that "the proportion of fit characters, be not less, in the large than in the small Republic,"[25] a large state will contain a greater number of such characters than a small one. By the same logic, however, a large state will also include a greater number of base and unfit characters. Since the people are less likely to know the characters of their representatives and will be unable to directly supervise their conduct in office, a large republic is no guarantee against political corruption.[26] And although an extensive republic is relatively immune to petty demagogues, it is vulnerable to demagogy on a grand scale.[27] Size and diversity are insufficient protections, by themselves; republics also need leaders, Hamilton argued, in whom "principle or the love of glory" elevates mere ambition, just as a republican citizenry needs virtue and morality.[28] Yet even Hamilton took it as a rule of political prudence that virtue, when it cannot ally itself to interest, will be defeated by it. Consequently, he was content to rest the Constitution on formal representation and the complex balances that pit interest against interest.[29]

As Anti-Federalist writers observed, the Constitution subjects representatives to no test of character or opinion. It avoids even those objective signs that might be taken as some measure of a representative's inward qualities; representatives are not required to be educated, to own property, to profess any religious belief, or even to have been law-abiding.[30] "A Pagan, a Mahometan, a Bankrupt," the Anti-Federalist "Samuel" wrote, "may fill the highest seat and any and every seat; nothing but age and residence, are required, as qualifications, for the most important trusts."[31] Another Anti-Federalist, "A Watchman," objected to the Constitution's age and residence requirements for holding office because they exclude newcomers and the young, even when they "are endowed with the wisdom that is from above."[32]

Though "A Watchman" would have preferred some religious test for representatives, he appears to have regarded *no* restrictions as more desirable than the Constitution's superficial, objective requirements. Few Anti-Federalists would have agreed, but "A Watchman" was typical in his concern with the inward qualities of those who rule.

The Anti-Federalist Response

More than their Federalist opponents, the Anti-Federalists inclined toward the ancient view that, just as the soul's excellent qualities have a natural title to rule over base impulses, public spirit is entitled to govern private interests. This older doctrine—rooted in classical Greek philosophy and articulated, in eighteenth-century America, largely by Christian teachers— suggests that political society is natural to human beings and has priority over any private rights or liberties.[33] Individuality is possible only because political society protects and nurtures our individual strengths and attri- butes, making it possible for each of us to do what he or she does best. Preacher and state legislator (and, eventually, Vermont Supreme Court jus- tice) Nathaniel Niles argued in 1774 that there are no private rights in the state of nature; all the legitimate rights of individuals derive from the politi- cal society as a whole.[34]

The Anti-Federalists generally employed a rhetoric far more modern than the ancient ideas they espoused. They characteristically spoke of a state of nature, for example, in which individuals were endowed with rights, a vir- tually inescapable idiom of American political discourse in the eighteenth century.[35] Even so, a certain number of Anti-Federalists willingly asserted the less contemporary view that civil society and government were natural for human beings.[36] Others used Lockean language to develop views that rejected the primacy of private rights and liberties. It was common for Anti- Federalists to argue, for example, that political societies, once created, be- came "one body,"[37] a collective second nature that subsumes and supersedes all or most individual rights. "William Penn" added a moral component to the individual rights debate; recognizing that individuals have natural rights, he maintained that our natural liberty is only an "*unlimited power of doing good,*" implying that there is no natural right to do wrong.[38]

Penn suggested, further, that what is good is not known by instinct or de- sire but is, instead, discovered through learning, reflection, and discourse.[39] Penn's reasoning, therefore, leads to the conclusion that natural liberty re- quires society. Our natural freedom cannot be enjoyed in a separate state but only within a wisely governed political regime.[40] William Penn went on to indicate that because philosophers are most able to inquire into the good, natural liberty is most fully comprehended by them.[41] In its highest forms, consequently, liberty is ordinarily the preserve of the philosophic few. Penn asserted, however, that this philosophic understanding of liberty had been embodied in American manners and institutions to a remarkable degree. Americans were uniquely suited to widespread political freedom and republican government because they had been taught by their laws and customs that liberty must be guided and restrained by moral goals and principles. In Penn's view, the Constitution's threat to America's political habits—and, especially, its encouragement of private interests and liberties—struck at the foundations of republican life and civil freedom.[42]

This persuasion helps account for the fact that even though the Anti-Federalists appreciated the danger that a majority might become tyrannical, they concerned themselves far less than the Federalists with the danger posed by the majority to strictly private rights. In advocating a bill of rights, the Anti-Federalists most zealously defended public freedoms and the right to a republican civil life.[43] The Maryland minority, for example, proposed amendments to limit the power of the central government and the army, to safeguard freedom of the press, and to provide for trial by jury and other judicial rights, emphasizing public institutions and the right to participate in political deliberation.[44]

Private rights were generally absent from Anti-Federalist pronouncements. Aside from proposals to limit warrants to search and seize and to forbid the quartering of soldiers in private homes in time of peace, the Maryland minority, for example, advanced few amendments designed to secure specifically private liberties.[45] In fact, they could not even agree to amendments providing for religious liberty and conscientious objection to military service.[46] Richard Henry Lee sought to rectify that omission, but his proposed bill of rights was also preoccupied with public institutions—juries, frequent elections, an increased representation, and a privy council.[47] Even where Lee sought to limit the power of majorities to impose commercial regulations, he explained his position as an attempt to defend "the minority of the community" from oppression based on "motives of interest," an argument that implicitly appealed to the common good as opposed to private aims.[48]

Despite many ambivalences, Anti-Federalists were more disposed than their antagonists to the notion that any political society has a common good or ruling principle, higher than and inclusive of the good of its parts. Justice, in this view, is something quite independent of consent, although all Anti-Federalists regarded consent as an element of a good polity. Similarly, representation—their form, not the Federalist version—is valuable chiefly as a mode of political education, a way of helping citizens discern what is just. The Federalists adhered to the modern doctrine that just government is government in which we consent to be represented; Anti-Federalists leaned toward the proposition that representation is just when it leads us to consent to just rule.

Following traditional political theory, Anti-Federalists regarded civic virtue or public spirit as the first principle of republican government. Self-government, they contended, implies more than a say in making law; it must include a willingness to observe law in one's own life and conduct.[49] America vindicates republican liberty because government is "respected from principles of affection and obeyed with alacrity."[50]

The Anti-Federalists were not utopians. They acknowledged the existence of vice and temptation, and they knew that any political society will contain lawbreakers.[51] They hoped merely that the "sensible and virtuous part of the community" would be law-abiding, and for those that did not obey the laws, they recognized the need for coercion and constraint.[52] They believed that government is defined by one of two ruling principles: *force,* the basis of despotism, or *persuasion,* the foundation of republican government.[53] To the extent that a republic depends on force, it ceases to be *republican*—the laws may retain their form, but the regime will be governed in and by a different spirit.[54] Republican policy, therefore, should cherish civic spirit and seek to increase the number of sensible and virtuous citizens—"to arm persuasion on every side," the Federal Farmer wrote, "and to render force as little necessary as possible."[55]

It is worth emphasizing that the Anti-Federalists believed this gentle rule possible only because it rested on stern and moral foundations. In the Federal Farmer's argument, republics hope to make deliberation forceful, seeking to base government on speech. Since all human beings can use argument to further private purposes, persuasion will *rule* only those who will listen to reason and put the public good before their own. Republican policy thus demanded the shaping of republican souls.[56]

Civic education posed a problem for the Anti-Federalist ideal, however, in that our bodies are autonomous and our senses private and both strain against public spirit.[57] Reason may discern that we are parts of a whole, but the body nonetheless inclines toward self-centeredness.[58] To some degree, however, the Anti-Federalists thought that passion and sentiment could be trained to support public spirit—that habit and discipline could lead the people to associate security and gratification with decent rules and the common life.[59] Similarly, my affection for and attachment to things that I regard as "mine"—my family, my property, or my way of life—can extend my idea of myself beyond my body and link my personal well-being with that of the community.[60] Democratic laws and manners, the Anti-Federalists believed, can and must be "well-digested," that is, made part of each citizen's identity by custom and practice.[61]

It takes powerful loves and loyalties to challenge self-centeredness. Public reason appeals to private feeling only through benefits that are palpable. It was almost axiomatic for eighteenth-century Americans that "Bodies in Contact, and cemented by mutual Interests, cohere more strongly than those which are at a Distance."[62] Affection and attachment are strongest "within our domestic walls," and each step away from intimacy weakens the sense of affiliation.[63] Civic spirit attenuates wherever common "acquaintance, habits and fortune" lose ground to impersonality and diversity.[64] The Anti-Federalists insisted, therefore, that small states and local communities were the natural and necessary primary schools of civic education. They thought strong assent possible only in small polities and worried that even states would be too large for republican rule.[65] In a nation as large as the United States, the Anti-Federalists feared that patriotism would become little more than a "denomination," stronger than "sameness of species" but ordinarily feebler than the more immediate bonds and relationships existing within private circles and smaller communities.[66]

The Anti-Federalists also argued that small states could better satisfy the human demand for dignity. Citizens would be bound to resent any regime in which they were not recognized and respected; in large states, rulers could know their people only as so many abstractions. Anti-Federalists urged local forums in which citizens could hear their rulers and be heard by them, regarding such deliberative communities as indispensable in overcoming feelings of indignity and in fostering relationships of trust between the people and their government.[67]

Small polities also provide a greater chance of holding office, an Anti-Federalist goal because it encourages citizens to regard public life as a source of honor.[68] Arguing for a larger number of representatives in an annually elected Congress, "Cato" contended that affording the many the opportunity to win offices and honors will "fill them with a desire of rendering themselves worthy of them."[69]

Similarly, Melancton Smith argued that rotation of office in the Senate would "diffuse a more general spirit of emulation" and would further the "true policy" of disseminating "knowledge of government" because "the ambition of gaining the qualifications necessary to govern will be in some proportion to the chance of success."[70] Though even with rotation and annual elections only a small fraction of the citizenry could ever hold national office, the general principles advanced by "Cato" and Smith underline the importance to the Anti-Federalists of local government as a school for citizenship.

The Anti-Federalists' Doctrine of Representation

Despite their admiration for small republics, the Anti-Federalists did not advocate a closed society modeled after the classical city-state. Christian teaching insisted on a recognition of human equality, at least in principle; Niles wrote that because it is only "by reason of the feebleness of human powers" that the world is divided into separate states, "it is the business of these still to regard the good of the world."[71] Prudence, moreover, informed Anti-Federalists that a larger regime was necessary for eighteenth-century America.[72] Many Anti-Federalists actually preferred representative government, and even the staunchest defenders of direct democracy regarded representation as the next best alternative. "Government by deputation," when properly safeguarded, Zabdiel Adams maintained in 1782, could enable people to "be as free as the state of the world will commonly admit."[73] Nevertheless, Anti-Federalists insisted that representation be rooted in small communities and local forums, and no Anti-Federalist complaint against the Constitution popped up more frequently than the demand for "a more numerous representation."[74]

This "numerous representation" was needed in a country as large as the United States, the Anti-Federalists felt, because a constituency can be represented only to the extent that one person can credibly speak for many. Anti-Federalists were convinced that republics depended on a strong form of representation, a kind of representation in which a representative's voice and vote would commit his constituents even where important sacrifices were called for. That sort of empowerment, Anti-Federalists contended, requires a relatively coherent community. The trust of citizens in their representatives, Anti-Federalists observed, is proportional to their confidence that those representatives understand them sympathetically and hear them attentively.[75] Strong representation thus required districts small enough that representatives could know the feelings, opinions, and interests of their constituents.[76] Mere information did not substitute for common experience and shared understandings.[77] The people, the Federal Farmer argued, must "chuse men from among themselves, and genuinely like themselves."[78] Representatives and represented must be united by a kind of political friendship. This relationship, the Anti-Federalists believed, would afford a representative a more respectful hearing when defending measures that violated established custom, interest, or opinion.[79] The Anti-Federalists regarded speaking *for* constituents as only half a representative's charge; they must also speak *to* their constituents, "mix with the people and explain to them the motives which induced the adoption of any measure, point out its utility and remove or silence any unreasonable clamours against it."[80]

For the Anti-Federalists, every step away from the rough fellowship of the deliberative community diminished, if only imperceptibly, the quality and legitimacy of the representative's authorization.[81] If such a diminution went unchecked, Anti-Federalists argued, citizens would eventually "have no confidence in their legislature, suspect them of ambitious views, be jealous of every measure they adopt, and would not support the laws they pass."[82] The Anti-Federalists feared that without the support of a committed citizenry, tax collectors, bureaucrats, and—ultimately—the army would be required to enforce the laws: "the government will be[come] nerveless and inefficient, and no way will be left to render it otherwise, but by establishing an armed force to execute the laws at the point of the bayonet."[83] Inadequate representation could thus lead Congress, as established by the Constitution, to drift away from the true principles of republican governance.

Similarly, the Anti-Federalists contended that, as far as possible, each "order" of the community—each occupation, class, and group—must have a voice in representative institutions.[84] Drawing representatives from different social strata would, like rotation in office, decrease the distance between representatives and constituents.[85] It was not satisfactory, in their view, for a people to be represented only by "natural aristocrats."[86] A representative needed "brilliant talents" less than the trust and affection of his constituents, and, in fact, Anti-Federalists warned that those with "mighty talents" might be dangerous.[87] Great abilities exposed their possessors to great temptations, exacerbating what Anti-Federalists took to be the inherent tendency of representative government, already a form of rule by the few, to further degenerate into oligarchy.[88] A legislature composed of persons of middle rank would be less threatening to republican principles.[89]

Many of the Anti-Federalist arguments grew directly out of their belief in small districts and local forums. Citizen participation in government and civil life would be fostered, they said, in the kind of republic they envisioned. "The great easily form associations," Melancton Smith observed, "the poor and middling class form them with difficulty."[90] Small districts, like small states, would help to redress the balance, making it easier for ordinary citizens to organize and act in concert. "Substantial . . . and informed" citizens might easily be overlooked because they keep "generally silent in public assemblies"; they would never be known in "dispersed" districts where only the "conspicuous"—the prominent and self-advertising—would attract the public eye.[91] Moreover, simplicity and virtue marked the best republican politics, affording participants a dignity that Anti-Federalists believed drew citizens toward public life.[92] By contrast, large-scale politics tended to produce only "meanness and submission" and passive citizens preoccupied with private life.[93]

Madison argued that the "republican principle" of majority rule, established in law, would virtually prevent minority rule.[94] The Anti-Federalists were not persuaded. In *practice,* they believed, a large republic with a fragmented and dispersed citizenry gave decisive advantages to organized elites—specifically, government officials, the wealthy, and men of commerce.[95] In large districts, as in large republics generally, the Anti-Federalists presciently reasoned that election by plurality would be the rule, since citizens could not be assembled to cast repeated ballots.[96] Citizens would naturally tend to vote for local favorites and for candidates known to them, which would result in a dispersion of votes to the benefit of organized minorities.[97] To make their votes effective, citizens must cast their ballots for a candidate with a real chance of election.[98] To identify those candidates, Patrick Henry predicted, they will take their guidance from "men of influence," who will determine the terms of choice if not the choice itself.[99] Henry argued that politics naturally tends toward elite rule and weak representation in large districts, reducing most voters to a state of impotence and dependence.[100]

In Anti-Federalist theory, then, representative institutions rest on two pillars: (1) districts that are places of political fellowship, affording representation to every significant community among the people, and (2) rotation in office, combined with frequent elections, designed to keep representatives attuned and accountable to their constituencies and to broaden the number of potential officeholders.[101] Conceived in these terms, a legislature is bound to be relatively inexpert and very large—"so numerous as almost to be the people themselves," the Federal Farmer said, referring to legislatures in the states.[102] At best, such a legislature will be somewhat unwieldy and very talky. Since there is a practical limit to the size of any deliberative body, a fully "adequate" representation on Anti-Federalist terms is possible only in a small polity.[103] The state legislatures in 1787 were acceptable representative bodies for most Anti-Federalists, but "Cato" regarded even the states as straining the proper limits of representation, and he expected—correctly, as it turned out—that some states would soon have to be divided.[104]

The Anti-Federalists had no hope that a federal legislature could be both workable and "properly numerous."[105] In the sense that Anti-Federalist ideals for representation were so clearly impracticable at the national level, Federalists were correct to regard their opponents' doctrines—such as the idea of an "actual representation of all classes"—as "altogether visionary."[106] The Anti-Federalists, however, maintained that their theories defined the standard that federal representation should attempt to approximate. "Necessity, I believe, will oblige us to sacrifice in some degree the true genuine principles of representation," the Federal Farmer wrote. "But this sacrifice ought to be as little as possible."[107] Anti-Federalist spokesmen, like Melancton Smith, hoped to "approach . . . perfection by increasing the representation and limiting the powers of Congress."[108] Somewhat despairingly, they remained defenders of the ideal of strong representation in a deliberative republic.

Representation and Party

The Anti-Federalists failed to change the formal, legal basis of representation, and congressional districts today are more than seventeen times as large as those to which the Anti-Federalists objected two hundred years ago. For most of us, it has become second nature to speak of representation in the Federalists' terms. At the time of this writing, my representative in Congress is James Courter, a conservative Republican with whom I almost never agree, as easily as Mr. Courter says that his representatives in the Senate are Bill Bradley and Frank Lautenberg, who rarely share his views. Our ideas of representation seem to have little connection to the Anti-Federalist attempt to reconcile private feeling and public reason through speech and political friendship.

Yet, Anti-Federalist concerns did find a reflection in American political parties. The Anti-Federalists were no admirers of partisanship, fearing its divisive effect on the community, but they did recognize a more or less natural foundation for political parties in the social orders of society.[109] In the United States, the Federal Farmer argued, the line between the "natural aristocracy" and the "natural democracy" is to some extent arbitrary, with many individuals "wavering and uncertain themselves on which side they are."[110] Nevertheless, "it is easy to perceive that men of these two classes, the aristocratical and democratical, with views equally honest, have sentiments widely different" on the issues of the day.[111] The conflict of these "great parties"—organized around the rival principles of equality, on one hand, and what Mercy Otis Warren called the "desire of distinction," on the other—is reinforced by the competition between narrower interests and lesser parties.[112] "Thus, in every period of society, and in all the transactions of men, we see parties," the Federal Farmer concluded—and every class and order needs its own "centinels" in government.[113]

The Anti-Federalists correctly noted that the Constitution's large-scale politics would make it difficult for the people to select and hold accountable representatives like themselves. To neutralize the advantages of the favored and powerful, the "poor and middling class[es]" need the tribuneship of permanent public associations that can yield new political loyalties, nurtured by habit and memory but adequate to the politics of a complex, commercial regime.

> On the preservation of parties, public liberty depends. Whenever men are unanimous on great public questions, whenever there is but one party, freedom ceases and despotism commences. The object of a free and wise people should be so to balance parties that *from the weakness of all, you may be governed by the moderation of the combined judgments of the whole.*[114]

Years after the Constitutional Convention, John Francis Mercer wrote Jefferson of his fear that two great parties that alternately command a majority would "inflict increasing injuries on each other," a cycle that could only end in despotism. In an argument akin to Madison's, Mercer noted that "like sects in Religion," parties could be properly balanced only by "multiplying their number and diversifying their objects."[115] Martin Van Buren recognized the defect in this sort of reasoning. Multiplying the *number* of parties may be unnecessary if the *objects* of each party are diversified, so that the other interests of its members temper any zeal for common, unifying principles. In this respect, the diverse republic that Madison celebrated is modestly compatible with an Anti-Federalist goal. It allows for a party system that combines moderation with accountability.[116]

A party system offers the best republican answer, albeit a partial one, to the riddle of accountability in a large regime.[117] As the Anti-Federalists warned, government under the Constitution is "intricate and perplexed"; representatives easily diffuse and confuse responsibility under the "cloak of Compromize."[118] Hamilton essentially conceded this point in his defense of a single, more easily accountable executive. The "two greatest securities" for the "faithful exercise of any delegated power," Hamilton wrote, are

> First, the restraints of public opinion, which lose their efficacy as well on account of the division of the censure attendant on bad measures among a number, as on account of the uncertainty on whom it ought to fall; and secondly, the opportunity of discovering with facility and clearness the misconduct of the persons they trust.[119]

The same principle, of course, suggests at first glance that the executive is a more accountable and hence more republican representative than the legislature.[120] Anti-Federalists did not need our recent experience to see the danger in this praise of the executive, for they knew that executive power is most needed at times that render accountability most difficult. Republican institutions—preeminently the legislature, which epitomizes the "force of persuasion"—may mobilize strong assent, but these institutions are slow moving, discursive, and apt to be late in noticing perils. Crisis government, "Cato" conceded, might call for rule on the basis of the discretionary authority and force of executive prerogative, at least on a short-term basis.[121] A republic's commander, however, could not be trusted to recognize that the time had come to relinquish his authority. The people would need a representative legislature to control a representative executive.

Still, Hamilton's argument cannot be dismissed. A legislature can rival the executive's claims to public confidence only to the extent that it is accountable, which presumes a principle of *collective* responsibility. In English history, the legitimation of party grew out of the effort to control the prerogative and executive power generally.[122] Similarly, American parties developed out of conflicts in Congress, hardening in the dispute over the Jay Treaty.[123] Presidents can be strong, it was argued, and "above party"; presidential power derives largely from the institution and the personal qualities of the incumbent. By contrast, Congress cannot be effective, let alone powerful, without the extraconstitutional institution of party.[124]

Perhaps most important, Anti-Federalist thinking points toward party as one means of narrowing the affective distance between citizens and their representatives. For virtually all citizens in a republic as large as the United States, partisanship is the closest possible approximation to the Anti-Federalist notions of political friendship and strong representation. We cannot play, in essence, but we can cheer those who wear our colors.[125] Legislators from territorial districts represent us according to law, but despite the fading of party loyalty, those of our fellow partisans who hold office are more likely to represent our hearts and speak with our voices. Party brings us closer to strong assent, and party leaders often draw us toward public goals even when interest and ideology pull in opposite directions.[126] And when citizens are discontented, punishing the party in power is still one means of holding government accountable.[127] In representing "the poor and middling class[es]," those objects of Anti-Federalist solicitude, parties today are indispensable, "the only devices . . . which with some effectiveness can generate countervailing collective power on behalf of the many individually powerless against the relatively few who are individually—or organizationally—powerful."[128] In modern democracies, as Herman Finer wrote, "representative government is party government."[129]

Traditional American party organization paralleled Anti-Federalist ideas of representation. The traditional party was rooted in local communities and in political fellowship. It also aspired to forge a chain of personal relationships and deliberative bodies linking citizens to the federal government.[130] As the Anti-Federalists expected, each link in the chain—each step away from the citizenry—weakened the bonds of trust and civic friendship.

Parties, however, found (and find) a compensating source of strength in the political combat of elections—a kind of sociopolitical battleground that encourages partisans to overlook their differences in the interest of victory. Those who built the American party system accepted party controversy and legitimate opposition because they recognized its contribution to strong assent and to the representative qualities of party. Even the spoils system took on special value because it increased the stakes of political conflict and the motives for party solidarity.[131] Party loyalty, like strong assent generally, is inseparable from political turbulence. It was for that reason that the Federalists distrusted the "spirit of party."[132] Provided public liberties were guaranteed, the Anti-Federalists were more inclined to accept a measure of disorder to draw citizens into public life.[133]

Despite their contributions, however, contemporary political parties are less and less effective as representatives and civic educators. American life grows more specialized, more mobile, and more pervaded by the media; local communities and personal bonds of all kinds are becoming increasingly fragile.[134] Allegiance to party is also declining.[135] And parties have suffered from reform legislation that, following the tradition of the framers, regards them as only coalitions of so many individuals.[136] Increasingly impressive national party bureaucracies are no substitute for strong and stable loyalty; still invaluable, American political parties stand in need of revitalization.[137]

The first principle of a republic, as the Anti-Federalists taught, is not party. It is the character of its citizens. In political extremity, republics depend on citizens willing to subordinate individual rights to the common good and to sacrifice life, liberty, and property. Contemporary America faces crises that will strain the rather spiritless devotion of citizens and representatives. We must retrain ourselves in the discipline of republican habits. The Anti-Federalist tradition can jog us toward strengthening and restoring the deliberative communities that, for citizens and representatives alike, are the wellsprings of public vitality.

PART II
America's Two Voices

5

Science and Freedom: America as the Technological Republic

FROM THE BEGINNING, AMERICANS, in appreciation of technology's comforts and conveniences, its relief from drudgery and want, have honored the nation's great inventors. This is not surprising: even technology's critics are appalled by hunger's shadow on a child's face, and a plague such as AIDS turns laboratories into temples of hope. But technology also brings nuisances and deadly perils, and that dark side is something Americans have always known or suspected. Our schools teach that the cotton gin strengthened slavery, with the implicit moral that the machine can corrupt the garden as subtly as the serpent.[1]

Technology is more than gadgets and machines: it is associated with a frame of mind, a preoccupation with ways of getting results, a dangerous spirit that strains against limits and for rule. And America's oldest wisdom teaches that when the people of Babel set out to build a tower to heaven, the Lord scattered them and confounded their speech, political disaster following technological pride.[2]

From their religion, early Americans learned that human beings are naturally subject to limits, parts of a good whole. Men and women are granted "dominion" only within creation and subject to rule; the alienation of humanity from nature, like the estrangement of human from human, is the result and mark of sin. According to this doctrine, the goal of human life and prudence is to achieve, as far as possible, the reconciliation between human beings and nature and, finally, to reconcile humanity and God. Redemption is ultimately the work of grace, but law, religion, and family, all the great institutions of human education, are naturally intended to promote a loving

Originally published as "Science and Freedom: America as the Technological Republic," in *Technology in the Western Political Tradition,* ed. Arthur M. Melzer, Jerry Weinberger, and M. Richard Zinman (Ithaca, N.Y.: Cornell University Press, 1993), 85–108. Copyright © 1993 by Cornell University. Used by permission of Cornell University Press. This essay was originally prepared as part of a symposium on the theme "Science, Reason, and Modern Democracy." The symposium was sponsored by the Department of Political Science at Michigan State University in 1989.

attachment between human beings and their fellows and an adoring recognition of the wonder of the created order.

Science and technology, consequently, were to be cherished insofar as they revealed the excellence of God's design, and to that extent, there was an affinity between early American religion and the new science. Even champions of orthodoxy supported technologies, such as vaccination, that bettered human life, provided that the highest honor was reserved not for the device but for God as first cause.[3] Like all human works, science and technology were to be ruled by right subordination and attachment, governed by nature and the good life.

The strongest voices in early American religion rejected asceticism. Calvin argued that "delight," God-created, was meant to aid the soul, and John Wise maintained that God intended human beings to "banish sordidness, and live Bright and Civil, with fine Accomplishments."[4] But religious teaching also held that there are limits to what is needful, however difficult it is to define them in practice; beyond that boundary, wealth is luxury, a distraction to the soul. Most important, the doctrine of sin testified emphatically that some powers are not safe in human hands. The first principle of politics is the education and right government of the soul, so that implicitly the excellent soul sets the rule that measures the arts and the laws.

Human beings are made happy not by having much but by needing little, and Protestant teaching sought to develop the inner qualities necessary to make the best of any station, including the finite, human place within nature.[5] In Daniel Defoe's great celebration of resourcefulness, Robinson Crusoe saves what he can from his wrecked ship, but this remnant of technology leaves him vulnerable to loneliness and despair. The foundation of his industriousness is his conviction that providence is pervasive, so that if he bestirs himself, he will find all that is needed for an ordered life. Thus assured, Crusoe successfully champions right order against violations of natural duty (cannibalism) and civil obligation (mutiny), bringing his island a kind of decent governance.[6]

The new science, however, proved less governable, linked as it was to the modern political philosophy that had helped nurture it. In the education of the founding generation, the new sciences of nature and politics were so intertwined that, for Thomas Jefferson, Newton, Bacon, and Locke—the "three greatest men the world had produced"—were a secular trinity, almost as inseparable as the three persons of its Christian rival and certainly grander than ancient philosophy.[7]

The new doctrine described a natural order but one lacking moral authority in human affairs. In the new view, nature is matter in motion, its order defined by the mechanics of attraction and repulsion, at best indifferent to human hopes.[8] Human beings are moved by need and desire and by the effort to avoid pain and death; self-preservation, "the first and strongest desire God planted in men," is "the first principle of our nature."[9] Since the human conflict with nature, in these terms, is itself natural, human beings properly seek mastery over nature, a goal that requires them to become supreme mechanics with their hands on the levers of natural power. Technology, in this sense, is the answer to the human problem, worthy to be pursued through all methods and inventions that "let Light into the Nature of Things, tend to increase the Power of Man over Matter, and multiply the conveniences or Pleasures of Life."[10]

Nature furnishes the human goal—its own subjugation—but not the moral basis of human society. Benjamin Franklin's early *Treatise on Liberty and Necessity, Pleasure and Pain* (1725) located human beings wholly within the mechanisms of nature, reasoning that, given God's power, knowledge, and benevolence, the human world must be presumed to have the regularity of the natural world. "Man is a part of this great Machine, the Univers," for the "ingenious Artificer" would not have manufactured a second system "endu'd with an independent *self-motion,* but ignorant of the general interest of the Clock."[11] The young Franklin concluded that evil cannot exist; when human beings pursue their self-interested natural inclinations, it must be presumed that they forward the good of the whole.[12] Experience led Franklin to regret having printed this pamphlet because of what he regarded as its bad moral consequences. The fault, he concluded, was not in his logic but in his premises: neither God's nature nor his design is known sufficiently to furnish a basis for moral deduction. The moral order, then, must be seen as a thing of human making, to be judged in terms of its perceptible effects and utilities.[13]

Yet human reason is also an inadequate basis for moral and civil order. As Locke had argued, the fact that reason separates human beings from the rest of nature—making them conscious of the struggle with nature's limits—allows them to fall below the level of instinct as well as enabling them to rise above it.[14] Reason may moderate passion, but at bottom, it serves desire. Franklin reports that despite his vegetarian principles, he persuaded himself that it was not "murder" to eat fish, since fish ate other fish. Yet he went on to indicate, tongue-in-cheek, the instrumental quality of his own reasoning: "So convenient a thing it is to be a *reasonable Creature* since it enables one to find or make a Reason for everything one has a mind to do."[15] Reason can administer, but it cannot be trusted to rule, especially since human passion reaches beyond eating fishes.

In the characteristic political science of the founding era, the state of nature, when human beings have no stay or support but instinct and reason, is open to imperious desires and exposed to desperate dangers, so that—whether in the beginning or soon after—it comes down to a state of war.[16] Seeking to escape that condition, human beings, following the path sketched by social contract theory, agree to create political society, giving up certain rights in order to enjoy the rights they retain more safely and effectively.[17] Nature drives human beings into political society, but politics is not natural; it is a technological project, an instrument for protecting rights and effectuating essentially private desires, properly rooted in the consent of the intended users. Government's lodestar is not virtue but interest.

All human beings are self-interested, in the most general sense of the term, so that for the dramers, the public good is equivalent to a "judicious estimate of our true interests."[18] Most human beings, however, define themselves narrowly, thinking of their bodies and desires or, at best, identifying with their families and properties. Human judgment is chronically shortsighted and parochial: "Momentary passions and immediate interests have a more active control over human conduct than general or remote considerations of policy, utility or justice."[19] This is especially true because long-term calculations are uncertain and exposed to unexpected events. The "mild and salutary" constraint of law and the assurance of government policy are necessary to prod or prompt us toward our interests, "rightly understood."[20] In the conduct of government and even more in its founding, the majority of human beings need the guidance of that political minority who identify themselves with public things—power, fame, or the good of their kind—and are thus "disinterested" in the common sense of the word.[21] But these more public motives and goals have no superior moral title, since at bottom, they come down to self-interest, though more amply defined. In fact, such ambitions are dangerous because the desire for power, the quest for greatness, or the zeal to do good are expressions of the yearning for dominion.

Governments, consequently, must be so contrived that public officials represent and administer only private ends and are held accountable by private citizens. As Jefferson wrote in *A Summary View of the Rights of British America* (1774), the king "is no more than the chief officer of the people, appointed by the laws and circumscribed with definite powers to assist in working the great machine of government erected for their use, and consequently subject to their superintendence."[22] The framers' modern political science rejects rule, a government that measures and is measured according to a scale of excellences or virtues, in favor of *rules,* officials qualified by technical skill and "kept within their due bounds."[23]

The right design of the laws is the more urgent because government must be a house of power, forwarding the human effort to master nature.[24] Government, the *Federalist* insists, must possess "energy," power decked in the language of science. It needs force sufficient to overcome obstacles to its authority, to protect civil peace and the rights of citizens, to forestall foreign danger, and in general to protect the sphere of order against the disorder of nature.[25] More positively, government must help to promote the accumulation of power, wealth, and technique, supporting commerce and encouraging "science and useful arts."[26]

Power over nature, however, entails the growth of human power within political societies and between them, with a corresponding increase in the possibilities of abuse. The "science of finance, which is the offspring of modern times," Alexander Hamilton remarked, gives government new control over money and hence over politics, notably by allowing (and requiring) professional armies, with their potential for repression.[27] Similarly, commerce, though generally benign, also has prompted the trade in slaves, that "barbarism of modern policy."[28] Consequently, government needs power in relation to these challenges and outrages; its "means ought to be proportioned to the end" as causes to effects, for "wherever the end is required, the means are authorized."[29] The laws can rule only if they shape necessity or obey it, and either alternative demands power.[30]

Yet although government and order are the preconditions of any effective human freedom, liberty is first by nature, the end and purpose of political life, so that, James Madison argued, safeguarding "the diversity in the faculties of men" is "the first object of government."[31] Since reason is naturally connected to self-love, it is impossible to deal with the "causes" of faction without repression, but that solution is *morally* unacceptable. If faction is the price of freedom, it is one that a rightly constructed government must pay. Factions must be controlled through their "effects," just as human beings must be governed through their behavior, leaving them at liberty but shaping their choices, channeling human desires and actions through institutions scientifically designed to get results.

In fact, when the American framers appeal to the "improved" science of politics, they are thinking less of theoretical principles than of the very practical technology of institutions, such as representation and the separation of powers.[32] Of course, the framers recognized that political technology must be adapted to the people and the times to which it is being applied, especially since at the outset, new laws can only point toward a new political culture.[33] And the United States was not a perfect laboratory: the framers were forced to accommodate to slavery, a violation of natural right, and to certain attachments, such as state loyalty and trial by jury in civil cases, that many would have preferred to do without.[34] Still, foreign threats were not pressing, society was prosperous and without extremes of wealth and poverty, and the public was accustomed to personal and political liberty. So favored, America was relatively free to test the new science and to establish whether, in principle, it is ever possible for a people to give itself laws on the basis of reason and choice.[35]

Moreover, American experience and reflection convinced Madison that the efficacy of political technology was less dependent on political culture than had been supposed. Montesquieu was a Bacon, Madison wrote in 1792, but no Newton or Locke; writing "before these subjects were illuminated by the events and discussion which distinguish a very recent period," Montesquieu exaggerated republican government's dependence on civic virtue, falling short of the discovery that an extended republic, properly contrived, could uphold *both* personal and political liberty.[36] Under the Constitution, Madison claimed, the United States was "without a model," virtually a prototype of the technological republic.[37]

Schooled in the civic catechism, most of us will immediately think of the system of checks and balances that Madison described as the "internal" control on government.[38] And as Madison's vaunt suggests, the Constitution involves two departures from established ideas on the separation of powers. In the first place, the legislature is not based on the classes or orders of society. The framers expected that the Senate's dignity and longer term would attract men of wealth and position, but the Constitution sets no requirement of property or station. The differences between the two houses are purely formal—terms, constituencies, and mode of election—which is what Patrick Henry meant when he sniffed at the "paper checks" of "a sort of mathematical Government" with no necessary connection to social interests.[39] Second, the framers departed from a strict separation of powers, giving each branch significant power in the affairs of every other, increasing the occasions for contention. As David Epstein points out, the American framers regarded the separation of powers as a set of devices shaped to avoid the concentration of power that is the aim of human beings in general and public people in particular. The clash between the branches of government in the American system is intended to derive largely from the competition between individuals ambitious for prominence and power, collected in institutions jealous of their prerogatives, a mechanical safeguard against the dependence of private citizens on the politically minded.[40]

This use of rival interests as a substitute for "better motives" is not confined to government: as Madison suggested in the *Federalist,* it is carried into the "whole system of human affairs, private as well as public," where it helps to solve the great riddle of republican politics, the problem of majority faction.[41] Popular habits made republican government a practical necessity in America, but the framers were also convinced republicans in theory, since majority rule approximates the natural equality and "consent of the governed," which they saw as the origin of all legitimate regimes.[42] Moreover, the "republican principle" follows directly from the determination to avoid an evaluation of souls or ruling qualities. Majority rule makes no judgment on these matters. Given a rule of suffrage and reasonably honest elections, it settles government on a quantitative and objective basis: majoritarianism moves from the rule of speech to the rule of number.

Nevertheless, this solution is delicate. The "just powers" of government may derive from consent, but its *effective* power depends on force or energy. Only in the state of nature is majority rule also the rule of force; in civil society, the command of armed forces, wealth, or strategic position gives unequal advantages, so that force is ordinarily on the side of minorities.[43] The "republican principle" is a legal bar to minority rule, but if majorities are factional, pursuing a narrow idea of self-interest, there is every danger that strong minorities will refuse to accept the results of elections and appeal to a test of strength.

The framers' answer, of course, is the large republic, its "orbit" expanded by representation to take in a bewildering variety of interests and factions.[44] Majorities in such a regime are bound to be shifting coalitions, composed of mutually distrustful groups and conflicting interests. Evidently, such majorities are assembled through bargains and compromises and are unable to strike too high a moral tone. The mediocrity of majorities teaches citizens to limit their political enthusiasms and allegiances. In a large republic, any group or party whose program we wholly support and in which our views matter will almost certainly be too small to succeed. An extended republic tends to produce a limited-liability politics in which moderation is the fruit of disaffiliation and disenchantment.

In fact, in the framers' thinking, detachment is a kind of substitute for civic spirit. All attachments are suspect, since the bonds of love and community limit liberty, tying individuals to particular persons, places, ideas, and institutions without regard to their usefulness. Worse, attachments ordinarily chain us to the past, since they are likely to result from early education and long familiarity, just as ancient examples and teachings—most obviously, religion—tend to double the strength of opinion. Even the reasoning associated with political attachment is dangerous and unreliable. "The reason of man," Madison wrote, "like man himself, is timid and cautious when left alone, and acquires firmness and confidence in proportion to the number with which it is associated."[45] Bold reason is the quality of human beings in a state of association, and—especially in the "noblest minds," driven by the passion for fame—it can enter into "extensive and arduous enterprises for the public benefit."[46] And on rare occasions like the American Revolution, when private passions are disciplined by threat and indignation, ordinary citizens may become a fraternal public capable of heroism and virtue. Such unusual excellence, however, is not the foundation for "a system we wish to last for ages."[47]

In the ordinary course of things, individuals are more apt to be rational in isolation. Statesmen and teachers who are visible and accountable may be able to govern passion. For most citizens, however, the combination of personal anonymity with strength of numbers tends to unite private passion with public daring, an invitation to faction and party spirit. The Athenian assembly would have been a mob, Madison asserted, even if every citizen had been a Socrates.[48] Whatever is gained in human excellence by a fraternal politics is purchased at too high a price. The "bright talents and exalted endowments" produced by the ancient city-states, Hamilton claimed, have only "a transient and fleeting brilliancy," tarnished by the "vices of government" that helped to produce them.[49]

By contrast, the framers hoped that the design of the laws would weaken attachments, setting individuals free but leaving them somewhat isolated in psychological terms, confronting within civil life a mild version of the order-inducing vulnerability of the state of nature. The reasoning of human beings who are "left alone" is timid, not dazzling, but it can slow even great passions by its very fearfulness, edging the desires toward safe, if petty, objects. And timid reason develops "circumspection," the effort to seek safety by seeing things from all sides, which, though not truly public-spirited, is still public-regarding.

This strategy of detachment is evident in the Constitution's provisions with respect to the states. In the framers' view, the states, like all political societies, were no more than artifacts intended to serve the purposes of individuals. James Wilson told the Constitutional Convention that "a private citizen of a state is indifferent whether power is exercised by the General or State Legislatures, provided it be exercised most for his happiness." Madison agreed: "The people would not be less free as members of one great republic than as members of thirteen small ones."[50] Yet a citizen of a small republic does enjoy a better chance to be heard or to hold office and to that extent can be said to have more political freedom. The freedom that concerned Madison and Wilson was the liberty of private persons, and it is by that standard that they preferred to judge the states.

In practice, however, the states could not be evaluated in strictly utilitarian terms. They enjoyed old loyalties—"antecedent propensities"—and were emotionally close to their citizens, the beneficiaries of "the first and most natural attachment of the people."[51] The state governments, consequently, had an interest in established ways and in parochiality, and since "all public bodies" are ruled by avarice and ambition, the state regimes sought to hold their citizens to narrow and outdated interests, using attachments to limit liberty.[52]

The government of the Union, consequently, is given direct access to individuals within its sphere of authority, without the need for any "intermediate legislation" by the states, in order to make a claim on "those passions which have the strongest influence upon the human heart."[53] At a distance from the bodies, senses, and day-to-day lives of citizens, the central government will always be at a disadvantage as far as affection is concerned.[54] The framers were confident, however, that interest is naturally sovereign unless confused and opposed by overwhelming attachment. By ending the states' monopoly over "those channels and currents in which the passions of mankind naturally flow," the national government allows interest to make itself felt, eroding state attachments over the long term. Since the federal government can be expected to have a "better administration"—combined with sovereignty over commerce, money, and war—it will gradually detach affections from the states.[55] To be sure, the Union will attract only diffuse affections and relatively weak attachments, but this tepid patriotism, the counterpart of timid reason, suited the framers' hope of holding government in the role of servant, securing liberty for individuals.

In this version of political hydraulics, commerce is a millrace. Acquisitiveness is the great civilizing passion—it was the "taste for property," Gouverneur Morris argued, that prompted human beings to leave the state of nature—and the new national market opens new opportunities for specialization and gain, liberty and power.[56] Commerce also broadens, gentling some of the self-centeredness of avarice and forcing consideration of other interests.[57] Moreover, since values vary with supply and demand, commercial life promotes detachment and flexibility, an emotional distance from any particular set of products, techniques, and relationships, especially a sensitivity to changes in opinion.

At the same time, the framers regarded economics as essentially political, a set of contrivances to be fitted to human wants.[58] The chief "task of modern legislation," Madison observed, lies in regulating the diverse kinds of property.[59] Inequality resulting from differences in ability is acceptable and even desirable, since the protection of differing faculties is government's first aim. But wealth will always be tempted to try to shut out competition, just as social and political power can be used to hold others in a disadvantaged position.[60] Commerce should consequently be governed to ensure a reasonable opportunity for all. On the whole, the framers trusted that the advantage of the large republic—the competition of many interests, denying more than short-lived ascendancy to any—would be effective in economics as well as politics, allowing regulation to be left largely to "the silent operation of the laws."[61]

Yet despite their confidence in political technology, the framers recognized that a republican people needs some element of moral and civic virtue, a "vigilant and manly spirit" that "nourishes freedom."[62] Self-preservation and self-interest, for example, do not support military virtue; in defense of a standing army, Hamilton observed that a commercial people can never be a "nation of soldiers."[63] But unless citizens are patriotic enough to defend their liberties, a republic is wholly dependent on and vulnerable to an army of mercenaries or dedicated soldiers, employees who are doubly dangerous, since they are apt to despise the soft and ignoble values of a liberal regime.

The problem of the military is only an instance of a more basic problem. It is clearly in my interest for a political society to exist and for other citizens to obey the law, but it also appears to be in my interest to break the law whenever it seems advantageous, enjoying the benefits of law without being limited by it. The framers' doctrine can only answer that, in practice, lawlessness risks too much: I am likely to be found out and punished; moreover, any crimes that I commit endanger the social contract and political society, especially if I escape punishment, because they weaken the trust and fidelity of others. This argument is plausible in the case of the great and powerful, who are too prominent to escape notice and whose wrongdoings may seem to justify others in disregarding the law. For private persons, however, these dangers are greatly diminished; the obscure and unpropertied have a good chance of escaping detection, and their conduct is less likely to set a destructive example. The poor and desperate, moreover, may feel that they have nothing to lose. Such people, the framers observed, need religion and moral education to make good the deficiencies of private interest and public power as supports for law.[64]

In these terms, however, moral education is a kind of equivocal fabling, practiced on behalf of the "aggregate interests of the community" on individuals who are unable to reason or to discern their interests (that is, according to the framers, children and perhaps women) or whose very interests may nudge them in a lawless direction, such as "desperate debtors" like Daniel Shays and, even more clearly, slaves.[65] It is not true that promises should always be kept, but it is useful for people to believe so; not all crimes are detected and punished here below, and a belief in a supreme judge sustains many who might otherwise falter.[66]

Moral education, in other words, is necessary but vaguely questionable, too dangerous to be trusted to the state and also incompatible with the dignity of a regime devoted to reason and freedom. At the same time, there are distinct problems in entrusting moral education to the private sphere or to the states. Lacking a proper foundation in reasoned consent, early education's authority and moral education's deceptions can be justified only if they develop or support the individual's capacities for independence and reason. The civic foundation of the technological republic requires an appropriate "education for liberty."[67]

John Locke and his American followers supplied the founding generation with just such an educational technology, one distrustful of authority and attachment, the mirror of the framers' political principles.[68] In Locke's view, children, like all human beings, are driven by the desire for freedom and mastery and hence are naturally inclined to resist commands and overt rule. Education, accordingly, is best understood as a problem in human hydraulics: once their nature is understood, children are "flexible waters" whose courses can be channeled, so that by rightly designed training, even defects of nature can be at least "a little remedied."[69]

In the American tradition, this emphasis on malleability has often been exaggerated into a belief in the almost limitless power of "socialization." Locke's view was soberer, since he regarded nature as a limit on education. Nevertheless, he did teach that apart from certain basic impulses, such as hunger and the yearning for liberty, human desires have no natural objects and can be directed by proper technique, so that, for example, play can be made burdensome for children by imposing it as a duty, making study relatively more attractive.[70]

But Locke also sets out to *promote* a flexible soul that will be responsive to socialization and to opinion through a family government that is severe, to say the least. He argues that parents must attempt to discipline children's minds and habits from their "very Cradles," when they are "most tender, most easy to be bowed," and especially "before Children have Memories to retain the beginnings of it."[71] This intervention is to be stern: apart from satisfying a child's physical needs, spartanly defined, parents must make a special point of denying children what they want and must also ignore crying except when a child has suffered some bodily hurt.[72]

This program has two aims. First, it is intended to make the habit of self-denial and self-control second nature. The desires aim at natural goals (in fact, there are times when it may be necessary to stimulate them), but the ability to defer gratification is necessary for great or long-term projects and for the defense of liberty, which often calls for sacrifice and pain.[73] Second, Locke's program for early education is designed to avoid the fostering of dependence. It teaches children that they cannot simply or safely rely on others, a negative spur toward managing for themselves. And because, on this view, women are too prone to indulgence, the role of the mother in early childrearing should be diminished, overruled by the government of the father, the voice of civil reason overriding natural affection.[74]

At the same time, the frustrations children suffer under Locke's scheme are intended to drive home the lesson of their weakness and practical vulnerability. Parents are to curb their children's desire for dominion and to break their pride, brooking no "Obstinacy or Rebellion," using milder modes if possible but, if necessary, falling back on force.[75]

These formative severities reproduce, psychologically, the experience of the state of nature, leaving children free but driving them into society. Forgotten but written in the secret places of the soul, early harshness reduces the need for external authority and physical constraint later in life. In Locke's system, rule is replaced by repression.[76] Detached but sensitive to the power of others, Locke's citizen is intended to develop a "relish" for "the Good Opinion of Others" and with it the polite circumspection the framers valued.[77] Classical education aimed at souls who love what is true more than what is honored, a virtue defined by inner quality rather than outward behavior. Locke's standard is lower but more accessible, and it is less dangerous to civil peace than pride. The Lockean school aims to rear civil competitors whose desire for supremacy is defined in terms approved by society and by law and whose very self-interest is bent toward generosity—liberal souls for a liberal regime.[78]

There were evident problems, however, in translating Locke's prescriptions into an American idiom. He wrote primarily of an education that, after early childhood, would be entrusted to tutors, but such training was out of reach for most Americans, and even schooling still seemed beyond the needs and resources of ordinary citizens.

It was apropos, then, that when Benjamin Franklin resumed his *Autobiography* in 1784, he redirected the book from his son to the public, as if acknowledging that the new republic needed an education in which the family would yield to the polity.[79] The change was also consistent with Franklin's long-standing hope of developing a model for self-education within the power of the many. This secular "apparatus" of moral training would be more reliable than Christianity—since "all Men cannot have Faith in Christ"—and thus "adapted to universal Use."[80] Taming lightning was less ambitious: aiming to improve on Christianity, Franklin was also aspiring to outdo Locke, in so many ways his master. A practiced enchanter, Franklin spoke to generations of Americans with unique authority, and he still casts a long shadow.

Most Americans know Franklin's technology of the virtues, if only in a somewhat distorted mirror, since it has become one of the hazards of American childhood. He recommended making and retaining a chart of thirteen virtues; each week, the individual is to practice one of these graces, grading his or her achievement daily to enlist pride on the side of good performance. After the thirteen weeks of practice, Franklin confided, individuals will be greatly strengthened in the habits of virtue, by no means perfect but better and happier.[81]

His method presumes morally serious individuals who desire to lead good lives "but know not *how* to make the change."[82] The system, consequently, depends on an adequate early rearing, affording that "tolerable character" with which Franklin, by his own account, had begun his career.[83] But Franklin did not recommend his own rearing to others, substituting a more modern education based on his adult experience.

He "often regretted," Franklin tells us, that he devoted much of his early reading to his father's books of "polemic Divinity," but he has kinder things to say about Bunyan's *Pilgrim's Progress*, Defoe's *Essay on Projects*, Mather's *Essays to Do Good*, and Plutarch's *Lives*. His bow to Mather is often the object of comment, but Franklin notes only that Mather's book "perhaps" gave him a "Turn of Thinking that had an influence" on his later life. Similarly, though expressing no regret at reading Bunyan and Defoe, he has no praise for their teachings, only for their prose styles, which he subsequently lauds. By contrast, reading Plutarch—the only pagan text on Franklin's list—was "time spent to great advantage," a lesson underlined by his decision to sell Bunyan to buy histories, the progress of the soul giving way to progress in time. And as that might suggest, even Plutarch's wisdom proved inferior to the "peaceful, acquiescing manners" of Franklin's teaching: ancient virtues must also yield to modern experience and science.[84]

For Franklin, the heroic virtues, anciently praised, have no just claim to rule. The love of honor provokes contention and violence, so that warriors and statesmen ("public cutthroats and intriguers"), together with contemplatives and poets, have failed to pacify existence, a goal that requires the reconstruction of human nature.[85] Philosophy is a somewhat better guide, since Franklin admired Socrates' guileful rhetoric, his pose of "lithe humble Inquirer and Doubter." But by confuting one's opponents, one provokes them; skill in debate brings victories but not goodwill.[86] Ultimately, Socratic rhetoric is not safe because it teaches too openly and too much in public. Instruction and mastery must be more thoroughly hidden.[87] Speech—for Aristotle, the political quality par excellence—is less effective than experiments that others can "repeat and verify" and need no verbal defense.[88] The model of government is not the Bible's God, who creates by speech, but the silent deity who orders inanimate nature through the laws of attraction and motion.

"Publick Religion," for example, should be devoted to morals rather than faith or doctrine, and preaching should aim to make "good Citizens" at least as much as it tries to make "good Presbyterians."[89] Stripped to its "essentials," religion is reduced to a belief in God, the immortality of the soul, and the due reward of vice and virtue "either here or hereafter."[90] This faith lacks any Christian dimension, even the ambiguous affirmations of Locke's *Reasonableness of Christianity.* A maker and creator, Franklin's God does not redeem the world, except possibly in the next life; here below, he supports the quest for mastery, so that it may be "the Design of Providence" to extirpate the Indians "to make room for Cultivators of the Earth."[91]

Humility, that high Christian excellence, was included in Franklin's list of virtues but as an afterthought, added only at the urging of a Quaker friend. Yet humility did not fit: a desolating sense of one's own shortcomings combined with wonder at God's glory, humility is a state of the soul as paradoxical as Socrates' knowledge of ignorance, the gift of grace and not human teaching. As Franklin winkingly observed, even if it were possible to cultivate the virtue, success would have made him "proud of [his] humility."[92] Nevertheless, Franklin argued, the *appearance* of humility is of great value, since its disguise allows one to lead those for whom appearances are everything. Since to "raise one's Reputation" is to invite envy and opposition, the truly great teacher or founder conceals himself behind an apparent humility, sustained by an inner pride in his creation that does not need public recognition.[93] Out of sight, it is possible to appeal to and channel the lesser pride of less perfected human beings, holding up the lure of honor and success. For Franklin as for Locke, pride and vanity, the most tenacious of the passions, become the bases of social morality. The desire for approbation can tame selfishness into civil competition, where it can be guided toward benevolence and the common good.[94]

The truly reigning virtue, in Franklin's system, is sincerity, which he makes central in his list of excellences. Unlike more modern versions, Franklin's sincerity is an *inward* quality, compatible with useful trickeries, limited only by the injunction to "use no hurtful deceit."[95]

To be sincere is to be honest *with oneself*, to maintain a directing will at the center of all the social and political roles it may be necessary or useful to play. Like self-mastery, sincerity requires that one never identify with such disguises, keeping psychological distance between oneself and one's relationships.

This detached self-command is the motif of the "Party of Virtue" that Franklin suggested, based on a new elite, a secret "Society of the Free and Easy" composed of persons who—having followed Franklin's course of the virtues—would be free from vice and debt and able to set their own directions. The vanguard of liberty, the society was to operate behind the scenes "until it was become considerable."[96] Ordinary political parties, Franklin argued, remain united by common principles only when out of power; once successful, parties tend to fragment, divided by the interests and vanities of their members. His projected party, Franklin thought, would be an exception because its members, practiced in his discipline, would be free from the itch for public esteem. Franklin hoped to school a new class, and perhaps a public, that would be literally utopian, detached from everything except the project of mastering nature—suitable citizens for the technological republic.

Two centuries later, we are all participants in the framers' project, and the great majority of us appreciate its benefits and cherish its liberties. At the same time, we know that power has proved more difficult to control than the framers had hoped. The "silent operation of the laws" has failed to avoid monumental inequalities of wealth and power, both of which constrain private opportunity and political freedom. Moreover, citizens—so many parts of a complex division of labor in an integrated market and world—are radically dependent on and exposed to national and international events. As Michael Ignatieff comments, this vulnerability, so thoroughly beyond the control of individuals or their social relationships, tends to transform needs into rights that must be protected by public authority.[97] Even those political scientists who discern a somewhat self-regulating mechanism in the competition among interest groups see a need for government to broker compromises and maintain fair rules of the game, and conservative administrations acknowledge the need for an economic safety net and use public money to protect private savers. The need to curb private inequalities and to provide citizens with minimal security—both necessary to republican life—has created and continues to require a government more active and more inclined to intervene in the private sphere than the one the framers brought into being. Moreover, the growth of power and pace of change demand swift, sometimes secret decisions, so that the president's prerogative strains against and sometimes overruns the barriers and forms in which the framers sought to confine it.[98]

Meanwhile, the republic's citizens—its "human resources"—seem increasingly less suited to control its energies. The framers trusted that the scale and moderation of public life would limit the confidence and enthusiasm of citizens, turning them toward private life. As Tocqueville taught us, however, mass politics magnifies this design until it becomes grotesque. Contemporary majorities, all but incomprehensible to most citizens, are certainly beyond their power to change. Even public leaders scurry to adapt to opinion, and presidents and their staffs anxiously watch the polls. Private citizens quickly learn that public life is a sphere of weakness and indignity in which they matter only as statistics and in which they are safe only if they confine their thoughts and voices within the bounds permitted by the "tyranny of the majority."[99] Small wonder that the retreat into private life becomes a rout or that the republic suffers from a chronic shortage of allegiance.

Private life, however, is no safe citadel. Gradually, American society has been yielded to the laws and logic of technique.[100] The temptations of commerce bribe us, and change forces us, to fear commitments to places or persons, institutions or ideas. Attachments make us liable to pain, loss, and abandonment, just as they are obstacles between us and new opportunities. And individualism, in alliance with the laws, offers justifications and routes for escape.[101]

As families and communities have weakened, they have become more exposed and more apt to conform to the dominant institutions and ideas. Today, the technological republic pursues Americans into the most private places and to the very foundations of the self. From Locke to our times, Americans have been attracted to technologies of child-rearing ranging from the sensible to the bizarre. For us, however, the impact of technology grows ever more direct: the media play an increasing role in the education of children, before literacy and even before speech, encouraging the development of spectatorial personalities careful to preserve their flexibility and their distance. That teaching is reinforced by the discovery, through observation if not personal experience, that families and friendships are unstable relationships in which it is wise to limit one's liabilities.[102] The sources of commitment and loyalty are becoming anorexic in the private order as well as in public life, so that Tocqueville's bleak fear—that in the end, each human being would be confined "in the solitude of his own heart"—takes on a disturbing immediacy.[103]

Lacking the support of communities of faith and remembrance, individuals face oblivion as well as insignificance, so it is not surprising that more Americans grasp at immediate or short-term gratifications or that they find them hollow.[104] As the sphere of individual liberty shrinks in practice, Americans seem more insistent on being unrestrained in what remains. In intellectual life, the accurate perception of our dependence on other human beings and on the environment is accompanied by a desperate insistence on the individual's freedom in theory and in the soul. The very idea of a "self" is widely regarded as a violation of the freedom of subjects to construct themselves, and even words are asserted to be so many chains imposed by power.[105]

Yet this rebellious distrust of language mirrors the official doctrine of technological government, always disposed to substitute rules and procedures for speech and judgment.[106] In contemporary public life, this inclination comes to seem a virtual necessity: citizens, disdaining politics and inadequately informed about it, are ill equipped to deal with the modern world's intricacies and perils. Power and scale, the artifacts of technological politics, have magnified its original theory and practice into the ideology of the administrative state and the search for scientific or quantitative measures by which objective data can displace civic deliberation.[107] Just as power moves from the legislature to the executive in the quest for expert decision, it has tended to pass from the executive into the bureaucratic "technostructure," sliding "into the body of the organization," increasingly out of the public's sight and reach.[108]

Even if this pattern reduces many political risks, it also lessens the public's support for government. It convinces a growing number of citizens that public life is a sham, manipulated by secret powers and hidden strategists, at best no answer to and possibly complicit in their own indignity. Resentment, thus far, is largely held in check by perceived weakness and the consolations of affluence, expressed in private fantasy or self-destructiveness, but it is no comfortable ground for the republic's future.[109] The public's indifference to politics and its disposition to indignation—exploited by so many investigative reporters—are warning signs of the despair and rage rooted in the technological project itself. Not only does the mastery of nature entail the possibility of mastering human nature, but the elimination of human need seems to erode the need for what is human—our labor and art as well as our allegiance and aspiration.

Tocqueville described two ways of mitigating and perhaps healing the ills of the technological republic. In the first place, he argued for the decisive importance of the "art of associating together" as a protection against the impotence felt by individuals in mass regimes.[110] This craft is not easily learned in modern America: Franklin contrived voluntary associations for street paving and fire protection, but we depend on the public funding of public services. Of course, it is possible for us and for the government to seek to expand the sphere of association wherever possible. We could abandon or reverse the hostility to party that has informed our legislation throughout this century, or we could follow the Wagner Act's more positive example, encouraging association by the support of law. In the same way, public policy can attempt to do more to assist families and communities, acting—against the teaching of the laws—on the principle that strong and secure attachments are the foundations of self-esteem and freedom.[111]

Any such policies, however, also point to the need—one Tocqueville observed—for "constituted authorities" to support "theoretical studies," allowing and if necessary compelling Americans to consider the truth that is beyond possessions and beyond associations, the nature in which humans and political societies have their being. The artist Jacques Louis David was inferior to Raphael, Tocqueville commented, even though he followed nature like a good anatomist, capturing the details of the human body. Like technology, David "dragged nature to the easel," attempting to know it through its parts and to master it by force. Raphael, by contrast, drew from the inside out, from first principles rather than appearances, informed by a sense of the whole that gives his work greater "life, truth and freedom."[112] Compare this trinity of Tocqueville's with Locke's: truth deprives liberty of the central position, and property is displaced altogether. In the most fundamental sense, Tocqueville implies, freedom is not the mastery of persons and things; it is being what we are, subject to truth's authority. No teaching is more necessary if the technological republic is to rediscover its soul.

6

In Good Faith: On the Foundations of American Politics

AMERICA IS A LAND OF MANY FAITHS where faith itself means different things. The faith to which George Gilder appeals—the "morale and inspiration of economic man"—is not the faith of the prophets and the apostles. Leslie Fiedler detected a new "age of faith" immanent in the creeds of "liberation," where others saw only the despairing celebration of an empty faithlessness. Variously, faith is identified with a transcendent sanction for the existing order and with a covenant which weights American life and finds it wanting. In America, the Ark and the calf both go by the name of faith.[1]

This cannot be dismissed as no more than a healthy pluralism. Contemporary America is experiencing a crisis of political faith—one which visibly raises, among other things, the question of the place of faith in politics.[2] More and more Americans, from diverse points on the political spectrum, suspect that there is something unsound at the foundations of American political life, and their doubts point in the right direction. Any effort to understand our present discontents must retrace the relationship between faith and the founding principles of American politics. I will try to mark part of that trail by considering, first, the nature of faith—and, especially, the distinction between "good" and "bad" faith—and second, the rejection of "good faith" in the Machiavellian and liberal roots of modern political science. In the end, I will argue that America needs to restore good faith as the standard of public policy. I will be covering old ground, but that is the only way by which we can reclaim the land of our parentage.

Faith, Trust, and the Public Good

Let us begin with the obvious: Americans are inclined to praise faith, but they are uncomfortable with any discussion of it. Faith, in common

Originally published as "In Good Faith: On the Foundations of American Politics," *Humanities in Society* 6 (1983): 19–40.

parlance, means religion, a subject that makes us anxious because—like politics—it can so easily disturb and fragment private relationships. Faith is a public subject, at least in the sense that it threatens the order of private life. In America, however, religious faith seems unsuited for serious political discussion, since the Constitution forbids penalizing or rewarding any confession. In this setting, the discussion of religious faith is as frustrating when it leads us to a conclusion as it is when it does not. Religion, paradoxically, is a public subject without a public forum.[3]

Most Americans do not, consequently, think very much about the meaning of faith and are content to take their understanding of faith from common usage and opinion. Our culture and language, however, are deeply influenced by the liberal tradition that informed the framers and pervades our political institutions and speech.[4] For the moment, it is enough to observe that the founders of liberalism, although they valued religion as a support for morality, feared and suspected faith, associating it with persecution, fratricidal strife, and superstition.[5] Liberal political philosophers, consequently, were at least as concerned to *confine* faith as they were to *define* it, and that intent shaped and clouded the terms in which liberalism speaks about faith.

First, liberalism sought to exclude faith as well as religion from political life. It is in keeping with that tradition that our ordinary patterns of speech limit faith to the relationship between the faithful and God. Yet even though this is the most exalted form of faith, it is also the most elusive. Faith has many more possible objects and forms in secular life, and these lesser, more accessible varieties of faith are the logical place to begin any effort to understand faith as such.[6] In fact, it is even necessary to think of faith in this broader sense to appreciate liberalism's case for confining faith to a narrower sphere, but this—like the argument to follow—is a position I will develop later.

Second, liberalism sought to substitute trust for faith as the standard for public relationships. The success of this effort is indicated by the fact that we treat "trust" and "faith" as virtually synonymous, although the two terms are anything but the same.

Trust puts the burden of obligation on the person trusted. If I trust you, it is up to you to prove that you are trustworthy. Trust, consequently, is a means by which subjects attempt to control objects; the self seeks to establish moral claims on the other.

As this suggests, trust involves private property in the broad sense of that term: when I trust you, I *entrust* you with something that is properly mine—my possessions, the care of my loved ones, or my reputation. When I "put my trust in you," I am making an investment, and I expect you to return my trust intact or enhanced.

Trust is a matter of behaviors, not souls. If I trust you, my values and expectations precede and control my trust; it is not your job to teach me better values or improve my character. In the same sense, you are trustworthy if you act in ways that fulfill my trust; your motives, unless they affect your conduct, are quite irrelevant. By the same token, if your actions fail to live up to my expectations, you have forfeited my trust. The claim that you meant well, even if true, is not enough to make you trustworthy. As Locke put it,

> all power given with trust for the attaining of an end being limited by that end, whenever that end is manifestly neglected or opposed, the trust must necessarily be forfeited, and the power devolve into the hands of those who gave it.[7]

Trust, in other words, is a relation between *separate persons* with distinct interests, concerned with conduct and not conscience, ideally suited to the liberal premise that human beings are by nature free, isolated beings concerned with their own welfare and preservation.[8]

Faith, by contrast, obliges the subject as much as the object. If I say that I have faith in you, you may feel inspired or burdened, but my faith itself is likely to be put to the proof. My faith in you presumes that you can do well, not that you will or must. In fact, we ordinarily say "I have faith in you" out of a desire to reassure someone who may fail or has failed. My faith, consequently, is always liable to the test of disappointment.

Faith, then, looks beyond behavior. My faith in you is premised on who you are, not on what you do. It involves the judgment that your failures or shortcomings—even if repeated—are not essential to your true self. Faith makes *a judgment of wholes rather than parts,* of you rather than this or that moment or incident of your life. In the same sense, when I speak of my faith in our relationship or my country, I am referring to wholes. I need not deny that in this or that detail, our relationship or my country falls short of the best or even does what is base. It is not accident that our times should spark so many eloquent appeals to civil religion: even Thomas Paine found it useful to appeal to faith and to the soul in times of trial and failure.[9] As this implies, faith is a necessary element of any realistic notion of the public good.

Faith, Reason, and Science

Necessarily, faith speaks of unseen things.[10] We see the parts of a whole; its unity is an idea discerned in and in spite of more or less discrete sense impressions. It is for that reason that liberalism tends to equate faith with the irrational. Liberal empiricism makes sense impressions the ultimate data of reason. It follows that only parts and separate bodies can be said to exist by nature. Ideas that unite discrete impressions are created or made, the products of convention, and can claim only a second-rate, artificial rationality. Notions of the whole, the products of men's minds, must always yield to the rationality of things sensed and especially of things seen.

Even Hobbes, more sympathetic to "names" and scientific concepts than a rigid empiricist would be, contended that everything beyond sense is "derived from that originall." The things "naturally planted" in man's mind are only those things that involve the "use of his five Senses." Religion, consequently, is either "natural"—derived from the "visible things of this world and their admirable order"—or the result of human imagination, "decaying sense" moved by the "feare of things invisible."[11]

Liberal philosophy was correct in its judgment that that faith is "blind" because faith does often ignore visible appearances. Yet faith certainly need not be "blind" in the sense of excluding doubt. Faith constantly tests and is tested. Shallow faith can grow deeper and weak faith stronger with experience and reflection, just as faith can be lost under the weight of embitterment. Faith, in other words, is a working hypothesis, held with more or less force and certainty. "Prove all things," Paul wrote, "hold fast to what is good."[12] Evidently, since every scientific hypothesis requires faith, if only of a weak sort, a scientist must believe that a hypothesis is worth the time and trouble of putting it to the test.[13] In this respect, at least, there is no conflict between science and faith.

One example of questioning faith is apposite. Abraham doubts the justice of God's purposed destruction of Sodom, and he persists in the argument until God concedes that he will not destroy the city if there are as many as ten just men in it. In fact, if God did not break off the discussion, Abraham's premise—that it is unjust to slay the righteous with the wicked—would lead to the conclusion that God cannot justly destroy Sodom if there is *one* just inhabitant. Abraham's view necessarily implies that God's decision, though irresistible, is unjust. The defect of Abraham's faith, however, does not lie in this challenge to God's justice. It is in his premise, which sees guilt and innocence in terms of *individual* wickedness and righteousness. Abraham ignores the possibility that a city—a political whole—might be collectively guilty. God spares Lot because of his defense of the principles of hospitality that the native Sodomites ignore: in these quasi-private terms, Lot is a righteous man. But Lot *has,* after all, lived in and profited from Sodom, and his bond to the city goes beyond mere utility. Even when he knew God's purpose, Lot "lingered," unwilling to leave the city, and his wife, of course, looked back nostalgically. Lot, in fact, needs a city, if only a small one, for the life of his soul; he depends on the city for what is most excellent in him. The excellent soul, however, is likely to be tainted by the corrupt city. Certainly, since the polis is prior to the individual, the part cannot escape involvement with the sins of the whole.[14]

This interpretation only emphasizes, however, that faith prefers the "evidence of unseen things" to that of visible things.[15] This is particularly damning to modern political philosophy because it regards sight as the master sense. Sight is quicker and reaches farther than our other senses: taste and touch are limited to what is close at hand; hearing makes its fine discriminations only slowly and with care; smell is both limited and evanescent. Vision, consequently, is suited to large and rapidly changing political societies that the founders of modern political philosophy prescribed and in which their successors live. "Men, in general," Machiavelli wrote,

> judge more according to the eyes than their hands, since everyone is in a position to observe, just a few to touch. Everyone sees what you appear to be; few touch what you are.[16]

Machiavelli had no illusions about the qualities of vision. Sight is quick and applicable to men in general; it is also superficial and, consequently, unreliable. For Machiavelli, preference for sight is a political, not an epistemological, principle, something his successors have often forgotten. Vision is also a distinctly *private* sense because it is content to observe and mark the boundaries of separate things. To that extent, sight is defective as a source of political knowledge: it distracts us from the foundations of political life, the presumption of some inner likeness uniting human beings who differ in work and appearance, on one hand, and the deliberate effort to determine the "good life," on the other.[17]

Opinion and Knowledge

There is another aspect to the critique of appearances. As Plato knew, our senses receive impressions, not objects, and these images are unformed until the mind organizes them into wholes. Even the simplest perceptions rest on such underlying ideas. Some of these ideas seem to be instinctive; most derive from our early and continuing education in doctrines about the nature of things that are implicit in the opinions of our society. Even our seeing, in other words, is shaped by unseen things. If we are to know the external world at all, we need to begin with faith (*pistis*) in these forms.[18] The alternative to faith is not reason or science but solipsism.[19]

As with all faith, experience and reflection may lead us to articulate, doubt, and revise these original assumptions. Yet our ability to question depends on the education our passions receive in political society. It takes courage to unsettle the foundations of one's life. To doubt one's first principles requires emotional security, which includes the conviction that the world is neither incomprehensible nor unyieldingly hostile, and the belief that the value of truth outweighs the pain of acknowledging one's past errors. If we do not need to believe that the world is a home for humankind, we do need to believe that it is not a prison.

Philosophy and science depend on that faith, but they come too late to teach it. Treatises on methodology proclaim that it is the duty of scientists to change their minds in the face of disconfirming evidence, and so it is. In fact, however, most scientists cling to their basic beliefs, tormenting the evidence until it supports that aim. They may surrender the periphery, but they will try to hold the citadel. As Max Planck observed, scientific theories do not prevail by converting old believers: such transformations are exceptional. They win out by persuading the young and the uncommitted.[20]

Consequently, as Plato taught, philosophy is always dependent on the foundation provided by opinion.[21] Higher forms of knowledge are to some degree analogies to what is grasped by the lower faculties. Knowledge derives from right opinion and right opinion from right faith.[22]

This argument, moreover, points to the dimensions of faith. The dependence of knowledge on opinion heightens the importance of opinion-makers, the poets and lawgivers who frame the institutions and imagery of a political society. In the *Republic*, Plato had Socrates argue that makers must acquire a "right belief" about the goodness and badness of what they make by being compelled to associate with and listen to the users of what is made.[23] On the surface, this is a democratic argument: shoemakers must listen to those who know whether the shoe pinches, and legislators must attend to those who are ruled. But the knowledgeable user is one who knows the right or appropriate use of a thing: a horse-trainer could not learn much from someone who harnessed a racehorse to a plow. Consequently, the argument implies that makers must have faith in those who know the right or natural end of what they make. Poets and lawgivers must believe in philosophers who understand the place of poetry and law in human life and of human life itself within nature as a whole.

There is a derogatory quality to this invocation of "right belief," since it presumes that poets and legislators will never know what the philosopher knows and can only believe what he reports. But it would be a mistake to take this assertion of the philosopher's authority as a deprecation of faith. Socrates argues that "imitators" know only the appearance, not the reality of things. Practical life—the life of makers—is necessarily primarily concerned with appearances. This is especially true because, although it is desirable for shoemakers to listen to those who know the right use of footwear, the practical condition of their craft is that they listen to their customers. Socrates goes on to argue that there are three things with which users, makers, and imitators are concerned: the virtue (*arête*), beauty (*kallos*), and rightness (*orthotes*) of every implement and action. The imitator, however, will not know whether what he portrays is beautiful (*kala*) or right (*ortha*).[24] Notably, *virtue* has been omitted from this second list, presumably because the imitator, caught up with appearances though he is, *may* know or recognize excellence. This is a striking concession to the imitators, and it demands explanation.

Socrates' argument begins with the fact that appearances show us only separate things, not the wholes of which they are parts. Appearances do, however, allow us to grasp the relations between separate things: they permit us, in other words, to compare larger and smaller, wiser and more foolish, better and worse. The appearances, in other words, are enough for pragmatic judgment. But these relative measures have two central defects: (1) they see only contention and competition, not harmony, and hence, they are unsuited to perceive the beauty of things, and (2) they do not comprehend what is truly best and worst, and lacking such an absolute measure, they fail to understand the radical shortcoming of all human excellence. The imitators, for example, hear only the irony, not the sincerity, in Socrates' assertion that he "knows nothing." Socrates' argument, then, maintains that makers have defective knowledge because they lack the philosopher's higher faith. To put it another way, the imitator can conceive of the whole only in terms of the relations between competitors (hence, for example, the poetic version of the gods); he possesses a species of faith, but it is wrong faith, corrigible only if he is compelled to listen to the truer voice of philosophy.

Good and Bad Faith

Plato's argument helps correct our tendency to speak of faith in terms of a dichotomy between those who have faith and those who do not. It draws us back to our own usage, which distinguishes between good and bad faith.

Bad faith, after all, is a species of faith. It differs from simple deception because bad faith involves malice. Although I have deceived you if I tell you a falsehood that I believe to be true, in such situations I am likely to claim that I acted in "good faith."[25] In the same sense, I may act in bad faith even if I tell you the truth, especially if I tell you the truth in such a way as to lead you to disbelieve it. (For example, consider the "reassuring" statement, "I'm certain your lover *really* is faithful.")

Bad faith implies that I have used words for some inappropriate end. An offense is involved because words are common things, belonging to all those who speak a language. As this implies, the meaning of bad faith reaches beyond words. Bad faith is defined by the use of public things for a private purpose, the exploitation of a whole for the benefit of a part.[26]

Faith conveys power by revealing the relationship between seemingly disparate things. What is distant is affected by what is close at hand, and the humble sway the exalted.[27] By observing the structure of the whole, even the lowly can do great works; for the sower who knows the earth and its seasons, the smallest of seeds will yield an abundant harvest.[28] Similarly, the New Testament makes a centurion the exemplar of faith because his knowledge of political relationships frees him from the empirical observation that Jesus must touch in order to heal. "For I am a man set under authority, with soldiers under me, and I say to one, 'Go,' and he goes, and to another, 'Come,' and he comes."[29]

But authority and power can be misused. Knowledge of relationships gives me power even if I determine to betray the whole of which they are parts. A traitor can move with relative freedom because he is a citizen and knows the culture of his people. Faith conveys a certain strength, but it does not guarantee righteousness: "Though I have all faith, so that I could remove mountains, and have not charity, I am nothing."[30]

It is quite possible to be convinced that God rules and must be obeyed and even that God loves and will redeem mankind and still resent his dominion.[31] It is not enough, Robert Neville writes, "to acknowledge the *truth* of faith."[32] Mere obedience may reflect only envy and the hope of gain; although Simon Magus "believed," he did so in bad faith, "in the gall of bitterness and in the bond of iniquity."[33]

Good faith, by contrast, involves the loving concern for the whole even at some cost to the part. I demonstrate my bona fides when I tell the truth even though a lie might serve my interest. Political good faith, consequently, is the creed of the good citizen. But just as there is distinction between the good man and the good citizen, there is a difference between political good faith and good faith as such.

Good faith, the apostles argued, requires a new perception of the relation between human beings and the world. This transformation allows people to see the world as a home, a place meant for them and their good rather than an arena of meaningless travail and mocked hopes. The visible sign of good faith is charity, but *caritas* must reflect the conviction that one cares for another—and, especially, for the other close at hand—because one cares for the whole.[34] This sort of charity is also a sort of public-spiritedness, open-handed because in helping another one helps oneself as part of the whole.[35] The analogy to civic spirit is not at all strained: when God grants human beings good faith, he reconciles himself and his governance to them.[36] It is hardest to excuse God's injustice in forgiving the ungodly, but the desire that they should be redeemed follows from the love for the whole and the wish that it should be made more lovely.[37] God's governance, through good faith, becomes more desirable because the faithful see the outlines of his purpose and "rejoice in the hope of the glory of God."[38]

Good faith, in this high sense, inwardly envisions the "beauty and rightness" of the universe. They may reach it by different paths and in different degrees, but good faith is the common ground of true religion and philosophy.[39]

Reason and law may encourage and support this exalted form of good faith, but they cannot produce it. Reason may lead to faith, just as law demonstrates the existence of a common order. *Ex nihilo nihil fit*—an undeniably rational principle, whatever criticisms may be leveled against it—can lead to the First Cause, but that stark doctrine falls very short of proving that God is a loving father and a just king.[40] The Word, Augustine remarked, is not enough to mediate between God and humankind; it was necessary for the Word to become incarnate.[41] Yet the ministry of Jesus transformed the feelings only of those who were capable of perceiving it, and that number included only a few of those who met the living Christ. For subsequent generations, the historical life of Jesus changes only what may be *said* about reality; it leaves us with a new Word but the old flesh.[42] Religious faith, like the philosophic soul, ultimately depends on a blessing. The highest form of faith is inseparable from good fortune.

Consequently, like the best city, this high good faith cannot be enacted as the rule of social or political practice. It can, however, serve as the standard by which we measure practice: the best is the rule by which reason measures the better. In day-to-day life, for example, we most often refer to "faith" in relation to marriage.[43] Marital "fidelity," however, commonly is limited to sexual conduct, a narrow standard at best. The scripture goes much further: it ordains that husband and wife should be "one flesh," a *gesammtperson* with new and superior claims and interests.[44] To be faithful to one's marriage, in those terms, requires the subordination of all individual interests to the good of the whole. Even to speak of a conflict between "my marriage" and "my career" reflects an element of bad faith, since it treats marriage as one of my interests rather than an interest superior to me.[45] In the New Testament rule, we cannot be freed from marriage, although we may be parted.[46] Yet Jesus is careful to remark that "all men cannot receive this saying."[47] Jesus's teaching, in other words, cannot be commanded by civil society. It is a rule for the best case that can be reflected in the law: even in these lesser days, our law concedes that spouses cannot be forced to testify against their partners. To do so would, on the scriptural rule, violate the privilege against self-incrimination. And it makes a difference if the law regards matrimony as a covenant rather than a contract, an estate superior to the claims of individual interest and freedom.[48]

Machiavelli and the Art of Bad Faith

I have emphasized the distinction between good faith and bad because the modern tradition in political philosophy begins with a revolt against the standard of good faith. In only one of the chapter titles of *The Prince*, the eighteenth, does the word "faith" occur. It is the central of seven chapters dealing with the princely virtues; Friedrich Meinecke thought it the "most notorious and evil" chapter in the book.[49]

This crucial chapter promises a discussion of the "manner in which the faith of princes should be carried out." Machiavelli implies, in other words, that he will be discussing means and not ends, "manner" rather than faith itself, but a discussion of means requires some answer to the question, "What *is* the proper faith of a prince?"

Machiavelli begins with the comment that "everyone knows" that it is laudable for a prince to keep his word (*mantenere la fede*). It is far from clear, however, that everyone understands the same thing by "faith," an ambiguity that is especially important because, as the chapter proceeds, it becomes clear that Machiavelli is referring to religious as well as to narrowly political faith. He goes on to argue that princes who have achieved great things have taken little account of faith: this can be seen by the experience of "our times," but it appears that Machiavelli means the observation to be valid for all past time. The first paragraph ends with the argument that those who know how to manipulate men's minds prevail over those who base themselves on loyalty.

This last assertion is more specific than those that have preceded it: in a conflict between cunning and loyalty, *astuzia* will prevail. On the face of it, however, these alternatives are not mutually exclusive. Machiavelli appears to be saying that those who are *skilled* at rhetoric defeat those who do not *attempt* it. But craft is not the issue: even those who oppose Machiavelli would presumably urge that a prince ought to possess *astuzia* just as the best guardian is also, in a sense, the best thief.[50] The issue is not skill but first principles, ends and not means: some princes "found themselves" on loyalty, and others do not. This sort of principle, moreover, is even more fundamental, since it refers to the personal "foundation" of the prince himself rather than to the principality he founds.

The first paragraph, then, begins with the assertion that it is laudable for a prince to uphold or keep faith and ends by contending that it is a mistake for him to be loyal to it. This seeming contradiction can be resolved by a prince who *has* faith but *opposes* it, who regards what his faith discloses as an enemy to be overcome. That logic is close to the example with which the chapter ends: a "prince whom it is well not to name" (ordinarily thought to be Ferdinand the Catholic) preaches peace and faith and is an enemy to both.

Machiavelli goes on to argue that human beings are part beast and part man, and princes should know how to use force as well as law. This, too, is axiomatic, and yet it turns on a more subtle point: one cannot speak of the rational or spiritual side of humanity as its true or higher nature. *Nature* shows no preference for law over force, for the human over the bestial. Quite the contrary, in the usual case, human beings are a contemptible lot, especially in being faithless.[51] So far as nature gives any indication, she stands with what is bestial against what is human. A prince, consequently, must be prepared to break his promises in the interest of self-defense. This, of course, only amplifies Machiavelli's earlier assertion that a prince must learn how *not* to be good and to use goodness and badness according to necessity.[52]

Political scientists have often praised the "realism" of Machiavelli's teaching without understanding that his defense of undesirable means is not original. The medieval tradition, for example, took account of expediency and made an axiom of the proposition, "Necessity knows no law."[53] That doctrine, however, presumes that necessity is lawless. The law revealed by God or philosophic reason is always *morally* obligatory; it yields only grudgingly and to nothing less than necessity.[54] In this traditional view, the gap between physical and moral necessity is closed by the faith that both are parts of a good whole, that in the end physical necessity serves morally worthy ends.

To Machiavelli, on the other hand, necessity *is* the law, the only real law of nature. This law must be obeyed—in part so that it can be used against itself—but it is indifferent or hostile to human excellence. The order that includes humanity, like human nature itself, is mixed, combining good with (much more frequent) base potentialities. Human beings, by nature, are basely mediocre, lacking the aesthetic grandeur of great evil as well as the moral splendor of great good.[55]

Machiavelli, of course, never justifies a surrender to this low nature: necessity is to be used, not revered. That, in turn, calls attention to the importance of high purpose. Alexander VI, Machiavelli comments, "did nothing and thought of nothing" but deception. This is a shocking statement, since it contends that Alexander *never*—in his professed faith as well as his statecraft and his moral lapses—thought of anything but deceit. The jarring impact of that assertion probably concealed, for much of Machiavelli's audience, an even more damning verdict: Alexander was *trivial,* since his only purpose was to deceive; and since he practiced deception as an end in itself, Alexander must have sought to deceive himself as much as his antagonists. Moreover, in practical terms, Alexander was a fool. Breaking laws or customs (and one's word) is dangerous for an *established* prince because it undermines his authority. An established prince must struggle to keep his word and to uphold law. Only at the beginning or founding of regimes is ruthlessness justified and then only by serious purpose.[56] Alexander VI had the *astuzia* of the fox, just as the murderous Agathocles had the *ferocia* of a lion, but both were less than human.[57] A prince needs the qualities of both beasts, but he also needs the purpose, the *virtù ordinata,* that makes him master over means.[58]

Human beings are pathetic, but they are not without good qualities. They admire the greatness they do not possess, which is the reason that a prince must at least appear to have noble qualities. This admiration, however, is not to be trusted, and a prince must not found himself on it, since it is petty and composed of envy and irresponsibility. Nevertheless, human beings are not to be blamed for their condition. Nature makes human beings faithless, since she so frequently denies them the means to what they desire and subjects them to a degrading necessity. Human faithlessness may be lessened, if not overcome, by success in a war against nature.[59]

Machiavelli, in other words, celebrates bad faith. In his teaching, it is necessary to see the whole, human and nonhuman, and to obey the necessity nature imposes. The power conveyed by this recognition, the knowledge of necessity, is to be used in the service of a private artistic vision, the elevation of mankind through the triumph over nature and fortune. In Machiavelli's political aesthetic, humanity can be beautiful only in appearance, and the political poet contrives to use the lower forces in human life to make an excellence lacking in nature.

Good faith is the enemy of this vision, since it moralizes the whole. Machiavelli scorns the construction of "republics and principalities which have never been seen or known to exist in reality," but it is not the invisibility of such regimes that inspires his disdain. Machiavelli recognizes the value of things unseen: human beings in general and the citizens of self-governing cities in particular prefer a "dominion which they do not see," even if it is severe, to a rule that, "being seen every day, appears . . . to flaunt their servitude."[60] His real complaint against ideal cities lies in the different charge that they are not known to exist in reality (*essere in vero*). Machiavelli's phrasing is ambiguous, but he is clearly rejecting the claim that such cities derive their authority from nature: they cannot, despite the pretentions of their authors, be known to have a real existence—let alone a preeminent place—in some design of nature. "How we ought to live" is separate from nature, not a final cause immanent in it. Nature is no friend to right, and those who rely on her betray their own hopes.

Christian tradition taught that Europe's peoples and polities were only so many parts of a Christian republic, mutually obliged to justice and good faith. Yet that doctrine, though strong enough to undermine the authority of secular governments, was too weak to rule. In fact, Machiavelli contended, the church and "good faith" kept Christendom divided. Europe would be happier and more united if it returned to the original form of Christianity or, to be more precise, to the "principles of its founder." The meaning of this profession is established by the fact that Christianity, as Machiavelli understood it, was originally a deception, like all religions, and hence a species of art. The true "origin" of Christianity, in this view, does not lie in Jesus's words but in the will to power that moved him. A return to this earliest foundation of Christianity requires the freeing of the will to universal dominion from the teachings and traditions in which Christian faith had sought to confine it. Christianity humanized war; it thereby softened the "terrible apprehension" of defeat that, in ancient times, had supported patriotism and political virtue. The Christian restraint on war and expansion also kept alive small regimes and petty princes. The liberation of war, consequently, would drive humankind in the direction of larger polities and political virtue. We live, all too obviously, in the shadow of that teaching.[61]

Yet Machiavelli's doctrine involves a contradiction. His belief that human beings are ranged against a hostile nature led him to reject the idea of right defeat. Good faith argues that sacrifice may prevail: Socratic and Christian kingliness alike presume that human beings are moved by a courage that is not swayed by the threat of defeat or the bribe of success. Even if Israel is destroyed, Isaiah prophesied, God will preserve a "remnant," and his view suggests that the death of a polity may matter less than its fidelity to truth. Even if the witness of such a polity goes unheeded, good faith tells us that nothing of value is ever truly lost. Survival, all things being equal, is desirable because the whole is a good one, but the survival of a part is never a self-justifying end. Individuals and polities are required to offer up their lives, when called, in the service of the greater city.[62]

Machiavelli scorned that understanding, believing that since the good exists only by convention and by the genius of makers, it is ineffably vulnerable. The duty of the good is, above all else, to *survive*.[63] By making survival and success into first principles, Machiavelli hoped to strengthen the will to resist evil. His doctrine, however, also saps human courage. Cravens and libertines can find reassurance in the principles of Machiavelli's creed if not in the details of his design.

Liberalism: Public Trust and Private Faith

Liberalism boldly and unabashedly followed this logic to its conclusion. Liberal political science begins with the rejection of political aesthetics as well as good faith. Hobbes will have none of Machiavelli's effort to dignify or adorn politics or to rest it on the esoteric genius of the founder-poet. In the same spirit, Locke wrote that it is "ambition enough" to remove "some of the Rubbish, that lies in the way to knowledge." This sort of philosophy seems humbler than what has gone before, but it is a noble pursuit, slower but surer because it speaks to ordinary men. "He that hawks at Larks and Sparrows, has no less Sport, though a much less considerable Quarry, than he that flies at nobler Game."[64] Liberalism rejects the prince as well as the priest: it begins by *democratizing bad faith* as the first principle of public life.

Liberal thought postulates separate and self-interested human beings, each pursuing his own power and survival. By nature, human beings are at war with nature and one another. The natural order is niggardly, the life of human beings is mean, and any hope for excellence of the good life depends on mastering nature.

Given this natural individualism, of course, political society is a contrivance invented to protect and further private rights and goals. The public order is "invisible," an "artificial being, existing only in the contemplation of law."[65] Once this ghostly public person is created, however, human beings will seek to capture it for their private, truly natural, ends. Bad faith is nearly universal in public life. The classical distinction between the "healthy" and the "corrupt" forms of a regime is deceptive nonsense. Since good and evil are only "names" for our appetites and aversions, any distinction between monarch and tyranny only reflects our like for the one and our dislike for the other, decked out in public terms to take in the credulous. There are genuinely common interests, but they are (as Madison termed them) aggregates, made up of private claims, and even so, self-seeking humanity will always tend to prefer its immediate good to such distant interests. All appeals to patriotism and public spirit are to be distrusted; the presumption of bad faith must be the working rule of public life.[66]

Yet this public teaching leaves liberalism with the problem of obligation. If it is naturally right for me to pursue my desires and if public claims mask private interests, why should I obey a law that conflicts with my interest? Granted that I have promised to do so and that the continued existence of political society is valuable to me, why should I observe a rule if I can break it and remain undetected? I would combine the advantages of law and lawlessness, and if my crime goes unnoticed, I will not even have weakened political institutions.

Liberalism has no real answer to this radical appeal to bad faith, yet to grant it would amount to an invitation to anarchy. Hobbes, attempting a response, argues that it is an error to maintain that the "Kingdom of God" can justify lawlessness or to assert that "Successful wickednesse" in the pursuit of political power can excuse itself.[67] In other words, Hobbes remains silent about the most difficult case, the private man who wishes to break his promise obscurely, as opposed to those who wish to achieve great ends and public power. He chooses to debate priests and princes, zealots and Machiavellians, and to pass quickly by the fantasies of economic man.

Even on his chosen ground, however, Hobbes suggests that his opponents' position is *heathenish* before he turns to a more philosophic criticism, and he ends by indentifying a violation of covenant with Breach of Faith. He invokes religious imagery because, even against the most vulnerable opposition, his case is weak. It is "not against reason," Hobbes contends, to keep one's promises, since it is risky to break rules or to rely on escaping detection. Since human beings need society desperately, they cannot afford to chance exclusion from it by relying on the errors of others.[68] Yet to argue that it is not unreasonable to keep promises is a far cry from maintaining that it is unreasonable to break them. At best, Hobbes offers a utilitarian calculus based on the likelihood of detection. But this calculus is unreliable: the crimes most liable to be noticed are public crimes like rebellion, and it is arguable that great ends are worth a measure of risk. Despite his choice of antagonists, Hobbes is most likely to persuade the timorous, especially those whose petty ends are not worth the gamble. In any event, Hobbes has no reasoned answer to the proposition that breaking promises when it suits one's interest is always *desirable*.

To make good this deficiency, Hobbes appeals to good faith, arguing that any hope of the "felicity of Heaven" requires the keeping of covenants. Yet our knowledge of life after death, as Hobbes takes pains to point out, does not rest on "naturall knowledge" but on "other men's saying."[69] He introduces the contention in order to dispute the claim that heaven will reward those who rebel in a religious cause, but the same case lies against Hobbes's own reliance on the next life.

In fact, Hobbes despairs of a scientific answer to the appeal of bad faith. His own view is premised on the good faith this his version of scientificity requires him to discard, "a certain Noblenesse or Gallantnesse of courage (rarely found) by which a man scorns to be beholding for the contentment of his life to fraud or breach of promise."[70] Since faith is the only ultimate protection of covenant, Leviathan is threatened by any faith or covenant that does not derive from the sovereign. Private life and faith, consequently, must be ruled in the interest of public order, and all private right (save the right of self-preservation) must be treated as a concession from the sovereign.[71]

Locke, however, discovered another answer, more favorable to private liberty, in the *idea of trust*. English law had developed the trust as a fictional person, treating this contractual relationship as though it were a whole. The trust strengthens the principle of obligation: a trust holds a trustee liable to act in "good conscience" beyond the narrower, merely legal terms of his promise, requiring a species of good faith. By the time of Locke's writing, this fiction was well established in custom and law. English society provided an alternative to faith, "a liberal substitute," Maitland wrote, "for a law about personified institutions."[72] Since Englishmen were accustomed to think in these terms, it was reasonably safe to permit them a freedom quite unsafe in the hands of human beings more radically self-interested because not so socialized. Locke, consequently, applied the principle of trust to the constitution of political society itself. The legislative power is given in "trust" by "society and the law of God and nature." The legislative, similarly, is "only a fiduciary power to act for certain ends," and the people retain a right to "remove or alter it" when the legislative power acts "contrary to the trust" reposed in it.[73]

In Locke's teaching, individualism is afforded a variety of obligation through a fictional whole inculcated by society. That only emphasizes, however, the radical dependence of liberal political society on certain forms of private life, a reliance that reaches far beyond my argument here. Liberal theory shied away from the moral consequences of its own (and Machiavelli's) doctrine. It urged a limited self-interest, recognizing that in private life and society, "good faith" is necessary to human moral education and even to the capacity to act effectively. Some private relations, in other words, must be *treated* as wholes endowed with "personality," even though the only true persons are the individuals who are parties to the relationship.

Liberal society is a kind of moral school that must be protected against the logic of liberal theory, walled off and governed according to different precepts. The relations of citizens to the sovereign can alter and dissolve, Justice Marshall argues, but their "relations to each other . . . remain undisturbed."[74] In order to treat public life, this argument implies, on the principles of trust, we must rule private life on the principle of good faith. In his first dissent, Marshall appealed, against the current, to that founding doctrine: to allow legislative interference in private relations, he lamented, will undermine the "sanctity of private faith" and ultimately "destroy all confidence between man and man."[75]

Liberalism hoped to preserve public life as a sphere for moderate bad faith by resting it on a foundation of good faith learned in private life. In like manner, the distinction between faith and goodness helped persuade modern moralists that a concern for true faith might be politically irrelevant as well as dangerous. In this view, the services faith performs, such as they are, are best guaranteed by a diversity of faiths.

> For modes of faith, let graceless zealots fight.
> His can't be wrong whose life is in the right.
> In faith and hope the world will disagree,
> But all mankind's concern is charity.[76]

Perhaps this is so, so long as the vast majority of mankind combines charity with faith in some form. But charity without faith—compassion without a sense that humanity is part of an ordered whole—is quite a different matter. That conviction lends itself to the belief that the world is "absurd," arbitrary and alien to men but possibly manipulable by them. Faithlessness combined with moral passion is the root of modern millennialism, with all its familiar horrors. Even in moderate forms, that combination preaches the mastery of nature in the service of humanity, regarding all limits to human will as only so many obstacles to be overcome by material progress and technology. Babel built towers toward heaven; rocketry extends our range, but the end is likely to be the same.[77]

Faith and Politics in Contemporary America

In our own society, the public principle of liberalism—individualism and bad faith—is gradually devouring the residual havens of good faith, as Tocqueville predicted it would.[78] This is evident in the teaching of our highest institutions as well as in the patterns of family and personal life.[79] In *Griswold v. Connecticut,* the Supreme Court spoke of a "right to privacy" belonging to the marital relationship, rooted—although Justice Douglas avoided the term—in a law of nature protecting marital good faith.

> Marriage is a coming together for better or for worse, hopefully enduring and intimate in the degree of being sacred. It is an association that promotes a way of life, not causes; a harmony in living, not political faiths; a bilateral loyalty, not commercial or social projects.[80]

Yet within a few years the Court proclaimed

> the marital couple is not an independent entity with a mind and heart of its own, but an association of two individuals. . . . If the right of privacy means anything, it is the right of the *individual* . . . to be free from unwarranted governmental intrusions into matters so fundamentally affecting a person as the decision whether to beget or bear a child.[81]

The language ("or bear") was advised, of course. Within a year, the Court discerned a right to an abortion during the first trimester among the "activities relating to marriage," which included procreation and the rearing of children.[82] More recently, however, the Court has affirmed that this concern for "activities relating to marriage" does not imply the right of one spouse to a say in such a decision if that would involve any interference with the individual rights of the other.[83]

Liberal individualism, in other words, is continuing the historic pattern—so visible in capitalism—of destroying its own moral foundations, extending radical freedom into every sphere of life.[84] Liberal individualism, in fact, is reducing Machiavellian bad faith to a farce without decreasing its danger. Our public life seems dominated, at least for the moment, by petty self-seeking and a preoccupation with "images."

Political science has played its own role in the decay of liberal society. Modern political science tended to follow Hobbes in proclaiming that all appeals to the public good are made in bad faith and, at best, should be seen as "a promotional device by means of which a particularly extensive group or league of groups tries to reduce or eliminate opposing interests."[85] Pluralist argument of this sort follows the liberal tradition in asserting that *groups*, however, have real interests and may be regarded as wholes. But the same argument that is thought sufficient to dispense with the idea of a public interest—the fact that there is always disagreement about the just and unjust within a political society—also is enough to eliminate the claim of groups to an interest separate from that of individuals.[86] Moreover, if conflict between parts disproves the existence of a whole, the individual will have to surrender any claim to identity in favor of the "reality" of warring faculties and passions. In order to affirm the rights of the person, political science must defend the just claims of wholes over parts. That, in turn, points to the priority of political society over the individual and of nature over the polis. The ancient language of good faith, after all, reminds us that human beings depend on their world and had best revere it.

Fortunately, there are resources in America beyond the liberal tradition and its dying light.[87] We still believe, for example, in the doctrine of human equality. The idea of moral equality is beyond the ken of bad faith, which sees only individuals who differ in excellence and virtue. In the liberal tradition, human beings are "equally free," not equal in dignity. Equality before the law is a kind of concession, a political fiction necessary to persuade free and self-centered individuals to enter political society. Like politics itself, "equal protection of the laws" is a second-rate standard in liberal theory, justified by the fact that its existence permits the real, underlying inequalities to emerge in private life.[88]

Our religious heritage, however, teaches equality in a different sense (witness the earlier discuss of *caritas*). It insists that our equal human nature, considered in the whole of which humanity is a part, is the supremely important human fact, and it teaches equality in our feelings as well as our conduct. "Thou shalt not harden thy heart," Deuteronomy enacts, "nor shut thine hand from thy poor brother."[89] Generosity is not enough: we are commanded to give gladly and without the secret aim of establishing supremacy by beneficence.

The religious view is rooted in the ancient understanding that equality is an end, the goal of all justice.[90] To those who are truly devoted to God's purposes and the ends of nature, it is not an offense to ask human beings to receive the same "pay" for different "work."[91] The realization of our humanity is enough, a proper limit to ambition (even if not all human beings, or even a majority, ever attain it), just as in a good city, no man asks to be more than a citizen or is content with less. Equality and good faith are twins, and both were present at the founding of the Republic. They are difficult teachings, yet even if obscured by individualism and neglected amid abundance, they are among those qualities, "somehow more divine," that never lose their capacity to draw humankind.[92]

7

The Discipline of Freedom

Defining Liberty

"THE WORLD HAS NEVER HAD a good definition of the word liberty," Abraham Lincoln told a Baltimore audience in 1864, "and the American people, just now, are much in need of one."[1] Lincoln was speaking of the struggle to end slavery and praising Maryland for repudiating the "wolf's dictionary," with its idea of a freedom to hold others in bondage. Perhaps he was speaking carelessly or for the moment, but taken at his word, Lincoln was pointing to a problem more enduring and more fundamental. His assertion amounts to a criticism—startling, given Lincoln's reverence for the Declaration of Independence and the Constitution—of the political theory of the American founding. Lincoln tells us that the framers, who "brought forth" a nation "conceived in liberty," did so without a "good definition" of freedom, leaving a fault in the philosophic cornerstone of the Republic.[2]

He was right. The framers' view of liberty is at best a partial truth, and Americans have reason to wonder whether that flawed foundation can bear the weight of the Republic's contemporary problems. I will be arguing that American democracy needs to recall a teaching, more ancient than the framers', that holds that liberty is found in and through political life, that civil manners are inseparable from civil liberty, and that liberty itself is no more than a means to higher ends, a great spirit but no god.[3]

Originally published as "The Discipline of Freedom," in *To Secure the Blessings of Liberty: First Principles of the Constitution*, ed. Sarah Baumgartner Thurow, Constitutionalism in America series, vol. 1 (Lanham, Md.: University Press of America, 1988), 31–63. Reprinted with the permission of the Rowman & Littlefield Publishing Group. This chapter was originally prepared for a conference at the University of Dallas on October 18–19, 1985, as part of the University of Dallas Bicentennial Project. The published volume also includes comments by respondents to each panel. Jeffrey K. Tulis was the respondent to this essay, and his published response is well worth reading, including his contention that McWilliams offers a "Presbyterian slant" on a "forgotten Aristotelian world." Still, Tulis commends the "exceptionally thoughtful" essay that offers a challenging kind of "republican soulcraft."

The framers taught us differently. They held that human beings are by nature free beings who are morally independent and primarily self-centered. In this doctrine, nature is defined by origins and hence by the body; the decisive evidence of human freedom is the fact that we come into the world in separate bodies and so remain.[4] By nature, individuals are unencumbered, without duties to others or claims on them. There is no natural restraint on our desires, and we seek to do as we like. Above all, we strive for self-preservation, "the first principle of our nature" and the hard core of human self-concern.[5]

This natural liberty, however, is insecure and obstructed in practice. Nature, indifferent or hostile, gives us little and in the end will deny our desire to survive. Our fellow humans, confronting the same fundamental scarcities, seek to despoil or dominate us: in the state of nature, Samuel Adams declared, "the weaker was *by force* made to bow down to the more powerful."[6] Yet even the powerful, as Hobbes had observed, could not rest easy, since the "weakest has the strength to kill the strongest, either by secret machination or by confederacy with others."[7] Hence, by the well-known logic of social contract theory, human beings eventually agree to give up some of their natural liberty in order to make what remains more secure and more effective.

Legitimate political society rests on consent of the governed, since morally free human beings cannot otherwise be bound. Consequently, it frees us from rule by the will of another, the "only distinction," Hamilton once remarked, "between freedom and slavery."[8] In an even more fundamental sense, however, political society is created because we desire to be able, as far as possible, to *do* as we please. Civil society frees us—provides us with civil liberty—to the extent that it protects or adds to our power, especially when it enhances our mastery over nature.

In the framers' teaching, civil society embodies the "two concepts of liberty" discerned by recent political philosophers.[9] We retain a considerable sphere of "natural liberty" and moral independence, especially in our inward, theoretical freedom to want and choose what we please. In individual conscience and in private life, we enjoy "negative liberty," the absence of restraint. Civil liberty, on the other hand, offers us power, safety, and efficacy, the practical and positive freedom to act and achieve associated with participation in an ordered whole.[10] Government aims to afford the maximum power and safety consistent with the minimum limitation on natural liberty and individual rights, "the perfect balance of liberty and power."[11] However, since political society exists to serve the private purposes of free individuals, the balance must always tilt toward individual rights and liberties, the moral center of liberal civilization.

In our time, the balance at which the framers aimed is threatened in two different ways. Most obviously, the institutions and organizations of civil society have come to constitute a power that overwhelms any practical notion of individual independence. Thinkers in the past—Jefferson and Rousseau come easily to mind—feared that this would be so; today, however, the power of civil society is not a fear but a fact, one close to the heart of modern political life and thought.[12] The power of government is unmistakable, armed as it is with weapons of destruction and technologies of surveillance and capable as it is of great terrors and petty interferences. We need to emphasize, however, that the power of civil society is a *general* characteristic of our civilization, present in the private sector as well as in public life.[13] The vulnerability and dependence of individuals is ubiquitous, not only in economic and political practice but also in the life of the soul. Modern civil society challenges the *moral*, as well as the practical, independence of the individual.

I will be developing this argument at some length in order to make clear that the protection of personal and civil liberties can no longer derive from the private resources of the individual. Contemporary freedom requires the support of political community. That argument, in turn, points to the more basic problem to which I have already alluded. The idea of an original, natural, individual liberty that we derive from the framers threatens our most important civil liberty—our political freedom as citizens—and, with it, our capacity to cope with the looming dangers around the Republic.

A Freeing Market?

We speak of the American economy as providing "freedom of choice," referring to the array of products, the range of services, and the diverse employment it offers us. For most of us, moreover, the economy provides freedom from want and affords us a chance, probably unequaled, to do what we do best.[14]

At the same time, our economy is a vast, complex, interwoven, increasingly international system of constraining interdependencies. It makes us free from particular persons and places but only by involving us in a sphere in which individuals matter less and less. It protects the "diversity in the faculties of men," but it makes us more dependent on the economic whole, the great network of specializations of which our work is a part. The division of labor, after all, is a principle of dependence as well as individualism.[15]

Of course, this is as the framers intended. They preferred a large, commercial republic because such a regime could, at one and the same time, free individuals and promote national unity. They saw and valued the subtle ways in which commerce dovetails individuals and localities.[16] Yet it seems at least possible that the modern American economy has gone beyond even their Promethean vision.

Today, if our lives are to go on, millions of others must perform their specialized tasks. We "provide for" ourselves and our families by earning money, but very few of us come close to providing in the literal sense: we need public services to bring us water and rid us of garbage, and our homes and cities can scarcely survive without electricity. Even the freedom of choice we celebrate indicates the extent to which we are passive, dependent on alternatives created by others. Valuable though it is, the freedom of choice is a *civil* liberty that derives from the nature of the regime.

In fact, the civil discipline called planning has become incorporated into the definition of economic liberty. The interdependencies of modern life make it necessary for us to take thought about others who may be involved in what we do and—if only as a form of traffic control—to give them notice of what we intend. If I want to fly to another city on a particular day, I will need to make reservations, but I do not experience this constraint as a violation of my liberty. I *do* feel interfered with, however, if the airline overbooks and decides to "bump" me.[17] Similarly, if I must spend time thinking about your business—wondering, for example, whether my bank is sound or whether the elevators I ride are safe—it impinges on my freedom to do *my* work. My freedom is bound up with the regularities of economic life; my self-determinations rely on people behaving in expected ways and making good on their implicit promises.

We are all exposed to economic and social forces and to reasons and policies of state on which our individual labor has little effect. American farmers were not less productive or hardworking during the 1980s. They suffered because the Reagan administration's economic policies, resulting in a strong dollar, shut American products out of the international market.[18] Especially because it is so often part of the problem, public authority has a duty to afford us and our legitimate expectations some insurance against our vulnerabilities.

At the same time, modern regimes are themselves noticeably fragile. Disruption at any one of a number of strategic points can produce disproportionate disorder. In fact, an individual's capacity to do harm to society greatly outweighs the positive significance of his or her labor to the economy as a whole. Outraged dignity is presented with a constant temptation to outrage.[19] Modern political life thus encourages a politics of disruption, which in turn leads to demands for a government strong enough to cope with the danger.

This is only a dramatic instance of a more general tendency toward an expansion of the role of government.[20] Given the mutual dependence of individuals in modern regimes, it is no longer enough for government to *protect* my private resources, since those resources are not sufficient to sustain me. I need a government that can guarantee that the economic system as a whole will *provide* those things that are needful on terms that are at least reasonably fair. As Michael Ignatieff observes, the division of labor transforms needs into rights, claims on political society mediated through public authority. The details are matters of political controversy, but the principle is conceded: even the Reagan administration acknowledged a duty to maintain a "safety net." This public responsibility, Ignatieff writes, "gives us whatever fragile basis we have for saying that we live in a moral community"; it is also a vital dimension of freedom.[21]

For most Americans, both political community and economic liberty are summed up by the phrase "equality of opportunity."[22] Yet, in practice, equality of opportunity depends on civil discipline and public support. As a matter of theory, the idea of equal opportunity "assumes the possibility of a fresh start, regardless of past history."[23] In the contemporary United States, however, past history presses on us: property accumulates in some hands to the disadvantage of others; inequalities in early rearing give some a great advantage and others a fatal handicap; for a terrible fraction of our population—especially in families headed by women—economic inequality is radical and cumulative; and all of this says nothing of the ancient and durable barriers of race, gender, and ethnicity.[24]

Soften the rebuke to the United States: the theory of equality of opportunity wars with the institutions of *any* complex civil society. Taken literally, it would require us to bring into civil society the conditions the framers associated with the state of nature: a leveling of convention, reducing each of us to a "poor, bare, forked animal" without the burdens or the benefits of civil life and station.[25] Even memory, which brings past history into present life, limits equality of opportunity. In civil society, no start is ever truly fresh and equality of opportunity is never more than partial.

The promise of equal opportunity, however, encourages a "fatal passion for sudden riches," the dream of a miraculous moment that will put us on an equal footing with wealth. Traditionally, that yearning was held in check by the culture of work. Americans could argue with some plausibility that opportunities for instant wealth were phantoms. They told stories that emphasized the perils of speculation, and they left us with a great cautionary proverb, "Easy come, easy go." Earlier generations of Americans recognized that the *existence* of instant ways to wealth, even if rare and infrequent, threatens the discipline of work, and they outlawed gambling—an infringement of individual economic liberty—to encourage honest labor. The more positive basis of the culture of work was hope, the conviction that one's small gains might lead to a fuller measure of equal opportunity for one's children.[26]

In contemporary America, however, radical and unpredictable change threatens our sense of connection to future generations. Americans may have recovered their optimism, but they are borrowing against the future, not saving for it. Moreover, there are now a considerable number of nearly instantaneous routes to wealth. For the children of the disadvantaged, the lure of professional athletics, rock music, gambling, or even less respectable ways of "striking it rich" helps to undermine work, especially given the attenuation of middle-income industrial employment, the traditional avenue for upward mobility.[27] In any number of ways, the demand for economic liberty to do as one pleases threatens to overwhelm the older bourgeois virtues.

The defense of *civil* opportunity is impossible without a government committed to encouraging a measure of social stability and protecting middle-income employment, the high-wage labor we associated with manufacturing.[28] Employment is the heart of contemporary economic liberty. Most of us are wage earners; we depend on jobs, and this makes us, to some extent, "unfree," even though we sell our labor voluntarily.[29] To the framers, this was no small matter. "It is a general remark," Hamilton declared, "that he who pays is master," and Gouverneur Morris doubted that "mechanics and manufacturers" who "receive their bread from their employers" could ever be "secure and faithful guardians of liberty."[30] If such worries seem archaic to us, it is because we are less concerned with individual employers and more dependent on employment and, hence, on general economic conditions.

Nevertheless, the individual employee's need for work—a source of dignity as well as a way to provide—is virtually always far greater than an employer's need for his or her particular work. Employers are also freed from personal dependence by the market; they need labor the commodity, not laborers as individuals.[31] Consequently, as we have known for a long time, genuine freedom of contract for workers demands collective bargaining, recognized as a right and afforded governmental protection at least comparable to that given property.[32] Moreover, freedom for wage earners requires full employment at socially adequate wages. The vision of labor hired at below the minimum wage entrances some economists and employers; it does not promote economic freedom.[33]

I have been arguing that employment is comparable to property as an essential element of economic freedom. In fact, we are coming to view property in a rather new way. The framers regarded property as a natural right, something very personal, closely tied to the self. They also thought of property as a "taste" that leads human beings into civil society; in that sense, property is the foundation of civil liberty, the bedrock of social stability. By contrast, corporate property is not possessed by individuals, and it is only by a fiction of law that corporations are defined as "persons" whose property is protected by the due process clauses.[34] The physical property of great corporations is not ordinarily connected to the selves or the ways of life of its owners; the relation of stockholders to the corporation is largely instrumental. The owners and upper-level managers of a large-scale firm have no real stake in its operations; they are concerned with particular businesses only as investments. It is not enough, consequently, for a plant to show a profit; its rate of return must be competitive with other possible uses of its capital. These days, as the headlines tells us, capital is only too likely to move out of plants and between regions and countries. In fact, the corporation's physical assets and operations are much more likely to be bound up with the lives and liberties of its workers, its lower-level managers, and the communities that depend on its taxes and payrolls. Property defined simply in terms of the rights of capital disregards and threatens the claims of social stability and civil freedom. That so many legislatures have considered legislation regulating plant closings reflects an appropriate concern for those neglected aspects of the rights and obligations of property.

There is increasing support for defining property as the right to participation in civil society. Citizens, Frank Michelman contends, have a right to the "maintenance of the conditions of fair and effective participation in the constituted order," including the economic bases of citizenship. Michelman leaves room for considerable inequality and for loss. But his doctrine does introduce a public obligation to protect citizens against "sudden changes" in the "crucial determinants of one's established position in the world."[35] The framers defined politics as existing to protect private rights, making civil freedom derive from natural liberty; contemporary theorizing is becoming more disposed to defend private rights because it conceives them to be necessary to political freedom.

This sort of thinking is not confined to theory. In recent years, the Supreme Court has acknowledged that expectations of benefit, encouraged by laws and policies, create a new kind of property right that cannot be abridged without due process of law. In 1970, the Court ruled that welfare benefits cannot be cut off without a hearing.[36] In 1976, it went much

further, holding—against the historic practice of the Republic—that non–
civil service public employees cannot be discharged simply because of their
political affiliations, a ruling it later extended to lower-level policymakers.[37]
In its most controversial decision, the Court found that the seniority rights
of firefighters, established by collective bargaining, take precedence over
programs for affirmative action unless there is evidence of discriminatory
intent.[38] One need not agree with all the decisions of this sort—to me, some
of them seem plainly outrageous—in order to recognize that the Court is
groping toward an understanding of economic freedom appropriate to our
time. Individuals are not free if they are simply left alone; even private liberties have their roots in public freedom.[39]

Freedom Today

In politics and in the psyche, separate individuals also are more prone to
frailty than to freedom. As Tocqueville observed, in a vast republic like the
United States, democracy makes us depend on masses of unknown others.
In a small group, a majority of 6–4 is no great matter; each member of the
majority is perceived as a person with a face and with foibles, and I can turn
the tables simply by persuading two people. In a national election, the same
margin—Reagan's in 1984—is a landslide, a fact of nature. The majority
is made up of millions of minds, a task beyond my powers. Even powerful
organizations and great leaders seek to read and adjust to the "mandate" of
opinion. For an individual, isolation only accentuates the weakness, push-
ing the soul toward the conviction that the only safety lies in conforming to
the "tyranny of the majority."[40]

Up to a point, the framers understood this. They knew and relied on
the fact that individuals, set free and left alone among multitudes, would
be "timid and cautious."[41] Part of their case for a large republic was this
tendency to unite individual liberty with civil order. Yet even though the
framers expected that individuals would be guarded, circumspect, and even
fearful in behavior, they believed that inwardly, the mind still would be free.
They accepted and reasoned on the basis of Spinoza's proposition that the
mind cannot be controlled as the tongue is controlled.[42] The fundamental
condition of political liberty, in this view, is that the body be free from
physical threats and restraints, leaving the soul to take care of itself.

Experience taught Tocqueville otherwise. The "civilization of our age has
refined the arts of despotism" and no longer needs the "coarse instruments"
of physical repression. The distinctly modern form of tyranny is:

as entirely an affair of the mind as that will which it is intended to coerce. . . . Under the absolute sway of an individual despot, the body was attacked in order to subdue the soul, and the soul escaped the blows which were directed against it and rose superior to the attempt, but such is not the course adopted by tyranny in democratic republics; there the body is left free and the soul is enslaved.[43]

With hindsight, it seems clear that the framers—and the liberal philosophic tradition of which they were a part—underrated the anxieties that can imprison the human soul. The liberal tradition relied on the lure and consolation of material well-being, but, Tocqueville noted, the more devoted we are to material possessions, the more we will be haunted by the certainty of their loss. The fundamental scarcity for human beings is not lack of wealth but lack of time.[44]

Enshrined in law and custom, individual liberty accentuates the desperate restlessness Tocqueville associated with the pursuit of worldly welfare. The combination of individualism and change makes all forms and relationships seem transient and insecure; home ranks high among the things from which individual liberty sets us free. Having learned to expect all bonds to be fragile, we fear to commit ourselves deeply to any relationship or community. To care about something or someone is to give part of oneself as hostage, to make oneself liable to pain, desertion, and loss. Love, after all, scandalizes individual liberty: though it must be freely given, love *obliges*. The logic of individualism, by contrast, makes "every man forget his ancestors . . . hides his descendants and separates his contemporaries from him; it throws back forever upon himself alone, and threatens in the end to confine him entirely within the solitude of his own heart."[45]

Today, our rather frantic mobility and juggernaut of change are wearing away what remains of our communities of remembrance. Individualism continues to deny that we have any obligation to such communities, and change makes the past seem outdated and distant. Yet the weakening of our bond with the past reminds us how swiftly our words and days will be forgotten. In the framers' teaching, human beings fear for their lives; contemporary Americans, as Tocqueville expected, are likely to fear for the self.[46]

It does not help that individual liberty tears down the social barriers to great achievement, encouraging each of us to aim high and to judge our worth by the standard of our dreams. Obviously, the more who compete for the highest prizes, the more who are certain to fail, and the more we feel at liberty to succeed, the more we will experience such failure as a personal defeat. A healthy realism, by limiting our aspirations, helps make us content with our achievements and ourselves. In our time, however, the dynamism of change undermines that discipline: "The impossible of yesterday becomes the possible of today, and the mind loses its sense of distinction between dream and risk."[47] An increasing number of Americans, drawing their aspirations from dreams, are destined to suffer shattering blows to self-esteem and to experience that "disgust of life" that Tocqueville already observed among the Americans of his time.[48]

In contemporary America, individuals are aware of their weakness and insignificance within the mass democratic public, and they are all too likely to be lonely and anxious. The mass media have an awesome power to shape our images of life and community by appealing to our desires for potency, for love without commitment, and for heroic stature.[49] In fact, as Solomon Asch demonstrated years ago, isolated experimental subjects, confronted with an apparent consensus, came to have doubts about—and, in a considerable number of cases, to deny—the contrary evidence of their senses.[50] The lesson is, by now, a familiar one: the more isolated we are, the more likely we are to depend on opinion for our definition of reality.[51]

Alone, individuals are very likely to lack the psychological and social bases of freedom.[52] We need the support and counsel of friends to set us free from fears and, for that matter, to liberate us from motives allied with our fears. As the Supreme Court recognized in *Miranda v. Arizona,* we have every reason to doubt the validity of consent offered by isolated individuals. A confession may be involuntary, the Court argued, even though no physical coercion is employed to obtain it. Consent, at least in the case of a confession, presumes an individual informed of his or her rights and provided with counsel.[53]

In fact, the quality of counsel is a serious problem for our political institutions. The framers taught us that "consent of the governed" is the sole basis for legitimate government, let alone political freedom.[54] Now, however, far too many of our citizens feel dependent, baffled, and constrained in politics and, consequently, experience their consent as less than free.[55]

Even if we accept the narrow definition that equates citizenship with voting, it is clear that citizens are limited to alternatives defined largely by others. Primary elections were supposed to "open" the selection of candidates to ordinary citizens, but the mass electorates associated with primaries are more apt to be swayed by the media, by money, and by opinion polls. Primaries are probably less subject to influence by individual citizens than the convention system they succeeded.[56] Citizens chronically complain about the quality of their choice—with reason, in recent presidential elections—and they know how little their individual votes matter. Consent given through voting—for those who go to the polls at all and even for those on the winning side—is conditional and halfhearted, only marginally more voluntary than confessions made in ignorance of rights and without counsel.[57]

That citizens should be so constrained and this constraint should weaken the quality of their consent is in part as the framers intended. Citizens who do not find their views and feelings perfectly mirrored in platforms and candidates will be restrained in their enthusiasm, resulting in a kind of political moderation.[58] Disenchantment constitutes a standing limitation on government.

Today, however, political disillusionment has taken on alarming proportions; the United States suffers from a chronic lack of legitimacy, a weakened sense of the obligation to respect and obey the law.[59] Tocqueville trusted that in local community and in society, Americans would learn the "art of associating together," thereby discovering that affiliation and loyalty can give individuals a political freedom they could never know alone.[60] Now, local communities are attenuating, and in social life, organizations are yielding to purely private activities. Contemporary Americans are apt to see groups as a time-consuming and probably futile nuisance. For citizens who share this view, political life leads to frustration, not freedom. Whatever his other accomplishments, Ronald Reagan did not lessen our doubts about government and public life; many of Reagan's policies and more of his popularity are based on a radical distrust of government and politics. American democracy can no longer rely on the arts of association; it needs to promote them.

I suspect, moreover, that the framers would be alarmed by the increasing role of organized power in our political life. Contemporary citizens confront a political world dominated by organizations so powerful that they amount to private governments. The media and the other great private associations have a considerable power to shape the market, to set terms for social life, and to mold political opinion. Ordinary citizens, in practice, have little or no ability to create alternatives; these private governments can be controlled only by equally giant public bureaucracies.[61] But private governments are often so important that government, at least in the short term, cannot *allow* them to fail. This is not a matter of ideology: the Reagan administration rescued the Continental Illinois Bank just as the Carter administration delivered Chrysler. At a certain level and size, the great private governments virtually become institutions of the Republic.

The relative invulnerability of our private governments, however, emphasizes the distinction between such organizations and the small businesses and individuals who can be and are allowed to fail because they are not important to the Republic as a whole. The lesson is not lost on citizens: for individuals, public life is a sphere of indignity as well as of weakness, a sphere of activity in which only a few are heard and still fewer matter.

Popular literature reveals our yearning for individuals who can outwit and undo bureaucracies. In crime fiction, our first heroes were private detectives, individuals who, though outside the system, were partisans of law. But the power of bureaucracy and large-scale organization is making itself felt even in fiction: more and more, private detectives are yielding to the novel of police procedure in which the hero—his intuition and imagination intact—has moved *into* the bureaucracy.[62] There is, as we know, less and less room for the independent individual. Public careers require a strength of character that goes beyond individual freedom; Frank Furillo of "Hill Street Blues" chafes at bureaucratic politics, but he recognizes that the real enemy is "the despair that goes with the territory."

In one supremely dangerous way, after all, our politics does leave space for individual liberty. We can identify vicariously with the power of presidents and leaders who we hope will prove able to master bureaucracy and political complexity, validating the voluntaristic ideal. Individualism has always taught us to suspect laws and forms, and millions of Americans, consciously or unconsciously, now see the law as their enemy. Ronald Reagan's favorite quotation from Tom Paine, "We have it in our power to begin the world over again," expresses the old faith in the possibility of mastering nature, and many Americans admire Reagan's assertion of the power of will and choice against those who speak of limits and necessities.[63] That our yearning for "strong leadership" has its dangerous side is obvious, and it is doubly perilous because, in practice, we cannot do without executive power.[64] Our fascination with leaders, like our adoration of celebrity, is strengthened by our passion for individual liberty, and we cannot be cured without a better sort of love.[65] We need a new appreciation of the liberative power of laws and civil forms and a recognition that both love and freedom are founded on a common life.

Social Contractarianism Restated

Despite all contrary evidence, however, the idea of individual liberty continues to dominate American thought and speech about freedom. Especially, Americans retain their belief in the moral autonomy of the individual, the heart of the framers' teaching.

This persistence of thought is not surprising: political scientists are even less willing than individuals to abandon habits of mind. It is more disturbing that, as Robert Bellah and his associates found, contemporary Americans have no moral language *except* the idea of individual liberty. Our older traditions—Bellah and his associates identify them as civic republicanism and biblical religion—are becoming inarticulate. Bellah's subjects justified themselves in the language of utilitarian or expressive individualism, calculated self-interest or spontaneous feeling, even when their conduct seemed better explained in other terms (for example, by reference to a duty to one's community).[66]

It is a striking illustration that both sides of the abortion debate cast their arguments in terms of individual rights. Supporters of "choice" are willing to appeal to a woman's "right to property" in her body even if they scorn property rights in economic life. It seems even more dissonant that the religious opponents of abortion should speak of a "right to life" rather than a duty to nurture.

As a general rule, our growing recognition of the dependence of individuals in practice has only inspired a more determined defense of their freedom in theory but without the philosophy of nature that gave the framers' teaching its coherence and grandeur. The great philosophic dogma of the time, the separation between "facts" and "values," owes much of its intellectual popularity to the effort to protect individualistic values against the onslaught of disconfirming fact.

Total war and totalitarianism, for example, made political scientists and political philosophers zealous to guard individuals—so terribly vulnerable to repression and mass persuasion—against the moral claims of the state. In the years after World War II, political scientists became all but universally devoted to "debunking" claims to the public good, unmasking them as only this or that private interest.[67]

Relativism and positivistic skepticism were urged because, by denying the claims to superiority of any moral doctrine, they seemed to provide a kind of negative validation for liberal democracy.[68] The relativistic critique, however, also denies any superior claims to tolerance, to fairness, or even to liberty itself.[69] Criticizing relativism for just these faults, Hans J. Morgenthau praised the liberal idea that "the individual is the ultimate point of reference for the political order and as such, owes nothing to any secular order or institution" as an invaluable restraint on power.[70] But, as Howard White pointed out in response, Morgenthau was unwilling to maintain that his theory of natural rights is *true* as well as useful. Finding no basis for the teaching in political practice, Morgenthau also did not believe that nature grants, guarantees, and limits our liberties. Without that grounding, however, natural rights are only one set of preferences, a doctrine that sets us free from decency as well as from nature.[71]

More recently, John Rawls and Robert Nozick have endeavored to find firmer footing for the doctrine of individual rights. Both Rawls's relatively egalitarian doctrine and Nozick's libertarianism began with an idea of the individual as an "end in himself." In this view, human beings are separate persons and free moral agents, each able to establish his or her own idea of the good: "The self is prior to the ends which are affirmed by it." Since rights are prior to the good—and since nothing strictly can be said to be good by nature—any moral order must derive from and respect the moral autonomy that is our fundamental right. "Individuals have rights," Nozick writes, "and there are things no person or group may to do them."[72]

Beginning with these premises, Rawls follows Locke and the framers, presuming that "free and rational persons concerned to further their own interests" will agree to limit their liberty in order to make their rights more effective, although individual liberty will always retain its "priority."[73]

Yet Rawls and Nozick do not speak of our rights as "natural." Both are unpersuaded that there is an order of nature; certainly, they doubt whether such an order can be demonstrated (and hence Rawls's appeal to an abstract "first position" instead of a "state of nature"). Against teleological ideas of nature, Rawls argues that it is an advantage of contractarian theory that it needs "much weaker assumptions" about our natural attributes.[74] In any case, Rawls and Nozick must reject the idea of nature because any whole would limit the liberty of its parts, violating the claims of individuals to be ends in themselves.[75]

Rawls and Nozick, however, do rest their theories on an implicit idea of nature. The body and "the fact of our separate existences" is the foundation of our rights.[76] Our "natural talents and abilities," in Rawls's arguments, are distinguished from "social circumstances" in the old distinction between nature and nurture, and—Rawls contends—we have a right to those natural abilities, provided the social process is "fair."[77]

Rawls recognizes the human need for social support; he knows that, to a considerable extent, the self is developed in and through politics and that civil society is needed to guide and nurture the individual. Nevertheless, Rawls seeks to retain moral autonomy for the self. As the fashionable idea of "realizing one's potentialities" implies, political society is limited to developing our "powers." The political order is only an instrument, restricted to the development of our individual means—our talents and our capacity to plan. Rawls confides that realizing our capacity as free moral agents will be associated with moral sentiments and psychology; these, in turn, prove to be a higher utilitarianism, similar to Tocqueville's "interest rightly understood."[78] Even if this is so, however, moral character is a by-product of politics, not its aim. Ends, even though they are developed in and expanded through political society, are not a concern of political society. Despite the expanded role that Rawls allows to political society, he maintains in principle that political society exists only to enhance our capacity as moral agents to do as we will.[79]

The language of moral individualism, in fact, goes far beyond Rawls's utilitarian doctrine of rights. Inherently, it leads toward the nihilistic conclusion that any moral claim on the individual—even the existence of moral standards—restricts freedom. To be ruled or limited by a norm perceived as external to the self—the idea of an objective human nature, for example—is heteronomy, a surrender of liberty. Human freedom requires that all forms as well as goals be things of one's making, authentic expressions of the self. The framers, in this doctrine, violated the principle of individual liberty because they believed in the existence of a self that needs to be "preserved." In reality, the argument goes on, "man makes his own essence": the self is produced (Marx) or created (Nietzsche) in an assertion of mastery.[80]

Most Americans, of course, do not yet carry the argument to so grand an extreme. Increasingly, however, they *do* reject almost all restraints on their private liberty to do as they please. The logic of individualism, as Tocqueville foresaw, is being carried into private life. As the sphere of individual liberty shrinks, Americans are more likely to insist on being untrammeled in what remains.[81]

The signs are all around us: it is increasingly acceptable to be divorced, to remarry or to remain unmarried, and sexual conduct is regarded as a matter of personal taste, part of one's "lifestyle" and hence an appropriate expression of freedom.[82] We are not accustomed to such arguments in secular society, but the same currents are visible in contemporary evangelicalism. The Christian life, in the new rhetoric, is portrayed as an "exciting, abundant adventure"; discipline and self-sacrifice are at least de-emphasized, and Christianity is presented as a version of expressive individualism in which "subjectivism has displaced . . . traditional asceticism."[83]

Yet this stress on liberties of private conduct and styles of life ignores the extent to which our lives and tastes are only too likely to be shaped by broad social currents or by fashions and putative trends proclaimed by the media. "I could very easily imagine," Arnold Gehlen wrote, "a society of termites in which each one imagined itself free."[84]

Civil and Civic Speech

That we so commonly speak of the "freedom of expression" is one indication of the privatization of liberty. Of course, the term also reflects a generous desire to broaden the definition of the First Amendment to include the arts and the symbolic acts that are so often necessary to capture public attention in this age of mass media and mass politics.[85] In that sense, we are compelled to refer to the "freedom of expression" by the increasing ascendancy in our political life of what is visible over what is said.

Yet we can scarcely be deaf to the desperation in much symbolic expression. So often, it involves a kind of sacrificial witness in the faces of forces one cannot hope to persuade. Thus, Camus, anguished by the Algerian war:

> If one dares to put his whole heart and all his suffering into such a cry, he will hear in reply nothing but laughter and a louder clash of arms. And yet we must cry it aloud."[86]

The decision to "throw yourself into the machine," which Mario Savio urged in 1964, does not mean that one has freedom; it is more likely to signify that one has *lost* one's voice.[87]

In order to command attention—especially from the media—it is ordinarily necessary to reduce speech to slogans if not to violence, debasing the content of one's messages to the point of inarticulateness. Justice Harlan's opinion in *Cohen v. California* aside, a protestor carrying a sign bearing a four-letter word is not writing lyric poetry. His evangel, if it is effective at all, is exhausted by the shock it is intended to produce.[88]

For citizens and for the Republic, the freedom of expression is no substitute for the freedom of speech. Speech edifies in a way that mere expression does not. In dialogue with myself, "I" argues with "me" at the cost of my identity; passion is all too likely to gain the ascendancy, and self-centeredness is the rule.[89] By contrast, if I desire to speak to an audience, my thoughts must be ordered in a way that makes them at least minimally intelligible. The silent, listening other gives reason a kind of ascendancy in speech that it is much less apt to have in private reflection.[90] Speech creates a whole that is ordinarily greater than the sum of its parts, a discourse more rational than would be possible for either party alone. Justice Brandeis was right: "It is the function of speech to free men from the bondage of irrational fears."[91]

Free speech is more than a "right to utter." In the most fundamental sense, speech is a political act, a participation in deliberation.[92] Speech is not free without the opportunity to *be* heard by an audience that is *able* to hear: even if we gain the rostrum, we will be effectively silenced if the audience speaks a different language, unless it is willing and able to learn ours.[93]

The ability to hear implies an openness to deliberation, a willingness to receive evidence and to consider argument that has at least two vital aspects. First, it presumes confidence, a relatively low fear of being deceived, a conviction that one's critical skills will enable one to evaluate both the matter and manner of what is said. Second, an audience is able to hear only to the extent that it perceives listening as compatible with dignity. Listening is most dignified when one chooses to hear even though one might have spoken. Like other mass regimes, modern America denies that choice to all but a handful of citizens, depriving listening of its dignity. Moreover, dignity in listening varies with the matter being discussed. I am relatively willing to attend to a discussion of national politics even though I have no chance to speak myself, but I feel furious and ill used when I must listen to a colleague ramble about trivia, even if I will have the chance to reply. In these terms, freedom of speech is enhanced by (1) civic education, including the study of rhetoric, and (2) access to forums in which we have the opportunity to speak, providing that these have at least some important powers and responsibilities.[94]

In our time, free government needs to foster, as well as protect, the conditions of free speech. Civic education is acknowledged already as a public responsibility, although that responsibility is discharged in an inadequate way. By contrast, public policy has ignored or undermined our local forums, which are now in urgent need of support. There are any number of ways of providing this assistance. We could mandate primaries by district caucus (as in Iowa) rather than by mass electorates; instead of requiring a certain number of signatures to qualify an initiative for the ballot, it would be possible to ask for the favorable vote of a number of district assemblies.

Perhaps most important, we could direct campaigning back to the local level. Public funds, for example, could and should go to state and local parties as well as to candidates and national committees. Above all, it would strengthen the freedom of speech if we found ways to restrict the role of money in political campaigns. Of course, the Supreme Court has eviscerated the Campaign Reform Act by finding that monetary contributions are a form of expression protected by the First Amendment. In practice, this means that Congress may not limit the amount of money that an individual (or corporation) contributes to a political campaign, although it may require that the money be distributed through a number of nominally

Chapter Seven

independent committees.[95] But money does *not* talk: we participate in politics by giving money, but most of us do so privately, without engaging in civic deliberation. The gift of money is an expression of sentiment that may or may not issue in speech.

Free expression in the form of money can, in fact, easily undermine free speech. In the first place, there are necessarily great inequalities in the extent to which citizens can participate by donating money, and the implicit indignity is likely to reduce the public's willingness to listen. Second, money tends to gravitate into the mass media, drawing campaigns with it. Even if we accept the Court's defense of unlimited contributions, we might choose to limit the amount of political advertising on television (on those networks and channels subject to regulation).[96] Such a regulation would rechannel money to the local organizations and forums in which broadly based free speech is possible.

Finally, civil liberty implies the public protection of *civil* speech. When we argue about public questions, we have a right to attack the ideas and doctrines of our fellow citizens but not their persons. The two things overlap, of course, but the principle is clear.[97] Moreover, the protection of the person includes more than the prohibition of assaults on the body. An attack on the identity or dignity of another citizen does violence no less than a physical blow.

The Supreme Court long ago noted that there are "fighting words" that public authority has a right and duty to forbid in public speech, even though—to say the least—it has hesitated to apply that doctrine in recent years.[98] As Alexander Meiklejohn has argued, rules of order and civil manners do not restrict content; such forms may challenge our creativity in speech and writing, but they do not make it impossible to say what we mean.[99]

For many years, we could take our civilities more or less for granted. Public debate was limited by a broad consensus on private morals—or at least, by the dominance of white, middle-class, Protestant proprieties.[100] For many reasons, this is no longer the case: groups that were once excluded or invisible now demand consideration; things once unthinkable and unspeakable are now items on the public agenda; our militant insistence on individual freedom in private life has helped to shatter older ideas of respectability.[101] The social order, in other words, has only a diminished capacity to maintain civility. We are likely to need public authority to uphold the good manners appropriate to contemporary civil speech.

In a variety of ways, government already bars racist or sexist speech, and in forbidding sexual harassment, governments look behind words to determine their intent.[102] This is as it should be. Our persons are not defined simply in terms of our separate bodies but by the groups with which we identify. A slur on a gender or on a racial or ethnic group involves an offense to its members and is intended to do so. This is especially true in mass society, since where individuals are dwarfed, the group takes on added significance as a source of strength, dignity, and personal freedom.[103] Given the unsettled state of civil manners, there is a good case for entitling the victims of such group libels to some sort of civil damages.[104]

All of this presumes, however, that civil freedom ranks higher among the liberties than the right of individuals to do as they please. As a matter of theory, however, that is a proposition that the framers' teaching denies.

A Better Kind of Freedom

This brings me back to the fundamental point: part of the contemporary problem of freedom derives from the inadequacy of the framers' view. Of course, the framers were wiser than today's fashions in political thought and opinion, especially in the value they set on government and civil restraint. Nevertheless, the framers' doctrine inherently involves a threat to the order of civil life, since it makes private, prepolitical rights the end of human society, superior in principle to all the forms (i.e., contracts and laws) created to "secure" these rights.[105] The framers hoped that the principle of natural liberty could be contained within scientifically designed forms, and Madison disagreed with Jefferson, his mentor in so many things, by seeking to make any "recourse to first principles" rare and extraordinary.[106] Even so, the framers' theory gives the rights of morally free individuals a priority in defining the terms and setting the direction of political life.[107]

By contrast, Aristotle held that human beings develop in and through political society. The ends of political regime are not established in some prepolitical state; they are characteristic of the political society as a whole. In this view, the forms and ends of a regime are closely related, defining a "way of life" that constitutes the political society.[108] In Aristotle's terms, the end of a democracy is political freedom, embodied in the form of equal citizenship, ruling and being ruled in a shared responsibility for the common good. The danger to democracy, Aristotle argued, lies precisely in that idea of liberty that the framers made their first principle—that individuals are most free when they can do as they please.[109]

As Aristotle's arguments suggest, there is something base about the framers' idea of liberty. Freedom is a relationship with three parts. I am free, in ordinary speech, when I am not kept from doing what I choose, a notion that involves (1) subjects, (2) the goals they pursue, and (3) the restrictions that are absent or the means that are available in the attainment of these goals.[110] If this is so, then unfreedom in *any* of these parts will limit liberty. Modern political doctrine, however, focuses entirely on the question of my power to do as I will.[111] Doctrines of negative liberty contend that I have the power I need, provided that you do not restrain me; ideas of positive liberty insist that I lack the power unless you help me and, hence, that I am restrained by your indifference.[112] For both, power virtually subsumes freedom.

At least implicitly, these modern ideas of liberty identify freedom with domination, the struggle to master nature that cannot be separated from the ability to master other human beings.[113] To that extent, as Lincoln appears to have understood, one cannot reject the "wolf's dictionary" without rejecting the framers' teaching as well. When freedom is separated from ends and defined in terms of an independent self, Schelling recognized, any "objective power" is a limitation on liberty. Even in the sphere of ideas, any "system of theoretically universal applicability" threatens my subjective freedom, since it denies my uniqueness and limits my creativity. It follows that I am free only to the extent that I can overcome nature in *theory* as well as in practice.[114] In other words, the idea of natural rights—which makes my independence derive from nature—has a tendency to destroy itself.

The ancient teachings that the framers rejected spoke of freedom in a more comprehensive way. In the first place, they regarded liberty as a quality of soul, an attribute of a particular *kind* of subject—one who is "free in spirit"—rather than a characteristic of subjectivity as such. Second, the older doctrines denied that freedom can be separated from worthy and appropriate ends. Whatever the means at our command and whatever the opportunities open to us, we are not free if we slavishly pursue a goal that enslaves us.[115]

Freedom is more than a matter of outward form. The fact that my body is physically separate does *not* endow me with moral autonomy. Quite the contrary, as Aristotle reasoned, the body is essentially slavish. On its own terms, the body, devoted to "mere life," pursues pleasure and self-preservation. It can, consequently, be controlled by pain or threats to life. The processes of the body offer automatism, not liberation; we must look elsewhere to find freedom.[116]

In his essay "The Turning Point of My Life," Mark Twain begins with a hyperbolic determinism, deriving the events of his life from Caesar's crossing of the Rubicon (and explaining that only limitations of space kept him from going back to Adam and Eve). Later in the story, however, Twain makes clear that the real turning point of his life came during his early adolescence. The town was visited by an epidemic, and Twain's mother, following the practice of the day, kept him isolated in a darkened room. Twain decided, he tells us, that "life on these miserable terms was not worth living." He escaped from his room and visited the sickbed of a friend, succeeding in his attempt to catch the disease rather than live in fear. It was this particular act of defiance that led Twain's mother to apprentice him: it was, in other words, a transition from the estate of a child to that of a man.[117]

This decisive "turning point," Twain is telling us, is premised on a liberation from the body and its fears. We are emancipated by the sort of courage that, acknowledging that death is fearful, recognizes that there are things still more dreadful. The free spirit will, like Twain, prefer to share death with a friend rather than live alone. To that extent, the need for friendship and conversation—the heart of politics—works to set us free.[118]

Similarly, an ageless wisdom instructs us that a free person is able to do without many things. In this understanding, the modern notion—that we are unfree unless we have what we want—bespeaks enslavement to desire.[119] Instead, one becomes free by distinguishing what is humanly needed from what is needless, trivial, or merely pleasant. Freedom is not so much an ability to do what we want as it is the capacity to *be* what we are.

In this sense, freedom expresses itself through a desire to know and be what one truly is, to be oneself fully. Yet this nobler self-seeking implicitly includes a need to know the whole of which we are parts and, hence, to see ourselves in our partiality. Freedom, in this elevated sense, strives to become unfree, and the higher dependence sets us free from lesser things.

Any such exalted idea of freedom, however, presumes that we have learned in humbler ways that attachments—the bonds of love and friendship—can make us free. An education in human freedom needs the kind of civil society that leads us, without indignity, out of the isolation of the body.[120] In that fundamental sense, the discipline of civility is the school of freedom.

8

On Equality as the Moral Foundation for Community

The gradual development of the equality of conditions . . . possesses all the characteristic of a Divine decree: it is universal, it is durable, it constantly eludes all human inference, and all events as well as all men contribute to its progress.
—Tocqueville, *Democracy in America*

EQUALITY IS APPARENTLY THE CONQUERING DOGMA of the age. Its march is increasingly aggressive; the gradual advance that Tocqueville detected in history has changed into a headlong rush. Hereditary political privilege, long in retreat, has been reduced to a few enclaves. Racism, the most stubborn manifestation of hereditarian thought, gives ground slowly and deviously but has few avowed partisans. Institutions, like property and empire, once the symbols of security and glory, have lost their moral aura and are pressed, even where they survive. The social distinction between the sexes, once unquestioned and considered part of the nature of things, is under confident attack. All cultures, evidently, dash as rapidly as they are able into the embrace of industrialism. As physical space shrinks under the impact of technology, it is not hard to imagine a future in which humanity rubs shoulders in the indistinction of Whitman's en masse.

It takes considerable temerity, given all this, to argue that contemporary humanity is at best ambivalent about equality or to maintain that the cry

Originally published as "On Equality as the Moral Foundation for Community," in *The Moral Foundations of the American Republic*, ed. Robert H. Horwitz (1977; 3rd ed., Charlottesville: University Press of Virginia, 1986), 282–312. Reprinted with the permission of the Greenslade Special Collections and Archives, Kenyon College. The contents of this book were originally delivered as part of the Public Affairs Conference Center Program at Kenyon College, which was a continuation of a similar program initiated by Robert A. Goldwin at the University of Chicago in 1961. The volume in which this essay originally appeared went through three editions and served as a model for many similar volumes that appeared at the time of the observance of the bicentennial of the Constitution.

for equality is too often only the rhetorical disguise for values much closer to the modern heart, but that is what I mean to contend. And I will argue that both the roots of our confusion about equality and the wisdom to resolve it may be found in our political inheritance.

Equality's Qualities

Equality is a matter of qualities. The statement "You and I are equal" means that we share in some essential quality: we are qualitatively the same in some significant respect. Equality does not exclude differences or imply identity. (The belief in human equality, Chesterton wrote, is not "some crude fairy tale about all men being equally tall or equally tricky.")[1] Quite the contrary: personal identity, a knowledge of what I am, logically demands a knowledge of what I am not and of those wholes in which I am *included* but with which I am not *identical*. If human beings are equal, it is because all are included in the whole, humanity, and, depending on it for their equality, retain their identities as parts of the whole. If I *identify* with you, I am not regarding the two of us as equals (although I may fool a superficial observer); I am denying either your separate identity or my own. Any such maneuver, however, rejects equality: equality is the middle term in an equation that must have at least two other parts, and human equality presumes a relationship between at least two equal but separate selves.[2]

The proposition that "human beings are equal," moreover, asserts that this equality is *intrinsic*. Adding modifiers—for example, stating that "human beings are equal in rank" or "equal in rights"—tends to make equality extrinsic, part of some condition external to humanity itself. Grammatically, a proposition like "human beings ought to be equal in treatment" transforms equality from a noun into an adverb; more properly stated, it would read, "human beings ought to be treated equally." And such an extrinsic usage, obviously, does not necessarily involve the belief that human beings *are* equal at all.

A claim to equality of treatment, for example, may be no more than a tactical demand reflecting the utilitarian calculation that equal treatment is the best that I can hope for but aiming at the maximum feasible personal advantage, not equality. A belief in equality of treatment or condition has no necessary relation to a belief in equality as a characteristic of human nature or as something to be valued in itself.

Tocqueville described two very distinct varieties of the "passion for equality." The first, which he thought "manly and lawful," perceived citizens as equal in fact and gave equality a relatively autonomous status as a value. It was a fundamentally political sentiment, public-spirited and patriotic and rooted in participation and political community. Those moved by it rejected superiority *for themselves* as well as resenting pretensions to it in others. Their desire for civic equality entailed their insistence that their fellow citizens share the burdens and responsibilities in governing. Demanding an equal share in ruling, such partisans of civic equality also claimed an equal right to be ruled.

The second "passion for equality," which Tocqueville considered a "depraved taste," did not believe in the reality of equality and valued it only as a second-rate alternative, at best useful and more often only a concession to necessity. It was a demand for equal *treatment* founded in a combination of individualism, self-concern, and felt weakness that, resenting being ruled, despaired of command. In public, the "depraved taste" insisted that "you are no better than I am," retaining the right to declare, privately, that "I am better than you." Supremacy was its real goal, and its "taste" for equality derived from a sense of failure and from resentment of more excellent or apparently more successful others. "Aye, he would be a democrat to all above," Starbuck mused about Ahab, "look how he lords it over all below."[3]

This distinction between a civic, or communitarian, equality, based on a sense of equal worth, and individualistic demands for equal treatment is paralleled by Erik Allardt's contrast between societies that aim at similarity and likeness and those whose institutions are based on exchange relationships.[4] The first aim at common values and interpersonal bonds; the second encourage differentiation and cannot afford high degrees of solidarity or common valuation. In societies that aim at likeness, dignity derives from the quality of one's devotion to the common values; and since commonality is one of those values, personal dignity entails a desire that others be equally devoted and equally dignified. In such societies, differences based on the division of labor, though useful and necessary, are neither encouraged nor valued; hence, it is relatively easy to acknowledge another's superior *ability* without associating that skill with superior *quality*. Where command is perceived largely as an instrumental value only, equality makes few demands for equal treatment. It will, instead, insist on the common good as defined by common values.

In exchange societies, however, dignity is a function of one's relative power in exchange. Society encourages me to demand, at least, the external validation of equal treatment as a proof of my equal worth. ("The *Value*, or WORTH of a man," Hobbes wrote, "is as of all things, his Price; that is to say, so much as would be given for the use of his Power: and therefore is not absolute, but a thing dependent on the need and judgment of another.")[5] Exchange societies value power; a "good trade" is one that is to my advantage, and I accept equality, a "fair trade," only from calculations of utility. But even if equality in exchange power is somehow imposed, we will not feel "the same": the principle of exchange is *difference*. I will have what you lack and vice versa, and I will feel a need to control those who command what I need and cannot have. Even under conditions of equal treatment, power over others—not equality with them—remains the highest social value.

Modern polities, obviously, more closely resemble Allardt's model of exchange society, and it is to be expected that our ideas of equality should be similar to the "depraved taste" that Tocqueville detected. There is, in fact, considerable evidence to support that suspicion.

In the first place, despite all the apparent triumphs of equality in our times, there are ways in which human equality is decreasing. The technology that has brought us closer in space has made us more distant in time; the "generation gap," still real and possibly widening despite the return of relative calm, is only one example. Science and technology have also tended to divide us into "two cultures"; Newton's knowledge, John Schaar observes, was far more accessible to the ordinary citizen of his day than is Einstein's in our own.[6] In the *Meno*, Socrates evoked geometry from a slave, but if we repeated the experiment with today's higher mathematics, we would at least require much more time—and by the time we reached our goal, mathematics, like Zeno's tortoise, would have reached a new, more abstruse point. Moreover, great political and social organizations, abetted by technology, increase the difference of power between rulers and ruled to an extent unhoped for by the tyrants of simpler times.

It is more to the point that the common symbol and slogan of radical movements in recent decades has been "liberation" and not "equality." The great themes of political passion and thought, "independence" and "autonomy," like Tocqueville's "depraved taste," strain toward mastery, supremacy, and rejection of the other. It may be argued that what is sought is "equal independence," but that does not change matters much. "Equal independence" implies an equal freedom from claims, obligations, and dependence. The goal, even if granted to all claimants, is liberation from the *shared* dependence and *mutual* claims of civic equality.

Nor has contemporary militancy often respected the "equal independence" of others when it conflicts with one's own will and desire. Advocates of abortion are largely unconcerned with their spouses; "doing one's thing" shows no great respect for those who may find that thing repulsive;

insistence on a volunteer army reflects at least the willingness to accept radically inegalitarian policies if they support one's own "freedom"; nationalists discount international comity and terrorists hold human beings as pawns in their political chess games.

Tocqueville's reflection on his own times is apposite in ours: "The sympathy with which it has always been acknowledged between the feelings and the ideas of mankind appears to be dissolved, and all the laws of moral analogy to be abolished."[7] Sympathy and moral analogy are the essence of any sense of likeness and equality, and where they are lacking, we must suspect that equality is little felt and not greatly valued.

That supposition finds considerable confirmation in the writings of contemporary philosophers. The case for equal *treatment* is explored in depth; arguments for human equality of *worth* are few and perfunctory. It can be argued that this neglect only reflects equality's status as an unchangeable dogma, but it is doubly unfortunate, whatever the cause. In the first place, it is precisely in relation to "worth" that equality is most at odds with common sense, which is offended by the suggestion that Hitler was as worthy as Martin Luther King or that Einstein was no more valuable than an imbecile. Second, without a belief in equal worth, even equality of treatment rests on the shifting and uncertain ground of utility and is reduced to something not very different (at best) from Tocqueville's "depraved taste."

Contemporary arguments normally begin with the proposition that human beings constitute a class or species and, consequently, should be treated alike unless good reasons are evinced. But any class or category is alike in that common quality that defines it. "All blonds are equal" in being blond, but in order to justify the unequal treatment of blonds, we do not require that "good reasons" be very numerous or very powerful. The equality of a class is morally and politically important only to the extent to which we assign value to that category that defines the class.[8] Certainly, we have been confronted often enough with arguments that assert implicitly that "all human beings are equal in respect of their humanity, but humanity is not worth very much." Unless it is worth a great deal, however, exceptions to equal treatment will be justified readily if, in fact, they do not become the rule.

The importance of our common humanity, unfortunately, is only weakly defended in contemporary political philosophy. William Frankena argues, for example, that human beings are equal in possessing desires and emotions, the ability to think, and the capability of "enjoying a good life in a sense which other animals [cannot]." Similarly, Bernard Williams speaks of the human capacity to feel pain and affection for others and to desire self-respect in relation to one's own purposes.[9]

Arguments of this sort, however, are both usually abstract and radically nonqualitative. It is doubtful, John Schaar remarks, that human beings are "equal" in any of these respects—some individuals seem, as least, to have stronger desires, affections, capabilities for thought and anguish, or concern for self-respect and the good life than do others—and it is certain that the quality of these feelings, reflections, and strivings differs radically from one human to another.[10] Frankena's argument seems to prove only that humans are more like one another than they are like "other animals," but even though the distinction between men and beasts may establish that I am more like Socrates than either of us is like a dog, it does not mean that I am very much like Socrates. If granted, it proves that we should treat animals differently, not that we should treat humans alike; it argues that animals are not our equals, not that our common humanity makes us equally worthy. (Like many arguments for inequality, it is also dangerous; we should be aware of slighting our common animality, a point to which I shall return.)

The strongest elements in contemporary arguments point to human potentialities and aspirations—"the striving to make himself something worthy of his own respect"—as the basis for equal worth, not what human beings are at present. Evidently, it is the striving and not its end that is thought important. Hitler sought to make himself "worthy of his own respect," but the something for which he struggled was hardly equal in worth to that sought by Martin Luther King. Nor would it be hard to argue that Hitler's moral respect was not worth having. The fact that such arguments are made, however, suggests that contemporary philosophers are led toward teleological arguments regarding the natural end of humanity, even though their presumptions and training compel them to stop short of that teaching.

This is not surprising. The belief in human equality is necessarily at odds with empiricism or positivism. It demands a radical deprecation of appearances and insists on a distinction between humanity's essential equality and its differing accidental manifestations. As Schaar comments, the doctrine of human equality "was meant to deny precisely what observation confirmed."[11]

The most virulent inequalities in American life have been at least accentuated by the tendency of our dominant institutions and philosophies to glorify appearance. The protagonist in Ellison's *Invisible Man* was unseen because a "blindness of the inner eye" prevented white Americans from discerning (or valuing) his humanity. Those who verbally insisted on his equality were "half blind," either denying the existence of a separate black experience or proclaiming that blacks were *only* their experience. Both the blind and the half-blind were unable to see that essential humanity that is affected and educated by society but that naturally seeks self-knowledge and the good life.[12]

The idea of an equally valuable "natural end," a good life that human beings naturally seek, makes it possible to resolve the most difficult problems posed by apparent inequality. Those who feel or act basely or who strive for base ends do not do so because they are inferior; rather, the argument contends, they do so because they have been deprived or misled by rearing, experience, or teaching.

This argument is conventional in social science and social policy, but it is at odds with the prescription of formally equal treatment. A case for unequal treatment, in fact, follows logically from the notion of equality as an end. If we regard Hitler's pathology or King's virtue as due in large measure to rearing, education, and experience, then clearly we do need to encourage one set of family patterns, teachings, and institutions and to discourage others. The mere fact of *having* values, including the value of equality, guarantees that some qualities, institutions, and behaviors will be rewarded and others discouraged, and it creates some sort of hierarchy.[13]

We may even require authority in the interest of the end of equality. If it is true, for example, that Nazism and similar doctrines reflect the absence of authority—"a longing for the father"—as well as a rebellion against brutal, rigid, or indifferent authority, it would seem to follow that a humane or nurturant authority is needed to develop both equalitarian convictions and a naturally equal worth of the individual.[14]

Those who are devoted to equality as an end must reject the idea that "equal treatment" is a mechanical standard. In fact, equal treatment requires *analogous* treatment. That is, it commands that each be treated as every other would be in the same situation, but it recognizes that the "situation" includes social circumstances, abilities, education, "moral development," and the like. (The punishment of juvenile offenders is a matter of controversy, but very few of us would insist that an eight-year-old be punished by the same standard as an adult who committed a like offense.) Against this thesis, Hugh Bedau urges that a principle of difference, like the Marxian maxim "from each according to his abilities, to each according to his need," though possibly *just,* is not equality.[15] In insisting that "equality" means formally equal treatment, however, Bedau ignores the fact that a defender of the maxim would regard abilities and needs as accidents and equality as the essence (and the natural end) of human nature.

It was precisely because they agree that justice was in some kind of equality that the classics insisted that distributive justice was a kind of equality. If we are equal in worth by nature, then we are due equality by the law of that nature. But we are evidently not equal in abilities, needs, or the attainment of wisdom and virtue. To treat us alike would violate equality as an end: it would demand too little of the advantaged and too much of the disadvantaged. That, after all, is the basis of the graduated income tax, as well as the more complex argument that we have a right, however unlikely to realize it, to demand that philosophers be kings.

I will be arguing that the "liberal tradition" erred in relation to equality, partly because it attempted to make equality an empirical proposition dependent on an inaccurate and irrelevant "science" but more importantly because liberalism reduced equality to a *means,* making it ultimately dependent on assessments of its utility. So considered, equality is reduced to the rule of equal treatment, not a divine decree, but a human device and contrivance and the servant of other ends. This lowering of the status of equality is a crucial part of the real meaning of much of the teaching of our times.

This contemporary argument discussed earlier regarding the relaxation between human beings and beasts makes a distinction not only more extreme than is warranted by natural science but one more radical than that developed by traditional philosophy and theology. Socrates compared men to a variety of beasts, suggesting that there was at least some likeness in their virtues.[16] Genesis declares that God made man master over the beasts, but it insists that both are creatures. Indeed, man's first sin is the effort to transcend that creaturehood. Traditional thought contended that man was *more* than a beast, but it did not deny the commonality of men and beasts in some aspects of their natures.

Rejecting the notion of a nature that includes and governs humankind, modern thought has also drawn a radical distinction between humans and beasts. Following the new routes opened up by the subtle Machiavelli, which were then clearly charted for all to see by such thinkers as Hobbes and Bacon, modern thought has directed man to master nature itself. Denying the distinction between God and man, it derives equality from the distinction between human and nature. We are all equal because we are all destined to be masters, but it is mastery and not equality that constitutes the goal.

This, however, greatly anticipates the argument. For the moment, it is enough that there are evidently problems and ambiguities in the modern theory and practice of equality. Robert Frost acknowledged our doubts and confusions when he mused on Jefferson's understanding of equality:

That's a hard mystery of Jefferson's.
What did he mean? Of course the easy way
Is to decide it simply isn't true.
It may not be. I heard a fellow say so.
But never mind, the Welshman got it planted
Where it will trouble us a thousand years.[17]

So it does, and if we would understand our present concerns, we must retrace the path of the idea of equality as it came down to those who proclaimed its self-evidence to a somewhat astonished world.

Civic Equality

It is evident that Plato and Aristotle and most classical philosophers with them were not believers in equality as we understand it. They considered that some men were naturally more fit to rule, that it was unjust to treat unjust things alike, and that it would be unjust to give the excellent only an equal share.[18] Aristotle, as we are often reminded, defended a form of slavery, and many other examples could be offered to the same purpose.

But Plato and Aristotle also held that equality rightly understood was an end for any true polity. "A *polis* aims at being," Aristotle declared, "as far as it can be, a society of equals and peers."[19] Similarly, the Athenian stranger in *The Laws* asserted that the only truly just regime, or *politeia*, was none other than the one created in speech in *The Republic* (the Greek title of which is *Politeia*). Then and always, he contended, "*polis* and *politeia* come first, and those laws are best, where there is observed as carefully as possible throughout the whole polity the old saying 'friends have all things in common.'" For a number of reasons (to which we will recur), the Athenian Stranger noted that such a regime can never be brought into being. Still, he reemphasized the point that "one should not look elsewhere for a model constitution [*politeia*], but hold fast to this one, and with all one's power seek the constitution that is as like to it as possible."[20]

Equality in the classical view was not merely formal or material; it involved an internal sense of equality, a concern for the good of the whole, a perception of the common political life all citizens share as being more important than private goods. Criticizing Phaleas of Chalcedon, Aristotle remarked, "It is more necessary to equalize men's desires than their properties, and that is a result which cannot be achieved unless men are adequately trained by the influence of the laws."[21] Material equality, Aristotle argued, is superficial and unstable if men remain covetous, for their inegalitarian spirits will resent equality and will find means to circumvent it.

By contrast, if citizens have an inward sense of quality and commonality, of mutuality and reciprocal duty, they will not resent outward inequalities that serve the common good, nor will those who command misuse their position as a basis for contempt, arrogance, or oppression. (In fact, distributive justice, "due measure according to nature," given the goal of equality, demands more from the powerful for the good of the weak.) Recognizing that "what is equally right is what is for the benefit of the whole *polis* and for the common good of all its citizens," the citizenry will restrain the tendency of equality to level down, neither excluding the excellent nor being resented by them.[22]

Mere formal equality, on the other hand, may even teach inequality. It is possible, Aristotle observed, for citizens to receive the same education and yet be more greedy and ambitious than others. Democratic institutions may be governed, in practice, by the belief that the members of the minority are not equal and need not be considered because the majority is the stronger. That "the many" is a numerous, collective tyrant does not change the fact. In such a case, it shares with individual tyrants the belief that supremacy is good and that the victor is entitled to superiority over the vanquished.[23] In such a polity, each citizen will be taught implicitly that possession of Gyges' ring is the touchstone of happiness.

Athenians praised equality, but they meant an "equality of opportunity" that let each man make the most out of his private liberty. Equal freedom, in other words, gave all citizens a chance to become unequal and made "each man zealous to achieve for himself." Athenian law liberated and stimulated competitiveness, as Pericles detected, and thereby produced citizens who were at their best when they saw in others an excellence they could hope to equal. But when confronted with a greatness they despaired of emulating, Athenians became envious and sought to discredit or destroy what was beyond their grasp.[24] There was little love of equality; Athens taught a hatred of superiors, dependence, and limitation. Her collective bond lay in Athenian power and in the sense of superiority over others; Athens needed the inferiority of outsiders to preserve equality at home. She valued unlikeness, individuality, and supremacy; equality was lauded in speeches but was hated in the heart.

Creating an inward sense of equality and commonality is obviously no easy task. Property in things and in persons (such as slaves, wives, and children), the Athenian remarks in *The Laws,* is merely "called" private by convention. The senses, however, are private by nature and can be trained to act in common—so that all citizens, "so far as possible, are unanimous in the praise and blame they bestow, rejoicing and grieving together and honoring the laws that made the *polis* unified with all their hearts"—only by contrivance of the laws and education. (Yet even with the best laws and teaching, some private self-centeredness would remain.)[25]

Sparta, which exemplified equality to the Greeks even more than Athens, understood the privacy of the senses. But Sparta did not believe that the emotions could be educated to support *isokratia*. The passions in the Spartan view could only be conquered by an education that taught men to resist pain, an austerity that limited pleasure and forced the practice of self-denial, and a rigid obedience to law supplemented by the constant watchfulness of fellow citizens. "Nor ought we to believe that there is much difference between man and man," Archidamus said (according to Thucydides), "but the superiority lies with him who is trained in the severest school."[26]

Sparta, the Athenian remarks in *The Laws,* made "each man his own enemy."[27] She did not create in her citizens a love of equality; she made them fear the consequences of their desires for private gratification and supremacy. But her citizens could not eradicate their desires, and the passions were powerful, ever-present enemies of the law. Sparta was haunted by fear; she saw her equality as artificial, fragile, and embattled and sought to shut out all influences of the foreign world that might undermine it, distrusting the unknown yet fearing the knowledge that might make it familiar. Spartan equality, like Spartan courage, was a surface phenomenon. Outside the control of public opinion and the laws, Spartans were notoriously avaricious and prone to ambition, submitting to those inegalitarian passions they had been taught they could not control alone.

As the Athenian suggested in *The Laws,* Sparta made citizens familiar with pain but not with pleasure and left them unable to resist its temptations. True education, as some great philosophers saw it, sought to educate the pleasures, leading men to see the connection between joy and community and between friendship, equality, and shared dependence, winning the support of the emotions, as far as possible, for equality with the common good. At this point, however, philosophy encountered a paradox, for much that is necessary for human political education and that contributes to the formation of philosophic character conflicts with the insight of philosophy itself.

In an important sense, philosophy must define equality, for it develops the idea of the universal, of a *cosmos* governed by a single law. All human beings are subject to the law; all are parts of the whole. Moreover, knowledge of the whole can never be complete or certain. Philosophy requires a "knowledge of ignorance," the recognition that human beings do not know adequately and cannot even be certain that they are in error. Human reasoning begins with opinion and ends with speculation; the most that can be hoped for is progress toward knowledge.

This is a paradoxical doctrine that cannot be "taught" in any simple sense because its meaning can be understood only by those already schooled in humility and equality. The paradox inherent in the statement "I know that we do not know" can be resolved, after all, if the "I" is not included in the "we," and that is how many, if not most, students hear the teaching. Knowledge of ignorance is understood as a weapon for discrediting conventional opinion, an excuse for shamelessness, and a justification for rejecting restraint. It is turned against philosophy itself, as an argument for regarding its discipline as pointless and for evading the obligation to seek painful knowledge or discommoding virtue. Cynicism, a vehicle for envy, may wear an egalitarian mask. It pretends to debunk the pretensions of elites, but whatever its guise, its understanding opposes equality.

Very different results follow from the humbling awareness that self-knowledge is radically incomplete and defective and that we reject and fear our mortal limitations, hoping for immortality and omnipotence. Living under the spell of illusions about the self, we despise the real self and the limited and mortal things that might otherwise bring us joy. Aware of our imperfections at some level of the mind, we seek to disguise them. Seeking perfection in others, we fear—while in the grip of our self-induced enchantment—that they will discover and desert us, and when disillusioned regarding their "perfection," we scorn what we once admired. The tyrant dreams of love but can never trust it; like him, humans who lack self-knowledge hope for omnipotence and are convinced of unworthiness. They are locked in a psychic dialectic between supremacy and servility that has no understanding of the basic value of equality.

Those who "know" the self, who have emotional as well as intellectual awareness of human nature, are in a sense "elevated" men. But what elevates them is a knowledge of equality in the nature and condition of humanity: "No man is an island entire of itself." But any such knowledge of ignorance and of equality depends on a prior education of the emotions in security, dependence, and the proper occasions for joy and pain.

It is now possible to return to the basic point that what is necessary for political education and hence required for the best politics and the broadest development of philosophic character conflicts with philosophy and especially with the philosophic understanding of equality.

Philosophy discerns the universal, but Plato and Aristotle agreed that the good polis, or political association, must be small. The universal state cannot be just because it cannot know individuals or their due. Moreover, it dwarfs the individual, making him feel insignificant; emotionally, it teaches withdrawal rather than equality. Speaking of religious institutions, Plato's Athenian in *The Laws* asserted the need for a polis small enough that "the people may fraternize with one another at the sacrifices and gain knowledge and intimacy, since nothing is of more benefit to the polis than this mutual acquaintance; for wherever men conceal their ways from one another . . . no man will ever rightly gain his due office or honor or the justice that is befitting."[28] Still, the polis involves a kind of injustice peculiar to itself.

Love for one's country and one's fellow citizens tends to slight the broader likeness that is humanity. The sense that "we are alike" in a given country leads easily to the perception of a categorical difference between "us" and "them," like the conventional Hellenic distinction between Greeks and barbarians.[29] If philosophy teaches that country may be artificial and accidental, however, it endangers the very patriotism that is so valuable in leading the emotions out of the fortress of the self. Patriotism is natural in general, though conventional in detail, but that logical distinction does not solve the practical problem, for most human beings are prone to identify the "conventional" with something *contrary* to nature.[30]

In a similar sense, reverence for age is useful in human education, if for no other reason than it teaches the passions to see life as an ascent, not a rise to maturity followed by a decline. But we all know wise youths and foolish dotards; age is no proof of venerability. Also, as the earlier argument suggests, in some respects men are like the beasts, and the line between them is an uncertain one. But *for that reason,* we do not wish to legitimate beastliness, and we may find it educationally useful to treat the distinction as categorical.

There are, moreover, quite unnatural institutions that may be necessary in a given political context. Aristotle defended a form of slavery, but he approved Alcidamas's saying "nature makes no man a slave" as an example of natural law. Plato refrained from attacking slavery, though he held no brief whatever for its naturalness.[31] Given the economy of the time, both thought slavery was necessary for excellence. In our own time, the division of labor is thought equally necessary, but it would not be hard to argue that extreme specialization is artificial and creates lives not essentially different from what slavery meant among the Hellenes.

In all these areas, classical philosophy thought it wisest to limit discussions of these propositions to the old, whose character is already formed (or to be more exact, to those old men whose character is not corrupt) and who can be presumed to understand the limitations of necessity. Some conventions that violate equality, however, even though partly necessary, are both unnatural and educationally corruptive. Plato certainly believed that rigid distinctions between men and women fell into this category, teaching men to despise dependence and women to seek to live vicariously and avengingly through their sons. In such cases, philosophy is permitted and obligated to discuss equality with the young, whereas prudence may dictate silence with the old, who might be shocked without learning any better lesson.[32]

The philosophic perception of human equality, then, was a kind of mystery, an ideal and a truth safe only for adequately prepared initiates. Plato quarreled with the tragedies because some spoke ignorantly but also because greater tragedians spoke promiscuously, without regard for the limits in human life and education. Socrates presented himself in the humbler mask of comedy, but his life was high tragedy, and to its initiates, philosophy offered a knowledge of equality that fulfilled its tragic aim: "Now the slave emerges as the freeman, and all the rigid, hostile walls which necessity has erected between men are shattered."[33]

Liberal Equality

These classical views in their various interpretations and modifications (some of which stemmed from Christian doctrine) held sway in the Western world for nearly two millennia. Conventional educators in the eighteenth century continued to emphasize the study of classical languages and literature. Yet even as the eighteenth-century student acquired some familiarity with the classics, they no longer held him enthralled. Their spell had been broken by those modern philosophers who had, as it seemed, successfully attacked both classical and Christian thought. The most influential of the American founders must be included among those bold statesmen who rejected, by and large, both the classical and Christian philosophic and theological traditions. It was the "new science of politics," one based on a new understanding of human nature, that served as their guide. Machiavelli, Hobbes, Locke, Montesquieu, and others had successfully laid new philosophic foundations, and the architects of the American Republic were acutely aware of the political order they were building on them. Their political doctrine and their philosophic vocabulary were drawn from modern sources, especially from the English tradition of contractarian theory, the common philosophic currency of reflective statesmen and men of affairs in the British Empire of that era.

Hobbes, as the founder of that tradition, confronted the issue of equality with his customary directness, but in his argument, the claims of equality are less extensive than they may seem. In a rough sense, human beings are equally able to kill each other and, given time, to acquire equal prudence. Science, however, is *not* naturally equal; it is something that "few have," and each has it in only "few things."[34] This argument is qualified but deceptive, for Hobbes regarded science as supremely important and vital to the right ordering of human affairs. Logically, Hobbes's argument might seem to lead to the conclusion that scientists—or, at least, political scientists—are natural sovereigns over other human beings.

Hobbes would have replied that such a conclusion is irrelevant, whatever the logic. Those who have science are few, men will not believe that many are as wise as themselves, and the many have both the force and the freedom to make their "conceit" effective. As the term is ordinarily used in civil society, men are by nature unequal in worth, but this inequality is ineffective in the "state of nature," in which equal freedom and roughly equal power produce a state of war. Self-concern and relatively equal force require that human beings be treated *as if* they were equal, for otherwise, they will not consent to be governed at all. In practice, then, equality is a premise without which it is impossible to *create* civil order. Once created, civil order affords a security and freedom from anxiety that the state of nature inhibits. It does not matter whether equality is true or not; it is an indispensable means to civil society and to those human goods unrealizable in a condition of war.

In fact, Hobbes feared the teaching of an inner equality of worth because it was associated with the idea of a sovereign "conscience" and hence with the sectarian disorder of his times. It justified men in a stubborn insistence on that desire for mastery that was natural to them. Men could not truly escape the state of nature without *some* recognition of equality, but so powerful was the natural desire for independence that men could only be driven to acknowledge equality by a desperate, violent confrontation—a kind of drawn battle in which both contestants abandon the hope of victory.[35]

Hobbes's argument is radically different from the classical notion that the passions can be gently seduced into a recognition of equality. In the first place, the classical theorists presumed that the natural place of man was in the polis and that political education, consequently, was also natural to human being; Hobbes saw civil order and the rearing associated with it as the products of convention, artifice, and contract. The classics considered that civic equality and genuine community were the end in view by which all political inequality must be justified; Hobbes justified the premise of equality as a means to civil order, which was itself justified by the fact that it permitted the development of the unequal faculties of private life.[36]

Locke's teaching, rhetorically more beguiling than that of Hobbes, was not fundamentally different. In the state of nature, men's "perfect equality" is, in fact, a perfect freedom, an equality of "power and jurisdiction" and not of worth. Indeed, the "fall" from the *apparent* gentleness of Locke's state of nature into the state of war cannot be explained unless *some* human beings are naturally more prone than others to violate the law of nature, thereby proving morally inferior to those they attack.[37]

Locke did not in fact regard human beings as equal in virtue, in potentiality, or in "excellency of parts." Each mind might begin as a tabula rasa, but there was an inequality of ability—a considerable one—among men of equal education. Locke argued, however, that there was no inconsistency between the inequality of worth he discerned in human nature and the equality of the state of nature: "I there spoke as proper to the business at hand, being that equal right that every man hath to his natural freedom."[38]

Thus, for Locke, as for Hobbes, man's natural freedom and equality of force made it necessary to regard human beings as equals, despite their inequality of worth, in order to make civil government possible. Locke, however, carried the argument a step further. Although unanimous consent was necessary to create civil society, it could hardly ever be realized afterward. The rule of the majority corrected that defect by relying on the only equality that counted in politics, the equality of force and freedom: "It is necessary the body should move whither the greatest force carries it, which is the consent of the majority, or else it is impossible it should act or continue one body, one community."[39]

For both Locke and Hobbes, equality was a concession to political necessity, a recognition of the rights inherent in the individual, and the basis for orderliness, not a reflection of equal worth. The classics had recognized the utility of equal treatment as a protection against disorder but had regarded that consideration as prudential, not as a first principle.[40] Hobbes and Locke reduced equality to a means that permitted the establishment of inequalities. Indeed, Locke's effort to limit government to a relatively narrow sphere in part reflected his conviction that government, a creation of artifice and convention, was necessarily based on the principles of equality of rights that could not properly be extended beyond the political realm. The broader area, "society," separated from the state, was reserved for those inequalities in the interest of which human beings—and especially human beings of the better sort—were constrained to accept government and, with it, legal equality. The "Lockean tradition," in that sense, ranked equality with constables and prisons as part of the price required for civil peace and order.

The leaders of the early Republic, however, did not restrict their reading to Locke and his epigones. The "celebrated Montesquieu," for example, had a great vogue, and Montesquieu's theories expressed a somewhat different tradition of modern theorizing.

In Montesquieu's state of nature, human beings were governed by fear and felt weakness, but those feelings led them to avoid one another; isolation and not war was the rule of nature. Men were equal in being independent, but that equality had little hold on their loyalties, since, almost unaware of each other, men were unaware of equality and, for that matter, were unable to make those comparisons that might have suggested inequality of ability or worth. When society begins, equality ceases. Relations of need and dependence develop, and those inequalities hidden by the state of nature become visible. From that state of unequal ability and mutual dependence, conflict and war result, and political society, in its turn, develops as a necessary response to war.[41]

As should be evident, this argument is quite similar to Locke's. Natural equality has no moral significance and exists under conditions of grinding necessity that keep men at a level with the beasts. When humanity escapes that subhuman condition, it enters a state of nature akin to Locke's and passes from thence into a condition of war.

Montesquieu, however, lauded democracy as a political order that required, demanded, and encouraged virtue. Civil equality was a noble idea, especially when contrasted with the privatism, self-concern, and greed of corrupt polities. Democracy, Montesquieu argued, requires *love of country* and the allied passion of *love for equality,* the latter an inward sentiment, like that praised by traditional thought, that involves a devotion to the good of the whole such that all "serve with alacrity" even though they cannot serve equally. What matters is not difference of talent but equal devotion to the common good. Extreme equality corrupts democracy, for such a leveling spirit destroys reverence and distinction of ability, leading to faction, dissension, and, eventually, to despotism. "As different as heaven is from earth," the true spirit of democratic equality accepts leaders but demands that they be "none but equals."[42]

Despite this praise, we must not forget that the two "loves," patriotism and equality, are both unnatural. They are creations of custom and law alone, since for Montesquieu, no less than for Hobbes and Locke, the political order is conventional and not natural for human beings.

Moreover, democracy requires a *love of frugality* because the state must be small and hostile to the acquisitive passions that make for successful commerce. Frugality, however, is decidedly something that, in Montesquieu's view, human beings do not naturally *love,* and even laws and customs can persuade them to be frugal only when allied with necessity and external limitations. Success in mastering the environment makes citizens realize that more is possible and that self-denial is forced on them by the laws; resentment and the decay of democracy follow in train.[43] In Montesquieu's theory, democracy is admirable, but its virtuous equality is unnatural and is too severe for human beings to long endure.

Commercial republics, by contrast, face the corrupting impact of private fortune, individualism, and the sense that one's own estate may be independent of (or even at odds with) the public good. They are, however, more comportable with human nature, allowing greater well-being and permitting some scope for self-concern, while submitting it to the discipline of work and the market. So long as excessive wealth is prevented, commercial republics may acquire riches without utterly corrupting morals, and competition helps achieve that limitation. Commerce is a kind of mean, corrupting but curing prejudice and parochiality, rejecting both robbery and suspicion of private interest. In the long term, commercial republics serve the material interests of human progress.[44]

All republics, however, must be small, and all are threatened by war and by the rise of great powers. The development of large states is a by-product of historical necessity. The dynamics of international politics drive out small states, and republics can only survive in confederation.[45]

American statesmen read Montesquieu with an eye to the separation of powers he saw in England, but that specific analysis was an example of a concern with the equilibrium of power that is fundamental to his doctrine. To summarize his argument: equality is associated with virtue, but it is stern and unnatural, unstable at best and possible only when the polity is environed by strait natural necessity. External political threats demand that a state expand to meet the threat or perish. Commercial republics and confederated commercial republics are not only more practical; they also satisfy the truly fundamental human desires for survival and mastery over nature. Such republics can, moreover, preserve some of the virtue associated with equality by substituting *equilibrium* for equality, the external balance of interests for an internal concern for the public good. Equality becomes a functional attribute of a *system* of exchange relationships, not of human beings and their immediate relationships. Feeling the call of the small state, Montesquieu gave self-preservation and historical necessity higher status as political principles. Although he accorded more moral stature to equality than many theorists of the "new science," Montesquieu also deserted that communitarian ideal as an end, accepting in its stead an equality that was only a means, useful to the extent that it served the more "natural" ends of naturally private men.

The Framers' View of Equality

The American heritage was, then, compounded of rather different and conflicting strains of thought that were often in conflict and sometimes poles apart. If the Declaration of Independence had evoked "harmonising sentiments," as Jefferson wrote in 1825 (by which time he had conveniently forgotten the numerous Loyalists), it is in part a tribute to ingenious political rhetoric that concealed the ambiguity of its terms and avoided other areas of conflict in the public mind.[46] Jefferson's draft, for example, referred to humanity "created equal and independent," and, it went on, "from that creation they derive rights, inherent and inalienable." Franklin, always prudent in matters of religion, apparently suggested substituting "endowed by their Creator" for Jefferson's more scientific "from that equal creation": the elimination of the reference to original independence also avoided conflict with those who held that humanity was naturally social and political. Similarly, the phrase "governments are instituted among men" avoided the term "social contract," using instead a phrase familiar in Calvinist rhetoric. These persuasive turns of phrase reflect more than the guile of the Declaration's authors; they reveal how much public considerations affected the Declaration as it finally appeared, decisively affecting it as a document for the education of future generations. In American political thought, one must never forget the people.

Nevertheless, there is a minimal political theory incorporated in the Declaration. What it does proclaim is that men have an original, natural liberty and equality of rights. In the state of nature, those rights, as we have seen, may not be utterly ineffective, but they are not secure. Hence, governments are "instituted" to protect them. Popular consent is needed to establish government, and this, along with equal rights, requires equality as a public norm but not because equality is especially desirable in itself. As Robert Ginsberg points out, "Deprivation of equality does not figure in the extended list of grievances against Britain, nor does equality reappear in the Declaration's portrait of civil society except as holding between distinct societies." In fact, Ginsberg comments, the Declaration "builds a case against equality in society."[47] Like Locke and like Montesquieu's commercial republic, the founders limited equality to a necessary public norm and presumed inequality in the social, private sphere.

The Declaration's sketchy but typical version of contract theory reflected a broad consensus, as Jefferson asserted. The *Federalist*, more "realistic" in rhetoric, says very little about equality, but its authors make clear that they are devoted to republican government and that they accept the principles of the Declaration.[48] It was generally agreed that in the state of nature, men were equal in possessing equal rights; all, that is, had a "natural liberty" in being free from obligation or authority.[49]

Paine was more direct than many, but most would have agreed with his arguments that the distinction between rich and poor could be "accounted for," whereas "male and female are the distinctions of nature, good and bad the distinctions of heaven." Nature creates physical distinctions and the passions by which men are naturally impelled; convention and reason create institutions like property; moral distinctions beyond this are supernatural or simply unnatural. In the state of nature, then, morality as conventionally understood did not exist, and this equal lack of moral obligations is critical, for human beings in the state of nature are equal in little else. Even power is only approximately equal; society, Paine argued, was created by the weak out of a desire to equalize their relations with the strong.[50]

The dominant desire of human beings, the first law of nature, is self-preservation, and that natural egotism places man at war with nature and, derivatively, with other human beings who may frustrate or endanger him. Natural egotism and power-seeking, however, although they define the individual's "interest," are only part of his desires. The "affections," gentler and more social passions, bind human beings together in "civil society." Sympathy and the moral passions, James Wilson wrote, exert the "force of confederating charm."[51]

In civil society, however, inequalities emerge, and ties of dependence and obligation limit men.

In nature or in simple society, affection is either allied to self-preservation and interests or yields to it. Abundance or greater security, reducing the pressure of necessity on self-preserving men, leads to a division between the social bonds (affection) and ambition (interest) and hence to social decay and conflict. It was in that spirit that the authors of the *Federalist* criticized the excessively democratic state constitutions, documents that had proved workable at all, Publius contended, only because of the unity imposed by war, which could no longer be relied on.[52] "Unaided virtue" cannot govern except under conditions of dire necessity, and governments are necessary to protect both the "equality of rights" found in nature and the inequality of talent and property characteristic of society.[53]

Government did not exist, however, to strengthen the hold of the affections and moral feelings. The affections were parochial, shortsighted, and concerned with comfort and immediate relationships. They restricted the fulfillment of human interests, limiting human effectiveness in the war against nature. (Even in America, Paine commented, where the absence of customary barriers and the size of the land drew men toward broader visions and humanitarian sentiments, few were able to see the effects of others' misfortunes on themselves.)[54] Liberty and interest were primary in nature, and affection should only follow and assist.

In *Federalist* 10, Madison contended not only that it was impossible to give citizens the same feelings, interests, and beliefs but also that it was undesirable. Public spirit and the inward conviction of equality are rejected as ideals in favor of more reliable, "scientific," and mechanical institutions that avoid dependence on virtue and that permit liberty and progress. Equality is limited to the uniform rules of the public sphere.[55]

Political prudence and scientific legislation, in fact, aimed at fragmenting those smaller communities and loyalties where affection is powerful and individual liberty is restricted and hence the logic of that overlapping "division of powers" that allows both federal and state governments to appeal directly to the individual (contrary to Montesquieu's prescription for confederacies) and the argument that many factions render any one group too weak to hope for success or to make total claims on the individual.

The small polis, the model of classical theory, was thus rejected by the Federalists because it was too weak to serve human interests and because it demanded an austerity that people cannot naturally and *ought* not endure. The polis had shown itself to be a "wretched nursery of faction" and had encouraged discord by opening the way to factions that were too large in relation to the whole. In consequence, it had often been too oppressive in the attempt to repress these factions in the interest of unity. Paine admired both public spirit and simple democracy, but he questioned the feasibility of simple democracy because it could not effectively govern an extensive state. He preferred representative government because it was "the greatest scale upon which human government can be instituted."[56]

Progress was a central goal, even though it was assumed that progress, arising from initiatives in the unequal private sphere, would result in greater inequality. In the debates in the Constitutional Convention, Pinckney argued that an upper house was superfluous given the equality of condition in

America. Madison responded that Pinckney should remember "the changes which the ages will produce. An increase of population will of necessity increase the proportion of those who will labor under the hardships of life and secretly yearn for a more equal distribution of its blessings."[57] But Madison did not argue that change should be resisted; he proposed to guard against its effects, for change was essential to liberty. In any event, Madison's fears of "agrarian attempts" helped Jefferson achieve the acquisition of Louisiana; Madison hoped to check the "leveling spirit" by satisfying it.

As Schaar observes, the *Federalist*'s constitutionalism designed a public realm fundamentally limited to utilitarian concerns, the acquisition of power, and the maintenance of order. Political life was only indirectly creative, and such moral purpose as it could claim derived from the hope that success in the war against nature would gradually allow the emergence of humanitarian sympathy and a diffuse sentiment of fraternity. Right was fundamentally a private matter; as Arendt comments, the framers aimed at a government sufficiently controlled to enable individuals to devote their attention to private life.[58] Yet private life and society were reserved for inequality, not only in social teaching but also in the attitudes of individuals "freed" from ties of loyalty to community, pursuing their interests and kept in order by the personal weaknesses each felt amid the multitude.

It is ironic that this privatistic vision should have been formulated by men whose vocations were so public and who so delighted in political life. Hamilton could not abide a private destiny, nor could Jefferson. Adams contented himself with the reflection that he was enabling his descendants to be private men (though one of them, Henry, did not thank his ancestor for the favor). It was, nevertheless, a theory from which very few of the framers ever departed. Furthermore, it may well have contributed significantly to the rapid changes in the character of the American regime, as Gordon Wood suggests in his discussion of the "Democratization of Mind in the American Revolution."[59]

The "conservative" statesmen among them were, like Adams, men who had become alarmed at the implications of their principles. The French Revolution only strengthened Adams's fear that the idea of equality might lead to attacks on property or on the law itself. Still, though that anxiety led Adams to insist that men were not equal by nature and that there must always be an unequal distribution of property and rank, he never ceased to believe in and hope for a recognition of equal treatment to the extent of "equal rights and duties" and the human claim to "equal laws." His argument shifted its emphasis from a concern for public equality to a zeal to defend social and private inequality, stressing the need for "equilibrium or counterpoise," but no departure from the characteristic principles of his contemporaries.[60]

Similarly, Hamilton never doubted the need for that "equal opportunity to obtain inequalities" that formed the core of the general creed. Hamilton, however, had less faith than some of his colleagues that the "self-regulating" mechanisms of government could eliminate the need for statesmen and public men. He feared that wealth, commerce, and power would produce public decay (if only from lower-class resentment) and felt that governmental control was required for the common good. Distrusting the wealthy, he hoped that they would have education enough to take a broader view of their interests and wealth enough to be tempted by honor (a more credible hope when wealth meant either landed property or a cosmopolitan commercialism that demanded considerable political knowledge).[61] But Hamilton hoped that those statesmen would devote themselves to protecting equal freedom and opportunity, and had his hopes been realized, his ruling class would have allowed competition, specialization, and privatization— emotional and evaluative, as well as social, inequality. Hamilton, like his fellows, never doubted that we should follow that "course of nature" that he discerned in history.

Jefferson, his great opponent, undeniably theorized in the same modern and "enlightened" terms then fashionable. He believed devoutly in natural rights, in the doctrine that self-preservation is the first law of nature, and in the notion that reason teaches utilitarian self-interest. He preferred large states because of the greater stability arising from the ability to play factions off against each other, and he believed passionately in the "new science."[62]

Indeed, as Daniel Boorstin observed, Jefferson's scientific beliefs led him to seek evidences of equality in the "similarity of men's bodies," in empirical and sensory "proofs" emphasizing the biological unity of the species rather than the inward likeness of souls. Even on its own terms, however, Jefferson's quest for evidence indicates a desire to *prove* an equality of which he was already deeply convinced despite the evidence of his senses.[63] Jefferson's egalitarianism led him to the conviction that apparent inequalities would subsequently be proved to result from environmental or related influences and, in fact, spurred him on to a teaching that avoided appearances almost entirely.

Reason taught self-interest, but morality (and hence moral worth) was an affair of the "heart," a "moral sense" that provided an instinctive knowledge of right and wrong. Akin to the qualities his contemporaries attributed to affection, the "moral sense" certainly made stronger claims on man and on political legislation. The creed that men were equal in "heart" allowed Jefferson, despite his belief in the intellectual inferiority of blacks, to insist that Negroes were equal. The "moral sense" allowed Jefferson, too, to trust and value a variety of minds and a freedom of opinion, confident that this would result in neither social conflict nor moral relativism. Moral notions with which Jefferson disagreed he tended to classify as the result of some "infirmity"—a dangerous teaching, which foreshadowed later abuses in the name of "mental health," but one that shows how little Jefferson's moral convictions were affected by his nominal "first principles."[64]

Jefferson was too sophisticated, moreover, not to realize that the "moral sense," like the other senses, was originally private and required nurture and education. That knowledge led him to the belief (rare among his contemporaries) in the value of political community for moral education and especially for education in the perception of equality.

Men in "barbaric" societies, Jefferson asserted, had affections that, like our own, responded to the appeals of benevolence, gradually receding in intensity as they extended away from the self. Because barbaric societies were small, political obligation coincided with intense affection, and little formal government or coercion was required.[65]

But material deprivations aside, barbaric society was morally inferior, restricting sympathy too narrowly—most perceptibly in its brutal treatment of women and its penchant for cruelty toward outsiders.

"Civilization" advanced the material lot of man and broadened his sympathies, but, associated with larger states, it eventually reached the point where sympathy became too weak to override vice, avarice, and self-concern. European states, with cities filled by a resentful and brutalized "*canaille*" and "higher orders" lost to arrogance and vice, had accentuated the faults of civilization by bad government, but they also reflected the general rule of civilized society.

Jefferson hoped that America could establish a mean between civilization and barbarism. Some of the worst excesses of civilization could be checked by economic austerity, but Jefferson knew his Americans too well to rely on the durability of that condition. He did, however, prescribe policies to avoid excess wealth by subdividing property and graduated taxation. Economic equality of a limited sort—and Jefferson never meant it to be more than that—would still, however, be a thing of surfaces.[66]

The small community was the natural limit of democracy, small enough to foster strong affections and to ensure that political duty could be closely allied through daily participation and friendship. The sense of commonality and inward equality of the "ward republics," as Jefferson came to envisage them, would make it easy for citizens to identify and trust their "natural aristocracy," men characterized as much by greater benevolence and sympathy as by greater talent. These local natural aristocrats, meeting in a representative "ward republic" of their own, could select others, until an ascending chain connected small communities to the Republic while trusted leaders, returning to their communities, could educate their fellows in the requirements of broader prudence and sympathy. It was this sort of idea that made Jefferson incline toward indirect election of the House of Representatives as more likely to produce truly able legislators, though he was easily persuaded that the benefits of immediate popular election outweighed that advantage.[67]

Jefferson's vital interest in civic education was part of his hope for a republic that could develop moral faculties, identify natural leaders, and evoke an inward sense of equality. That his education vision was limited, by our standards, is a relatively slight criticism; the very "utilitarianism" that Boorstin finds fault with is an indication of his desire to extend education to include classes for which it had been thought irrelevant.[68]

Nevertheless, Jefferson was committed to modern theory with a loyalty that threatened many of his other aspirations. Progress entranced him, and his zeal for change included a desire not to impose on future generations. Jefferson departed from the rule of equal human rights in one vital respect. In his theory, the dead have no rights and are excluded from the human community; future generations have at least the right to be considered.[69] Jefferson knew the values of veneration and stability, but they found small support in his teaching. When the dead are excluded from the embrace of equality, the living are reminded that they are destined for a similar rejection and are trapped in a present without continuity, driven to a fever to achieve or enjoy that endangers equality and community alike. "Thus," Tocqueville wrote, "not only does democracy make every man forget his ancestors, but it hides his descendants, and separates his contemporaries from him; it throws him back upon himself alone, and threatens in the end to confine him entirely within the solitude of his own heart."[70]

The Prospects for Equality Today

It will be no surprise that in my view, the classics were right in believing that human beings are meant to live in the polis, and their high objective of civic equality associated with the polis should not be neglected. Of course, we cannot realize that goal in our great industrial states; size alone prevents it, and those who have attempted to impose civic equality on such states have only created monstrosities. We may, however, hope to revitalize our political life as far as circumstances permit, but that requires that we recognize the nature of truly political life and that we find a place to begin.

Ours is a polity dominated by exchange relations and shaped in the image of those modern theories that informed the framers. But in value and desire, to say nothing of institutions, America has never completely accepted "the liberal tradition." Our political history has involved a conflict between modern, dominantly liberal ideas and those derived from religion and traditional philosophies and cultures, and that "check" to exchange relations has been the source of much of our political resilience. If America feels disoriented today, it is because the resistance of the "private order" seems finally to have been overcome.

Jefferson's thought was most distinctive in his sense of the potential of the small community as a school for public virtue and equality alike. Only infrequently did that idea ever coincide with our formal legislation, but it did find reflection in that private order that the framers saw simply as an area for inequality. Localities, churches, and ethnic communities, to name only the obvious examples, provided Americans over the years with "homes," communities of orientation that conveyed tradition and substantive values and, at their best, the foundations of knowledge about genuine equality and therefore true community.

I am not making a case here for the wisdom or value of all our traditional communities: some taught basely and many more inadequately; many, too, behaved badly in more than one respect. I am arguing that the private order formed a vital part of our political life, that it is increasingly fragmented and unstable, and that political wisdom counsels us to strengthen and rebuild it, hopefully in ways that will enhance the virtues and minimize the vices of the older private order. And in relation to equality, political memory was not the least of those virtues.

Nowhere do we appear in a worse light than in our tendency to equate memory with nostalgia. To estrange the past and the dead prevents us from truly learning the lesson of our own mortality. Mourning and remembering, we come closer to that truth, and in the sadness of the sense of loss, we find joy in the discovery that other persons, alike but not identical to those we have lost, can be found to replace them. Reminding us that we, too, can be replaced—a powerful but painful testimony to human equality—nature offers us the consoling knowledge that love and worth are abundant.[71] Stable communities make that lesson easier, for they have memories that may include us, guaranteeing that our unique identities will not be altogether lost. If we are troubled by the knowledge that all memory, too, fades with time, we may consider the mystery that knowledge of equality hints at: if our nature yearns for a love and worth more perfect than even that which abounds in nature, it may be that it *is* our nature to seek a love and a worth beyond nature itself.

PART III
American Politics, Public and Private

9

Ambiguities and Ironies: Conservatism and Liberalism in the American Political Tradition

BACK IN 1963, WHEN MY FATHER SPOKE at the University of Oregon, the local reporter had a hard time squaring the man with the liberal paragon. For one thing, he didn't look the part; among other things, he parted his hair straight down the middle (a habit he had learned, although the reporter didn't know it, from H. L. Mencken). And as the reporter told it, while he ended his speech sounding like John Kenneth Galbraith, he "took off like Billy Graham" with an indictment of public morals—including the quiz show scandals, recently brought back into memory—that had the accents of an evangelical revival.[1] In fact, a few months earlier, when my father participated in a forum with Russell Kirk, the conservative publicist, the *Minnesota Daily* headline ran, "KIRK, MCWILLIAMS CALL FOR RETURN TO TRADITIONAL ETHIC."[2]

Not that such conflicting images are unusual in American politics. In the past century, the most liberal Protestant denominations, the Friends and the Unitarians, have been represented in the White House by Hoover, Nixon, and William Howard Taft; the three Baptists to hold the presidency—Truman, Carter, and Clinton—have been at least a little to the left of center. Ronald Reagan was a hero for conservatives and religious conservatives in particular, even though he had been divorced, rarely attended church, and had a habit of quoting Tom Paine, that old infidel. Reagan even had a special fondness for Paine's dictum that "we have it in our power to begin

Originally published as "Ambiguities and Ironies: Conservatism and Liberalism in the American Political Tradition," in *Moral Values in Liberalism and Conservatism,* ed. W. Lawson Taitte (Dallas: University of Texas at Dallas, 1995), 175–212. This chapter is clearly based upon written remarks that were delivered as part of the Andrew R. Cecil Lectures on Moral Values in a Free Society, held at the University of Texas at Dallas in 1994. Among the participants was a former professor of economics at North Texas State University and member of the House of Representatives, Dick Armey, who would shortly go on to become House majority leader following his appearance in this lecture series.

the world over again," a proclamation of human mastery that, Paine goes on to say, holds out the possibility of undoing the pattern of human history since Noah, a vision that implies overcoming the alienation of humanity from nature, if not original sin itself.[3] Go figure: in American usage, the terms "liberal" and "conservative" are profoundly ambiguous, including elements that are often inconsistent and never without a proportion of irony.

In the first place, we preserve the original and enduring meanings in which liberal and conservative refer not to ideologies and parties but to temperaments, dispositions of the soul. (Even at the outset, I need to introduce a caveat and an ambiguity. Nobody is all one thing or the other; every soul has its liberalities and its Tory corners. Still, the distinction helps in identifying patterns and dominant principles.) Understood in relation to character, a conservative is someone who is inclined to cherish what has been received and to transmit an inheritance not strictly unaltered but in a way that preserves continuity, a link with the past and with origins. Conservatives value rituals, the old ways of doing and remembering, and they hold up examples from the past as models for aspiration, footsteps on a path to excellence that is both tried and distinctively one's own.

A conservative, Ambrose Bierce wrote, is "enamored of existing evils, as distinguished from the liberals, who wishes to replace them with others."[4] Just so: in the conservative view, change is suspect, and though conservatives acknowledge its inevitability, they do so without enthusiasm or moral celebration. The hope of reform, conservatives know, often results in something worse; meddling can damage parts of a regime that prove to be unsuspectedly fundamental. Order is precious and at least a little fragile. Conservatives treat it delicately, observing the forms; at least outwardly, they accept the limits of convention and respect established authority. And they regard it as the task of moral education to shape individuals to fit the existing order of things, developing those virtues and attitudes that suit the regime and its laws.

Liberals, by contrast, are defined by liberality. They are more inclined to give than to save, and since growth permits generosity without loss, liberals are temperamentally prone to look for the possibility of improvement. When liberals speak of continuity or traditions, they are likely to be thinking of ways in which an inheritance can be amplified or perfected; their vision is generally promethean rather than epimethean. Even in a relatively good society, liberals are apt to embrace change, trusting in their ability to separate what is essential from what is accidental or excrescent, crafting new skins from the wine of new times.

The liberal imagination deprecates forms in favor of substance and is likely to be attracted to theory at the expense of practice, asking us, as John Rawls does, to step behind a "veil of ignorance" that, by obscuring the lessons of experience, is thought to clarify first principles.[5] As that suggests, liberals habitually question and challenge authority, holding convention to the standard of the unconventional—to nature, or more recently, the creative will—so that "conventional," in liberal rhetoric, connotes contempt. A regime, in the liberal view, should adapt itself to the needs and wants of individuals, who are the measure of politics and perhaps of all things, as in Protagoras's ancient humanistic affirmation.

Similarly, liberals incline to see communities and social relationships in terms of their utility to the individuals they comprise and hence properly redefined or abandoned in response to changes in one's stage of life or historical developments. Individuals should be freed from the constraint of particular bonds to move toward relationships that are more inclusive, liberals hold, even though such broader relationships may sacrifice depth and intensity. A conservative, on the other hand, will be more concerned to preserve existing communities and bonds that are particular, historic, and hence relatively exclusive. In Marxist terms, in any choice between the dynamic "modes of production" and the "social relationships of production" that "fetter" them, a conservative will pick the social relationships every time; a liberal will be more willing to identify the modes of production with progress and freedom.[6] Liberals, in other words, look to make new friends, conservatives to keep old ones.

Finally, each temperament has its distinctive vices or excesses. Liberals are tempted to be profligate, squandering inherited cultural resources as well as money. Their ostensible warmth is often superficial, without intimacy or willingness to sacrifice, loving humankind but neglecting their own. Conservatives, by contrast, can be narrow and mean-spirited, hoarding in a way that loses sight of the future, clinging to outworn forms, sometimes gracefully, but indifferent to human pain. If the liberal nightmare is Mrs. Jellyby in *Bleak House,* conservatives are haunted by *A Tale of Two Cities* and the Marquis St. Evremonde.

But personality is not the whole story. Conservative and liberal also refer to more or less coherent ideologies that took shape from the late seventeenth century through the age of the democratic revolution, down to sometime around 1848. A sketch of those doctrines seems in order.

Rooted in the teachings of Hobbes and Locke and given a new, idealized form by Kant, liberalism begins by approaching politics in a secular spirit, holding that religion is properly governed if not defined by social and political utility. Liberty is liberalism's lodestar: individuals are endowed with rights or moral autonomy. Nature, at most the source of rights, poses obstacles but no moral limits to human striving; human beings are naturally engaged in a struggle to master nature. Society possibly and government certainly are humanly contrived and constructed, designed to protect rights and satisfy desires, so that ideally, government—lacking independent moral authority—is reduced to a matter of administration and technique.

Since human beings, in liberal theory, properly begin with equal rights and opportunities, inequalities are justified only as the prize of individual achievements, especially in the war against nature. Class conveys no moral title. Liberalism is at best suspicious of inheritance (although inclined to concede its utility) or of any claim based on birth; liberal teaching, consequently, strains against inequalities of race and gender, even when liberals accept them in practice. The free market—in goods but also in ideas—emerged as liberalism's ark of the social covenant. Commerce commended itself to liberal theorists for its ability to undermine boundaries, weakening custom subtly and ordinarily without violence. In the age of the bourgeoisie, Marx and Engels wrote of the market, "National one-sidedness and narrow-mindedness become more and more impossible. . . . The cheap prices of its commodities are the heavy artillery with which it batters down all Chinese walls." Like liberalism itself, the market works to erode the ideas of natural qualities or ranks. "All fixed, fast-frozen relations . . . are swept away," Marx and Engels observed; "all new ones become antiquated before they can ossify," a tendency liberal doctrinaires equated with progress and with freedom.[7] To sum up, historic liberal ideology rests on three pillars—secularism, individualism, and free exchange—simplified still further by the nineteenth-century battle cry, "Free markets and free men."

Conservatism is a somewhat more complicated matter because in its origins, it combined those who upheld the Old Regime from principle and those, like Burke, who did so chiefly from prudence. Still, conservative doctrine has its characteristic tenets and commonalities. (I am influenced, in what follows, by Russell Kirk's "six canons of conservatism.")[8] To begin with, conservatism admires reverence and is often disposed to regard religion as a shaping authority in secular life, one that defines what is truly human and truly useful, an inclination at least sympathetic to a religious establishment.[9] Nature assigns human beings a place in the order of things, accompanied by laws and duties, and nature's teaching speaks less of natural rights than of what is naturally right. Conservative theorizing tends to view human beings as social and, sometimes, as political animals, and it is certain to affirm that political society is necessary to any fully human nature. As a moral being the individual is a product of society or culture or history; the terms vary with the theorist, but all conservatism sees humans as *situated* animals, decisively shaped if not defined by context. Necessary to human nurture, family and civil society have autonomous roles, but the "little platoon" is part of a larger regiment; the state has a magisterial mission and superintending authority.[10]

Rank, the distinction of what is excellent from what is base, is inherent in moral ordering, and conservative teaching—respecting birth and tradition—regards the established classes as having at least "presumptive" virtue.[11] That doctrine, it should be obvious, admits a defense of inequalities based on race or gender, although the great conservative ideologues were chiefly concerned to support the hierarchies and continuities of social class. Conservatism suspected or despised the "sophists, economists, and calculators," the market's tendency to displace quality in terms of quantity, with the pursuit of honor yielding to the quest for economic gain.[12] For the sake of parallelism, conservative ideology can be reduced to three principles—religion, community, and ordered stability—that help to highlight its conflict with its liberal rival.

Obviously, there is an affinity between a liberal or conservative temperament and its corresponding doctrine, enough so that the two have often seemed all but equivalent. Early in the age of ideology, for example, Jefferson wrote Lafayette that the parties rested on a natural distinction between "healthy, strong and bold" Whigs, who cherished the people, and "sickly, weakly, timid" men, who, fearing the people, were Tories "by nature."[13] It ought to be clear, however, that the two things are not *identical*; by referring to some men as Tories by nature, Jefferson indicated that there were also Tories (or Whigs) by convention. In any given time, what a conservative person hopes to preserve may or may not accord with conservative doctrine. In the last years of the Soviet Union, for example, conservative inclinations pointed in the direction of Marxist-Leninism, as the media recognize when, reporting politics in the former Soviet republics, they group Communists with other "conservatives."[14] In the same way, as Selden Delaney observed back in 1923, a liberal temper presumes an open mind, but one can adhere to liberal ideology with a mind that is closed or even "ultramontane."[15] Delaney was thinking of Lord Acton, a devoted Catholic who was committed to liberalism; earlier, G. K. Chesterton, a converted Catholic, had expressed a similar thought: "As much as I ever did, more than I ever did, I believe in Liberalism. But there was a time of rosy innocence when I believed in Liberals."[16]

The ambiguous relation between doctrine and personality points to the irony of American conservatism, which many of us learned from Louis

Hartz or Clinton Rossiter.[17] America's oldest regime was decisively new: there was no feudal aristocracy; neither was there a church—even the established churches in the colonies and early states were, as often as not, what Burke called the "dissidence of dissent."[18] "Born equal," Americans did not have to become so.[19]

Moreover, the American polity originated in a revolution, not justified in the discrete evasions of Burke's "politic, well-wrought veil" but in an appeal to natural rights.[20] What the American Republic came to call conservatives were—with a few exceptions like William Johnson of Connecticut—erstwhile revolutionaries who had participated in dispossessing, expelling, or repressing American Tories and whose language, at least, often had indicated a willingness to tear up the social fabric. "I would have hanged my brother," John Adams said, "had he taken part with our enemy." American conservatives have no "ancient constitution"; the origins of our laws are only too well remembered. In the Massachusetts Constitutional Convention of 1820–1821, the aged John Adams argued for retaining a property qualification for voters, a provision, he said, instituted by "our ancestors." There must have been titters; the rule in question had been written, forty years earlier, by Adams himself. Adams the old man appealed to the wisdom of Adams the young man.[21]

So it goes. Necessarily, American conservatives are not conservative in *doctrine*; Burke, Harvey Mansfield discovered, "does not sell well in Reagan's America."[22] Rather, they are ideological liberals of conservative temper, whose task is not to protect the regime from alien principles but from its own precepts, carried too far or too recklessly. At their worst, American conservatives advocate a liberalism without generosity, that liberal grace; at their best, they defend the forms and the formalities of a liberal regime against liberal neglect.[23] And that irony points to another.

Liberals—and with them the American Left—have an enormous stake in their political birthright, the antiquities and founding doctrines of the Republic.[24] In America, liberalism is a tradition and an inheritance, a bequest from the past at least as much as a triumph achieved from reason and will. Even those who have a quarrel with the Constitution characteristically invoke the Declaration of Independence, trumping the Republic's second thoughts with its first principles. And whereas liberal theorizing is often rationalistic, in America, experience—that conservative refuge—mirrors the liberal account of the nature of politics, with governments constructed through a kind of social contract on the basis of individual rights, the separation of public and private spheres, and a more or less successful balancing of powers, interests, and claims. When I came to Rutgers University's

Livingston College in 1970, then a self-proclaimed bastion of liberalism and experimentation, I was fascinated to watch students, left to their own devices, create a government with a two-house legislature and a superabundance of checks and balances. Somewhat imperfectly, American custom and practice mirror liberal political philosophy; even the maddeningly abstract world of John Rawls's *A Theory of Justice,* John Schaar writes, "looks distressingly like the one we have."[25]

Not so long ago, American liberals were able to fend off an amendment excluding flag-burning from the protections of the First Amendment, relying heavily on the contention that we should not "tinker" with the Bill of Rights. That argument was doubly ironic: it passed lightly over the fact that the First Amendment itself is the result of meddling with the Constitution, and by claiming that this ancient tinkering should be exempt from present tampering, it offered one of many examples of the conservative dimension of the American liberal soul.

Almost from the beginning, Americans were a "people of paradox," adhering to both biblical religion and modern secularism, the law of love and the ethic of self-interest, their "bittersweet" attempts at synthesis reflected in the careful ambiguities of the Declaration of Independence.[26] And the enduring ideological anomalies of our political culture are evident in the way in which we remember and relate to the American founding. In the ratification debate, conservatives and liberals have their favorite voices, but they also find (and often try to forget) reasons for discontent with those paladins. Political heroes, in America, come with ambiguities included.

Conservatives are ordinarily more ardent in their support for the Constitution and the *Federalist;* at least since Beard, it has been commonplace for liberal and progressive discussions of the founding to introduce at least some criticism of the drift to the right in the Federalists' design.[27] Unmistakably, the leading spirits among the framers were preoccupied with order—"you must first enable the government to control the governed"—and with the protection of property.[28] They were even determined to avoid a declaration of rights and principles that might imply a criticism of convention—especially of slavery, that violation of natural right—settling instead for the relatively flat cadence of the Preamble.[29] The *Federalist,* moreover, is an "elitist" document, at least in favoring government by the able and talented, suspecting democracy, particularly in its local and participant forms, and applauding "the total exclusion of the people in their collective capacity" from any share in government.[30]

But the framers were also daring innovators and not overscrupulous about law. Rejecting traditional political thought in favor of the new science of politics, disregarding the Articles of Confederation, they set out to create a new, unprecedented regime, a large republic ordained in an almost absolute moment of political creativity.[31] They crafted a constitution that is empirically secular, not only rejecting an established church but lacking—unlike the Declaration—any acknowledgment of divine authority. By contrast, the framers' admiration for science and technology, shared enthusiastically by Jefferson, is reflected in the constitutional provision directing Congress to "promote the progress of science and the useful arts" (article 1, section 8). In fact, the framers' theorizing followed a liberal trail: they believed in natural rights and in an idea of freedom that emphasizes the individual's private capacities, treating the public good, for the most part, as an aggregate of private interests.[32] Taking the struggle to master nature as a human given, they regarded acquisitiveness as a foundation of policy. Hamilton was anything but unique in arguing that narrow self-interest needs to be regulated to safeguard "orderly commerce" against "ruinous contentions."[33] But this sort of concern did not entail much worry about the danger of luxury. Since nature sets no limits, demand alone sets goals, and in that sense, the framers took a hesitant but crucial step in the direction of a consumer society. Moreover, despite their distaste for ancient democracy, they had no doubt that rightful authority derives from popular consent, and the Constitution establishes a politics that is at bottom democratic, albeit in the "thinned" form of voting for representatives.

Finally, the framers rejected the ideal of a closed, coherent community in favor of an inclusive, diverse society comprising a great variety of interests—virtually as many as possible, or so Madison seemed to imply in *Federalist* 51. Their new Republic was already essentially "multicultural," enfolding a plurality of sects, many divided by ancient animosities, aboriginal peoples in conflict with Europeans, and, above all, the distinct and tenacious culture of slavery.[34] In the Constitutional Convention, Gouverneur Morris sought to uphold the claims of usage and shared memory, proposing fourteen years of residence (and he might have preferred native birth) as a qualification for membership in the Senate. "Citizens of the World," Morris argued, are politically suspect; "men who can shake off their attachment to their country can never love another." As conservative doctrine, Morris's sentiments were faultless, but his proposal did not even get the vote of his state, and he was lucky to get half a loaf. No one was unkind enough to point out the irony—Morris and his fellows, after all, themselves had broken their political attachments to king and country—but Franklin did observe that many foreigners had supported the Revolution, whereas many natives had opposed it. Madison, James Wilson, and Franklin all deplored the "illiberality" of Morris's notion, and it is worth noting that Madison attributes the word to all three. America, Madison contended, should want to attract "men who love liberty and are eager to partake in its blessings," and it should not discourage immigrants by imposing too many disabilities.[35] In the framers' vision, American nationality was not a given but something subject to reshaping within the Constitution and the laws, and its watchword was not tradition but rights and liberties.

Meanwhile, the Anti-Federalists, the other side of the ratification debate, have often won approval from the American liberal-Left. A diverse persuasion, the Anti-Federalists included most of the eighteenth century's warm supporters of democracy, and their doctrine, with its emphasis on citizenship, at least resonates with contemporary ideas of political participation—especially since, like Jefferson, Anti-Federalists were inclined to see a need for the ongoing refounding of political community through a more or less heroic politics. Anti-Federalists like "Cato" and Melancton Smith warned that government under the Constitution, too complicated for ordinary citizens to understand, would be dominated by elites. Accordingly suspicious of the state and jealously protective of the prerogatives of citizens, Anti-Federalists were insistent advocates of a bill of rights. Finally, although Anti-Federalists respected property and were largely persuaded by the moral case for commerce, they were much more emphatic than their opponents in ranking republican self-rule above any merely economic rights or aims. All of this, in short, sounds like a program compatible with a fairly advanced sort of contemporary liberalism.

But precisely *because* of their democratic sympathies, Anti-Federalists were profoundly conservative, fiercely guarding the political virtue of American ways against the threat of innovation. Popular understanding, Anti-Federalists recognized, is local and empirical; just as ordinary citizens cannot keep close watch on a government beyond a certain scale and level of complexity, so they cannot rapidly deal with laws and policies that change too rapidly. Democratic politics, in the Anti-Federalist view, depends on stable laws tied to the slow pace of public deliberation.[36]

The Anti-Federalists, moreover, were not enthusiasts for purely individual liberty. They were close to the ancient teaching that self-government consists in sharing in the life and rule of a political community. The rights they championed were less often private immunities than guarantees of a certain kind of politics—adequate representation, for example, or trial by jury, which they celebrated not so much as a protection of the rights of the accused than as the "democratic branch of the judiciary power."[37] They regarded a coherent moral community as the basis of republicanism, as in

Tocqueville's contention, based on his understanding of American Puritanism, that a moral world in which "everything is classified, systematized, foreseen, and decided beforehand" provides the foundation for a political world in which "everything is agitated, disputed and uncertain."[38] Sharing with Federalists like Madison the hope that commerce would promote understanding and overcome privilege, they feared luxury and distrusted foreign commerce and worried, as Jefferson did, that the pursuit of private gain would overcome public spirit.[39] Welcoming comfort and well-being, Anti-Federalists defended the principle that those goods are not ends in themselves and that austerity with self-government is preferable to abundance without it.

There is an ironic side to the Anti-Federalists' great victory, the adoption of a bill of rights. Like the Virginian who wrote under the singular pseudonym "A Delegate Who Has Catched Cold," Anti-Federalists advocated a declaration of rights as a basis for civic education in a large republic—a sort of formal, primary schooling in politics in a regime where practice and experience no longer could be relied on to teach the essentials and dignity of citizenship.[40] But the eventual Bill of Rights, shaped so much by Madison, was cast in a negative, largely individualistic language, with a corresponding tendency to be read as a set of private protections against politics. In our time, one example is graphic: the Second Amendment is the most didactic provision of the Bill of Rights—and arguably of the Constitution as a whole—indicating that it proceeds from the principle that a free state depends, through a "well regulated militia," on popular service in the military. It implies, at least, a citizen's duty to serve; it surely deprecates professional soldiers. Yet in our times, the amendment is widely read by conservatives as establishing a private right, and though contemporary liberals are critical of this interpretation, they are a long way from adopting the sterner teaching that the lives of citizens, like their goods, should always be at their country's command.

The American founding, in short, is an ideological muddle, full of tangled inconsistencies, especially when seen from our perspective. For most historians, John Adams is as close to an exemplar of conservatism as early America offers, just as Jefferson symbolizes liberalism, and though their theories are subtler and more ambiguous than that, the interpretation is no caricature. Yet both Jefferson and Adams served on the committee that drafted the Declaration of Independence, and both approved the Constitution, though in different ways and with different reservations. As far as our fundamental institutions are concerned, it is appropriate to paraphrase Jefferson's first inaugural: we are all conservatives; we are all liberals.

As I have already suggested, chief among the inherited commonalities that have come to unite American liberals and conservatives is the language of individual rights, the very altar of contemporary political discourse.[41] Our political speech, in other words, is cast predominantly in the terms of liberal political philosophy, and both conservatives and liberals are more comfortable referring to political society as a device intended to meet individual needs than as a whole with claims superior to those of its parts. Tocqueville saw it: Americans, he observed, almost always explained their conduct in terms of "interest rightly understood," even when their actions reflected compassion and public spirit. In their speech, Tocqueville concluded, Americans were concerned to honor their "philosophy"—the doctrine that human beings are separate individuals acting from private motives—rather than their own, often nobler, qualities of soul.[42] Gradually, he expected that way of talking to shape American life. And he was right.

Recently, American conservatives, although devoted to the liberal public institutions that come to them from the past, have made the defense of the "private sector" their special solicitude, hoping to wall off and preserve traditional morals, authorities, and relationships in the family, the church, and the community (just as, for a long time, many conservatives hoped to preserve the older relationship between the two races). They admired, in other words, at least a version of that combination of a closed moral order with an open politics that Tocqueville saw as the *fons et origo* of things American.

The ambiguities of American politics are not escaped so easily. Inevitably, the laws intrude on the private sphere, regulating property, defining enforceable rights and obligations, and marking off the limits of private authority. Since the ruling precept of the laws is what Tocqueville called the "spirit of liberty," even conservatives upholding moral obligations are apt to speak in terms of personal rights. Opponents of abortion, for example, appeal to a "right to life," not a duty to nurture, and recent advertising on that side of the question refers to life as a "beautiful choice," virtually conceding a great deal of that right to choose that has been their opponents' stock in trade.

The ironies of American conservatism are most evident in economic life. In the United States, capitalism and the market are pillars of established authority, and in that sense, it is no surprise that for most of our history, the championship of economic liberty—relatively unregulated competition for wealth—has been a centerpiece of conservative doctrine. But the market is anything but conservative: it teaches that property is acquired not for transmission to succeeding generations but for gain in exchange. In market capitalism, the view is dynamic, bound up with growth and continuous transformation.[43] The logic of the market reduces qualities to quantities and especially to the standard of money. At the "bottom line," capitalism is utterly disdainful of tradition or of any relationships that cannot pass the test of profitability. Speaking of the chronic need to refound corporations, Albert J. Dunlap, chief executive officer of the Scott Paper Company, remarked that "you must get rid of the people who represent the old culture . . . and you have to get rid of all the old symbols."[44] These sentiments are no less relevant to business culture today than when they were spoken in 1994—by a corporate leader who would be lionized by Wall Street with the nickname "Chain Saw Al." The moral language of the market does not speak of virtues but of values, a set of preferences molded by desire and opinion. "The Value or Worth of a man," Hobbes proclaimed, "is as of all things, his Price, that is to say, so much as would be given for the use of his Power; and therefore is not a thing absolute; but a thing dependent on the need and judgment of another."[45] In a word, the catechism of the market is relativism, its foundations resting on the sands of supply and demand.

This doctrine cannot be confined to economics, more or less narrowly defined; encouraging individualism, capitalism presumes and legitimates the "sovereignty of the passions."[46] The market values and rewards mobility, human beings who anticipate and respond freely to the currents of change. Its preferred social unit is the relatively free-floating individual or one-worker household, and it regards attachment to community, to extended family, or to craft as "frictional," if not essentially irrational. Historically, capitalism saw marriage and family as useful stimuli to ambition that also gave employees' lives a desirable stability. Increasingly, however, corporate America is inclined to view marriage as a problem involving possible impediments to mobility. At best, hiring policy is no longer a reliable ally of the family, and it is probably more accurate to say, as Elizabeth Fox-Genovese does, that economic forces and technology are "tolerating, when not financing, the destruction of the family, church and every other institution that aspires to a measure of autonomy."[47] In other words, the conservative effort to defend both traditional values and unregulated capitalism amounts to trying to square a moral circle.[48]

For a long time, modern American conservatism was held together by anticommunism and by the need to combat an ascendant liberalism, both of which militated against overniceness in relation to allies, present or potential.[49] Today, by contrast, greater strength on the right and the collapse of the Soviet empire make conservatives readier to air their disagreements in public. On the libertarian side, Robert Nozick promotes a radically individualist doctrine of rights, rooted in the philosophy of liberals like Locke, carried to an extreme in its suspicion of authority.[50] By contrast, from a position closer to historic conservatism, Harvey Mansfield rejoins that libertarian zeal for the "sovereignty of the self" threatens the "self-government of the self," an ideal that requires moral character, pride, and the willingness to sacrifice one's personal interests and liberties for one's country, the political whole of which personal freedoms are a part.[51] And in political practice, there are now regular, frequently bitter contests that pit social conservatives of various sorts—religious rightists are only the most visible—against their more economic or libertarian rivals or against each other. The discord is escalating beyond ambiguity; the new thunder on the right may prove to be rumblings along the fault lines of American conservatism.

But of course, liberals have parallel problems of their own. Modern liberals have always been ambivalent about market capitalism. They value the dynamic commercial economy that, after all, was largely a liberal invention, looking to it to provide abundance, appreciating its contribution to the easing of human life, and hoping for the well-being that prompts generosity. And like earlier liberals, they admire it for breaking down narrowness, exclusiveness, and prejudice; opening communities to new ideas and influences; and linking peoples in the bonds of trade and acquaintance. On the other hand, where the founders of liberalism allowed themselves to hope that free competition would limit the range and permanence of inequalities, by the mid-nineteenth century their successors learned that the market permits the development of towering inequalities, with differences of power deriving from large-scale institutions at least as alarming as disparities of wealth. Private power modifies, if it does not escape, the logic of competition, which—in economics and in its influence on government—has long since become oligopolistic, the power of the few constraining the opportunities of the many. Moreover, modern liberalism also recognizes that the combination of inequality with instability—especially the threat of unemployment—increases social insecurity and the fear of indignity. That in turn accentuates the dark side of market psychology: it prods human beings toward becoming more unambiguously self-interested and grasping and hence exclusive and lacking in sympathy, concerned only for their own, narrowly defined. In other words, free market liberalism endangers liberality; historic liberal doctrine threatens the liberal soul.[52] This tension increasingly has been accentuated by the weakening of the moral and social foundations of liberal politics. The American Constitution, of course, gives no formal support to any social institution other than property: like the founders of liberalism generally, the American framers were inclined to think that, whenever possible, government should leave social life and moral education to the devices of others. Any government effort to shape the soul entails threats to liberty; the great liberal teachers were more concerned to keep religion and concern for the soul from dominating political life, preferring religions and souls that are law-abiding and willing to surrender their this-worldly claims to rule. On liberal principles, moreover, public life is a sphere in which nominal equals are governed on the basis of reason and consent; the private sphere includes authorities established without consent and rules often tailored to human emotion. Intervention in private life, consequently, requires a liberal public authority to violate either its own principles or those of the private order, so that it is far less troublesome to leave the two spheres separate.

Both the framers and their opponents took it for granted, however, that families, churches, local communities, and schools would nurture and develop the civil sentiments and decencies. A liberal polity rests on rather definite moral premises. In the first place, it relies heavily on civility and tolerance and hence trust and reasonable personal security, manifested through citizens who keep their promises and fulfill their obligations even when doing so no longer seems in their interest. The laws can help protect that last excellence—the Constitution demands that states respect the "obligation of contracts" (article 1, section 10)—but the risk of being caught and punished affords only an inadequate guarantee; all human beings are tempted by the calculation that the potential gains from breaking a rule outweigh the chance of being detected. *Strong* security for pledges demands the support of personal convictions and perhaps of higher authority.[53] Second, a truly liberal citizen is generous-spirited, and even those liberal theorists who regarded benevolence as part of a "moral sense" or "instinct" recognized that it is a quality that requires cultivation through appropriate doctrines and ways of life. Any damage to the private order, consequently, endangers the basis of liberal citizenship.[54] By the late nineteenth century, liberal voices were warning that those institutions were becoming embattled and too often overthrown by the dynamics of modern life.

Willy-nilly, more and more liberals felt compelled toward the task of economic and social reconstruction, invoking government to safeguard and amplify a lifeworld suited to the liberal spirit.[55] This adventure drew on archetypically liberal qualities—sympathy and inclusiveness, for example, as well as a disposition to innovate—but it also moved into areas and policies traditionally associated with conservatism. Herbert Croly appealed to Hamilton, with more enthusiasm than he showed to Jefferson, and the leaders we now regard as the founders of modern liberalism typically preferred to call themselves "Progressives" to avoid association with radical individualism and the night-watchman state.[56] In many ways, the beginning of the Progressive era was signaled by Frederick Jackson Turner's warning of the passing of an American tradition, the end of the frontier that had provided, Turner argued, the environmental basis for American democracy. Nothing epitomizes Progressive concerns more than the policy of conservation, and in general, Progressives hoped to refurbish the rough equality, full employment, and moral coherence they remembered in the American past. And they were surely moralists, albeit of a bourgeois sort. Theodore Roosevelt, Mencken observed, had the instincts of a "property-owning Tory" even when he adopted liberal postures; "no one ever heard him make an argument for the rights of the citizen; his eloquence was always expended in expounding the duties of the citizen."[57]

It should be emphasized, however, that Progressives were attempting to conserve the moral basis of a liberal society. They distrusted traditional, merely customary, or ethnic institutions and cultures, and even those who were most welcoming toward "hyphenated" Americans wanted to liberate individuals from the prejudices of locality or the past. They called the forms and proprieties into question, seeking to reform and refound social institutions on liberal bases—choice, reason, or science—using schools as a key to overcoming "cultural lag" and working to produce "habits of mind and character . . . that are somewhat near even with the actual movement of events."[58]

As that indicates, modern liberals began with confidence in the moral direction of history, convinced that change and science work to promote cooperation and democracy. They saw little difficulty, consequently, in reconciling their moralism with the relativism that was their characteristic weapon against established institutions.[59] The relativity of cultures and codes was thought to entail a broad tolerance or even egalitarianism—a notion similar to the conceit that, paradoxically buttressed by the authority of Nietzsche, one finds so often in universities today.[60] But the Progressive period and our own times are separated by the era of totalitarianism and total war.

Experience has made contemporary liberals much more skeptical about technology and the redemptive logic of history; these days, historicism speaks about history's ineluctabilities, not its promise. Among political philosophers, John Dewey enjoys a new vogue, but his admirers lack the serene assurance of Dewey's faith in science when they are not, like Richard Rorty, agnostics or unbelievers.[61] There is no shortage of reasons for this incertitude.

Economic inequalities of wealth and power have grown even more staggering, enough to raise serious questions about the possibilities of liberal citizenship. Observation taught Jefferson that economic inequality is tolerably compatible with political equality when work at a "comfortable subsistence" is sufficiently certain that no worker feels dependent on a particular employer.[62] Today, by contrast, socially adequate jobs are scarce, and with corporations celebrating "downsizing," they are insecure even for those who have them. Americans are feeling pressed, growing less generous and more anxious to defend their own. The very affluent increasingly feel able and driven to insulate themselves from the problems of other Americans; society seems to be dividing into the exempt and the trapped.[63] Meanwhile, more and more liberals worry about crime, the apparent rise of domestic violence and abuse, and the increase in social isolation and self-concern.

All of this reinforces the tendency of liberals—joined by conservatives more often than the Right likes to admit—to look to government to redress the order of things. In economics, at least, liberals have something like a standard for policy—full employment at adequate wages—however difficult it is to achieve in practice (and however many differences there are between liberals—often bitter ones—about the best road to that goal). Socially, however, contemporary liberals are far less willing than their predecessors to establish a public definition of a desirable family or social order. In part, this reflects a greater awareness of marginal groups and cultures, combined with a generous liberal desire to include them in the body politic; there is simply a lot more *pluribus,* these days, in the American *unum.* And since liberals tend to be defenders of the freedom of "lifestyle," a great many are unwilling to "stigmatize" single-parent families or other unorthodox unions. (As the number of such families grows, moreover, political leaders also have reason to hesitate about giving offense, as Dan Quayle learned.) As a result, liberals, warmly willing to help single-parent families, are apt to be left with only a narrowly economic basis for doing so; conservatives, with every reason to recognize the difficulties under which single parents operate, are just as likely to be unwilling to do more than blame them.

It makes matters worse that liberals have become less enthusiastic about democratic politics and not just because of their experience in recent elections. Since marginal and vulnerable groups have a more or less desperate stake in supportive public policy, liberals have been unwilling to leave them to the vagaries of majority opinion, especially in these crabbed times. Instead, liberals have developed the habit of setting themselves to establish such policies as rights, relatively immune to politics (a process that almost all of us participate in where our own interests are concerned).

This parallels the ironic fact that the more individuals are dwarfed by private power, on one hand, and the state, on the other, and the clearer it becomes that a free spirit depends on attachments and social supports, the more liberals—to say nothing of right-wing libertarians or Americans generally—seem to insist on their belief in the moral autonomy of the individual. Robert Bellah and his associates found, in fact, that Americans have virtually no moral language other than individualism.[64] The putative freedom of an inner world, in other words, is invoked against an increasingly constraining outer one.[65]

It is part of this process that, unlike the founders of liberalism, contemporary theorists do not attempt to root the "priority" of individual liberty in nature.[66] Quite the contrary, the current tendency is to diminish or reject the idea of human nature because it constitutes a restraint on liberty. The human self, in this persuasion, cannot be ruled by any norm external to itself; human beings are bound only by principles of their own making.[67] Postmodernism and deconstructionism are only a new stage in the logic of this argument, appealing to liberals because, irreverent toward canonical authority, they seem to affirm a more inclusive liberty.

Even on its own terms, however, this line of argument moralizes and contributes to social fragmentation, and individuals left alone are no match for the dominations and powers of the time. In fact, the most strident voices on today's American liberal-Left recognize that, like the market in material goods, the free marketplace of ideas does not guarantee social justice and can work to the detriment of culturally disadvantaged groups. Often hamhanded and self-interested, the demands for "political correctness" include a largely appropriate insistence on civility toward women and toward minority races and sexual orientations. Yet ironically, this consideration is not ordinarily extended to others; those who require civil speech in the first set of cases resist any limit on "authentic" self-expression everywhere else.

As this hints, avant-garde liberalism has at best an uneasy relationship to democracy. Postmodern and deconstructionist teachings, for example, are disdainful of common modes of speech and understanding. Though far from conservative in principle, in practice thinkers who follow Derrida disparage the possibilities of political change in a way that recalls Burke.[68] Most important, their emphasis on the difference between human subjects and cultures, an old conservative set piece, is at odds with the principle of equality, the cornerstone of democratic life.[69]

Like their conservative rivals, American liberals are being torn by their own culture war, one that ranges economic egalitarians, often relatively conservative in social terms, against the libertarian-to-nihilist strain of the cultural Left.[70] All too visible in the Clinton administration, that conflict is another illustration of how problematic historical ideologies are as guides to American politics.

Liberal and conservative temperaments will always be with us, but liberal and conservative doctrines have become scrambled when they are not simply played out, although there are formidable obstacles to formulating a more adequate set of alternatives. If I have spent more time discussing the liberals' dilemma, it is partly because my heritage runs in their direction but also because I am persuaded that even cultural conservatives are too willing to accommodate to the market's relativistic dynamics.[71] Economic life has a kind of primacy: as Thoreau warned us, our ways of *getting* a living will always have a shaping effect on our ways of living.[72] But beyond economics, any effort to revitalize American politics also will have to deal broadly with civil society, the private foundations of public life. And Michael Sandel is right: we are becoming "more entangled, but less attached," personally "unencumbered" but caught in a network of interdependencies.[73] Seriously addressed, restoring or reconstructing the private order is bound to run up against deeply entrenched parts of the way we live—the pace of change, the scale of economic and cultural life, personal mobility, even the dream of affluence.

Understandably, most of our political leaders prefer to talk at the problem, not the worst idea, since in a republic persuasion needs to precede law. But even when conservative and liberal speakers abandon the language of rights, they invoke "values," the idiom of the market, asking us for better preferences rather than improved but demanding ways of living. Our older biblical language—the first grammar of American life—speaks of virtues and of righteousness, qualities beyond choosing, bound up with the fundamental order of things. From that teaching, we learned to regard our rights as unalienable, not made by us nor subject to our surrendering. But we also were taught that community is a fact of life: human beings are parts of nature, stewards and not masters, and subject to a law that assigns them duties to nature and to each other. For both liberals and conservatives, reclaiming that voice is a first step toward rearticulating the inner dialogue— the ambiguity and the irony—that is the soul of a liberal republic.

10

Political Parties as Civic Associations

IN THE CONSTITUTION OF THE UNITED STATES, political parties are like a scandal in polite society: they are alluded to but never discussed.[1] The importance of parties in political life has led the federal and state governments to intervene increasingly in the affairs of the parties, regulating primaries and the selection of party officials, but the political parties grew up as private associations, outside the sphere of our formally public institutions.[2] In this sense, political parties began outside the law, and they have never become quite respectable.

Paradoxically, the private origins of American political parties enhanced their understanding of public things. Public institutions in America use language that speaks most often of private things, referring to individuals, their "interests" (conceived chiefly in terms of their private estates and power), and their "rights" (defined, for the most part, as immunities against public interference). Our public institutions reflect, if imperfectly, the "science of politics" on which the framers based the Constitution: the theory that human beings are by nature free, private, and self-preserving animals caught up in a struggle for the mastery of nature, warring with their fellows for scarce resources, and willing to "give up" some rights to the group only to escape that state of war and to gain more effective enjoyment of the rights they "retain." Human beings, in the "liberal tradition" that informs our constitutions, are political and public only by artifice and from necessity.[3]

By contrast, many "private" institutions—most notably, families, churches, and local communities—have often taught an older creed that speaks more easily of the public as a whole, appealing to patriotism, duty, and the common good. Of course, these private bodies have been influenced, increasingly, by the liberalism and "modernism" of our public culture, and they articulate the more traditional view only infrequently, incoherently,

Originally published as "Parties as Civic Associations," in *Party Renewal in America: Theory and Practice*, ed. Gerald M. Pomper (Westport, Conn.: Praeger, 1980), 51–68. Copyright © 1980 by Praeger Publishers. Reproduced with permission of ABC-CLIO, LLC.

and apologetically.[4] Nevertheless, the "private" order shaped the American character, in part, in terms of a teaching that human beings are limited creatures, subject to the law of nature, born dependent, and—by nature—in need of nurturance and moral education. In the old phrase, we are by nature "political animals." Family, friends, and polity are essential to the development of human personality. "My self" is never separate from "my people"; I owe them my life and can rightly be asked to sacrifice it for the common good.

Rooted in the private order, political parties often voiced its doctrine. Tim Campbell's famous question, "What's the Constitution among friends?" amounts to an epigram summarizing the charge of traditional teachings against the public order and the framers' theories that shaped it.[5]

I will attempt to show the crucial role played by political parties in relating the private order to the public life of the United States and, correspondingly, the extent to which American party politics depended on the private order for its vitality. I will argue that the increasing fragmentation of the private sphere is an important cause of the decline of American political parties, and, finally, I will maintain that genuine reform—for the country as well as for the parties—requires the reconstruction of the private foundations of public life.

Private Lives and Public Virtues

When President Carter referred to a "crisis of confidence" in a speech delivered in 1979, he observed that Americans have too little trust in their political leaders to allow those leaders to govern effectively. He argued that various "special interests" block needed legislation, and he urged public opinion to force Congress to act in the public interest. Carter's argument presumed that public-spiritedness was not strong enough to prevail, and though the president was too politic to say so, he implied that the American people were then too preoccupied with private affairs and concerns. In other words, the public is generally disaffected and denies the government the resources of allegiance and dedication necessary to pursue the common good. It could be argued that little has changed in the intervening thirty years.

Contemporary problems, most visibly the ongoing energy crisis, make us unusually aware of the need for public spirit. In fact, however, civic virtue is always in demand. Public-spiritedness is never easy. My senses are always private, my own and no one else's. The more my reason and reflection tell me that I am like other human beings, that we are all parts of a whole or members of an interdependent political society, the more my senses and my feelings tend to insist on my uniqueness and my separateness. In reflection, Chesterton wrote, "Any man may be inside any men," but to look at others is to "leave the inside and draw . . . near the outside," emphasizing differences rather than similarities.[6] This is to say the obvious: that public spirit is to some extent at odds with our feelings and sensations. We are, for example, notoriously unjust about our families. Parents value children disproportionately, and children see parents as larger than life. Plato saw no "solution" other than eliminating the private family altogether for his guardian class, and in regimes less ideal than *The Republic,* the family is a constant limit on our willingness to be public-spirited. No citizen is perfect in his dedication to the common good, and any sort of civic spirit requires the discipline and governance of some of our most profound feelings and desires. Hence the classical saying that those who would learn to command must first learn to obey.

The more our feelings and our private interests are at odds with public interests and policies, the more we will experience law and government as a kind of tyranny. The more law and government make us feel impotent, undignified, and confused, the more we will withdraw into private refuges to protect whatever dignity we can salvage—if we do not react furiously, seeking to hurt a regime that injures our self-esteem. The more we *need* such a regime, the more we will resent its injuries. Under such conditions, we may be forced to obey; we do not learn to do so.

The government of our private feelings, however, need not be a tyranny. Our emotions can be charmed out of their preoccupation with self and educated to be allies—if never entirely reliable ones—of reason and community. Until modern times, political philosophy argued in favor of the small state because such states, keeping the polity within the emotional compass of the individual, reduced the distance between private feeling and public life and promoted civic virtue. Public spirit needs the shelter of limited space. In small communities, I can see, experience, and benefit from policies enacted for the common good. A bridge in Minnesota or a job-training program for the poor benefits me but very indirectly; I may reason that such benefits exist, but I will not feel them.[7]

Similarly, small groups and communities help create trust, commitment, and allegiance. In the first place, the small community enhances our knowledge of one another. Small societies are personal; people know me, my leaders know who I am, and I in turn know them. The most frequent complaint against small communities, in fact, is that we are known too well. Ideally, such communities are stable because stability increases interpersonal knowledge. In a small but mobile community, like most suburbs, I know who you *appear* to be, but I do not know your past and still less do I share it. I know you, in other words, only superficially and will trust you accordingly. Even more important, if I suspect that either you or I will move away soon, I am not likely to commit myself deeply to you or to the life of the community. It is a place where I *live,* not a part of what I *am.* Stability increases the feeling that I am with people who will not surprise me even if I do not like them and that we can pledge ourselves to one another without fear of being abandoned. Plato wrote,

> Nothing is of more benefit to the *polis* than . . . mutual acquaintance; for where men conceal their ways from one another in darkness rather than light, no man will ever gain either his due honor or office or the justice which is befitting.[8]

The small community also makes me feel important. Its smallness increases my relative impact as an individual. In the great state, I am a statistic; what I say has only an insignificant effect on society as a whole. In small societies, I can participate in common affairs if I choose; in large societies, only a small percentage of citizens can participate effectively. There is an upper limit to the number of citizens who can play a full role in public deliberation. Even if we were willing to spend twenty-four hours a day dealing with public affairs, if it took fifteen minutes to present one's views effectively, less than one hundred of us could speak on any given day. In a community of a hundred, this is almost enough time for all of us; in a community of a thousand, either only 10 percent of us can speak or we will be able to speak only for a minute and a half. In large states, most of us are silenced and even those who talk are forced to speak in slogans.[9] Participation itself is not crucial; the important thing is the dignity that the possibility of participation reflects. In the small community, I can decide to listen and let others lead because I have the possibility of doing otherwise. In the large state, I will have no choice in the matter.

The case for the small polity is a strong one. In material resources, however, such societies were always relatively weak, and the advent of "modernization"—industrialization and commercialization—shattered the autonomy of local communities, tied their economic life to a national and international market, permitted easy migration, and introduced strangers and strange ideas into local life. Modernization and its attendant benefits rooted local communities and traditional peoples in massive, ill-comprehended, and threatening societies ruled by impersonal forces. It offered the individual freedom from the restraints of local community but only because no individual mattered enough to be worth more than superficial attention. In the modern world, the large state became a necessity because only such states could hope to give some control over the forces that shaped their lives. That necessity, however, does not create anything like public spirit or civic virtue.

In large states, disaffection—the retreat of emotion, trust, and commitment into private places—is the *rule*, not the exception. Madison and the framers were content to have it so, provided that such private havens be numerous and, taken as parts of the whole, too weak to endanger society. In general, the framers were willing to rely on the appeals of material interest and power in foreign affairs to foster national allegiance, trusting that an admittedly diffuse "affection" would, in the long term, follow where interest led.[10]

But material advantage, though it may bribe us into complaisance, is counterproductive if the common good demands sacrifice, and "foreign danger" has its limits as a basis for national unity. Lacking an alternative, presidents term every major civic need the "equivalent of war," but few dangers really equal war in the sense of immediate personal danger they inspire, and those that do—the Depression is the only salient example—do not do so for long. Even war, if the enemy is far away, does not rule our feelings.

If there was once a significant degree of commitment and loyalty to public institutions in America, that fact is more surprising than the "disaggregation" we seem to be experiencing today. Political parties, as "mediating strata," helped build the emotional and personal bonds between local communities and the Republic as a whole. An examination of the traditional theory and role of American political parties is essential to understanding the present and future of parties in America.

The Parties in American Thought

It is a truism that the framers disliked and distrusted political parties. Informed opinion, at the birth of the Republic, saw parties as divisive forces that demagogically exaggerated conflict. Based on the English parties with which they were familiar, American leaders also associated political parties with cliquish corruption.[11] Eager to multiply competing factions so as to reduce the likelihood of a majority faction, the framers could hardly admire an association whose purpose is the aggregation of majorities. The diversity of interests required to make up a majority in America might reduce party to the level of a more or less trivial nuisance, but no positive claims could be made for it.

Jefferson was more ambivalent, but he too was no friend to party. Partisanship, he wrote in 1789, is "the last degeneration of a free and moral agent. . . . If I could not get to heaven but with a party, I would not go there at all." In 1798, Jefferson went as far as he would go in defense of party: "In every free and deliberating society, there must, from the nature of man, be opposite parties. . . . Perhaps this party division is necessary to induce each to watch and relate to the people the proceedings of the other." That, however, was Jefferson in opposition; as Richard Hofstadter points out, Jeffersonians in power pursued a "quest for unanimity."[12] Jefferson professed to be "no believer in the amalgamation of parties" because he saw parties as natural, rooted in temperament and biology, but he invoked this idea as much to deprecate his "sickly" opponents as to defend party.[13] Like Jefferson himself, the "first party system" he did so much to create accepted party only hesitantly; neither he nor his followers created permanent, institutional parties in the modern sense.[14]

In his "ward system," however, Jefferson advanced an idea that was to be seminal in the development of American mass parties. Jefferson was concerned to synthesize local communities and the central regime, combining the warm if parochial patriotism of the former with the broader, more enlightened perspectives of the latter. The secret of free government, he suggested, is that citizens retain all those powers within their competence, delegating others "by a synthetical process to higher and higher orders of functionaries."

> The elementary republics of the wards, the county republics, the State republics and the republic of the Union, would form a gradation of authorities. . . . Where every man is a sharer in the direction of his ward-republic, or of some of the higher ones, and feels that he is a participator in the government of affairs, not merely at election one day in the year but every day; when there shall not be a man in the State who will not be a member of some one of its councils, great or small, he will let the heart be torn out of his body sooner than his power be wrested from him by a Caesar or a Bonaparte.[15]

Jefferson, of course, was speaking of transforming the government, not of organizing a political party, but it was the party that attempted to put his doctrine into effect.

The first great champion of political parties in America was Martin Van Buren, and Van Buren's theory—which asserts an essential role for political parties in the republican government of a large state—has enduring value. On his credentials alone—a party boss, a statesman, a sage, and a third-party candidate—Van Buren's argument merits serious attention.

Staunch republican that he was, Van Buren recognized that elections can be shams. At least where mass publics are involved, nonpartisan elections work to the advantage of the well-to-do and the powerful, for they provide no organized alternatives and no basis, other than celebrity or prominence, on which the public could make a choice. The nonpartisanship of Monroe's administration, praised as the "Era of Good Feelings" by defenders of the antiparty tradition, was the worst variety of nonpartisan regime, since Monroe purported to be a republican but, in office, courted Federalists. Tacitly, if not consciously, Monroe was deceiving the public and, in the long term, courting a general public disillusionment. *All* nonpartisan systems encourage the belief that elections are a facade and that the "real" decisions are made somewhere else. Undermining the legitimacy of the regime, they encourage citizens to abandon a "fraudulent" public life in favor of their private interests.[16]

Public choice demanded organized, visible alternatives, and Van Buren envisioned three modes of organizing a mass electorate, only one of which deserved the name "party." In the first place, the electorate could be organized in what I will call *factions* on the basis of geography, with factions speaking for particular sections or localities, or on the basis of interests, with factions speaking for classes, economic sectors, or trades. Second, the people could be grouped as the rival personal *followings* of political leaders. Finally, the electorate could be divided into *parties*.

Van Buren's meaning was subtle. He saw no essential difference between sectional factions and organized interests because both were essentially parochial, based on different varieties of private self-seeking. Factions, whether geographic or interested, could easily fragment into multipartite confusion, but that defect is not essential to Van Buren's argument. Even if a sectional or interested "party" contrived to organize a majority, it would still be a faction because its constitutive principle would be private.[17] The Whigs, for example, were often condemned as a party of "interests" and "privilege," unconcerned with the moral unity of the people.

> The Whig professes to cherish liberty, and he cherishes only his chartered franchises. . . . He applies the doctrine of divine right to legislative grants and spreads the mantle of superstition round contracts. He

professes to adore freedom, and he pants for monopoly. Not that he is dishonest; he deceives himself; he is the dupe of his own selfishness, for covetousness is idolatry and covetousness is the only passion which is never conscious of its own existence.[18]

Discount the campaign rhetoric and one is still left with the contention that a faction, even a potential majority, based simply on private interests is a danger to republican government. Such factions are essentially oligarchic or aristocratic, "feudal" in the worst sense, concerned with private privileges and immunities against the community as a whole.[19]

Similarly, Van Buren rejected personal followings in part because they were ephemeral and because they encouraged demagoguery and "image" politics but also because they were essentially monarchic, emphasizing person rather than law and hierarchy rather than civic equality. In the same spirit, George Bancroft set "the tory principle" alongside whiggery as the enemy of democracy.[20]

Forced to choose between democracy's two enemies, Van Buren might have leaned—as his Whig critics charged—to the monarchic side. Better a king who sees his realm as one property and who gives unity to the sovereign, Hobbes had argued, than a host of private factions,[21] and I suspect that Van Buren agreed. Certainly, he argued that a "Tribunician executive" was needed to check the "interests" that tend to dominate the legislature. To control the executive, Van Buren relied on party to train, filter, and select leaders. As James Ceaser writes, "Party in this respect would be made 'prior' to leaders."[22]

Party, then, is the republican alternative, organizing the electorate on the basis of "principles" as opposed to the private concerns of factions and governing its internal affairs collegially as opposed to the hierarchy of followings. Van Buren used the term *party* judiciously. He meant an organization that regards itself as a part of the public as a whole, acknowledging higher political duties and regarding its own principles as an emphasis or priority—doubtless the right and correct one—within common values that give a people its "unity of character." Party, then, is not only a form of organization; it is a quality of spirit, a set of commitments, a dedication to public life.[23]

Van Buren intended that parties should teach, as well as reflect, this sort of civic virtue. In an otherwise superb article, Ceaser has observed that the "principles" on which Van Buren hoped to base parties would be necessarily "broad," since Van Buren aimed at a truly national coalition. Ceaser goes on to conclude that Van Buren aimed to extend the "Madisonian system" of "competing factions and coalitions" into the election of presidents.[24] Here, Ceaser goes astray.

Van Buren was, in fact, a shrewd critic of the framers as well as a respectful admirer. The framers, Van Buren maintained, took too mechanistic and formal a view of government. "Theoretic" dangers led them to a fear of the majority that Van Buren regarded as misplaced in America. All governments, Van Buren held, rest on "opinion," and it is this opinion, not formal rules, that ultimately limits and sets the direction of government. It is important that Van Buren referred to "opinion" rather than "opinions." Opinion, as Van Buren understood it, meant something like the term *doxa* in Greek antiquity: a "political culture," values, habits, and perceptions more fundamental than transient attitudes, rooted in the common language and experience of a people as a whole, shaping the very personalities of its citizens.[25] Hence Van Buren's assertion that the "truest service" one can offer one's country lies in "forming a right national opinion," akin to the *orthe doxa* of Plato's philosophy.[26]

Forming a right opinion is—to say the least—a formidable task. Fortunately, Van Buren did not think it necessary; a right opinion already existed in America. This opinion rendered pointless the framers' fears of majority rule. Experience demonstrated, Van Buren contended, that American majorities could be trusted to govern with restraint, common morality, and civic responsibility.

Right opinion, however, is only the first step toward civic virtue; it needs to be educated and led. The small community was the natural homeland of democracy. The people can most easily control matters that are near at hand, Van Buren observed, and "popular justice" required decision by the "nearest tribunal." A large state, then, weakens the public's control and the quality of its judgment. The friends of republican government must attempt to keep the central government on as small a scale as possible, and they must defend the rights of states and localities. Nevertheless, republican government also requires the attempt to lead opinion out of the localities and prepare it for the governance of a large state.[27]

The political party would begin, like Jefferson's "ward system," with the localities where popular judgment is sound and public control is possible. Following the logic of Jefferson's argument, local partisan groups were to choose their natural leaders. Natural leaders from several localities, united in a face-to-face society of their own, would select their natural leaders. Ideally, an ascending hierarchy of face-to-face societies, connected by relations of personal trust, would connect the locality and the central state. In one sense, the design of the party was a new departure in political life. In

another, however, it appealed to an older order of things, and the tradi-
tionalism of the party recommended it to the private order. "Aristocracy,"
Tocqueville wrote, "had made a chain of all the members of the community,
from the peasant to the king: democracy breaks that chain, and severs every link of it."[28] In America, political parties would attempt to reforge the
chain, giving its metal a new democratic casting.[29]

Van Buren was realistically aware that this hierarchy of allegiance was
precarious, needing guileful maintenance. The small communities at the
base of the chain were always tempted to fall back into purely private concern. The fraternities of leaders that made up the chain were always in danger of fratricidal rivalries, on one hand, and, on the other, might become
so intensely loyal as to develop their own exclusive parochiality, rejecting
their obligations to the people below and to the larger Republic above.[30]
There was no way to avert these perils altogether, but at every level the
party would use all its resources—patronage, personal friendship, and public honor—to enlist the feelings of its members and to win and renew their
allegiance.[31]

Van Buren prescribed broad principles as the basis for party because,
among other things, they were suited to his educational aim. Narrow principles, however desirable, would alienate citizens at the outset, reducing
the ability of a party to create a public (and, of course, also increasing the
chances of electoral defeat). Beginning with sound opinion, the party sought
to persuade citizens that the division between the parties, defined by broad,
civic principles, was the vital conflict in American politics and that all other
differences, for political purposes at least, were ephemeral. Parties sought
to create civic identities, leading people to set aside, in public affairs, differences of religion, ethnicity, and class—except, of course, where those differences *paralleled,* rather than intersected, the lines of partisan division.[32]

The rhetoric of parties urged their followers to set aside lesser differences
in order to defeat the greater enemy. In this, as in many things, party politics
remains unchanged. Given the ancient and present animosities that divide
groups in America, some greater fear is probably necessary to dispel hostility. But to define a common enemy presumes some common standard by
which we can identify enemies and judge which are greater. Implicitly, a
common enemy defines a common good. Baptists and Deists were at log-
gerheads theologically, but both detested the established churches, and the
"wall of separation between church and state" defined the common de-
nominator of their political creed.[33]

The political party gave Americans a new political credo: "Everything
for THE CAUSE, nothing for men."[34] Parties, in other words, rejected

"government by men." The party, as an institution, led voters a long step away from *merely* personal allegiance toward loyalty to the Republic. But at the same time, "THE CAUSE" was something warmer and more personal than the "government of laws" contrived by the framers' "science of politics."[35]

Over time, American political parties did create civic allegiances. Partisan allegiance, for example, checked and sometimes overrode sectional loyalties in the years before the Civil War. Given the forces making for sectional conflict, it is not surprising that party feeling was ultimately unable to prevent war. It is more notable that party leaders tried, stubbornly and with some measure of success, to find a "national solution" and that they almost certainly delayed the advent of the war for many years.[36]

The urban machine often sought to connect various ethnic "tribes" to the larger polity; sometimes, the machines even helped to create local communities. For immigrants and urban newcomers, especially, party provided jobs and social services (though rather less frequently than the machines' admirers imagine); opportunities for friendship and social life; and perhaps most important, a "master cue" to an otherwise baffling and alien polity. The machine did its business, as George Washington Plunkitt boasted, surrounded by the symbols and rhetoric of patriotism, and if the machine's orators ran to copybook maxims, they did inculcate loyalty to the Republic. "This great and glorious country," Plunkitt declaimed, "was built up by the political parties." In considerable measure, he was right.[37]

Van Buren's theory presumed that the parties would teach republican virtue. That George Washington Plunkitt was no Coriolanus would neither have surprised nor disappointed Van Buren. He recognized that the teaching of party would, of necessity, seem tawdry, diffuse, and compromised with private interest when compared with the standard of civic virtue established by classical political philosophy. That more exacting ideal, however, was possible only in small states. Van Buren aimed to teach and preserve that form of republican virtue suited to a large state and specifically suited to America. Van Buren weighed political life in ancient scales, even if America fell far short of their highest measure.

Party Renewal and Civic Renewal

Whatever their virtues in the past, parties and party allegiance today seem to be in decay, and their role in American politics is radically decreased.[38]

Of course, the established parties are to some extent outdated. It is nearly forty years, after all, since the end of the Great Depression, the cataclysm that still defines the major lines of partisan division. The Jeffersonian and

Jacksonian party systems did not last so long, and forty years after the Civil War, the party system was beginning to experience the ferment of Progressivism.

There is abundant evidence, however, that the contemporary decline of political party is part of a general political decay. Americans live lives that are more and more specialized, live in towns and neighborhoods that are less and less stable, live in families that are more and more likely to break up or—increasingly—in casual liaisons, and live in private havens more and more penetrated by mass media and mass culture and by the now thoroughly international economy. The private order is increasingly fragmented, and people are more and more alone in the face of a more gigantic and confusing political world.[39]

A growing number of Americans are preoccupied with desperate efforts to protect and gratify the private self, a *wounded* and incomplete self that lacks the ability to make strong commitments to others or to trust them and that certainly fears to give political allegiance.

Evidently, this "culture of narcissism" is ruinous for political parties. The search for common civic identities, after all, is radically at odds with specialization, and parties depend on citizens with a sense of self coherent enough to be able to make enduring commitments.[40] American political parties grew up presuming a "right opinion" in localities, and they continued to rely on the private order to form the personal foundations of political character. For a long time, in fact, American parties have taken those foundations pretty much for granted. They can no longer do so. Party identification has, increasingly, come to be an *individual* response reflecting personal history rather than any connection to party life and activity.[41] Even in these terms, however, contemporary parties are troubled. Families, the last bastion of the private order, have traditionally conveyed party identification. Today, they seem to be losing the power to do so.[42] The basic assumptions of American party politics no longer hold: the foundation of the house is washing away.

At least part of the malaise of the parties, however, derives from the theories of party that dominate political discussion. Both the reforming tradition and its most articulate critics see party as a central, national institution reflecting essentially private interests and values. Both reject the idea of party as a civic educator and its corollary, the integral relation of party to the local small communities in which political participation and civic education are possible. Both, consequently, misunderstand our political parties and blind us to the needs and resources of parties in the contemporary crisis.

Progressivism, from which the reform tradition derives, distrusted party generally and sought to reduce it to a vehicle representing voters as *individuals*. The Progressive movement was hostile to any "distortion" of existing public sentiment by party leaders, but it also disliked "bloc" voting, even though such voting reflected public perceptions and feelings. Politics and party, in the Progressive view, should represent individual citizens, their attitudes, and their interests. Progressives hoped for public-spirited citizens, but they saw this "public spirit" as essentially a matter of private character, to be produced by personal education or "communication" or by "social reform." In the eyes of Progressives, all communities between the individual and the state were suspect because they exerted power over citizens, shaping their feelings and their alternatives. Valuable in many areas of life, Progressive theory has been a disaster when applied to political parties. For Progressives, the preferred form of politics is a mass election—a national primary or the initiative and referendum—in which the power of party is reduced to the vanishing point and in which localities are lumped together in indistinction. The reform tradition, consequently, must bear much of the responsibility for mass politics.[43]

Plenty of political scientists have addressed these faults of the reform tradition. One of the ablest, surely, was E. E. Schattschneider, a warm and eloquent partisan of party government who assailed the reformer's view of the political party. Party, Schattschneider argued, derived from caucuses, from the attempt of an organized minority to outweigh a disorganized and indifferent majority. Politics always involves a passive majority and an active minority.[44]

In his distaste for primaries, Schattschneider went on to argue that partisan voters are not "members" of a political party. Party has no control over the admission of such "members." They pay no dues, and they take on no obligations.[45] Schattschneider drew the apparently logical conclusion that partisan voters have no right to control intraparty affairs. (Revealingly, he drew an analogy between party voters and baseball fans and hence between party and a private business.) Partisan voters exert influence through their ability to reject a party's nominee: "The test is, does it bind? Not, how was it done?" A party is an association of "working professionals," and democracy is "not to be found *in* the parties but *between* them."[46]

Schattschneider's argument presents party as a species of private property and voters as political consumers. Certainly, his position rejects any role for party as a civic educator. His thesis contends that the public has an interest in the product but not in the process. Presuming that the two can be so separated, locality is superfluous. A mass, centralized party can have its products "tested" as well as any number of local ones. In fact, competition between the parties—as Schattachneider knew—exists at the national level but is relatively rare at the local level.[47] To argue that democracy exists "between" the parties is to create an imperative for centralized parties that inhabit the more competitive environment.

"Interparty democracy," moreover, deals only with elections, and Americans see voting and party as different things. In the United States, unlike Great Britain, people often vote for "the other side" without changing their party.[48] For the most part, American voters do not even *think* of changing party. The vote is something ephemeral and transient; party is closer to personal identity.

Party, for Americans, seems to involve a stable alliance with some people, a shared stance in relation to the state and to the political past. Party, in this sense, presumes we know who we are *with;* it does not imply that we necessarily agree on what *for.*[49] Historically, the Democratic Party has attracted citizens who felt themselves outsiders in relation to Anglo-American culture, localists and traditionalists who adhered to a creed older than the liberal tradition as well as social critics who find Lockean liberalism not modern enough.[50] There is a commonality implicit among these outsiders, but disagreement about policy is almost an inevitable by-product of the effort to discover it. Intraparty conflict is likely to be particularly intense because party is a kind of political family where feelings run high (and no arguments, as we all know, are more intense than political arguments within families).

People do change parties, of course, but people can also change nationalities. Party's hold is less powerful than that of nationality, but in both cases, people feel that to change is to lose a part of themselves. (To judge from the statistics, we take party identification more seriously than marriage: we leave it less frequently, and we stay unattached unless we feel ready for something like a lifetime commitment.)

The relative stability of party identification indicates that leaders and followers are part of a political community; theirs is a political relationship between rulers and ruled. The *terms* of this relationship will depend on authority. The machines—and party leaders generally—profited from the deference of traditionalistic peoples; similarly, at times of intense party competition, voters may be disposed to allow their leaders greater discretion.[51] But even when authority is most autocratic, voters are "insiders" and must be treated as such. Schattschneider is wrong: partisans *are* members, just as in *The Republic,* where even the artisans are citizens.

The decline of authority generally in the society and in the parties specifically compels the parties to become more internally democratic.[52] Party organizations that resist such a demand obdurately simply lose the allegiance of their partisans. The "democratization" of the parties, however, does *not* require primary elections: mass elections are neither the only nor the most admirable form of democratic choice.[53] In fact, if parties wish to retain or regain the allegiance of voters, primary elections are out of the question. Primaries suggest an electorate dominated by the mass media and campaigns that are costly and closed to the average citizen. The new "professionals," the media specialists who shape such campaigns, have no ties to particular publics (or even, for that matter, to particular parties); they are part of the mass with which they deal, faceless and unaccountable. In such campaigns, the electorate is passive, and, individually, voters know that they are unimportant: the public may "choose," but its choice does not convey allegiance.

By contrast, open local caucuses leading toward state and national conventions have genuine possibilities for democracy, party loyalty, and public opportunity spirit. They may not increase participation, but they do increase the opportunity for it, and that may be contribution enough. A caucus system, in the great tradition of Jefferson's ward republics, provides a smaller setting that permits deliberation, personal relationships, and perhaps the beginnings of a sort of political community.

Even so, parties will need to continue to respond—as, willy-nilly, they have been doing—to the demand that they become more "issue-oriented" or "ideological."[54] In part, this reflects greater education and concern for the "issues." But it also is a symptom of the decline of the affective bases of interpersonal trust. Traditionally, "ideology" meant an implicit doctrine embedded in the life and habits of a group.[55] In American politics, it means an explicit doctrine that *defines* a group. In fact, ideological politics often involves an intense desire for friendship, community, and personal dignity.[56] Ideology is a kind of test, a more sophisticated loyalty oath, designed to tell me who is worthy of my trust, but the test always fails of its intended effect. Ideological parties provide no affective certainty: one learns quickly that cognitive agreements may mask great differences of personality, taste, and motive. In ideological groups, interpersonal distrust is the rule. The ideological partisan says, "I will trust no one who does not agree with me," which is a way of saying, "I will trust no one at all; I will not allow you to do as you think best; you must do as I think best." A common ideology often seems to promise public spirit and civic identity: in fact, such groups are all roof and no foundation.

Political parties grew up outside government and to some extent at odds with it. Today, they may need its support. Traditional American political parties presumed, with Van Buren, that Americans had a "right opinion" heavily influenced by the traditional and religious creed of the private order. They used the local communities and personal identities of the private order as the starting points from which to build support for public policies and programs. Contemporary parties must begin with opinions rather than opinion, and their resources of allegiance are waning. If they and Americans generally are wise, however, they will turn their resources to the support of any public policies that can help to reconstruct the local and private foundations of "right opinion" and democratic life.

11

Democracy and Mystery: On Civic Education in America

DEMOCRACY, ACCORDING TO ONE TELLING, has no mysteries; it is open, artless, and unshadowed, resting on "commonplace prosperity in broad and simple daylight."[1] Mystery, on the other hand, is the instrument of hierarchy, central among the three powers—"miracle, mystery and authority"—through which Dostoevsky's Grand Inquisitor hoped to outlast "freedom, free thought and science." In the end, the Inquisitor prophesied, "We shall sit upon the beast, and raise the cup, and on it will be written, Mystery."[2] On these terms, democracy and mystery seem to be sworn enemies, locked in mortal quarrel.

Yet the mystery story is also the great, popular, literary form of our democratic culture. It is also the most common public approach to political theory, since it involves reflection on the distinction between good and evil, an exploration of the relationship between justice and law, and—perhaps most important—a venture into forbidden things. The mystery story, consequently, is a major text in our curriculum of civic education, which is just as it should be.[3]

A mystery, my dictionary instructs me, is something unexplained, unknown, or kept secret, especially when it excites our curiosity. Clearly, a mystery cannot be *wholly* secret or obscure: we confront a mystery only when we know the surface or outline of something that remains elusive and tantalizing. Similarly, the term *mystery* implies that we think of a problem or puzzlement as soluble in principle. Of course, in practice a mystery may prove impenetrable. Even the best detectives do not solve all their cases. Nevertheless, the detective who is haunted by old and unsolved cases is a

Originally published as "Democracy and Mystery: On Civic Education in America," *Halcyon: A Journal of the Humanities* 11 (1989): 43–56. Reprinted by permission of the Nevada Humanities Committee. McWilliams presented his ideas on the subject of mystery and democracy at the University of Nevada, Reno, on April 15, 1988, when he participated in the Fifth Biennial Leonard Conference, "Higher Education in America." This chapter appeared as an article based upon the comments he made on that occasion.

literary cliché; mysteries nag us. One can prove a mystery is insoluble, in the familiar paradox, only if one has *solved* the puzzle, so that one can claim to know what is unknowable.

Mystery moves us to seek education, just as education, rightly conducted, confronts us with mysteries.[4] And the two, mystery and education, inhabit a middle ground between the experience of perplexity and the solutions we seek. Read closely, the Grand Inquisitor tells a sort of truth: it is the inability to face "marvels and insoluble mysteries" that leads to the self-destruction of democratic liberty.[5] When a dictatorial regime attempts to repress doubt and curiosity, it works to shut off inquiry—that grand and Deweyan word—but so do intellectuals who deny the possibility of solution to the great human questions, as do those who maintain that seeking such solutions is unprofitable. In either their relativistic or utilitarian forms, such teachings are dangerous to American public life.

Democratic civic education and democratic teaching begin with a puzzle if not a mystery. Democratic aspiration levels up, aiming to raise all citizens to the highest possible level of excellence, but democratic practice entrusts the judgment of excellence to ordinary human beings. This emphasizes the fact that democracy is the most ambiguous and mysterious of regimes: ancient wisdom and common experience testify that ruling and being ruled require different sorts of knowledge and qualities of soul, but democracy demands that its citizens have both.

We expect the ruled to revere and obey the laws, to follow social and political custom where the laws issue no contrary order, and to live a decent private life, keeping up the appearances and respecting the proprieties in manners and conduct. In general, the ruled must live within the familiar; one who is ruled is, in the deepest sense, a *conventional* person, part of the life of the cave. Rulers, however, must be at least inwardly unconventional, since they are confronted by and must address the limits of law, of custom, and of the familiar. This is most clearly evinced in foreign policy, in the transformations worked by social and political change, and in the disruptions of fortune and the unpredictable. Rulers, in other words, must mediate between convention and nature, recognizing that precedent and opinion are at best imperfect guides and that appearances, in the profoundest sense, may be deceiving. As the ruled, we are free to enjoy our apparent prosperity (if we are not numbered among the poor); as rulers, we must ask whether this well-being is soundly founded or conceals threatening faults. And in the same way, a ruling wisdom would have heard the "sounds of silence" in the 1950s that foretold the coming storm.[6]

Facing conflict between convention and nature, rulers ordinarily seek to mend the fabric of law and custom. However, there are times when the cloth is worn out, when the laws no longer teach or are even compatible with virtue. In the small town where Ronald Reagan grew up, reliance on the help of "friends and neighbors" was a rule that combined compassion with respect for dignity. In an impersonal state like California, where the "friends and neighbors" of the desperate are apt to share their distress, the same rule—invoked by then-governor Reagan as a standard for welfare policy—is a formula for indifference or hardheartedness. In modern regimes, we depend on the help of strangers.[7] Moreover, it is possible that the things a regime values are wrongly ranked or no virtues at all, requiring the correction of teaching, if not command.[8]

In short, rulers must be intellectually shameless and sometimes must act in ways that are shocking, violations of the ordinary code of right. For example, Lincoln was high-handed in his defense of the Union, but almost all Americans admire his statecraft. It ought to be clear, however, that rulers are also dangerous; even well-intentioned leaders bear a terrible responsibility for the times when their calculations are not correct. Richard Nixon appealed to Lincoln's precedent at the time of Watergate, Franklin Roosevelt authorized the evacuation of Japanese Americans, and we must consider ourselves fortunate that Harry Truman did not act on his belief that, contrary to appearances, Stalin was an avuncular soul, the prisoner of the Politburo.[9]

Ruling, at the very least, requires learning and practice, but American democracy gives most of us very little practice in ruling. Ordinarily, a citizen is not a ruler who is ruled—Aristotle's definition—but a subject who has rights. Despite this lack of training, however, the Republic does ask us to be rulers, if only infrequently. We judge our rulers when we vote; sometimes, we hold office or sit on juries, directly engaging in the practice of rule; and the amending process makes it at least possible that we will have to pass on the adequacy of the Constitution itself. American citizens cannot be simply law-abiding; they must also be law-finding and law-making.

Aristocracy separates rulers and ruled by class, and class or rank establishes the boundary of political mystery (as in "the divinity that doth hedge a king"). By contrast, in a democracy, ruler and ruled are united in one person. However, in political practice, ruling and being ruled are separated by *times*, so that at certain times—that is, on election day—one is and should act like a ruler. As ancient wisdom taught us, this change of roles or states requires ritual and preparation, a separation from the world of the ruled and an entry, through the mystery, into the world of rulers. And ritual is just as necessary before we reenter the world of the ruled. Athens had both

Eleusis and the Dionysia, and as Plato taught in *Crito*, decent citizens may need to be shown a mystery in which laws give reasons as well as commands, the meeting ground between philosophy and the city.

In the United States, there is still some sanctity around the shrouded voting booth. One of my great-aunts believed that God would guide her when she marked her ballot, and he surely did, since she always voted the straight Democratic ticket. Even today, election years redivide the public, separating us from some friends and relatives and uniting us, temporarily, to "strange bedfellows" (as Harvey Mansfield recently had occasion to remind Richard Rorty).[10] But as boundaries and forms grow weaker in *social* life, they grow stronger in *public* life. Intellectually, the stakes of our politics have never been greater, but our feelings about politics do not match them. "Strange bedfellows," that echo of Eleusis, have become as routine in politics as they are in social life. Our politics is losing its mystery and hence its charm.

For all its problems, the university is—for the sizable minority who can attend it—the best chance for initiation into the mysteries of rule. Matriculation involves a separation from the world of convention, a time spent in a sphere of relative (and sometimes not so relative) shamelessness, justified by the contagion of high truths and puzzles. In this sense, Tom Hayden's early sixties description of student life as a "parenthesis" amounts to a form of praise. Universities are dangerous, like all the mysteries, but also necessary and invaluable.

Recall that democratic aspiration turns on a mystery, the conviction that the many have a capacity to appreciate excellence, if only in a rough, untutored way. This natural inclination requires example and education or, to use two richly archaic words, refining and edifying, especially through the study of excellent works that one could not produce (or not yet produce) oneself. The great work is a common standard of democracy, uniting the ambitious, who hope to equal or surpass the mark, and the humble, who are content to admire it. But who is to select the works that deserve to be called great?

Democracy's political first principle answers, "The people themselves," and the people—aware of how easily they can be deceived by the "artful and designing"—prefer to be guided by custom.[11] The people are also wedded to the idea of a practical or vocational education (to which I will return), but the great books, those symbols of elitism, probably receive their strongest support from ordinary citizens.

Teachers may interpose their own judgments, introducing new works or older but neglected texts. Nevertheless, those of us who teach must recognize that our authority depends on popular respect for teachers and for our vocation. In a democracy, academic authority and academic freedom are hierophantic, bound up with the mysteries of the city, democracy's higher truths.

American democracy, in fact, involves a dispute between high teachings, and American political life has been shaped by a contest between mysteries.

For what can be called "classical" democratic theory, the central mystery is *equality*. "All men are created equal" is a proposition clearly at odds with common sense: human beings, as G. K. Chesterton thought it necessary to remind us, are not equally tall or equally tricky; they are not equal in wisdom or passion or goodness. The Declaration's "self-evident" truth is not obvious; it is self-evident only to those who understand the term "men." Consequently, knowing this self-evident truth presumes a knowledge of human nature that is neither instinctive nor attested by the appearances.

Older republican theory held that coming to know human nature—and hence equality—requires political society. The Anti-Federalist "Republicus" accepted the proposition that human beings originate in an "unconnected state, or as some say, in a state of nature." But Republicus's phrasing—"as some say"—makes clear that he does *not* regard this unconnected state as natural. In his view, reason, and not preservation, is "the great, primary and never-ceasing law of nature," and reason demands that we govern our passions and our desire for dominion. For Republicus, a truly natural state, like truly natural liberty, entails awareness of "connections" and hence government according to "the greatest good of the whole, and of every individual as a part of the whole."[12]

Another Anti-Federalist, "William Penn," echoed the teaching: natural right is the liberty to do what is naturally right. Moreover, what is good by nature can be discovered only through reflection and in society. It was first discovered by philosophers—the first, if "Penn" is correct, to be truly free—and is ordinarily known only to the few. However, "William Penn" held, here in America, knowledge of what is naturally right has been planted in opinion as a part of common knowledge. This fortunate opinion, the bond between the people and philosophy, is far too unusual to be taken for granted; it must be preserved through education.[13]

This insistence on right education, an Anti-Federalist theme, reflected their recognition that the knowledge of equality is a high and imperiled mystery. It requires political society, yet no political society can *practice* equality. W. S. Gilbert's Inquisitor had it right in *The Gondoliers*: "When every one is somebodee / Then no one's anybody." Even the most egalitarian society must make distinctions between vice and virtue and rank us

according to our achievement, as in the argument that "elitism" is repre-
hensible. Moreover, as every Socialist regime has discovered, the division of
labor is bound to result in inequalities of power, if not property. In practice,
the Maryland Farmer wrote, an equality of rights may be the best we can
achieve, yet we cannot lose sight of equality as an *end*, an "ardent desire
and unceasing pursuit" written by nature in every human soul.[14]

The Anti-Federalists, following older republican teaching, held up the
ideal of a regime that is small, simple, and relatively austere. In the first
place, such a polity minimizes the tension between equality as an end and
politics as a means. Limiting the division of labor, it also makes politics
comprehensible, whereas a large republic, "Cato" argued, is "too intricate
and perplexed and too misterious for you to see and observe." Like his Anti-
Federalist fellows, "Cato" distrusted "misterious" political practice because
it excludes citizens from the mysteries of ruling. Further, the very limitations
on practice in small republics direct ambition toward the mysteries of the
soul. According to "A Customer," the "Principles of 1775" hold that
the people should be devoted "to the study of politicks and of religion"
as the pillars of human excellence. Instead, the Constitution, indifferent to
religion, usurps politics for the few.[15]

Originally directed against the Constitution, such arguments, *under* the
Constitution, emphasize the need for schools and seminaries to counterbalance the effect of "misterious" laws, upholding the doctrine of equality
against the idea of separateness. Advocates of such republican schooling
at the time of the founding—whether Anti-Federalists or supporters of the
Constitution like Benjamin Rush—were inclined to regard religious education as indispensable in the curriculum of citizenship. Though the Bible is
"a more difficult book to read *well* than many others," Rush observed, it is
still the surest defense of human equality.[16]

There are good reasons on Rush's side. I offer only one example, from
Paul, a galloping sexist and hence an unpromising interpreter of equality.
The eleventh chapter of Romans addresses the question: how can God's
promises to Israel be reconciled with Paul's reception of gentiles? To put it
another way, how can the division of human beings into political societies—
and a rank order among those societies, implicit in the idea of a "chosen
people"—be squared with the doctrine of equality?

Paul begins by arguing that the inward qualities of the soul are both the
crucial test of election and the aim of the law. Grace of spirit, however, is to
some extent unpredictable. In the first place, this excellence of soul does not
always come to people reared in the law, schooled by a good regime, just as
first-rate parents do not invariably produce first-rate children. And second,

inward grace is sometimes found in people who have not been raised in a good society; as we witness, there are towers of moral strength amid the most terrible deprivation. Both philosophy and common sense agree with this critique of the law, and Paul's readers can hardly have been surprised by it.

Paul goes on, however, to maintain that grace in the absence of a right political education is "contrary to nature," like grafting a wild olive onto a good olive tree. It is possible but only through art and fortune. Moreover, this grafting is possible at all only because of a still more fundamental likeness of species. In other words, Paul is arguing that Christian congregations are an unnatural second best, requiring attention and discipline and possible at all only because of equality. "For I would not, brethren, that ye should be ignorant of this mystery, lest ye be wise in your own conceits." What grace Christians can claim is due to God, whose wisdom is "unsearchable" and whose ways are "past finding out."[17]

Yet Paul himself searches and offers an explanation of this particular mystery.[18] His claim is not so much that God's ways are *unknowable* as that they are *inimitable*: human beings lack the wisdom and power to overthrow the ordinary rule of nature and must live subject to natural distinctions.

Nevertheless, the excellent soul, discerning equality—"the fellowship of the mystery which from the beginning of the world hath been hid in God"— will await the opportunity to realize it. Distinctions between human beings may be naturally necessary or useful, but they lack divine sanction. Distinctions bear the burden of proof; in Paul's teaching, equality is the *rule*.[19]

There is an element of conservatism in Paul's doctrine that may offend modern sensibilities. To wrestle with Paul's argument, however, is to comprehend equality better. In fact, we may need to confront antiquity to understand ourselves.

The ancients founded philosophy *on* mystery, the questions and perplexities that arouse wonder. For classical political philosophy, the starting point was incertitude, Socrates' knowledge of ignorance. American institutions, on the other hand, were framed in terms of modern theories that turn from the *puzzle* to the *given*.

Those newer teachings set out to banish mystery from theory, aiming to begin with certitudes that hold the keys to practical success, following Machiavelli's rejection of unseen cities in favor of *la verità effettuale*, that truth that gets results. Hence Descartes' familiar claim to found philosophy on "clear and certain knowledge of all that is useful to life" or the promise of his character, Eudoxe, to "reveal . . . secrets so simple that henceforth you will wonder at nothing in the works of our hands."[20]

The foundation of certitude, in this new method, is the self but not the self as an object of mystery, as when we ask, "Why am I here?" inquiring into the relation of the self to the whole. Rather, modern doctrines begin with that self that we know intimately, the bodily self, separate from all things.

Descartes' method led him to doubt all propositions about the world, about the self in its relationships. In order to carry methodical doubt to its ultimate conclusion, at important points in his argument Descartes was forced to posit a deceiving "evil genius" as the author of apparent truths. This view of the world regards nature as hostile rather than mysterious, and that enmity drives individuals back to the self as the only safe ground of knowledge. By contrast, Augustine derived knowledge *of* the self from its relationships, whether deceptive or not: "If I am deceived, I am."[21] This sort of self-knowledge, however, immediately raises questions. About what am I deceived? And how shall I separate the false from the true? Augustine's formulation entails mystery rather than the basis for deduction. Modern theory preferred to begin with the bodily self and its desires because such a starting point, if low, seems reliable and universal. And this new, theoretical certainty makes it possible to turn to a *new* mystery in practice.

Descartes, for example, envisioned an "infinity of artifices that would enjoy, without any pain, the fruits of the earth." Artifices—those "works of our hands" at which we are not to "wonder"—become infinite, equaling and even outdoing the creator. God, after all, made a world in which there was *one* fruit that could not be enjoyed "without pain." Descartes' artifices, by contrast, will remake humanity and enable us, as "masters and owners of nature," to painlessly enjoy all fruits.[22]

The new mystery of modern teaching is science or, more properly, technology. When my children speak the strange language of computers, I am reminded that in the contemporary world we more and more experience one another's knowledge and speech as mysteries. The Babel of specializations pervades the university and society. Ancient political philosophy held that the polis requires at least a language of the common good and that each regime implicitly defines a ruling type, an idea of the best life. Modern political philosophy, on the other hand, set out to rebuild Babel, the city of dispersed speech and the thousand and one goals, on the basis of political science, confident that this new Babel could really scale the heavens.[23]

The new science of politics designed and relied on complex, relatively incomprehensible institutions, through which "men are so led that they think themselves not to be led, but to live by their own mind and free opinion."[24]

In this way, the variety of human types, each moved by its own passions, can be channeled so as to advance mastery and freedom. Accordingly, political and social science have become preoccupied with mechanisms of great power, like the market or "checks and balances" in which "functional rationality" displaces substantive reason.[25]

The new mystery, to sum up, is not in the soul but in science and technology and in the laws. This establishes the rank order of the modern university, in which the humanities—still dealing with the soul—are subordinate to both the high-class natural sciences and technologies ("science and useful arts" in the language of article 1 of the Constitution) and the social sciences, still cursed with a middling station.

In the liberal teaching that shaped our laws, the goal or highest mystery is not equality but mastery and dominion over nature or (to use the gentler term) liberty. John Locke does speak of human beings as equal by nature, but as he later explains this really refers to "that equal right that every man hath to his natural freedom."[26] Locke's argument does reject any rank order in nature but also any obligation that interferes with one's own preservation. In any case, the absence of hierarchy is not the same thing as the presence of equality. Equality does not require the belief that there are no ranks or differences among human beings; rather, it demands the conviction that *one* quality, our common humanity, outranks all other differences. Locke's doctrine, by contrast, holds that we are alike chiefly in being separate.

Our laws and the modern side of our culture teach us to pursue individual freedom and technological mastery, and to an increasing extent, we do. Yet this quest tends to be haunted and more than a little desperate, for separateness within large-scale institutions proves to involve a new kind of domination. At the beginning, Hobbes taught us that in the market we may compete as individuals, but we are ruled by the opinion of others.[27] In the same way, Tocqueville indicated that individuals, overwhelmed by mass opinion, succumb even inwardly to the tyranny of the majority. On the quiz show "Family Feud," contestants win by guessing correctly what a hundred persons surveyed have responded to various questions: we are thereby instructed that knowing the opinion of the many is a more valuable skill than knowing whether the many are right.

Technology, of course, has its own terrors. Ancient myth was preoccupied with the line between beasts and men, concerned to defend the right order of nature. Many of our current myths, by contrast (I think of the Bionic Man and Woman or my particular antipathy, He-Man and the Masters of the Universe), are caught up with the distinction between human beings and machines. Our growing sense of likeness to our own artifacts involves the implication that we, artifact-like, can ourselves be made or shaped—presuming, of course, that we survive at all.

The dark side of our heritage prompts more and more Americans into desperate flight from the threatening and inconstant world of social and technological power to the private places of the soul. Relativism, now ubiquitous, fulfills Tocqueville's prediction, urging us to avoid bonds to places, to times, to persons, and to institutions—which are "all relative"—in favor of what works.

> Thus not only does democracy make every man forget his ancestors, but it hides his descendants, and separates his contemporaries, from him; it throws him back forever upon himself alone, and threatens in the end to confine him entirely within the solitude of his own heart.[28]

Americans are increasingly inclined to speak a language of radical individualism, proclaiming their uniqueness and denying that there is any commensurability—any dimension of equality—between cultures, persons, and genders. There may be a kind of ultimate portent in deconstructionism, which tends to see any speech as a form of domination (even if a failed one), suggesting that the only real freedom is found in the wordless privacies of the self.

Our citizens need to relearn common speech and common life, and both are founded on the great mystery of equality. Universities, for their part, need to resume (or assume) the role that classical republicans prescribed for them, as the counterbalance of the Republic, devoted to the mysteries of equality and of rule. I began with the fact that in the mystery story, popular literature touches fingertips with political philosophy. In *The Simple Art of Murder*, Raymond Chandler, that nonpareil, described the essence of his craft as a journey down mean streets by a human being who is "neither tarnished nor afraid," a detective who is "complete" because he is both "common" and "unusual" and engaged in an "adventure in search of hidden truth."[29] That is not a bad standard for our students or ourselves.

12

National Character and National Soul

CHARACTER IS A FINE, AUTUMNAL WORD, with echoes of Protestant gentility and sherry in the afternoon.[1] As for national character, it has an even more archaic ring: even when I was an undergraduate, we were taught to distrust the term as a generalization with racist undertones, at least vaguely associated with "soul stuff"—one of Arthur Bentley's dismissive descriptions of psychological analyses of politics, as opposed to his own focus on group behavior.[2] It is not surprising, then, that although our character as a people is much on our minds, we prefer to speak of it in euphemisms and neologisms, most often "political culture," that serviceable borrowing from anthropology.[3] Political theorists, however, have a long-standing claim to be unfashionable in speech; these days, some of them even refer to the soul.[4] So, when I use these older terms, I rely on your indulgence as due to my age and vocation.

The Nature of Character

"Character," the dictionary tells me, is "the aggregate of features or traits that form the *apparent* nature of a person or thing" (the emphasis is mine), and it goes on to list, among other definitions, a part or a role and a visual mark or symbol, also mentioning that in Roman Catholic theology, character is an imprint on the soul made by efficacious sacraments.[5] Character, in other words, is an appearance or external form, a role played with sufficient regularity that it becomes second nature. Still, we recognize that character is not entirely reliable, that individuals and peoples can be—and, at times, may even need to be—"out of character," as in the admiring saying that went around Warsaw during the Hungarian uprising of 1956, as reported by the late George Lanyi: "The Hungarians are behaving like Poles."

Originally published as "National Character and National Soul," *Willamette Journal of the Liberal Arts* 12 (Summer 2002): 25–35. Reprinted with the permission of Willamette University.

"Soul," by contrast, refers to something altogether more fundamental and mysterious, invisible and to some extent ineffable. Still, when we know someone well, over a long time—when we have puzzled over quirks and inconsistencies and unguarded moments—we can get at least some idea of the soul behind the appearances.[6] So, making all the necessary qualifications and allowances for exceptions, it is possible to say that, just as nations can be said to have character, they can be said to have souls.[7]

It should be noted, however, that national character is dependent on and manifested in generalized patterns of behavior, the conduct of the many. By contrast, the soul of a nation, its vital principle, is a quality of the whole, which may be reflected only in a few or even in one. In the *Apology*, Socrates is tried by the Assembly, Athens in its most democratic character. Against the charge that he corrupts Athenian youth, he leads Meletus to claim that Socrates alone does so and that ordinary Athenian citizens can raise excellent children. But in addition to other aspects of his response, Socrates shows that Athenians ordinarily assume it is "the one"—the best or most skilled teacher—who would elevate and the many who would achieve mediocre results.

Democratic in their public character, in other words, Athenians are far more "elitist" in their private lives.[8] Socrates' very example, horse-trainers, underlines this. In the first place, horse ownership was a characteristic of the Athenian upper class. More important, horse-trainers educate horses to compete and win, in races or battle, but not to evaluate the goal. And Meletus, by applying the principle to "all other animals," suggests that Athenians do not want children suited to democratic deliberation, with its sharing of ruling and being ruled, but single-minded pursuers of rank and victory.[9] The souls of Athenians, consequently, do not suit Athens as a polity: if Athens has a soul, it may be found in Socrates.

But souls are evidently hard to discern and hard to regulate: the American framers gave it up, holding that both practicality and right rule out any attempt to legislate directly about the soul. Character, however, is inevitably influenced, more or less strongly, by circumstance—by the audience to which a character seeks to send its message—and hence is more fit as a concern of the laws. "In all very numerous assemblies, of whatever characters composed," Madison wrote in a striking passage, "passion never fails to wrest the scepter from reason. Had every Athenian citizen been a Socrates, every Athenian assembly would still have been a mob."[10] Madison's reasoning is starkly illustrative: there may be exceptional souls, although Madison pointedly does not say so, but as a political rule, reason is the servant of the passions and character is more or less a pose and an act, dependent on the praise and blame of society.

Character, in that sense, belongs to the public sphere and is subject to shaping and legislative intervention. The soul, by contrast, belongs to the reserved order of private right. I take it as obvious that the framers shaped our laws and institutions in a way designed to build a broadly liberal civic character, that is, citizens imbued with a sense of their rights; convinced of a reasonable obligation to fulfill contracts (the only duty acknowledged in the Constitution) and extending to others a moderate, somewhat diffident trust; and disposed to tolerance, though recognizing the need for order—in short, devoted to private ends and, for the most part, private life but able to cooperate for public purposes. The Constitution, in those terms, is given over to a temperate version of liberal theory.

Yet the framers also relied on stronger, deeper foundations for obligation than calculations of interest can afford, if only—as Benjamin Franklin said in relation to the doctrine of Particular Providences—for "weak and ignorant Men and Women and . . . inexperienced and inconsiderate Youth."[11] They assumed a moral education, a soul-crafting, that was classical and religious, imparted by families, churches, communities, and schools. However, as Anti-Federalists fulminated, they gave that education no standing in the laws, partly because doing so would have run against the framers' ideas of legitimate politics as based in reason and consent rather than inculcation and partly because they relied on the promptings of an innate moral sense. Nevertheless, they looked to at least two teachings, religion and natural right—neither of which is invoked in the Constitution—to provide souls that, first of all, see contracts as sacred, secure against all but the most extreme temptations and reasons to break promises once made. ("The taking away of God . . . though but even in thought, dissolves all," Locke had written, and though the American framers were less dogmatic, they came close.)[12]

Second, republican souls require a certain manliness about their rights— a disposition to defend those rights at the price of comfort and risk and even a willingness to sacrifice those rights to defend the freedom of others. Thus, arguing for the defendants in the Boston Massacre trial, John Adams appealed to the unqualified claims of self-preservation and the right to kill anyone who threatens one's life. "That is a point I would not give up for my right hand," Adams declaimed, "nay for my life."[13] It was an argument that did not spontaneously arise from the theory, but it surely reflected a spirit that the framers valued.

Finally, the framers expected and desired souls notable for their generosity, for a humanitarian spirit that expresses itself in care for the helpless and dependent. Reason, Locke observed, had been insufficient, even in the "civilized parts" of the ancient world, to convince parents that they should not kill their children by exposing them. In forbidding infanticide, revealed religion is consistent with reason, Locke held, but extends its obligations and gives them force.[14] The framers relied, in other words, on a largely Christian soul informed by natural right, to support and supply the deficiencies of liberal character, building a republic that—in Tocqueville's formulation—depended on a certain equilibrium between the "spirit of liberty," embedded in the laws and in economic life, and the "spirit of religion," whose strong citadel was the heart.[15]

America's Character

Every great analyst of American character and culture, I think, has recognized that America is conflicted, paradoxical, or ironic, a regime whose reality is not confined to what is apparent: the American character, in short, cannot be understood without reference to the American soul.[16] For example, Perry Miller, that nonpareil, wrote a predictably splendid study, *The American Character,* back in 1962, in which he argued that America is framed by the tension between the "business civilization," ostensible in America's life and conduct, and the "inner propulsion" of the American soul, whose basic qualities—guilt for falling short and the obligation to redeem—Miller traced to Puritanism.[17] (If it needs saying, Miller regarded the soul as in danger, given the American temptation to pursue a material prosperity—fulfilling Winthrop's foreboding—that would end in a society based on machines and technique rather than human craft and virtue.)[18]

Many years before Miller, the marvelously urban Dr. Oliver Wendell Holmes—Holmes père, for the uninstructed—always recognized that the liberalism he cherished rested on more profound spiritual foundations, the "inarticulate major premise" to which his now more celebrated son referred us. Nowhere is this clearer than in *The Professor at the Breakfast Table* (vol. 2 of Holmes's Autocrat series). The central character in this story, "Little Boston," is a zealous American patriot, passionately devoted to personal and spiritual liberty and—descended from an ancestress hung at Salem—convinced of the need to "Americanize" religion as well as politics. A champion of progress as both opportunity and necessity (and hence, like most of his countrymen, indifferent to the fate of Indian cultures), he declares that "America . . . is the only place where man is full-grown."[19] Yet the appearances don't sustain his claim: Little Boston himself is shrunken and deformed. He has one good feature, a beautiful and muscular left arm (on which he wears a ring memorializing his martyred ancestress and hence the claims of liberty against religion), and he constantly puts that visibly best side forward. When Little Boston is dying, however, the Professor discovers that his heart is on the right side, and when his closely guarded secret cabinet is examined, it proves to contain an ivory crucifix. Holmes was saying, I think, that the best case for America, for all its deformities and occasional beauties, is that its heart is on the right side and that, at some deep level, it identifies with the agony of suffering humanity.

One final example: sketching American characteristics in 1948, Ralph Barton Perry began with a familiar list of liberal qualities. Americans, he argued, are individualists, albeit of a collective sort; optimists; people who expect success and want their achievements to be "observed, recorded, applauded and envied"; competitive, although in ways that are kept from being deadly by confidence in ultimate success; and inclined toward uniformity by the universal, egalitarian quality of their competition and comparison (on that point, I am reminded of a recent Toyota commercial that tells us that Americans want to be number one, the very best; most of us, therefore, want the best; and thus—with a logic that would stun either Aristotle or Ramus—that what most of us want is best and that we should buy a Toyota because it is best-selling); and finally, that Americans are relatively law-abiding but inclined to resist legislation where it interferes with valued aspects of private life, particularly where it involves drink, taxation, or (in a portentous observation) sex.[20]

Even today, this is a shrewd list. But at the end of his book, Perry indicates some "fundamental principles of Americanism" that he calls "simple and trite" but that, I think, seem quite different from the characteristics with which he began: individual responsibility; dedication to the good as one sees it; accepting the "burden of service"; cooperation toward "an end which is greater than anyone because it embraces all"; intelligence; love; kindness, generosity and sympathy; and the Golden Rule.[21] In other words, Americans, as Perry saw them, have characteristics that are not easily compatible with their souls. In American history, that dialectic, often bitterly argumentative, has generally been respectful, a civil rivalry defining the distinctive equilibrium of the Republic.[22] To Tocqueville, however, the long-term problem was obvious. Allied with the strength and authority of the law, the "spirit of liberty" is increasingly strong in shaping the "habits of the heart," so that over the years, character wins a growing dominion over soul.[23]

In *Democracy in America,* Tocqueville argues that "self-interest rightly understood," the all but universal moral language of Americans, is probably the theory "best suited" to the times. But his tempered appreciation is limited further by the fact that Americans, who frequently act from nobler and less interested motives, are embarrassed to admit it. "They are more anxious to do honor to their philosophy than to themselves."[24] In this respect, American speech—and hence American politics—denies or distorts the American soul: the soul is denied a voice for its discontent, hampered in the effort to find through discourse a new basis for the "implicit self-sacrifice and instinctive virtue" that, in Tocqueville's view, were "already flitting away."[25] Yet Tocqueville also thought that the demands of the soul are "constituent principles of human nature," more fundamental than any civic character and bound to make themselves felt, at least periodically.[26] Secular society that ignores the soul, in these terms, has defined its own inner nemesis, and so it is in contemporary America, as increasingly the national soul speaks incoherently and ineffectively in its attempts to refine and educate our national character.

Character Building

In the first place, civil society—especially in the schooling of the soul—is characterized by much greater moral and cultural diversity; not yet a cacophony, it falls considerably short of harmony. The great traditional religious confessions are divided by the "culture war," a contest that defines itself morally at least as much as theologically.[27] At the same time, new religious communities are growing rapidly. Even Islam has come to seem relatively familiar, so that Pat Robertson was moved to comment that it at least has biblical roots.[28] And though upwards of 90 percent of Americans continue to say they believe in God, that datum, closely examined, also shows cultural fragmentation: 12 percent of these say that they believe in a "life-force" or "spirit"—including astrology, New Age spiritualism, extra-terrestrial influences, or neopaganism—rather than a personal deity.[29]

Beyond religion, American culture was once characterized by a broad familiarity with the Anglo-European past, a tradition that was the particular province of schools but that is fading into memory. Our areas of cultural commonality, in that sense, are growing thin, especially in contrast to the ways in which we are being unified by an ever more integrated economy, linked instantaneously by the media and information technology. To the extent that we have common texts, they are likely to be derived from the media—in fact, increasingly from commercials—in images that rival or pre-empt socialization and displace the ancient oral traditions of childhood. In relation to politics, the evidence is overwhelming and not much relieved by its comic dimension: in an introductory American government class at Rutgers in 1998, 54 percent of students could name the president's pet, but only 11 percent could name even one member of the Supreme Court, so it is not surprising that the best-known American jurist was not Chief Justice Rehnquist but Judge Judy.[30]

American character is defined by an increasingly radical individualism suited to the logic of the market and technology. Consider, for example, Laurence Tribe's criticism of efforts to prohibit human cloning. Any distinction between "natural" and "unnatural," Tribe argues, inhibits "experiment," particularly alternative forms of "erotic attachment, romantic commitment, genetic replication, gestational mothering and the joys and responsibilities of child rearing."[31] There should not be much need to point out the chilling implications of Tribe's elevation of "experiments" by and on humans to a preferred status in law. (Nor is there much comfort in Richard Rorty's happy assurance that "experiments with new forms of individual and social life will become unthinkably diverse"; the ones we can remember, let alone think of, are troubling enough.)[32] And there should not be much more need to remind us that the identification of our natural rights was meant to "inhibit" experiments at surrendering what belongs to us unalienably. However, I do want to draw attention to the ways in which even Tribe's argument is limited, even contradicted, by the residual influence of America's national soul. Tribe insists that child rearing has numerous acceptable forms but—or am I missing something?—that it naturally has "joys and responsibilities." So it does. But isn't Tribe worried about chilling the freedom to experiment with irresponsibility? Better not ask: like Tocqueville's Americans, he might feel obliged to honor his philosophy rather than himself. A good deal of contemporary opinion, after all, shows signs of leaning in that direction.

The great majority of Americans continue to assert at least a belief in traditional values and institutions.[33] At the same time, they are disinclined to constrain people who deviate from those standards: in a recent *Washington Post* poll, a sizable majority worried that America is "on the wrong track" morally, but 70 percent also declared that we should be "more tolerant of those who choose to live according to their own moral standards, even if we think they are wrong."[34] This zealous toleration reflects a shadow on the national soul. Responding to such questions, Americans are apt to cite

"Judge not, that ye be not judged," almost their only spontaneous reference to scripture.[35] So much for the good news; it is also a very distorted reference. In Matthew 7:1, Jesus is not arguing that you should not judge but that you should be willing to have the same standard applied to yourself: "For with the judgment you pronounce, you will be judged, and the measure you give will be the measure you get" (7:2). Jesus is not urging a passive toleration but a generous, egalitarian engagement: he does not suggest we should leave a speck in our brother's eye, only that we should clean our own first (7:5). Christian teaching, however, in the language of American character, is translated into the idiom of unfettered personal choice and the public principle that one should not interfere with others, the tendency that Harvey Mansfield calls "creeping libertarianism."[36] Increasingly, at least in their public character, Americans are apt to be complaisant, following convenience, avoiding conflict, and making commitments only with escape routes carefully preserved. They do not show any notable willingness to sacrifice and not even much generosity; unwilling to constrain their fellows, Americans are also not greatly disposed to help them.

David Levering Lewis recently asked, if Americans are really so tolerant, how do we explain their apparent indifference to the country's growing economic inequality?[37] Yet surely, it ought to be evident that one can be tolerant of inequality; to care about it would require a standard of duty, not toleration. And though I am happy to criticize the market, the media, and the bad guys in Washington, intellectual fashions are part of the problem, most obviously in the emphasis on our differences and diversities that discounts the ways in which we are akin. Even more egalitarian thinkers often fail to help much.

Richard Rorty's *Achieving Our Country*, for example, appeals to us to put "social justice" above "individual freedom" as our principal goal and to love our country for its "promise" of "being kinder and more generous than other countries." These ideals, held up as a standard for practice, Rorty defines as loyalty to a "dream country."[38]

Yet Rorty's heroes, Whitman and Dewey, whatever their faults, saw the American promise as growing out of the facts, the extension of experience, following the logic of science if not moral necessity. Similarly, Dr. King's echoing dream envisioned Americans coming awake, seeing their fellows as they truly are, by the light of nature. "Dreams" in Rorty's sense, only so many preferences and fantasies, tend to remain that: they leave us excited by night and discontented during the day (like George Babbitt's image of himself as a woodsman), but they do not compel us, particularly in the face of opposing inconveniences and powers. Kindness and generosity as dreams lack the force of obligations that we owe our kind and genre, debts that command and that can help to free us from fears, temptations, and superficialities.[39] Moreover, Rorty's ideal itself is profoundly deficient. Americans want more than kindness and generosity, just as they are "restless amid their prosperity."[40] They yearn for dignity in a world that makes its possession ever more difficult and insecure. The media and, more generally, the weakening of community confront us with superstars, making our local honors seem tawdry.[41] Jobs are unstable and insecure; inequality is escalating; there is sharper competition for good jobs and within the workplace, which, as Kristin Downey Grimsley writes, may have become "leaner" but is definitely "meaner."[42] And home is altogether too likely to have its own uncertainties when it is not, as it is for too many of us, a place of loneliness and silence.[43]

Above all, we feel ourselves caught up in a world ruled by great interests and forces, like globalism and technology, no less powerful for being shadowy, half visible, and less comprehended.[44] That they have benefits and great ones only heightens our sense of dependence. Government, so overwhelming in relation to individuals, increasingly appears unable to do more than qualify or adapt to these dominations and powers. Across the industrial world, allegiance to political institutions is on the decline, and to a growing number of Americans, self-government looks to be little more than myth and memory.[45]

Most Americans, however, are still convinced, despite their disenchantment with the folly and ineptitude of those who occupy high places, that democratic institutions offer our best hope for a dignified character. The common ground of the American character and the American soul was and remains citizenship, the principle that Chesterton saw as the ruling tenet of this "nation with the soul of a church," the doctrine that "no man must aspire to be anything more than a citizen, and that no man shall endure to be anything less."[46] And although the practical problem of revitalizing citizenship is enormous, it is challenging rather than insuperable.

More fundamentally, however, we have to be concerned for the education of American souls. All the institutions of civil society are involved, but churches and schools have a special need to articulate first principles, the great texts and traditions of philosophy and theology, cultivating the mystery on which reason relies and that faith explains, that the universe is humanly intelligible.[47] In this spirit, I come back—as Americans always must—to the Declaration of Independence, which tells us that we indeed have rights but as endowments from the creator. Paradoxically, then, our liberties are entails that we cannot renounce, and they include a duty to act worthily if not rightly. And those rights, as Lincoln recognized, also dedicate us to the soul's highest vision and obligation, the proposition that all human beings are created equal.

NOTES

1. Democracy and the Citizen

1. Most political scientists probably share this view. The Constitution, Robert Dahl writes, "given the right circumstances . . . could become the government of a democratic republic. And it did." See Dahl, *Pluralist Democracy in the United States* (Chicago: Rand McNally, 1967), 55.

2. For similar views, see Walter Nicgorski, "The New Federalism and Direct Popular Election," *Review of Politics* 34 (1972): 3–15; and Lane Davis, "The Cost of Realism: Contemporary Restatements of Democracy," *Western Political Quarterly* 17 (1964): 37–46.

3. Aristotle, *The Politics of Aristotle*, trans. Ernest Barker (Oxford: Clarendon, 1952), 258.

4. Delba Winthrop, "Aristotle on Participatory Democracy," *Polity* 2 (1978): 155.

5. John Locke, *Second Treatise on Government*, sec. 96.

6. Even Locke's argument is debatable, since majorities would be particularly unlikely to have superior force in the individualistic conditions of Locke's state of nature. There is a sense in which democracy, and the virtue of majorities, does derive from force, since democracy is akin to an army. As Aristotle knew, majorities acquire force only through discipline, the ability to trust and rely on one's fellows *as a whole*, and the willingness to obey orders (provisionally at least), the reason for which we cannot see from our part of the battlefield. See Aristotle, *Politics*, 182, 272, 308, and Plato *Apology* 28d–e.

7. Winthrop, "Aristotle on Participatory Democracy," 156.

8. Aristotle, *Politics*, 258.

9. Plato *Republic* 346a–347d.

10. Compare Franklin's advice to Tom Paine; see Benjamin Franklin, *Select Works*, ed. P. Sargent (Boston: Phillips Sampson, 1857), 488.

11. Aristotle, *Politics*, 258.

12. Because democracy emphasizes "free birth," it is more familial than its claim to freedom would suggest (ibid., 163–164). On the general point, the emphasis must be on finding friends within the city, for the friendship of all citizens is decidedly second-rate. Even though I begin by admiring what my friend appears to be, I aim at the friend I can value for what he truly is. See Aristotle *Nichomachean Ethics* 1164a1–30, 1168a27–1169b2, and Aristotle *Ethica Eudemia* 1236a–b, 1237a–b, 1238b, 1234b.

13. Aristotle *Metaphysics* 1018b9–29 discusses the varieties of "priority."

14. Winthrop, "Aristotle on Participatory Democracy," 166–167.

15. Peter Berger, "On the Obsolescence of the Concept of Honor," *European Journal of Sociology* 2 (1970): 339–347; Anthony Lauria, "*Respeto, Relajo,* and Interpersonal Relations in Puerto Rico," *Anthropological Quarterly* 37 (1964): 53–67.

16. Aristotle, *Politics*, 105.

17. Mancur Olson, *The Logic of Collective Action* (Cambridge, Mass.: Harvard University Press, 1965).

18. Plato *Laws* 738e.

19. R. E. Gehringer, "On the Moral Import of Status and Position," *Ethics* 67 (1957): 200–202.

20. Aristotle, *Politics*, 63–68, 209, 232, 268.

21. James Madison, Alexander Hamilton, and John Jay, *Federalist* 10, 39; Martin Diamond, "The Declaration and the Constitution: Liberty, Democracy, and the Founders," in *The American Commonwealth 1976*, ed. Nathan Glazer and Irving Kristol (New York: Basic Books, 1975), 48–49.

22. *Federalist* 43.

23. Hanna Pitkin, "Obligation and Consent, II," *American Political Science Review* 60 (1966): 39–52.

24. *Federalist* 15, 51. Madison's implicit theology is revealing. Angels are governed, after all, by an absolute monarch, but Madison seemed to assume that the government of heaven is not relevant to earthly politics. If men were angels, Madison asserted, they would be beyond the power of nature, though not masters over it. Even with that qualification, given a modern view of the purposes of politics, no *human* government would be necessary.

25. *Federalist* 49. Hegel regarded war as useful because it reminded citizens of their partiality and their need for the state. See Hegel, *Philosophy of Right*, ed. S. W. Dyde (New York: Cosimo, 2008), 192–196. Elections are a kind of "war without the knife" and hence both invaluable and dangerous.

26. *Federalist* 51, 10.

27. Julian Boyd, ed., *The Papers of Thomas Jefferson* (Princeton, N.J.: Princeton University Press, 1950), 6:308–309.

28. *Federalist* 10, 63.

29. *Federalist* 49.

30. *Federalist* 55.

31. Winthrop, "Aristotle on Participatory Democracy," 166.

32. Robert A. Rutland, William T. Hutchinson, and William M. E. Rachal, eds., *The Papers of James Madison* (Chicago: University of Chicago Press, 1962), 9:384; *Federalist* 49.

33. *Federalist* 49.

34. *Federalist* 16.

35. Alfred F. Young, "Conservatives, the Constitution, and the 'Spirit of Accommodation,'" in *How Democratic Is the Constitution?* ed. Robert A. Goldwin and William A. Schambra (Washington, D.C.: AEI Books, 1980), 117–147.

36. *The Life and Selected Writings of Thomas Jefferson*, ed. Adrienne Koch and William Peden (New York: Modern Library, 1944), 441.

37. *The Writings of James Madison*, ed. Gaillard Hunt (New York: Putnam's, 1900–1910), 2:336–340; Max Farrand, ed., *The Records of the Federal Convention* (New Haven, Conn.: Yale University Press, 1937), 1:162, 164, 168, 297, 463–464, 476, 489–490, 530, 2:390–391, 3:77.

38. Walter Berns, "Does the Constitution 'Secure These Rights'?" in *How Democratic Is the Constitution?* ed. Robert A. Goldwin and William A. Schambra (Washington, D.C.: AEI Books, 1980), 59–78.

39. Cecilia Kenyon, ed., *The Antifederalists* (Indianapolis, Ind.: Bobbs-Merrill, 1966), xcii, 148, 197, 205, 263, 309–310, 374, 388.

40. Ibid., 154, 210.

41. Ibid., lxi, 216–217, 377–378, 383–385.

42. *Federalist* 10; Kenyon, *Antifederalists*, lii.

43. Paul L. Ford, *Essays on the Constitution of the United States, 1787–1788* (Brooklyn, N.Y.: Historical Printing Club, 1892), 73; Kenyon, *Antifederalists*, 310–312.

44. *Federalist* 63.

45. *Federalist* 10.

46. Jonathan Elliot, *Debates in the Several State Conventions on the Adoption of the Federal Constitution* (Philadelphia: Lippincott, 1896), 2:295; Kenyon, *Antifederalists*, 72.

47. Kenyon, *Antifederalists*, liv; James Madison, *Notes of Debates in the Federal Convention of 1787*, ed. A. Koch (Athens: Ohio University Press, 1966), 235, 194.

48. James Ceaser, "Political Parties and Presidential Ambition," *Journal of Politics* 40 (1978): 725, 728.

49. Kenyon, *Antifederalists*, 310–311; Elliot, *Debates in the Several State Conventions*, 2:295.

50. On the rhetoric of the Anti-Federalists and its origins, see Kenyon, *Antifederalists*, xlv, and Harvey Mansfield, Jr., *The Spirit of Liberalism* (Cambridge, Mass.: Harvard University Press, 1978), 79–80.

51. Kenyon, *Antifederalists*, 45.

52. Ibid., lxxv, 212–213.

53. Ibid., 141.

54. Ibid., 265, 212–213, 43, 127.

55. Alexis de Tocqueville, *Democracy in America* (New York: Schocken, 1961), 1:383.

56. Kenyon, *Antifederalists*, 308–309.

57. Madison's comment is related in Bancroft's biography, *Martin Van Buren* (New York: Harper & Bros., 1889). Justice Johnson's comments are only a little more explicit than Marshall's opinion for the Court; see *Gibbons v. Ogden*, 9 Wheat. 1, 1824.

58. Tocqueville, *Democracy in America*, 1:176–177, 179.

59. Ibid, 1:298–318. James Bryce, *The American Commonwealth* (New York: Commonwealth, 1908), 2:358–368.

60. Tocqueville, *Democracy in America*, 2:118–120.

61. Ibid., 1:353–373, 2:22–32, 170–177.

62. Ibid., 1:181.

63. Ibid., 1:293; see also 1:216–226, 331–339.

64. I make a similar argument in "Political Parties as Civic Associations," in *Party Renewal in America*, ed. Gerald Pomper (New York: Praeger, 1980), 51–68. That essay has been republished as chapter 10 in this volume.

65. *National Labor Relations Board v. Jones and Laughlin Steel Corporation*, 301 U.S. 1 (1937).

66. See my essay "American Pluralism: The Old Order Passeth," in *The Americans, 1976*, ed. Irving Kristol and Paul Weaver (Lexington, Mass.: Heath, 1976), 293–320.

67. John H. Schaar, "Equality of Opportunity and Beyond," in *Equality*, ed. Roland Pennock and John W. Chapman (New York: Atherton, 1967), 228–249.

68. Christopher Lasch, *The Culture of Narcissism* (New York: Norton, 1979), and *Haven in a Heartless World* (New York: Basic Books, 1977).

69. Grant McConnell, *Private Power and American Democracy* (New York: Knopf, 1966).

70. Bertrand de Jouvenel, "The Chairman's Problem," *American Political Science Review* 55 (1961): 368–372.

71. Gerald M. Pomper, "The Decline of the Party in American Elections," *Political Science Quarterly* 92 (1977): 21–41.

2. The Bible in the American Political Tradition

1. Northrop Frye, *The Great Code: The Bible as Literature* (New York: Harcourt Brace Jovanovich, 1982).

2. When I refer to the Bible, I use the word in its most common American sense, embracing both the Jewish and Christian testaments. The idea of the "liberal tradition" is derived from Louis Hartz, *The Liberal Tradition in America* (New York: Harcourt Brace, 1955).

3. Christopher Lasch, *The Culture of Narcissism* (New York: Norton, 1978).

4. Alexis de Tocqueville, *Democracy in America* (New York: Schocken, 1961), 2:118–120.

5. Nathalia Wright, *Melville's Use of the Bible* (Durham, N.C.: Duke University Press, 1949); for a contemporary example, see Theodor Reik, *The Temptation* (New York: Braziller, 1961), as well as Reik's other studies of Genesis.

6. See Robert Bellah's generous discussion, "New Religious Consciousness and the Crisis of Modernity," in *Varieties of Civil Religion*, ed. Bellah and Phillip Hammond (San Francisco: Harper & Row, 1980), 167–187; see also Sydney Ahlstrom, *A Religious History of the American People* (New Haven, Conn.: Yale University Press, 1972), 1037–1054.

7. Georges Dumezil, *La religion romaine archaique* (Paris: Payot, 1966), 8.

8. I have, however, been instructed by such studies; see, for example, H. H. Rowley, ed., *The Old Testament and Modern Study* (Oxford: Clarendon, 1951); and Yehezekel Kaufman, *History of the Religion of Israel* (Chicago: University of Chicago Press, 1961).

9. Revelation 1:9–13. For a fine treatment of a satanic version of revelation, see James Rhodes, *The Hitler Movement* (Stanford, Calif.: Hoover Institution, 1980), 38–42.

10. Matthew 7:21–27; John Dillenberger, "Introduction," in *Martin Luther: Selections from His Writings*, ed. John Dillenberger (Garden City, N.Y.: Doubleday, 1961), 19. Robin Needham argues a similar point in "Terminology and Alliance," *Sociologus* 16 (1966): 156–157 and 17 (1967): 47–50.

11. Martin Buber, *On the Bible*, ed. Nahum Glatzer (New York: Schocken, 1968), 5.

12. Exodus 34:9; Deuteronomy 9:6, 10:16, 30:14; Ezekiel 2:4, 8.

13. Deuteronomy 32:46–47.

14. Perry Miller, *Nature's Nation* (Cambridge, Mass.: Harvard University Press, 1967), 214–215, 220; see also *Martin Luther: Selections*, 474.

15. Deuteronomy 32:46–47.

16. Hence, the Torah is "didactic-historical instruction" as much as—or more than—a set of specific laws and regulations. Calum Carmichael, *The Laws of Deuteronomy* (Ithaca, N.Y.: Cornell University Press, 1974), 18n3.

17. 2 Timothy 3:15; on wisdom and scripture, see Leo Strauss, *Jerusalem and Athens*, City College Papers no. 6 (New York: City College of New York, 1967), 5.

18. John 20:30–31; Carmichael, *Laws of Deuteronomy*, 7; George Mendenhall, *The Tenth Generation* (Baltimore, Md.: Johns Hopkins University Press, 1973), 8. Solomon Goldman's comment, "The Book of Genesis is the great clearing which the fashioners of the Jewish saga made in the jungle of primitive folklore," speaks to the point; see Goldman, *The Book of Human Destiny* (New York: Harper, 1949), xi.

19. Edmund Leach, *Genesis as Myth and Other Essays* (London: Jonathan Cape, 1969), 29–30; Julius Wellhausen, *Prolegomena to the History of Ancient Israel* (1878; repr., New York: Meridian, 1957). Spinoza anticipated this argument. See Leo Strauss, *Spinoza's Critique of Religion* (New York: Schocken, 1965), 267.

20. Buber, *On the Bible*, 36; Buber, of course, is speaking of the Jewish scriptures, but because Christian authors were concerned to show that the New Testament fulfills the Old, they were no less concerned with unity of composition. See Franz Rosenzweig, *Star of Redemption* (New York: Holt, Rinehart & Winston, 1971), 117. Strauss appears to reject this view. The compilers of the Bible, Strauss asserts, "seem" to have "excluded only what could not by any stretch of the imagination be rendered compatible with the fundamental and authoritative teaching." Hence, unlike a "book in the strict sense," the contradictions and repetitions in the Bible may not be intended; see Strauss, *Jerusalem and Athens*, 18. Strauss does not tell us the evidence for this view, but he concedes that the "traditional way of reading the Bible" *does* treat it as a "book in the strict sense"; ibid., 19. It is apparently a fair assumption that Strauss's nontraditional view is based on a modern reading, on things as they "seem" in the light of the historical criticism of Scripture. This principle of interpretation is curious because Strauss so often cautions his readers against historicistic readings and especially because he lays down the rule that "it is safer to understand the low in the light of the high than the high in the light of low. In doing the latter one necessarily distorts the high, whereas in doing the former, one does not deprive the low of the freedom to reveal itself fully as what it is." See Strauss, *Spinoza's Critique of Religion*, 2, also 7–8, 12–14, 21–25, and "On Collingwood's Philosophy of History," *Review of Metaphysics* 5 (1952): 559–586. Since it is unlikely that Strauss contradicted himself on so important a point in relation to so important a text, the safest assumption is that Strauss's approach to the Bible is compatible with his exegetic precepts. This is possible if (1) the view that the Bible is not a "book in the strict sense" is true to the *highest* possibilities of scripture, and (2) his view of the way in which the Bible's editors selected their texts is not a historicistic reading but reflects the way in which those editors understood themselves. In fact, Strauss's seemingly modern view itself emphasizes that scripture's editors *had* a guiding purpose, a "fundamental and authoritative teaching." Moreover, Strauss is contending that scripture's accounts and stories are compatible with this teaching, although we must sometimes stretch our imaginations to discern that compatibility. Closely examined, in other words, Strauss's argument maintains something like the traditional view: the Bible is not a "book in the strict sense" only because its fundamental teachings and unities are more difficult to discover. This is as it should be.

The Bible claims to speak about divine things; God is the unity underlying scripture. Human speech, however, must fall short of God, the Word that is the foundation of all language yet beyond all words. If the Bible is not a "book in the strict sense," it may be because it is written in an even stricter sense, with an understanding of the limitations of books and writings. (I find something like this view in Chaim Potok's essay "The Bible's Inspired Art," *New York Times Magazine*, October 3, 1982, 58–68.)

21. 1 Samuel 31:4; 2 Samuel 1:6–10.

22. Herbert N. Schneidau, *Sacred Discontent: The Bible and Western Tradition* (Berkeley: University of California Press, 1977), 214–215.

23. Carmichael, *Laws of Deuteronomy*, 23, 256–257.

24. Henry David Thoreau, *Walden,* ed. J. Lyndon Shanley (Princeton, N.J.: Princeton University Press, 1971), 106, 100, and 99–110. Thoreau's unorthodox inclusion of other sacred works along with the Bible does not make him less insistent on applying his principles of interpretation to the Bible; see also Buber, *On the Bible,* 30, 213, and the comments on stretching the imagination in note 20 in this chapter.

25. Wright, *Melville's Use of the Bible,* 12–13, 17–18, 45, 114–115; see also my *Idea of Fraternity in America* (Berkeley: University of California Press, 1973), 317–318, 331–332.

26. *Martin Luther: Selections,* 343; Jacques Ellul, *The Politics of God and the Politics of Man* (Grand Rapids, Mich.: Eerdmans, 1972), 113.

27. Buber, *On the Bible,* 1; Rosenzweig, *Star of Redemption,* 198–204.

28. Miller, *Nature's Nation,* 216, 219, 222, 234.

29. Exodus 20:4; Isaiah 40:15–25; Peter L. Berger, *The Noise of Solemn Assemblies* (Garden City, N.Y.: Doubleday, 1961), 131; Henri Frankfort, Henriette Antonia Groenewegen-Frankfort, John A. Wilson, and Thorkid Jacobsen, *Before Philosophy* (Baltimore, Md.: Penguin, 1961), 243.

30. Georges Dumezil, *The Destiny of the Warrior* (Chicago: University of Chicago Press, 1970), 3; Mendenhall, *Tenth Generation,* 7, 16.

31. Peter L. Berger, *The Sacred Canopy* (Garden City, N.Y.: Doubleday, 1969), 99, 112–124; Eric Voegelin, *Israel and Revelation* (Baton Rouge: Louisiana State University Press, 1966).

32. This, of course, helps account for the extraordinary capacity for self-criticism in the biblical tradition. For example, see Jeremiah 7:26, Ezekiel 20:25–26; on the general point, see Mendenhall, *Tenth Generation,* 15, Schneidau, *Sacred Discontent,* 14, Peter L. Berger, *The Precarious Vision* (Garden City, N.Y.: Doubleday, 1961), 219–238, Frank M. Cross, *Canaanite Myth and Hebrew Epic* (Cambridge, Mass.: Harvard University Press, 1973), 89–90, 190–191.

33. Frankfort et al., *Before Philosophy,* 241–243; the italics are theirs.

34. Genesis 1:31.

35. Buber, *On the Bible,* 195, commenting on Job 38:4–5, 9–10. Herbert Schneidau has a point in arguing that the Bible's attack on "the old mythology of the community and its culture" helps to lay the "groundwork" for the "mythology of the individual," so long as it is understood that this second mythology is no less contrary to the Bible's teaching than the first; see Schneidau, *Sacred Discontent,* 45.

36. Psalms 103:15–16; see also Ecclesiastes 1:11, 13.

37. Isaiah 64:6; John 2:19.

38. Isaiah 40:6–11, 29–31.

39. Mendenhall, *Tenth Generation,* xii–xiii, 5.

40. Schneidau, *Sacred Discontent,* 154.

41. Genesis 4:7.

42. Genesis 4:12–15.

43. Genesis 4:17.

44. A. M. Hocart, *Kings and Councillors* (Chicago: University of Chicago Press, 1970), 35, 38.

45. This helps to account for the Bible's deep and continuing suspicion of commerce and money. See 1 Timothy 6:10; Genesis 47:15–18; Exodus 22:25; Deuteronomy 23:19; Psalms 49:5–10; Jeremiah 9:23; Mark 10:23–25; James 4:13–56.

46. A. L. Oppenheim, *Ancient Mesopotamia* (Chicago: University of Chicago Press, 1964), 82–83; Mendenhall, *Tenth Generation,* 105–110, and "The Hebrew Conquest of Palestine," in *The Biblical Archaeologist Reader,* ed. E. F. Campbell and David Freedman (Garden City, N.Y.: Doubleday, 1970), 103, 105.

47. Genesis 11:4.

48. Compare Robin Needham, Editor's Introduction, in Hocart, *Kings and Councillors,* xxx.

49. Carmichael, *Laws of Deuteronomy,* 261–262; see also Buber's discussion of the distinction between a people defined by biology or history (*goy*) and a community (*am*), in Buber, *On the Bible,* 85–86.

50. John Bright, *History of Israel* (London: SCM Press, 1967), 132–137; see also Werner Muller, *Die heilige Stadt* (Stuttgart: Kohlhammer, 1961).

51. Genesis 8:21, 9:2.

52. This goes beyond material possessions because it includes "my ideas."

53. Proverbs 28:1; Ecclesiastes 4:7–14; John Hallowell, *The Moral Foundations of Democracy* (Chicago: University of Chicago Press, 1954), 99–100.

54. Genesis 1:31, 50:19–20; Deuteronomy 30:14.

55. Buber, *On the Bible,* 13, 87.

56. Genesis 50:20; see also Genesis 15:12–15, 21:1, 22:1–12, 33:3–4, 41:41, 45:28.

57. Buber, *On the Bible,* 36–43; Genesis 13:9–9, 20:9–11; Schneidau, *Sacred Discontent,* 133–134; Bright, *History of Israel,* 135.

58. Deuteronomy 10:1.8, 15:7–11.

59. Buber, *On the Bible,* 109–110.

60. Reinhold Niebuhr, *Moral Man and Immoral Society* (New York: Scribner's, 1932).

61. Genesis 18:17–33, 19:1–23.

62. Genesis 12:1, 24:4, 14, 17–21.

63. Genesis 40:12–19, 41:25–37, 47:13–21.

64. Compare the similar experience of the Babylonian exile: Bright, *History of Israel,* 415–420.

65. Buber, *On the Bible,* 85–86; Augustine, *City of God,* bk. 4, chap. 3, 15, bk. 5, chap. 12, 17, bk. 19, chap. 12, 21. Lassa Oppenheim favors the modernized version of Christianity, which teaches that "the principles of Christianity ought to unite Christians more than they have done hitherto," but he admits that applying this

precept to the case for an international regime requires that "the letter" of Christian religion—its biblical principles—yield to its "spirit"; see Oppenheim, *International Law*, 3rd ed. (London: Longmans Green, 1920), 1:60–61. On the development of this question in Christian thought, see Ewart K. Lewis, *Medieval Political Ideas* (London: Routledge & Kegan Paul, 1954), 2:430–466.

66. Isaiah 40:17; Psalms 2:10–11, 47:7–9; Martin Buber, *The Kingdom of God* (New York: Harper, 1967).

67. Jeremiah 1:10.

68. Buber, *On the Bible*, 170; see also 166–171.

69. Jonah 5:2.

70. Compare Socrates' teaching as Plato presents it in *Apology* 25c5–26e6 and *Republic* 335d.

71. On the other hand, Puritanism and the common law often followed parallel courses: see David Little, *Religion, Order and Law* (New York: Harper & Row, 1969). One relatively late example of the appeal to the Bible as the foundation of law is Lyman Beecher, *The Bible: A Code of Laws* (Andover, Mass.: Flagg & Gould, 1818).

72. John Winthrop, *The Winthrop Papers* (Boston: Massachusetts Historical Society, 1929–1947), 2:282–295; John Cotton, *An Exposition of the Thirteenth Chapter of Revelations* (London, 1656), 121; H. Richard Niebuhr, *The Kingdom of God in America* (Chicago: Willet, 1937), 59–62; Niebuhr, "The Idea of Covenant and American Democracy," *Church History* 23 (1954): 129.

73. For some recent studies, see Richard Gildrie, *Salem, Massachusetts, 1629–1688: A Covenant Community* (Charlottesville: University of Virginia Press, 1975); Stephen Foster, *Their Solitary Way* (New Haven, Conn.: Yale University Press, 1971); David Leverenz, *The Language of Puritan Feeling* (New Brunswick, N.J.: Rutgers University Press, 1980); Ernest B. Lowrie, *The Shape of the Puritan Mind* (New Haven, Conn.: Yale University Press, 1974); Emory Elliott, *Power and the Pulpit in Puritan New England* (Princeton, N.J.: Princeton University Press, 1975).

74. Alan Heimert, *Religion and the American Mind* (Cambridge, Mass.: Harvard University Press, 1966), 352–353; see also Robert Bellah, *Beyond Belief* (New York: Harper & Row, 1970), 187–188.

75. Robert Bellah and Phillip Hammond, eds., *Varieties of Civil Religion* (San Francisco: Harper & Row, 1980), 11.

76. John H. Schaar, "Some Ways of Thinking about Equality," *Journal of Politics* 26 (1964): 867–895; that the three attributes (or "persons") of God mentioned in the Declaration correspond to the three powers of government underlines, in my view, the extent to which the Creator of the Declaration is a civil rather than a biblical deity. See Harry V. Jaffa, "What Is Equality?" in Jaffa, *The Conditions of Freedom* (Baltimore, Md.: Johns Hopkins University Press, 1975), 153.

77. Isaiah 14:12–15.

78. *Federalist* 10, 51; Gordon Wood, *The Creation of the American Republic* (Chapel Hill: University of North Carolina Press, 1969), 429, citing the *Boston Independent Chronicle*, November 2, 1786; Thomas Jefferson, *Works*, Federal ed. (New York: Putnam's, 1904), 12:477; Martin Diamond, "Ethics and Politics: The American Way," in *The Moral Foundations of the American Republic*, ed. Robert Horwitz (Charlottesville: University Press of Virginia, 1977), 39–72.

79. Walter Berns, "Religion and the Principle," in *The Moral Foundations of the American Republic,* ed. Robert Horwitz (Charlottesville: University Press of Virginia, 1977), 163–164, 170; see also Thomas Pangle, *Montesquieu's Philosophy of Liberalism* (Chicago: University of Chicago Press, 1973), 249–259. Sidney Mead writes that "every Species of traditional orthodoxy in Christendom is at war with the basic premises upon which the constitutional and legal structures of the Republic rest"; Mead, *Old Religion in the Brave New World* (Berkeley: University of California Press, 1977), 2.

80. *The Writings of James Madison,* ed. Gaillard Hunt (New York: Putnam's, 1900–1910), 9:220, 2:183–191. Madison felt, in fact, that it would constitute an "establishment of religion" if the census counted ministers. Mark De Wolfe Howe, *The Garden and the Wilderness* (Chicago: University of Chicago Press, 1965), 62.

81. A. E. Dick Howard, *Commentaries on the Constitution of Virginia* (Charlottesville: University Press of Virginia, 1974), 1:290–293; see also Irving Brant, "Madison on the Separation of Church and State," *William and Mary Quarterly,* 3rd ser., 8 (1951): 3, 15–16, 23–24.

82. Gordon Wood, "The Democratization of Mind in the American Revolution," in *The Moral Foundations of the American Republic,* ed. Robert Horwitz (Charlottesville: University Press of Virginia, 1977), 111.

83. Thomas Paine, *Common Sense and Other Political Writings,* ed. N. Adkins (New York: Liberal Arts, 1953), 10.

84. Exodus 28:5–12.

85. Schneidau, *Sacred Discontent,* 244.

86. Paine, *Common Sense,* 32.

87. Ibid., 13–14.

88. Ibid., 51; it is almost certainly significant that Paine relegated this reference to beginning the world again to the appendix to *Common Sense.* The choice of Saul is referred to at 15.

89. Ibid., 25; John Milton, *Paradise Lost,* iv, 98–99.

90. Heimert, *Religion and the American Mind,* 479.

91. Mead, *Old Religion in the Brave New World,* 5.

92. Berns, "Religion and the Founding Principle," 165–166; Wood, *Creation of the American Republic,* 427–428.

93. Thomas Jefferson, *Notes on the State of Virginia,* ed. W. Peden (Chapel Hill: University of North Carolina Press, 1955), 159, 162–163; Harvey Mansfield, Jr., "Introduction," in *Thomas Jefferson: Selected Writings,* ed. Harvey Mansfield, Jr. (Arlington Heights, Ill.: AHM Publishing, 1979), xxvi; on Jefferson's idea of "Heart," see his letter to Mrs. Cosway, in *Life and Selected Writings of Thomas Jefferson,* ed. A. Koch and William Peden (New York: Modern Library, 1944), 395–407. John Chester Miller, *The Wolf by the Ears* (New York: Free Press, 1977), is an excellent study of Jefferson's views on slavery.

94. Jefferson, *Works,* 9:461; Jefferson, *Notes on the State of Virginia,* 148. See also S. Gerald Sandier, "Lockean Ideas in Jefferson's *Bill for Establishing Religious Freedom," Journal of the History of Ideas* 21 (1960): 110–116.

95. Wood, "Democratization of Mind," 114; Donald Stewart, *The Opposition Press of the Federalist Period* (Albany: State University of New York Press, 1969), 15, 624, 634, 638, 640.

96. Eldon Eisenach, "The American Revolution Made and Remembered," *American Studies* 20 (Spring 1979): 77; Mary Kelley and Sidney Mead, "Protestant-ism in the Shadow of the Enlightenment," *Soundings* 58 (1975): 335–338.

97. Isaac Backus, "An Appeal to the Public for Religious Liberty," in *Isaac Backus on Church, State and Calvinism: Pamphlets, 1754–1789,* ed. William G. McLoughlin (Cambridge, Mass.: Harvard University Press, 1968), 305–306, 328.

98. William G. McLoughlin, *Isaac Backus and the American Pietistic Tradition* (Boston: Little, Brown, 1951), 149, 212.

99. William G. McLoughlin, "Isaac Backus and the Separation of Church and State in America," *American Historical Review* 73 (1968): 1392–1413; Samuel Ad-ams, *Writings,* ed. H. A. Cushing (New York: Putnam's, 1908), 4:238, and see also 3:163.

100. Rhys Isaac, "Preachers and Patriots: Popular Culture and Revolution in Vir-ginia," in *The American Revolution,* ed. Alfred Young (De Kalb: Northern Illinois University Press, 1976), 125–150; Elisha Douglass, *Rebels and Democrats* (Chi-cago: Quadrangle, 1965), 115–161.

101. Heimert, *Religion and the American Mind,* 95, 140, 179–182, 403; Tocque-ville, of course, later endorsed this view in *Democracy in America,* 1:383.

102. Heimert, *Religion and the American Mind,* 32, 55, 87, 381, 496–497.

103. Ibid., 306; see also 298–299, 515–517.

104. Ibid., 40, 265, 455–456, 459, 468, 504. For a fine example of the polit-ical thought of the Awakening, see Nathaniel Niles, *Two Discourses on Liberty* (Newbury-Port, Mass.: Thomas & Tinges, 1774).

105. Heimert, *Religion and the American Mind,* 526.

106. Herbert Schneider, *The Puritan Mind* (New York: Holt, 1930), 106–110; Heimert, *Religion and the American Mind,* 15; Richard Birdsall, "The Second Great Awakening and New England Social Order," *Church History* 39 (1970): 345. On Edwards's rather different personal views, see Heimert, *Religion and the Ameri-can Mind,* 129; and Perry Miller, *Jonathan Edwards* (New York: Delta, 1949), 214–232.

107. Jonathan Edwards, *Religious Affections* (New Haven, Conn.: Yale Univer-sity Press, 1959), 300.

108. Heimert, *Religion and the American Mind,* 225; Niebuhr, *Kingdom of God in America,* 109.

109. Romans 10:12; Galatians 3:28; 1 John 4:21; Thessalonians 4:9–11.

110. Heimert, *Religion and the American Mind,* 61–68, 190; Nathan Hatch, *The Sacred Cause of Liberty* (New Haven, Conn.: Yale University Press, 1977).

111. Heimert, *Religion and the American Mind,* 288, 395–397.

112. Ibid., 104–105; Harvey G. Townsend, *The Philosophy of Jonathan Edwards* (Eugene: University of Oregon Press, 1955), 65.

113. Van Wyck Brooks, *The Flowering of New England* (New York: Dutton, 1936), 59–60; G. K. Chesterton, *What I Saw in America* (New York: Dodd, Mead, 1922), 16–17; William Sullivan, *Reconstructing Public Philosophy* (Berkeley: Uni-versity of California Press, 1982), 13.

114. Perry Miller, *The Life of the Mind in America* (New York: Harcourt, Brace & World, 1965), 3–95; Heimert, *Religion and the American Mind,* 546–552.

115. Heimert, *Religion and the American Mind,* vii, 534; Miller, *Nature's Nation,* 208–240.

116. Tocqueville, *Democracy in America,* 1:355–373, 2:22–32.

117. Schneidau, *Sacred Discontent,* 56; cf. Roland Barthes, *Mythologies* (New York: Hill & Wang, 1972).

118. Berger, *Noise of Solemn Assemblies,* 57–72, 112, 117; John Murray Cuddihy, *No Offense: Civil Religion and Protestant Taste* (New York: Seabury, 1978).

119. Ahlstrom, *Religious History of the American People,* 399.

120. See my discussion in *Idea of Fraternity in America,* 283–284; Randall Stewart, *American Literature and Christian Doctrine* (Baton Rouge: Louisiana State University Press, 1958), 43–65.

121. McWilliams, *Idea of Fraternity in America,* 282–289, 304–318, 338–342; Quentin Anderson, *The Imperial Self* (New York: Knopf, 1971), 3–87.

122. Herman Melville, *Israel Potter: His Fifty Years of Exile* (New York: Sagamore, 1957), 63, 74; Miller, *Nature's Nation,* 223.

123. Genesis 46:30, 47:9, 48:8–11, 49.

124. The King James Version translates Genesis 48:21 as "Behold, I die." Jacob does not die until 49:33.

125. See my discussion of Melville's ideas in *Idea of Fraternity in America,* 328–371.

126. Caleb Sprague Henry, *Considerations on Some of the Elements and Conditions of Social Welfare and Human Progress* (New York: Appleton, 1861), 220–226, 238–239, 241–242, 290.

127. John H. Schaar, "Jacques Ellul: Between Babylon and the New Jerusalem," *Democracy* 2, no. 4 (Fall 1982): 102–118.

128. 1 Corinthians 7:21; see also Ephesians 6:6–7.

129. Genesis 9:25; on scientific racism, see McWilliams, *Idea of Fraternity in America,* 258, 253–270.

130. Deuteronomy 23:15.

131. Henry S. Commager, *Theodore Parker* (Boston: Beacon, 1960), 216. This, at least, was Parker's report of the incident.

132. Niebuhr, *Kingdom of God in America,* 156–159; Melville made much the same point in *Benito Cereno* (Barre, Mass.: Imprint Society, 1972).

133. For a challenging commentary on Lincoln's speech, see Harry V. Jaffa, *Crisis of the House Divided* (1959; reprint, Seattle: University of Washington Press, 1973).

134. The other versions differ only in context, although this matters a good deal. Matthew, for example, preceded the story with a reference to the prophecies of Isaiah and his own attribution to Jesus of descent from David (12:17–23), and Matthew follows the story with a foretelling of Jesus's death and resurrection (12:40). Matthew, in other words, is concerned to establish the preeminent authority of Jesus, and he places the story of the "divided house" within that context. Mark, by contrast, tells the story in relation to Jesus's ordination of his disciples (3:14–19), a much more egalitarian setting.

135. Jesus himself makes this argument in Matthew 7:22.

136. Bright, *History of Israel,* 423, 427.

137. Mark 2:27, 3:4.

138. Mark 3:32–35.

139. Bellah, *Beyond Belief,* 177–178.

140. Horace Bushnell, *Building Eras in Religion* (1864; reprint, New York: Scribner's, 1910), 293–295, 298, 309, 317.

141. Orestes Brownson, *The American Republic,* ed. A. D. Lapati (New Haven, Conn.: Colleges and Universities Press, 1972), 27, 31–34, 98, 102.

142. Elisha Mulford, *The Nation* (Boston: Houghton Mifflin, 1887), v–vi, 5–23, 382–383, 390–391.

143. Elisha Mulford, *The Republic of God* (Boston: Houghton Mifflin, 1881), 189; Mulford, *Nation,* 319, 381, 395, 408.

144. Theodore Munger, *The Freedom of Faith* (Boston: Houghton Mifflin, 1883), 19–58; Lyman Abbott, *The Theology of an Evolutionist* (New York: Houghton Mifflin, 1897); Abbott, *The Evolution of Christianity* (Boston: Houghton Mifflin, 1892); Henry Drummond, *The Ascent of Man* (New York: Pott, 1894). For a contemporary version of this argument, see Thomas J. J. Altizer, *The Gospel of Christian Atheism* (Philadelphia: Westminister, 1966), 27–28, 77.

145. McWilliams, *Idea of Fraternity in America,* 383–388, 402–406, 479–483.

146. Eric Goldman, *Rendezvous with Destiny* (New York: Knopf, 1954), 93–94, 200.

147. The most notable omission is the failure to read seriously the account of creation in Genesis 1. To do so is to recognize that creation days are not necessarily identical to sun days and certainly not on the authority of the text; Strauss, *Jerusalem and Athens,* 8–9; and see also Anne Brennan, "The Creationist Controversy: The Religious Issue," *Commonweal* 109 (1982): 559–561. On the more general shortcomings of the religious Right, see Gabriel Fackre, *The Religious Right and Christian Faith* (Grand Rapids, Mich.: Eerdmans, 1982).

148. For one example, see Arthur Hallaman, *Christian Capitalism* (Akron, Ohio: Capitalist Press, 1981). By contrast, see Bob Goudzwaard, *Capitalism and Progress: A Diagnosis of Western Society,* trans. J. Zylstra (Grand Rapids, Mich.: Eerdmans, 1979); see also John H. Schaar, *Legitimacy in the Modern State* (New Brunswick, N.J.: Transaction, 1981).

149. Stewart, *American Literature and Christian Doctrine,* 136–146, has a good discussion of Faulkner and Robert Penn Warren.

150. Daniel Bell, *The Cultural Contradictions of Capitalism* (New York: Basic Books, 1976); Michael Novak, *The Spirit of Democratic Capitalism* (New York: Simon & Schuster, 1982).

3. Protestant Prudence and Natural Rights

1. Alexis de Tocqueville, *Democracy in America* (New York: Knopf, 1980), 1:43.

2. Robert N. Bellah, Richard Madsen, William M. Sullivan, Ann Swidler, and Steven M. Tipton, *Habits of the Heart* (Berkeley: University of California Press, 1985).

3. Alan Wolfe, *One Nation after All* (New York: Viking, 1998).

4. G. K. Chesterton, *What I Saw in America* (New York: Dodd, Mead, 1922).

5. Michael Kammen, *People of Paradox* (New York: Knopf, 1972).

6. This has been, of course, a very persistent pattern in American history. See John Murray Cuddihy, *No Offense: Civil Religion and Protestant Taste* (New York: Seabury, 1978).

7. Romans 13:3–4; John Calvin, *Commentaries on the Epistles of Paul to the*

Romans and to the Thessalonians, trans. Ross Mackenzie, in *Calvin's New Testament Commentaries,* ed. David and Thomas Torrance (Grand Rapids, Mich.: Eerdmans, 1980), 8:281–282.

8. Calvin, *Commentaries,* 8:282.

9. John Calvin, *Institutes of the Christian Religion,* bk. 4, chap. 20, sec. 32; Sheldon S. Wolin, *Politics and Vision* (Boston: Little, Brown, 1960), 188–189. Luther would have agreed with Calvin that those who would "bear rule over men's consciences" will find no support for their "blasphemous tyranny" in Romans 13. See Calvin, *Commentaries,* 8:283.

10. See my essay "The Bible in the American Political Tradition," in *Religion and Politics,* ed. Myron Aronoff (New Brunswick, N.J.: Transaction, 1984), 24. That essay has been republished as chapter 2 in this volume.

11. Locke's teaching treated human beings as social animals in fact; it regarded them as separate, rights-bearing individuals *normatively* and before the law. See Ruth Grant, "Locke's Political Anthropology and Lockean Individualism," *Journal of Politics* 50 (1988): 42–63. Notably, Locke rejects Christian virtue as a standard for public policy; see Locke, *Letter Concerning Toleration* (Indianapolis, Ind.: Bobbs-Merrill, 1955), 42.

12. Locke, *Letter Concerning Toleration,* 52.

13. Locke, *The Reasonableness of Christianity,* ed. I. T. Ramsey (Stanford, Calif.: Stanford University Press, 1958), 64.

14. For example, William Graham Sumner accepted a duty to children despite his general rejection of claims on "other people's labor and self-denial," but he asserted that this sense of duty is "spontaneous" and, in fact, the only such case known to nature. See Sumner, *What Social Classes Owe to Each Other* (Caldwell, Idaho: Caxton, 1978), 8, 64. Sumner's argument, obviously, can answer Locke's objection only by holding that the ancients were perverse.

15. There are "signs of divine origin," Hannah Arendt wrote, in what the American founders took to be self-evident truth just as, in the "enlightened conscience," they often heard "an inner voice which was still the voice of God." See Arendt, *On Revolution* (New York: Viking, 1963), 194–195. The principle of inclusiveness our contemporaries discern in liberalism has the same quality: liberal ideas of natural and equal rights imply the right to make contracts and to apply for admission to existing ones but on their own terms; they do not suggest a right to be included. See my essay "On Rogers Smith's *Civic Ideals,*" *Studies in American Political Development* 13 (1999): 221.

16. Willmoore Kendall and George Carey, *The Basic Symbols of the American Political Tradition* (Baton Rouge: Louisiana State University Press, 1979), 84.

17. In the same way, since natural rights are unalienable, there are limits to proper consent; the "consent of the governed" can convey only "just powers" to government.

18. "The Journal of John Winthrop," in Edmund Morgan, ed., *Puritan Political Ideas* (Indianapolis, Ind.: Bobbs-Merrill, 1965), 138.

19. Morgan, *Puritan Political Ideas,* 358, 367–368. Langdon does suggest that the "civil polity of Israel" has special claims as a regime.

20. Chesterton, *What I Saw in America,* 17; John H. Schaar, "Some Ways of Thinking about Equality," *Journal of Politics* 26 (1964): 881.

21. Locke, *Second Treatise on Civil Government*, sec. 54.

22. James Madison, *Federalist* 10; see Robert Ginsberg, "Equality and Justice in the Declaration of Independence," *Journal of Social Philosophy* 6 (1975): 8.

23. John Winthrop, "A Model of Christian Charity," in Edmund Morgan, ed., *Puritan Political Ideas* (Indianapolis, Ind.: Bobbs-Merrill, 1965), 77.

24. 1 Corinthians 12:12–31.

25. Winthrop, "Model of Christian Charity," 87.

26. Sheldon S. Wolin, "Contract and Birthright," in Wolin, *The Presence of the Past* (Baltimore, Md.: Johns Hopkins University Press, 1989), 137–150.

27. On the divisions of method and doctrine within American Protestantism, see Jerald C. Brauer, "Puritanism, Revivalism and the Revolution," in *Religion and the American Revolution*, ed. Jerald C. Brauer (Philadelphia: Fortress, 1976), 25.

28. Steven M. Dworetz, *The Unvarnished Doctrine* (Durham, N.C.: Duke University Press, 1990).

29. Calvin, *Institutes of the Christian Religion*, bk. 3, chap. 19, sec. 15.

30. Sidney Mead, "Christendom, Enlightenment and the Revolution," in *Religion and the American Revolution*, ed. Jerald Brauer (Philadelphia: Fortress, 1976), 40–41.

31. Joseph Haroutunian, "Theology and the American Experience," *Criterion* 3 (Winter 1964): 7–9.

32. Ellis Sandoz, ed., *Political Sermons of the American Founding Era* (Indianapolis, Ind.: Liberty Fund, 1990), 53.

33. Romans 1:19–20, 2:14–15.

34. Calvin, *Institutes of the Christian Religion*, bk. 1, chap. 5, sec. 1, 11, 14, and bk. 1, chap. 6, sec. 2, 4; see also St. Augustine, "The Predestination of the Saints," in *The Essential Augustine,* ed. Vernon Bourke (Indianapolis, Ind.: Hackett, 1985), 22.

35. Perry Miller, *The New England Mind: From Colony to Province* (Boston: Beacon, 1961), 426–427.

36. Ibid., 300.

37. Martin Luther, "The Freedom of a Christian," in *Martin Luther: Three Treatises*, trans. W. A. Lambert (Philadelphia: Fortress, 1960), 284; cf. Galatians 3:28, Romans 8:38–39.

38. Luther, "Freedom of a Christian," 313, 315; Ephesians 6:1–9.

39. Calvin, *Institutes of the Christian Religion*, bk. 3, chap. 19, sec. 10.

40. Luther, "Freedom of a Christian," 304, 312–315; 1 Corinthians 8:9. Following the divine example, Calvin argues, we should encourage our fellows to improve in spite of their imperfections, not crush them by insisting on their defects: our rule, consequently, should be to restrict the expression of our liberty in accordance with the demands of charity and moral education (*studendum charitati et spectanda proximi aedificatio*); see Calvin, *Institutes of the Christian Religion*, bk. 3, chap. 19, sec. 12, 5.

41. Alan Heimert, *Religion and the American Mind* (Cambridge, Mass.: Harvard University Press, 1966), 174.

42. The "love of our neighbor," Calvin wrote, must not be carried so far as to "offend God." See Calvin, *Institutes of the Christian Religion*, bk. 3, chap. 19, sec. 13.

43. "All things are lawful for me," Paul taught, "but not everything is expedient and not everything edifies." See 1 Corinthians 10:23–24; see also Ephesians 6:10–17.

44. 1 Corinthians 9:19–22.

45. Matthew 10:16; Genesis 3:1.

46. Nathaniel Niles, *Two Discourses on Liberty* (Newbury-Port, Mass.: Thomas and Tinges, 1774). I will refer here and there to Niles's second discourse, but that work, less concerned with civil liberty, is also less to the purpose here.

47. Heimert, *Religion and the American Mind*, 454. Niles (1741–1828) was never ordained but was much in demand as a preacher, and the printing and reprinting of several of his sermons indicates, on Nathan Hatch's argument, that he spoke for a significant body of religious opinion. See Hatch, *The Sacred Cause of Liberty* (New Haven, Conn.: Yale University Press, 1977), 181. His family eminently reflected the Puritan tradition: his grandfather, the redoubtable Samuel Niles (1674–1762), occupied the pulpit at Braintree, Massachusetts, for more than fifty years and was the author of such works as *Tristitiae Ecclesiarum; or, a Brief and Sorrowful Account of the Present State of Churches in New England* (Boston: Draper, 1745); Niles's father was a judge and a friend of John Adams. Niles himself graduated from Princeton (then the College of New Jersey) and later studied with Joseph Bellamy, thus coming to stand in the direct line of intellectual descent from Jonathan Edwards. See Heimert, *Religion and the American Mind*, 455. Niles tried his hand at various trades, but the consistent themes of his career were religious and political, like the tradition in which he stood: in the founding era, Niles served three terms in the Connecticut legislature (1779–1781); eight in the Vermont lower house, where he was Speaker in 1784; three years (1784–1787) on the Vermont Supreme Court; and—after participating in Vermont's Ratifying Convention (1791)—in the U.S. House of Representatives (1791–1795). An Anti-Federalist and a Jeffersonian, he was also antislavery and antibank.

48. In this, like his sometime teacher Joseph Bellamy; see Heimert, *Religion and the American Mind*, 167.

49. This was especially true because, in Connecticut, Joseph Bellamy's denunciation of upper-class Arminians had inspired disorders that came close to "civil war." Bellamy and his school, appalled, were delighted that a new "common enemy," the British, afforded the basis both for civic unity and for the effort to develop a new politics; see Heimert, *Religion and the American Mind*, 347–349.

50. Ibid., 301.

51. Craft of this sort was familiar in Niles's intellectual circle. As Heimert notes, Bellamy's writings, almost anathema to John Witherspoon, circulated furtively among Princeton students, and those attracted by Bellamy's teaching, facing or fearing persecution from more established clergy, developed a "private, highly metaphorical language" for communicating their views; see Heimert, *Religion and the American Mind*, 168n.

52. Niles, *Two Discourses*, 5.

53. A proposition, it will be noted, that assumes the end justifies the means.

54. At the beginning of his second discourse, while emphasizing that spiritual liberty is to be preferred, Niles points out that Jesus (in John 8:32, 36) uses the same word, *ĕlĕuthĕria*, to refer to both civil and spiritual freedom. See Niles, *Two Discourses*, 40, 41.

55. Ibid., 5, 6.

56. Philippians 2:5–8.

57. Romans 8:38–39; Niles, *Two Discourses*, 47. As in the argument discussed earlier, this evidently calls for restraint on self-expression. Love, one might say, frees us even from the sway of liberty.

58. Niles, *Two Discourses*, 9.

59. Ibid., 9.

60. For example, the Anti-Federalist who wrote under the name William Penn identified our natural rights with liberty, defined as the "unlimited power of doing good," and hence dependent on moral education. See Penn's essay in the *Philadelphia Independent Gazetteer*, January 2, 1788, in *The Complete Anti-Federalist*, ed. Herbert J. Storing (Chicago: University of Chicago Press, 1981), 3:169–170.

61. Aristotle *Politics* 1253a19–29.

62. Niles, *Two Discourses*, 14–15.

63. Ibid., 16.

64. Ibid., 23–24, 28. Niles was contemptuous of teachings that rely on sympathy and the benefactions of private individuals, finding them wanting in respect for reason, justice, and manliness, all of which speak of a duty to the common good that calls for public authority and the sanction of law. See Niles, *The Perfection of God, The Fountain of Good, Two Sermons Delivered at Torringford, Connecticut, December 21, 1777* (Norwich, Conn.: Green & Spooner, 1778).

65. Niles, *Two Discourses*, 26. See Joseph Bellamy's 1762 "Election Sermon," in *The Works of Joseph Bellamy, D.D.*, ed. Tryon Edwards (Boston: Doctrinal Tract and Book Society, 1850), 1:590.

66. Niles, *Two Discourses*, 28, 45; perfect justice and liberty would require perfect knowledge, not only of general rules but also of circumstances and occasions, down to the most minute. More important, human beings cannot know the hearts and souls of their fellows: political society must judge by external expressions. And all human judgment, of course, is at least tinged with self-interest (42–44).

67. Ibid., 26, 28, 45.

68. Ibid., 23–24n.

69. Ibid., 31–32. Our forefathers, Niles writes, "however they might greatly err in some particular instances," were inspired to risk their lives by this "generous scheme of liberty," and it is to be hoped that we will not allow ourselves "to be enslaved by an India herb, or English manufactures" (15n). That advice might be repeated, with less confidence, to contemporary Americans.

70. Ibid., 19–20. Part of the virtue of majority rule, Niles holds, is that most of those disposed to a genuine concern for the public good—partly because they are less tempted by the delusion of independence—are in the lower classes; only a "very small proportion" are found in the higher orders (45–46). See also Bellamy's "Election Sermon," *Works*, 1:590–596. The potential danger of majority rule is accentuated because so many take up the cause of liberty out of a desire for popularity, as opposed to real conviction; Niles, *Two Discourses*, 58.

71. Niles, *Two Discourses*, 36. Confronting McCarthyism, Elmer Davis found himself reminded of the hymn "Dare to Be a Daniel, Dare to Stand Alone." See Davis, *But We Were Born Free* (New York: Bobbs-Merrill, 1953).

72. Niles, *Two Discourses*, 37–38.

73. Ibid., 38.

74. Locke, *Second Treatise on Civil Government*, sec. 26, 27; notably, Locke begins his discussion of property by referring to natural reason and hence self-preservation, turning only afterward to revelation (sec. 25).

75. Niles, *Two Discourses*, 10n.

76. Ibid., 11–12n. Niles's typology parallels Harrington's distinction between ancient and modern prudence, the latter devoted to the pursuit of private benefit; Niles's emphasis on a "system of laws" also at least resembles Harrington's appeal to contrivance against either form of prudence, although Niles, of course, also depends on free-spiritedness. See James Harrington, *Oceana*, in *The Political Works of James Harrington*, ed. J. G. A. Pocock (Cambridge: Cambridge University Press, 1977), 161, 205.

77. Niles, *Two Discourses*, 24n.

78. See Niles's argument in *The Substance of Two Sermons Delivered to the Second Society of Norwich, July 12, 1778* (Norwich, Conn.: John Trumbull, 1779).

79. Niles, *Two Discourses*, 34.

80. Psalms 121:1–2.

81. Psalms 120:2, 6–7.

82. Niles, *Two Discourses*, 34.

83. Jude 9:11, 19.

84. Niles, *Two Discourses*, 34.

85. 2 Samuel 16:5–13.

86. 2 Samuel 19:16–23.

87. 1 Kings 2:8–9.

88. The allusion, needless to say, is to Mario Puzo's *The Godfather* (New York: Putnam's, 1969).

89. Niles, *Two Discourses*, 34.

90. Daniel 9:26

91. Niles, *Two Discourses*, 39, 55.

92. Ibid., 57–58.

93. Ibid., 48.

94. The phrases, of course, are taken from Hobbes's *Leviathan*, chap. 18.

95. Joseph Bellamy, *The Nature and Glory of the Gospel*, in *The Works of Joseph Bellamy, D.D.* (Boston: Doctrinal Tract and Book Society, 1850), 2:344, as well as his "Election Sermon," *Works*, 1:590–596.

96. Joyce Appleby, *Inheriting the Revolution: The First Generation of Americans* (Cambridge, Mass.: Harvard University Press, 2000); cf. Madison's *Federalist* 49. Timothy Dwight, whose political inclinations were at poles with Niles's, also advised postponing confrontations until the end of the war. Heimert, *Religion and the American Mind*, 348.

97. John G. West, *The Politics of Revelation and Reason* (Lawrence: University Press of Kansas, 1996); the "crisis of the house divided," of course, refers both to Lincoln's grand scriptural metaphor and to Harry V. Jaffa, *Crisis of the House Divided* (Chicago: University of Chicago Press, 1959).

98. Jonathan Edwards, *The Great Christian Doctrine of Original Sin Defended*, in *The Works of Jonathan Edwards*, ed. Edward Hickman (Carlisle, Pa.: Banner of Truth Trust, 1987), 1:170.

99. Joseph Bellamy, *The Millennium*, in *The Works of Joseph Bellamy, D.D.* (Boston: Doctrinal Tracts and Book Society, 1850), 1:445, 452, 460.

100. Niles, *Two Discourses*, 53.

101. Mark 8:12; Matthew 12:39, 16:4; James Davison Hunter, *Culture War* (New York: Basic Books, 1991).

102. Bill Joy, "Why The Future Doesn't Need Us," *Wired*, April 2000, 238–262.

4. The Anti-Federalists, Representation, and Party

1. "Letter from a Farmer to the *(Baltimore) Maryland Gazette* (February 29, 1788)," in Herbert Storing, ed., *The Complete Anti-Federalist* (Chicago: University of Chicago Press, 1981), 16, 18.

2. *Federalist* 14.

3. Jean Yarbrough, "Representation and Republicanism: Two Views," *Publius* 9 (1979): 77, 84.

4. Ibid. "The Federalists believed that the purpose of representation was to improve upon direct democracy by refining the interests *and opinions* of the people" (79).

5. The proposed amendment, the first submitted by Congress to the new states, provided that after the initial census, one representative for every 30,000 persons would be required until the number of representatives reached 100; subsequently, Congress would regulate such that not less than one representative for every 40,000 persons would be required until the number reached 200—with a minimum of 100 members. After reaching that plateau, the amendment provided that representation "shall be so regulated by Congress that there shall not be less than two hundred Representatives, nor more than one Representative for every fifty thousand persons"; see *Annals of Congress,* 1st Cong., 1st sess. (1789), 2034; R. Rutland, *The Birth of the Bill of Rights 1776–1791* (Chapel Hill: University of North Carolina Press, 1962), 238. Originally, the last sentence read "nor *less* than one Representative for every fifty thousand persons"; an eleventh-hour change on September 24, 1789, revised "less" to "more"; see *Annals of Congress,* ed. J. Gales, 1st Cong., 1st sess. (1789), 913 (emphasis added); Sol Bloom, Director General, *U.S. Constitution Sesquicentennial Comm'n, History of the Formation of the Union under the Constitution* (Washington, D.C.: Government Printing Office, 1946), 315. Had the amendment been ratified as originally worded, today's House of Representatives would be required to have more than 4,500 members. Even modified, it retained some implication that one representative per 50,000 persons is a desirable norm. Submitted to the states without time limit, the amendment could still, theoretically, be ratified.

6. The term "framers," necessarily imprecise at the edges, refers to those delegates at the Convention of 1787 who played a major role in shaping the Constitution and who were leaders in urging its ratification (most notably James Madison, Alexander Hamilton, James Wilson, and Gouverneur Morris). The doctrine of the framers derived from a number of sources, with the liberal tradition, exemplified by John Locke, arguably the most important of these. See Thomas Pangle, *The Spirit of Modern Republicanism* (Chicago: University of Chicago Press, 1988), 35. Self-preservation, Locke wrote, is "the first and strongest desire God planted in men";

John Locke, *Two Treatises of Government*, ed. Thomas Cook (New York: Hafner, 1947), 67. It is also a "fundamental, scared and unalterable law" (197). Locke—who provided the framers with first principles and "bases for establishing a government"—was the secular author most frequently cited in political writing in the 1760s and 1770s, rivaled only by Baron de Montesquieu. See Donald S. Lutz, "The Relative Influence of European Writers on Late 18th Century American Political Thought," *American Political Science Review* 78, no. 1 (March 1984): 189, 192–193. He was less cited in the 1780s but only because he wrote relatively little about the design of institutions. Authors—like John Trenchard, Thomas Gordon, and David Hume (and other of Hume's countrymen in the Scottish Enlightenment)—who rejected the important aspects of Locke's doctrine often followed him in defining human nature in terms of the body and its senses. See Wilson Carey McWilliams, "The Discipline of Freedom," in *Constitutionalism in America*, ed. Sarah Baumgartner Thurow (Lanham, Md.: University Press of America, 1988), 31, 32–34. (That essay is reprinted as chapter 7 in this volume.) For example, though Hamilton acknowledged some duty to humanity and to those who are "allied to us by ties of blood, interest, and mutual protection," he went on to argue that "humanity does not require us to sacrifice our own security and welfare to the convenience or advantage of others. Self-preservation is the first principle of our nature. When our lives and properties are at stake, it would be foolish and unnatural to refrain from such measures as might preserve them because they would be detrimental to others." See A. Hamilton, "A Full Vindication," in *The Works of Alexander Hamilton*, ed. Henry Cabot Lodge (New York: G. P. Putnam's Sons, 1904), 3, 12.

7. Thomas Hobbes, though no partisan of elective representation, originated the argument that the legitimate sovereign "represents" his subjects' desire to preserve their lives and well-being. Harvey C. Mansfield and Robert G. Scigliano, *Representation: The Perennial Issues* (Washington, D.C.: American Political Science Association, 1978), 22–23. In *Of the Office of the Soveraign Representative*, Hobbes argued that "the Office of the Soveraign, (be it a Monarch or an Assembly,) consisteth in the end, for which he was trusted with the Soveraign Power, namely the procuration of the *safety of the people*." See Thomas Hobbes, *Leviathan*, ed. C. B. MacPherson (New York: Penguin, 1968), 376 (emphasis in original).

8. Madison distinguished the demands of faction from "the permanent and aggregate interest of the community"; *Federalist* 10, 57. He also wrote of the need for rulers to discern and pursue "the common good of the society"; *Federalist* 57. Hamilton argued that the people "commonly *intend* the public good" but "that they sometimes err" about the "*means* of promoting it"; *Federalist* 70 (emphasis in original). Rulers, he contended, must guard the people's "interests" against their transient and subjective "inclinations." Other writers emphasized a similar theme. Noah Webster, for example, contended that although provincial interests should be voiced, "every [representative] should act for the *aggregate interest of* the whole confederacy. The design of representation is to bring the collective interest into view" See Webster, "An Examination into the Leading Principles of the Federal Constitution," in *Pamphlets of the Constitution of the United States*, ed. Paul Leicester Ford (Brooklyn, N.Y., 1888), 25, 40.

9. Locke argued that, in a state of nature, majority rule is necessary to create a political community because the majority is the "greater force"; Locke, *Two*

Treatises, 169. Once a civil society is created, however, a minority may well have more force than the many. A ruler commanding an armed force, for example, may be "a hundred thousand times" stronger than an individual (191). The majority may—even in nature—*decide* to create an oligarchy or a monarchy as more conducive to its rights and interests (187). Jefferson, for similar reasons, believed that a people may legitimately choose to be represented by "a Bonaparte or an Alexander"; see "Letter from Thomas Jefferson to Correa de Serra," in *The Writings of Thomas Jefferson,* ed. A. Lipscomb and A. Bergh (Washington, D.C.: Thomas Jefferson Memorial Association of the United States, 1904), 330.

10. "Has it not . . . invariably been found," Hamilton asked rhetorically, "that momentary passions and immediate interests have a more active and imperious controul over human conduct than general or remote considerations of policy, utility or justice?" *Federalist* 6, 31. See also *Federalist* 51, 71. Locke originally enunciated the principle. See Locke, *Two Treatises,* 127, 184. This is also the foundation of the need to separate legislative and executive power (194–195).

11. Locke, *Two Treatises,* 164. Hobbes argued that a commonwealth, whatever its form of government, is created by majority rule (a "plurality of voices"). Hobbes, *Leviathan,* 227. A commonwealth, he wrote, is "instituted" only when "whatsoever *Man* or *Assembly of Men,* shall be given by the major part, the *Right* to *Present* the Person of them all, (that is to say, to be their *Representative;*) every one, as well he that *Voted for it,* as he that *Voted against it,* shall *Authorise* all the Actions and Judgements, of that Man or Assembly of men, in the same manner as if they were his own" (228–229, emphases in original).

12. Strictly speaking, majority rule is required only in the state of nature, where natural equality is fully effective. Locke, *Two Treatises,* 164. Once the people have established government, whether or not it rests on majority rule, Locke—like Jefferson in the Declaration of Independence—holds that they are morally obliged to obey it, so long as it respects and protects their rights. The power of the people, however, remains real (196–197, 235–236). The determination that a government has become too oppressive must be made by the people and only by the people; their decision, moreover, is effective whether or not they judge government unjustly (245–246). Locke argues that if the people err, it is more likely to be by bearing with abuses than in unjustified suspicion (235–236). Since the public's resumption of its natural power is, at bottom, an appeal to force, it is prudent (if one hopes to avoid civil war and violence) to give the majority *civil* power and to derive government explicitly and by law from that public support that is its ultimate foundation. This is evidently the direction in which Lockean teaching tended, especially in America.

13. The Federalists' familiar arguments might be summarized like this: large republics are preferable because they allow for a great variety of interests and parties that, making coherent majorities unlikely, reduces the possibility of majority tyranny—and with it, the chance that desperate or strong minorities will appeal to violence. *Federalist* 10; J. Madison, *Notes of Debates in the Federal Convention of 1787,* ed. Adrienne Koch (Athens: Ohio University Press, 1966), 76–77. The Federalist writers also offered both practical and moral objections to the classical ideal of the small, coherent, and virtuous republic espoused by the Anti-Federalists. First, public spirit is an ineffective way to decide private interests, at least as a general rule; the "intervals of felicity" in ancient republics, Hamilton wrote, soon were

"overwhelmed by the tempestuous waves of sedition and party-rage." *Federalist* 9. Second, public spirit can rule only by repressing private concerns—in the individual's soul if not by legal coercion. This, Madison argued, is unacceptable, given the supreme value of liberty and the proposition that government exists to enable individuals to be different. Protecting the "diversity in the faculties of men" is the "first object of Government." *Federalist* 10. In this view, the division of labor necessary in a large republic is a good to be pursued, its value enhanced in that it supports order rather than endangers it. Some delegates at the Constitutional Convention of 1787 who generally agreed with the Federalists about representation issues, however, found elements of the small republic argument compelling. Roger Sherman of Connecticut, for example, argued that smaller states embody a kind of public spirit that should not be summarily dismissed. During the debate on the configuration of the Senate, he asserted that "each state like each individual had its peculiar habits[,] usages and manners, which constituted its happiness." Madison, *Notes of Debates,* 161. Sherman effectively used Anti-Federalist rhetoric—the "people are more happy in small than large states"—to secure equal representation in the Senate for small states (75, 208). On that issue, pertaining to the mechanics of representation, James Wilson rejoined that "a private Citizen of a State is indifferent whether power be exercised by the General or State Legislatures, provided it be exercised most for his happiness" (162). Wilson sought to ensure the representation of individuals, not the representation of states; he advocated a system of direct election for representatives, and he opposed any means by which states themselves—those "imaginary beings"— might frustrate the needs of the majority (221, 189). In a similar spirit, Madison maintained that "the people would not be less free as members of one great Republic than as members of thirteen small ones. A Citizen of Delaware was not more free than a Citizen of Virginia: nor would either be more free than a Citizen of America. Supposing therefore a tendency in the General Government to absorb the State Governments no fatal consequence could result." (166). Hamilton underlined the point when, conceding that Delaware would "lose *power*" in a large republic, he insisted that her citizens would not be "*less free,*" since the vote of each citizen of Delaware would be equal to that of a citizen of Pennsylvania (215, emphases in original).

14. Fisher Ames argued in the Massachusetts Convention (January 15, 1788) that popular assemblies create factionalism, violence, and "a government not by laws, but by men." Jonathan Elliot, ed., *Debates in the Several State Conventions on the Adoption of the Federal Constitution* (Washington, D.C.: By Order of Congress, 1881), 7, 8; *Federalist* 9 (ancient city-states were buffeted by the "tempestuous waves of sedition and party-rage").

15. *Federalist* 63.

16. *Federalist* 10.

17. Ibid.

18. Ibid.; Madison, *Notes of Debates,* 76–77; *Federalist* 51 (laws ordered by the principle of self-interest).

19. *Federalist* 55 (concerning the maximum and minimum number of legislators necessary to ensure effective representation); *Federalist* 58 (regarding the adverse effects of too many legislators).

20. Bertrand de Jouvenel, "The Chairman's Problem," *American Political Science Review* 368 (1961): 55.

21. *Federalist* 10, 56. Of course, districts can still be quite coherent in their subjective interests, so it is necessary to emphasize the relativity of the freedom and objectivity enjoyed by legislators under the Constitution.

22. *Federalist* 10, 63.

23. Ibid.

24. "Speech of James Wilson (December 4, 1787)," in *Pennsylvania and the Federal Constitution, 1787–1788*, ed. J. McMaster and F. Stone (Philadelphia: Historical Society of Pennsylvania, 1888), 313, 336; Elliot, *Debates*, 300, 302.

25. *Federalist* 10.

26. The argument that citizens in a large republic will find it difficult to know or supervise their representatives was a major Anti-Federalist theme. "Letter from Brutus to the *New York Journal* (November 29, 1787)," in Storing, *Complete Anti-Federalist*, 377, 384–385.

27. Demagogues, Hamilton observed, are not always petty men. See Max Farrand, ed., *The Records of the Federal Convention of 1787* (New Haven, Conn.: Yale University Press, 1911), 147 (notes of James Madison, June 6, 1787); "Letter from Alexander Hamilton to George Washington (August 18, 1792)," in *The Papers of Alexander Hamilton*, ed. Harold C. Syrett and Jacob E. Cooke (New York: Columbia University Press, 1961), 228, 252; Storing, *Complete Anti-Federalist*, 91n38.

28. "Letter from Alexander Hamilton to James Bayard (January 16, 1801)," in Lodge, *Works of Alexander Hamilton*, 417. The same principle informed his early denunciation of those who, lacking "virtue and ability," fell short of the trust and opportunity of membership in Congress. "Letter from Publius to the *New York Journal* and the *General Advertiser* (November 16, 1778)," in Syrett and Cooke, *Papers of Alexander Hamilton*, 580–581.

29. "First Speech by Alexander Hamilton to the New York Ratifying Convention (June 21, 1788)," in Syrett and Cooke, *Papers of Alexander Hamilton*, 42, 85; Gerald Stourzh, *Alexander Hamilton and the Idea of Republican Government* (Stanford, Calif.: Stanford University Press, 1970), 70–75, 95–106.

30. U.S. Constitution, art. 1, sec. 2, cl. 2.

31. "Letter from Samuel to the *(Boston) Independent Chronicle and Universal Advertiser* (January 10, 1788)," in Storing, *Complete Anti-Federalist*, 193.

32. "Address by a Watchman in the *Worcester Magazine* (February 1788)," in Storing, *Complete Anti-Federalist*, 232.

33. Aristotle, *The Politics of Aristotle*, ed. Ernest Barker (New York: Clarendon Press, 1946), 4–7.

34. Nathaniel Niles, "Two Discourses on Liberty," in *American Political Thought during the Founding Era*, ed. Charles Hyneman and Donald Lutz (Indianapolis, Ind.: Liberty Fund, 1983), 260–262.

35. In Storing, *Complete Anti-Federalist*, see the following: Luther Martin, "The Genuine Information Delivered to the Legislature of the State of Maryland (1788)," 27, 35; "Letter from Cato to the *New York Journal* (undated)," 109, 111; "Letter from Brutus to the *New York Journal* (November 1, 1787)," 372–373.

36. "Letter from Agrippa to the *Massachusetts Gazette* (January 29, 1788)," in Storing, *Complete Anti-Federalist*, 106–107.

37. "Speech by Melancton Smith in the Debate by the Convention of the State

of New York on Adoption of the Federal Constitution (June 20, 1788)," in Storing, *Complete Anti-Federalist,* 149, 153.

38. "Letter from William Penn to the *(Philadelphia) Independent Gazetteer* (January 2, 1788)," in Storing, *Complete Anti-Federalist,* 168–169 (emphasis in original).

39. Ibid., 169–170.

40. Reaching conclusions similar to those of William Penn by different reasoning, the Kentuckian Anti-Federalist "Republicus" referred to the original state of human beings as "unconnected," but he declined to call such a condition "natural," noting only that "some say" that independence is humanity's natural state. Republicus argued that reason—not self-preservation—is the "great, primary and never-ceasing law of nature." Obedience to this law is the condition of all that is right and good. Since the right of reason to rule the soul is more fundamental than individual rights, it is not surprising that Republicus believed that a community has "one common public interest"—"the greatest good of the whole and of every individual as a part of that whole." See "Letter from Republicus to the *(Lexington) Kentucky Gazette* (February 16, 1788)," in Storing, *Complete Anti-Federalist,* 164.

41. "Letter from William Penn," 170.

42. Ibid.

43. For an excellent discussion of the way in which such Anti-Federalist views became, during the ratification debate, the language of individual rights, see Michael Lienesch, "North Carolina: Preserving Rights," in *Ratifying the Constitution,* ed. Michael Gillespie and Michael Lienesch (Lawrence: University Press of Kansas, 1989), 343.

44. "Address of a Minority of the Maryland Ratifying Convention in the *(Baltimore) Maryland Gazette* (May 6, 1788)," in Storing, *Complete Anti-Federalist,* 93. For example, Anti-Federalists saw trial by jury—that "palladium of civil liberty"—as a "check on the judiciary authority" (95), reflecting their view of juries as the "democratic branch of the judiciary power." Juries served as much as vehicles for citizen participation as they did to protect individual freedom. The phrase "democratic branch of the judiciary power" is from "Essay by a Farmer in the *(Baltimore) Maryland Gazette* (March 21, 1788)," in Storing, *Complete Anti-Federalist,* 38. For similar Anti-Federalist views, see the following in Storing, *Complete Anti-Federalist*: "Letter from the Federal Farmer to the *Republican* (October 12, 1787) (fourth letter)," 245, 250; "Letter from the Federal Farmer to the *Republican* (January 18, 1788) (15th letter)," 315, 319–320; "Letter from a Farmer to the *(New Hampshire) Freeman's Oracle* and *New Hampshire Advertiser* (June 6, 1788)," 212, 214.

45. "Address of a Minority of the Maryland Ratifying Convention (May 6, 1788)," in Storing, *Complete Anti-Federalist,* 96.

46. Ibid, 97.

47. "Letter from Richard Henry Lee to Governor Edmund Randolph (October 16, 1787)," in Storing, *Complete Anti-Federalist,* 112, 116–118.

48. Ibid., 117–118.

49. C. Montesquieu, *The Spirit of the Laws,* ed. Franz Neumann (New York: Hafner, 1949), 34. "A free republic will never keep a standing army to execute its laws," Brutus wrote. "It must depend on the support of its citizens." "Letter from Brutus to the *New York Journal* (October 18, 1787)," 370.

50. "Letter from Agrippa to the *Massachusetts Gazette* (January 14, 1788)," in Storing, *Complete Anti-Federalist*, 94, 96.

51. Republicus commented that "as universal observation assures us, that mankind are more generally actuated by their passions and appetites, than by their reason; something is necessary to restrain, controul or at least counteract those passions: hence the necessity of civil government." "Letter from Republicus," 161.

52. "Letter from the Federal Farmer to the *Republican* (October 10, 1787)," in Storing, *Complete Anti-Federalist*, 234.

53. "Letter from the Federal Farmer to the *Republican* (December 31, 1787)," in Storing, *Complete Anti-Federalist*, 264–265.

54. "Letter of Richard Henry Lee (April 28, 1788)," in *The Letters of Richard Henry Lee*, ed. James Curtis Ballagh (New York: Macmillan, 1914), 463–464 (where obedience is not secured by the good opinion of citizens, government must rely on force, the "parent" of tyranny). A government based on liberty, another Anti-Federalist contended, cannot be "executed" without the public's confidence and good opinion; see "Speech by Melancton Smith," 149, 154–155. A Federal Republican, writing in Pennsylvania, insisted that reliance on enforcement by a standing army would emphasize fear, "a contracting principle of obedience," and would encourage a relaxation of the "chaste and severe manners" associated with public virtue; see "A Review by a Federal Republican of the Constitution Proposed by the Late Convention (1787)," in Storing, *Complete Anti-Federalist,* 76. This line of argument derives from but revises Montesquieu's teaching, in *Spirit of the Laws,* 19–28. Montesquieu concluded that there are three principles of government—democracy, monarchy, and despotism—and assigned to monarchy the spirit of honor. Anti-Federalist argument seems to presume that, at a minimum, honor is an uneasy balance between the love of virtue and the fear of shame. It is, consequently, not a true principle but a combination of the two fundamental bases of rule. Carefully tested, in this view, any monarchy will be found to tilt toward despotism.

55. "Letter from the Federal Farmer to the *Republican* (December 31, 1787)," 264. Mercy Otis Warren emphasized the union's dependence on "genuine republican virtue" and a "sublime code of morals"; see Warren, *History of the Rise, Progress, and Termination of the American Revolution* (Boston: Manning & Loring, 1805), 340. Even the Maryland Farmer, who took a more jaundiced view of American life than most Anti-Federalists, recognized the importance of virtue to effective and lasting democratic government; see "Letter from a Farmer to the *(Baltimore) Maryland Gazette* (March 7, 1788)," in Storing, *Complete Anti-Federalist*, 30. By contrast, the Federalists emphasized the need for coercion so strongly that they often came close to defining government simply in terms of coercion and force. "Why has government been instituted at all?" Hamilton queried. Answer: "Because the passions of men will not conform to the dictates of reason and justice without constraint"; see *Federalist* 15 and also Elliot, *Debates,* 260–261 (notes on the remarks of Charles Pinckney in favor of ratification of the Constitution, delivered before the South Carolina House of Representatives). Such views, of course, are not incompatible with the hope, expressed in *Federalist* 1, that human beings can found and frame governments—as opposed to conducting them—on the basis of reason and choice.

56. Anti-Federalists, as one might expect, had a variety of ideas about soulcraft. The Federal Farmer stressed the need to continually remind the people about

republican principles and supported a bill of rights because it would reinforce "the particular principles on which our freedom must always depend"; see "Letter from the Federal Farmer to the *Republican* (January 20, 1788)," in Storing, *Complete Anti-Federalist,* 324–325. Other Anti-Federalists emphasized the importance of religion and formal civic education to the preservation and success of republicanism; in Storing, *Complete Anti-Federalist,* see "Speech by Charles Turner to the Massachusetts Ratifying Convention (February 5, 1788)," 221; "A Friend to the Rights of the People, in the *(New Hampshire) Freeman's Oracle* (Anti-Federalist No. 1) (February 8, 1788)," 242; "Address by Denatus to the Members of the Virginia Federal Convention (June 11, 1788),"264–265; also see Warren, *History,* 412–414. Despite—or perhaps even because of—their general support for commercial society, Anti-Federalists thought it vital to restrain avarice, "the canker worm of public and private virtue"; in Storing, *Complete Anti-Federalist,* see "Letter from the Maryland Farmer to the *(Baltimore) Maryland Gazette* (April 22, 1788)," 68; "Letter from Alfred to the *(Philadelphia) Independent Gazetteer* (December 13, 1787)," 142; "Speech by Charles Turner to the Massachusetts Ratifying Convention (January 17, 1788)," 219. Some, such as the Maryland Farmer and George Mason, admired sumptuary laws regulating consumption thought to be luxurious; see "Letter from a Farmer to the *(Baltimore) Maryland Gazette* (March 28, 1788)," in Storing, *Complete Anti-Federalist,* 50; Madison, *Notes of Debates,* 488, 632.

57. Even Plato, who held that the best polity is one that most closely approximates the rule that "'friends' property is indeed common property,'" noted that the senses are "our *own,*" so that eyes, ears, and hands only "seem" to see, hear, and feel the same thing at exactly the same moment. Plato, *The Laws,* trans. Alfred Edward Taylor (London: Dent, 1960), 739b–e (emphasis in original).

58. "Letter from Republicus," 161 (contrasting reason—the part of the soul naturally intended for rule—and the "passions and appetites" that reject the law of nature). For similar reasons, Aristotle referred to the body as essentially slavish and in need of rule. Aristotle, *Politics,* 13.

59. "In educating children," according to Aristotle, "we must use the instrument of habits before we use that of reason, and we must deal with the body before we deal with the mind." Aristotle, *Politics,* 337.

60. An understanding of this process informed prevailing religious teaching in eighteenth-century America. Wilson Carey McWilliams, "Religion and the American Founding," *Princeton Seminary Bulletin* 8, no. 1 (1987): 46, 47–50. Similar ideas were even more important to secular Lockeans, as in Gouverneur Morris's observation that the "taste for property" is the great motive for and support of civil society. Madison, *Notes of Debates,* 244; Nathan Tarcov, *Locke's Education for Liberty* (Lanham, Md.: Lexington Books, 1984).

61. "Letter from Cato to the *New York Journal* (undated)," 118; "Address by Denatus to the Members of the Virginia Federal Convention (June 11, 1788)," 263–264 (arguing that the Constitution should be designed to prevent the triumph of passion over reason). Custom is especially important because "the stability and attachment which time and habit gives to forms of government" may be necessary to protect the people against the designs of "the enlightened and aspiring few." "Letter from Centinel to the *(Philadelphia) Independent Gazetteer* (October 1787)," in Storing, *Complete Anti-Federalist,* 137.

62. Richard Bland, "An Inquiry into the Rights of the British Colonies (1766)," in *American Political Thought during the Founding Era,* ed. Charles Hyneman and Donald Lutz (Indianapolis, Ind.: Liberty Fund, 1983), 85; *Federalist* 17 ("It is a known fact in human nature that its affections are commonly weak in proportion to the distance or diffusiveness of the object").

63. "Letter from Cato to the *New York Journal* (undated)," 112.

64. Ibid.; "Letter from the Federal Farmer to the *Republican* (October 9, 1787)," in Storing, *Complete Anti-Federalist,* 231 (need for force and coercion increases with the distance from the seat of government); "Letter from Brutus to the *New York Journal* (October 18, 1787)," 369–370 (union too diverse to have the unity of "manners, sentiments and interests" necessary for a republic).

65. "Letter from Cato to the *New York Journal* (undated)," 111. Hamilton dismissed the possibility of "split[t]ing ourselves into an infinity of little jealous, clashing, tumultuous commonwealths" as suited only to those "who possess not qualifications to extend their influence beyond the narrow circles of personal intrigue." *Federalist* 9.

66. "Letter from Cato to the *New York Journal* (undated)," 112.

67. "Letter from Brutus to the *New York Journal* (October 18, 1787)," 370–371. The Maryland Farmer proposed submitting all laws to deliberation at the local level (except in cases of emergency). "Letter from a Farmer to the *(Baltimore) Maryland Gazette* (March 28, 1788)," 50. Under this plan, local forums must be given real power, since—as John Smilie argued during the Pennsylvania Ratifying Convention, predicting the decline of state and local government under the Constitution—the people will not "idolize a shadow." McMaster and Stone, *Pennsylvania and the Federal Constitution,* 270.

68. Federalists, of course, accepted that office is relatively more accessible in smaller states and communities.

69. "Letter from Cato to the *New York Journal* (undated)," 118.

70. "Speech by Melancton Smith to the Convention of the State of New York (June 25, 1788)," in Storing, *The Complete Anti-Federalist,* 165.

71. Niles, "Two Discourses on Liberty," 264n.*. Jefferson found fault with the ancient philosophers because, although they "embraced . . . the circle of kindred and friends" and taught patriotism, they failed to extend their love and benevolence to "the whole family of mankind." On this point, Jefferson greatly preferred the teachings of Jesus. "Letter from Thomas Jefferson to Benjamin Rush (April 21, 1803)," in *The Life and Selected Writings of Thomas Jefferson,* ed. Adrienne Koch and William Harwood Peden (New York: Modern Library, 1944), 568–569.

72. Foreign trade concerns weighed heavily. Mercy Otis Warren called the idea that the United States could avoid "commercial and political intercourse with distant nations" a "pleasing reverie" but utterly impossible given the absence of any "mounds of separation, either natural or artificial," and the commercial ambitions of Americans. Warren, *History,* 381–382.

73. Adams, "An Election Sermon (1782)," in *American Political Thought during the Founding Era,* ed. Charles Hyneman and Donald Lutz (Indianapolis, Ind.: Liberty Fund, 1983), 543–544. Proper safeguards might include frequent elections and short terms of office for representatives (544); "Letter from Brutus to the *New*

York Journal (November 29, 1787)," 382; "Speech by Melancton Smith to the Convention of the State of New York (June 20, 1788)," 153–154.

74. "Letter from Cato to the *New York Journal* (undated)," 119 (number of representatives too few to resist corruption and the "temptation to treachery"); "Letter from the Federal Farmer to the *Republican* (October 9, 1787)," 230 (too few representatives to allow for the representation of "every order of men"); "Letter from Brutus to the *New York Journal* (November 15, 1787)," in Storing, *Complete Anti-Federalist*, 380–382 (Congress too small to represent all classes); "Letter from the Impartial Examiner to the *Virginia Independent Chronicle* (June 4, 1788)," in Storing, *Complete Anti-Federalist*, 192–193; "Speech by George Mason in the Virginia State Ratifying Convention (June 4, 1788)," in Storing, *Complete Anti-Federalist*, 258; "Speech by Melancton Smith to the Convention of the State of New York (June 20, 1788)," 154–155.

75. "Letter from the Federal Farmer to the *Republican* (December 31, 1787)," 268–269: Representatives under the Federalist Constitution, the Federal Farmer argued, are "too far removed from the people, in general, to sympathize with them, and too few to communicate with them: a representation must be extremely imperfect where the representatives are not circumstanced to make the proper communications to their constituents, and where the constituents in turn cannot, with tolerable convenience, make known their wants, circumstances, and opinions, to their representatives."

76. Representatives of the people, George Mason maintained, should "think as they think, feel as they feel . . . [and be] thoroughly acquainted with their interest and condition"; "Speech by George Mason in the Virginia State Ratifying Convention (June 4, 1788)," 257. "Speech by William Symmes to the Massachusetts Convention (January 22, 1788)," in Storing, *Complete Anti-Federalist*, 63 (desiring "a more *feeling* representation") (emphasis in the original). "If the people are to give their assent to laws, by persons chosen and appointed by them," Brutus contended, "the manner of the choice and the number chosen, must be such, as to possess, be disposed, and consequently qualified to declare the sentiments of the people"; "Letter from Brutus to the *New York Journal* (October 18, 1787)," 369.

77. Representatives should possess the "sentiments and feelings" as well as the interests of their constituents, Brutus declared, and should "bear the strongest likeness [to] those in whose room they are substituted." Each of the "several orders in the society," accordingly, should have the opportunity to be represented by someone "intimately acquainted" with its wants and interests—someone, moreover, with the "becoming zeal to promote their prosperity"; "Letter from Brutus to the *New York Journal* (October 18, 1787)," 379–380. "Speech by Melancton Smith to the Convention of the State of New York (June 21, 1788)," in Storing, *Complete Anti-Federalist*, 157 (representatives should "be a true picture of the people").

78. "Letter from the Federal Farmer to the *Republican* (December 31, 1787)," 266.

79. Brutus contended that "if the person confided in, be a neighbour with whom [the constituent] is intimately acquainted, whose talents, he knows, are sufficient to manage the business with which he is charged, his honesty and fidelity unsuspected, and his friendship and zeal for the service of this principle unquestionable, he will

commit his affairs into his hands with unreserved confidence and feel himself secure; all the transactions of the agent will meet with the most favorable construction, and the measures he takes will give satisfaction"; "Letter from Brutus to the *New York Journal* (November 29, 1787)," 385.

80. Ibid.

81. Brutus pointed out that "the confidence which the people have in their rulers, in a free republic, arises from their knowing them, from their being responsible to them for their conduct, and from the power they have of displacing them when they misbehave: but in a republic of the extent of this continent, the people in general would be acquainted with very few of their rulers: the people at large would know little of their proceedings, and it would be extremely difficult to change them"; "Letter from Brutus to the *New York Journal* (October 18, 1787)," 370–371.

82. Ibid., 371.

83. Ibid.; Herbert Storing, "What the Anti-Federalists Were For," in Storing, *Complete Anti-Federalist,* 84n12; "Letter from Cato to the *New York Journal* (undated)," 111, 121 (laws are too feeble to assure domestic tranquility and protection to all the Union's parts); "Letter from the Federal Farmer to the *Republican* (January 23, 1788)," in Storing, *Complete Anti-Federalist,* 335–339 (government's power of purse and sword should not be unlimited); "Letter from Brutus to the *New York Journal* (January 17, 1788)," in Storing, *Complete Anti-Federalist,* 409–411 (standing armies dangerous to the liberties of the people). Anti-Federalists would have found confirmation of their argument in contemporary efforts to draw the military into the enforcement of drug laws. See "Drugs: A Military Matter?" *Christian Science Monitor,* June 25, 1986, 15; Jonathan Fuerbringer, "House Approves Use of Military to Fight Drugs," *New York Times,* September 12, 1986, A1, col. 2.

84. "Letter from the Federal Farmer to the *Republican* (December 31, 1787)," 266.

85. On the desirability of drawing representatives from the "several classes of the people" who compose a community, see "Letter from Brutus to the *New York Journal* (November 15, 1787)," 380; "Notes of Speeches Delivered to the Maryland Ratifying Convention (April 1788)," in Storing, *Complete Anti-Federalist,* 89–90; "Speech by Melancton Smith to the Convention of the State of New York (June 21, 1788)," 157–159. Rotation in office is urged in "Letter from the Federal Farmer to the *Republican* (December 31, 1787), 269, and Letter from the Federal Farmer to the *Republican* (January 10, 1788)," in Storing, *Complete Anti-Federalist,* 290–292; "Letter from Brutus to the *New York Journal* (April 10, 1788)," in Storing, *Complete Anti-Federalist,* 444–445; "Letter from Republicus to the *(Lexington) Kentucky Gazette* (February 16, 1788)," 163; "Speech by Melancton Smith to the Convention of the State of New York (June 25, 1788)," in Storing, *Complete Anti-Federalist,* 164–165. On the same principle, Anti-Federalists tended to advocate annual—or at least very frequent—elections. "Letter from Cato to the *New York Journal* (undated)," 122; "Letter from John DeWitt to the *(Boston) American Herald* (undated)," in Storing, *Complete Anti-Federalist,* 28; [Mercy Otis Warren], "Observations of a Columbian Patriot on the New Constitutions and on the Federal and State Conventions (Boston, 1788)," in Storing, *Complete Anti-Federalist,* 275.

86. "Speech by Melancton Smith to the Convention of the State of New York (June 21, 1788)," 157–159.

87. "Letter from the Federal Farmer to the *Republican* (January 12, 1788)," in Storing, *Complete Anti-Federalist*, 298; "Letter from a Friend of the Republic to the *(New Hampshire) Freeman's Oracle* (Anti-Federalist No. 2) (February 6, 1788)," in Storing, *Complete Anti-Federalist*, 244.

88. In Storing, *Complete Anti-Federalist*, see "Letter from Brutus to the *New York Journal* (November 29, 1787)," 383–384; "Letter from Cornelius to the *Hampshire Chronicle* (December 18, 1787)," 141–142; "Letter from a Newport Man to the *Newport Mercury* (March 1788)," 252; "Speech by Melancton Smith to the Convention of the State of New York (June 23, 1788)," 162. The Maryland Farmer observed that since all representative government is aristocratic in practice, even the "perfection of political wisdom" could only "temper" this quality; "Letter from a Farmer to the *(Baltimore) Maryland Gazette* (February 29, 1788)," 20. Federalists, by contrast, argued that rule by natural aristocrats was desirable and that the measure of republican government was satisfied where office was open to all. Elliot, *Debates*, 277–278.

89. "Speech by Melancton Smith to the Convention of the State of New York (June 21, 1788)," 157–159.

90. Ibid., 158.

91. "Letter from the Federal Farmer to the *Republican* (January 4, 1788)," in Storing, *Complete Anti-Federalist*, 275–276.

92. "Letter from Cato to the *New York Journal* (undated)," 110–111; "Letter from the Federal Farmer to the *Republican* (January 18, 1788)," in Storing, *Complete Anti-Federalist*, 230 (trial by jury and democratic legislatures "are the means by which the people are let into knowledge of public affairs"); "Letter from the Federal Farmer to the *Republican* (January 23, 1788)," in Storing, *Complete Anti-Federalist*, 339 ("the people in a small state can act with concert and with vigor").

93. "Letter from a Farmer to the *(Baltimore) Maryland Gazette* (March 7, 1788)," 31–32.

94. *Federalist* 10.

95. "Letter from Brutus to the *New York Journal* (November 17, 1787)," in Storing, *Complete Anti-Federalist*, 380–381 (natural aristocracy, using its wealth and family connections, will "constantly unite their efforts" and will "generally carry their election"); "Letter from Brutus to the *New York Journal* (November 29, 1787)," 383–384 (small legislatures are susceptible to the intrigues and corruptions of "great and designing men"); "Letter from Cornelius to the *Hampshire Chronicle* (December 18, 1787)," 143 (mercantile interests, concentrated in seaport towns, will find it easier to organize and will dominate the federal government); "Notes of Speeches Delivered to the Maryland Ratifying Convention (April 1788)," 89–90 (wealthy will combine to elect persons of their own rank); "Letter from the Independent Examiner to the *Virginia Independent Chronicle* (June 4, 1788)," 192–193 (size and diversity of the country will divide the electorate; the wealthy, better able to organize, will have the advantage).

96. "Letter from the Federal Farmer to the *Republican* (January 12, 1788)," 297; "Letter from Cornelius to the *Hampshire Chronicle* (December 18, 1787)," 143.

97. "Letter from the Federal Farmer to the *Republican* (January 12, 1788)," 296–297.

98. The logic of single-member, plurality districts works to decrease the number of candidates to two, as we learn whenever we are warned against "wasting" our votes. Maurice Duverger, *Political Parties: Their Organization and Activity in the Modern State* (New York: Wiley, 1963), 60. Duverger also observed, however, that single-member plurality election is compatible with weak party articulation, particularly in the United States (45). Duverger ultimately confirmed an Anti-Federalist suspicion by concluding that "the size of the constituencies seems to be of greater importance than the nature of the ballot." (358).

99. "Speech by Patrick Henry to the Virginia Ratifying Convention (June 12, 1788)," in Storing, *Complete Anti-Federalist,* 243.

100. Ibid., 243–244.

101. On rotation and frequent elections, see note 85. The jury is probably the closest approximation of the Anti-Federalist ideal in American political practice, since jury service is a short-term, broadly inclusive rotating obligation. Accordingly, Anti-Federalists championed the jury as the "democratical balance" in the judiciary. "Letter from Hampden to the *Massachusetts Centinel* (January 26, 1788)," in Storing, *Complete Anti-Federalist,* 200; "Letter from the Federal Farmer to the *Republican* (October 9, 1787)," 230–231; "Letter from the Federal Farmer to the *Republican* (October 12, 1787)," 249–250; "Letter from the Federal Farmer to the *Republican* (January 18, 1788)," 319–320. The Maryland Farmer went so far as to proclaim juries "more necessary than representatives in the legislature," perhaps because of their role in civic education. "Letter from a Farmer to the *(Baltimore) Maryland Gazette* (March 21, 1788)," in Storing, *Complete Anti-Federalist,* 38.

102. "Letter from the Federal Farmer to the *Republican* (January 12, 1788)," 300.

103. In Storing, *Complete Anti-Federalist,* see "Letter from the Federal Farmer to the *Republican* (January 3, 1788)," 274; "Letter from the Federal Farmer to the *Republican* (January 4, 1788)," 277–278; "Letter from the Federal Farmer to the *Republican* (January 7, 1788)," 284. Legislatures in Vermont and New Hampshire retain some of this character (150 and 395 members, respectively, for populations, according to the 1980 census, of 511,000 and 920,000).

104. "Letter from Cato to the *New York Journal* (undated)," 111; "Speech by Melancton Smith to the Convention of the State of New York (June 20, 1788)," 153–154 (holding up the states, since the Revolution, as the nearest approach to perfection in representation, considering it "impracticable to have such a representation in a consolidated government").

105. "Letter from the Federal Farmer to the *Republican* (October 10, 1787)," 236; "What the Anti-Federalists Were For," 18; "Letter from Brutus to the *New York Journal* (October 18, 1787)," 369; "Speech by Melancton Smith to the Convention of the State of New York (June 23, 1788)," 162.

106. *Federalist* 35. This practical objection, of course, conceals the fact that the Federalists also rejected the Anti-Federalist ideal. On this rejection, see Norman Jacobson, "Parable and Paradox: In Response to Arendt's *On Revolution,*" *Salmagundi* 123 (Spring–Summer 1983): 60.

107. "Letter from the Federal Farmer to the *Republican* (January 4, 1788)," 277.

108. "Speech by Melancton Smith to the Convention of the State of New York (June 20, 1788)," 154; "Letter from the Federal Farmer to the *Republican* (January

7, 1788)," 284–285; "Letter from the Federal Farmer to the *Republican* (January 12, 1788)," 298.

109. Mercy Otis Warren feared "party feuds," but she also observed the conflict between the "equality of nature" in which human beings are created and the "inherent," also natural, "desire of distinction." Warren, *History*, 396–397. In fact, despite her high republican sympathies, Warren regarded the aristocratic principles as invaluable in republican politics because the yearning for honor checks the pursuit of wealth (415).

110. "Letter from the Federal Farmer to the *Republican* (December 31, 1787)," 267.

111. Ibid.

112. Ibid.; Warren, *History*, 415.

113. "Letter from the Federal Farmer to the *Republican* (December 31, 1787)," 268.

114. "Letter from a Farmer to the *(Baltimore) Maryland Gazette* (March 18, 1788)," in Storing, *Complete Anti-Federalist*, 36 (emphasis in original). Note that this balance limits the upper classes but empowers the lower ones.

115. "Letter from John Francis Mercer to Thomas Jefferson (October 27, 1804)," in Storing, *Complete Anti-Federalist*, 72n40. Madison's argument, of course, appears in *Federalist* 10.

116. James Ceaser, "Political Parties and Presidential Ambition," *Journal of Politics* 40 (1978): 708, 730. Edmund Burke, the British philosopher, argued that party government is respectable precisely where parties are not "great" or where their great principles are moderated by other claims. See Harvey C. Mansfield, *Statesmanship and Party Government: A Study of Burke and Bolingbroke* (Chicago: University of Chicago Press, 1965). In contemporary politics, for example, successful presidential candidates tend to be drawn from the center of a party's spectrum. In 1988, for instance, Pat Robertson's candidacy was doomed by the perception of his views as extreme, even within a Republican context; Jesse Jackson suffered from a milder version of the same disadvantage. At the same time, candidates—especially where the nomination is contested—are likely to be far enough from the center of national opinion to provide voters with significant choice. Wilson Carey McWilliams, "The Meaning of the Election," in *The Election of 1988,* ed. Gerald Pomper (Chatham, N.J.: Chatham House Publishers, 1989), 184.

117. Ceaser, "Political Parties and Presidential Ambition," 727.

118. "Letter from Cato to the *New York Journal* (undated)," 111; "Address by John Francis Mercer to the Conventions of Virginia and New York (April or May 1788)," in Storing, *Complete Anti-Federalist*, 103–104; "Letter from Centinel to the *(Philadelphia) Independent Gazetteer* (October 1787)," 139.

119. *Federalist* 70.

120. Speaking of a plural executive, Hamilton argued that "it is far more safe there should be a single object for the jealousy and watchfulness of the people." Ibid.

121. "Letter from a Farmer to the *(Baltimore) Maryland Gazette* (March 28, 1788)," 50. The prerogative, according to Locke, is the "power to act according to discretion for the public good, without the prescription of the law and sometimes even against it," conveyed to the executive by the "common law of nature" and,

especially, by the "fundamental law of nature and government—*viz.*, that as much as may be, all members of the society are to be preserved." Locke, *Two Treatises,* 203–204. Hamilton had this principle in mind when he asserted that "energy in the executive is a leading character in the definition of good government," essential to and more fundamental than any form of government. *Federalist* 70; Larry Arnhart, "'The God-Like Prince': John Locke, Executive Prerogative, and the American Presidency," *Presidential Studies Quarterly* 9 (1979): 121–130.

122. Mansfield, *Statesmanship and Party Government,* 4, 17–18 (observation that Burke's defense of party rests on "an attempt to avoid dependence on great men" and involves a "movement from statesmanship to party government"). Similarly, Woodrow Wilson traced American parties, like American institutions generally, to the Whig "struggle to curb and regulate the power of the Crown." See Woodrow Wilson, *Constitutional Government in the United States* (New York: Columbia University Press, 1908), 198.

123. James MacGregor Burns, *The Vineyard of Liberty* (New York: Vintage Books, 1982), 136.

124. Wilson, *Constitutional Government,* 202–203. Yet, as Wilson also observes, a president may be able to "break party lines asunder and draw together combinations of his own devising" (215).

125. Perry M. Goldman, "Political Virtue in the Age of Jackson," *Political Science Quarterly* 87, no. 1 (March 1972): 46.

126. Joel H. Silbey, *The Partisan Imperative* (Oxford: Oxford University Press, 1985). "There is a sense," Woodrow Wilson argued, "in which our parties may be said to have been our real body politic. Not the authority of Congress, not the leadership of the President, but the discipline and zest of parties, has held us together, has made it possible for us to form and to carry out national programs." Wilson, *Constitutional Government,* 218. In this respect, Wilson agreed with George Washington Plunkitt's famous saying: "This great and glorious country was built up by political parties." William L. Riordon, *Plunkitt of Tammany Hall* (New York: Penguin, 1948), 18. On parties and the "aggregation of interests," see Gerald M. Pomper, *Voters, Elections, and Parties: The Practice of Theory* (New Brunswick, N.J.: Transaction, 1988), 257–259.

127. Pomper, *Voters, Elections, and Parties,* 259–260.

128. Walter Dean Burnham, *Critical Elections and the Mainsprings of American Politics* (New York: Norton, 1970), 133; Burnham, *The Current Crisis in American Politics* (Oxford: Oxford University Press, 1982).

129. Herman Finer, *The Theory and Practice of Modern Government* (New York: Henry Holt, 1949), 237. To some extent, the courts have recognized the special role played by parties in representation. Parties cannot practice racial discrimination in primary elections, for instance. *Smith v. Allwright,* 321 U.S. 649 (1944); *Terry v. Adams,* 345 U.S. 506 (1953). At the same time, there is a public interest in the autonomy of political parties. Compare *O'Brien v. Brown,* 409 U.S. 1 (1972).

130. Wilson, *Constitutional Government,* 207–209; Mary Kingsbury Simkhovitch, "Friendship and Politics," *Political Science Quarterly* 17, no. 2 (June 1902): 189. Jefferson's hope for a "gradation of authorities" from the local ward-republic to the nation, similar to Anti-Federalist theories of representation, was never realized in the formal institutions of government. "Letter from Thomas Jefferson to Joseph C. Cabell (February 2, 1816)," in *The Life and Selected Writings of Thomas*

Jefferson, ed. Adrienne Koch and William Harwood Peden (New York: Modern Library, 1944), 661, 673; Richard K. Matthews, *The Radical Politics of Thomas Jefferson* (Lawrence: University Press of Kansas, 1984), 81–89.

131. The importance of patronage has greatly diminished in contemporary politics. Nevertheless, court decisions that limit patronage have contributed to the weakening of local party organization. *Branti v. Finkel,* 445 U.S. 507 (1980); *Elrod v. Burns,* 427 U.S. 347 (1976); Leon D. Epstein, *Political Parties in the American Mold* (Madison: University of Wisconsin Press, 1986), 141–143. It is worth remembering A. C. McLaughlin's observation that "we should have little hesitation in preferring the spoils method of financing party management to the secret system, whereby large corporations with special interests to be subserved furnish the funds in exchange for favors." Andrew C. McLaughlin, *The Courts, the Constitution, and Parties* (Chicago: University of Chicago Press, 1912), 128.

132. *Federalist* 49; Richard Hofstadter, *The Idea of a Party System* (Berkeley: University of California Press, 1969), 39–73.

133. Jefferson held similar views. See Matthews, *Radical Politics,* 85–86. Later, Martin Van Buren would write that when "the principles of contending parties are supported with candor, fairness and moderation, the very discord which is thus produced, may in a government like ours, be conducive to the public good." Martin Van Buren, *The Autobiography of Martin Van Buren,* ed. John Clement Fitzpatrick (Washington, D.C.: Government Printing Office, 1920).

134. Robert Bellah, Richard Madsen, William M. Sullivan, Ann Swidler, and Steven M. Tipton, *Habits of the Heart* (Berkeley: University of California Press, 1985).

135. Pomper, *Voters, Elections, and Parties,* 262–266, 282–304; William J. Crotty, *American Parties in Decline* (New York: Little, Brown, 1984).

136. Morris P. Fiorina, "The Decline of Collective Responsibility in American Politics," *Daedelus* 109, no. 3 (Summer 1980): 25–40; Everett Carll Ladd, *Where Have All the Voters Gone?* (New York: Norton, 1978).

137. Gerald M. Pomper, ed., *Party Renewal in America* (Santa Barbara, Calif.: Greenwood, 1980). On the burgeoning of national party bureaucracies, see Epstein, *Political Parties,* 200–238.

5. Science and Freedom

1. Leo Marx, *The Machine in the Garden* (New York: Oxford University Press, 1964).

2. Genesis 11:4–9.

3. Perry Miller, *The New England Mind* (Boston: Beacon, 1961), 2:345–363.

4. John Calvin, *Institutes of the Christian Religion,* bk. 3, chap. 10, sec. 23; John Wise, *A Word of Comfort to a Melancholy Country* (1721), cited in Miller, *New England Mind,* 2:329.

5. Calvin, *Institutes of the Christian Religion,* bk. 3, chap. 10, sec. 6.

6. Daniel Defoe, *Robinson Crusoe* (Philadelphia: J. C. Winston, 1925), 167, see also 118–119.

7. Letter to William Duane, August 12, 1810, in *The Life and Selected Writings of Thomas Jefferson,* ed. Adrienne Koch and William Peden (New York: Modern Library, 1944), 609.

8. Thomas Hobbes, *Leviathan,* ed. C. B. Macpherson (Harmondsworth, UK: Penguin, 1968), 118–119, 160–161. "On the basis of sensation, of matter and motion," Jefferson wrote, "we may erect . . . all . . . certainties," rejecting any knowledge except what comes to the body through the senses. *The Adams-Jefferson Letters,* ed. Lester J. Cappon (Chapel Hill: University of North Carolina Press, 1959), 568–569.

9. John Locke, *Two Treatises of Government,* 1, par. 86, 87, 2, par. 149; Alexander Hamilton, "A Full Vindication" (1774), in *The Works of Alexander Hamilton,* ed. H. C. Lodge (New York: Putnam's, 1903), 1:12; see also *The Writings of James Madison,* ed. Gaillard Hunt (New York: Putnam's, 1900–1910), 4:387.

10. Benjamin Franklin, "A Proposal for Promoting Useful Knowledge among the British Plantations in America" (1743), in *Benjamin Franklin: Writings,* ed. J. A. Lemay (New York: Library of America, 1987), 296.

11. Ibid., 61; cf. Locke, *Essay Concerning Human Understanding,* bk. 4, chap. 3, par. 18.

12. Franklin, *Writings,* 61, 63–64.

13. Franklin, "Letter to Thomas Hopkinson, July 1748," in ibid., 435; Benjamin Franklin, *Autobiography and Other Writings,* ed. Kenneth Silverman (New York: Penguin, 1986), 63.

14. Locke, *Two Treatises of Government,* 1, par. 58.

15. Franklin, *Autobiography,* 39.

16. Hobbes's view of the state of nature, Franklin wrote James Logan (1737?), is "nearer the truth" than the idea that the original condition was a "State of Love"; see Franklin, *Writings,* 425.

17. *Federalist* 2; *The Papers of James Madison,* ed. William T. Hutchinson and William M. E. Rachal (Chicago: University of Chicago Press, 1962), 5:83, 8:78, 300.

18. *Federalist* 1. Or, in Madison's phrase, "the permanent and aggregate interests of the community"; *Federalist* 10. When our duties and interests "seem to be at variance," Jefferson wrote to Say (February 1, 1804), "we ought to suspect some fallacy in our reasonings"; Jefferson, *Life and Selected Writings,* 575.

19. *Federalist* 6; see also Franklin, *Autobiography,* 103–104; even the best measures of government, Franklin remarked, are ordinarily "forc'd by the Occasion" (147).

20. *Federalist* 20; see also *Federalist* 15. Tocqueville's discussion of interest "rightly understood" may be found in his *Democracy in America,* ed. Henry Reeve (New York: Knopf, 1980), vol. 2, bk. 2, chap. 8.

21. David Epstein, *The Political Theory of "The Federalist"* (Chicago: University of Chicago Press, 1984), 6; Douglas Adair, *Fame and the Founding Fathers* (New York: Norton, 1974), 3–25; on the ideal of disinterestedness and challenges to it, see Gordon Wood, *The Creation of the American Republic, 1776–1787* (Chapel Hill: University of North Carolina Press, 1969), 471–518.

22. *Political Writings of Thomas Jefferson,* ed. Edward Dumbauld (New York: Liberal Arts, 1955), 16.

23. Locke, *Two Treatises of Government,* 2, par. 137; Sheldon S. Wolin, *Politics and Vision* (Boston: Little, Brown, 1960), 347–348; Norman Jacobson, "Political Science and Political Education," *American Political Science Review* 57 (1963): 561–569.

24. I take the term "powerhouse" from Henry Adams, *The Education of Henry Adams* (Boston: Houghton Mifflin, 1961), 421.

25. *Federalist* 15, 16, 23, and 70.

26. U.S. Constitution, art. 1, sec. 8. *Federalist* 12 refers to "multiplying the means of gratification" as a public good.

27. *Federalist* 8.

28. *Federalist* 42.

29. *Federalist* 31, 42.

30. *Federalist* 25, 41.

31. *Federalist* 10; Epstein, *Political Theory of "The Federalist,"* 144, 163.

32. *Federalist* 9; representation, Madison argued, is a "great mechanical power," discovered by Europeans but one that Americans have applied and can develop to its "full efficacy."

33. Michael Kammen refers to the framers' statecraft as "a blend of cultural relativism combined with theoretical universalism" in *A Machine That Would Go of Itself* (New York: Knopf, 1986), 65. In 1814, Jefferson wrote to Thomas Law that "men living in different countries . . . may have different utilities; the same act, therefore, may be useful, and consequently virtuous in one country which is injurious and vicious in another"; see Jefferson, *Life and Selected Writings,* 639–640.

34. Conceding that it was important to "annihilate" the states, Gouverneur Morris expressed the hope that the convention would "take the teeth out of the serpents"; see James Madison, *Notes of Debates in the Federal Convention of 1787* (Athens: Ohio University Press, 1966), 241. On trial by jury in civil cases, see *Federalist* 83.

35. *Federalist* 1; see also Epstein, *Political Theory of "The Federalist,"* 112.

36. *National Gazette,* February 20, 1792, in *Papers of James Madison,* ed. Robert Rutland (Charlottesville: University Press of Virginia, 1983), 14:233.

37. Letter to Edward Livingston, April 17, 1824, in *Writings of James Madison,* 9:188.

38. *Federalist* 51.

39. Herbert J. Storing, ed., *The Complete Anti-Federalist* (Chicago: University of Chicago Press, 1981), 5:233, 236.

40. Epstein, *Political Theory of "The Federalist,"* 141.

41. *Federalist* 51.

42. Martin Diamond, "Democracy and *The Federalist:* A Reconsideration of the Framers' Intent," *American Political Science Review* 53 (1959): 52–68.

43. Locke, *Two Treatises of Government,* 2, para. 96, 137.

44. *Federalist* 10, 14, 51.

45. *Federalist* 49.

46. *Federalist* 72.

47. Madison, *Notes of Debates,* 194. In *Federalist* 49, Madison listed the conditions at the time of the Revolution that ensured successful public constitution-making, observing that the United States could not expect any "equivalent security" in the future.

48. *Federalist* 55.

49. *Federalist* 9.

50. Madison, *Notes of Debates,* 162, 166.

51. *Federalist* 46.

52. Madison, *Notes of Debates*, 131; see the criticisms of the state regimes that Madison records as being made by Wilson and Morris, 90, 241.

53. *Federalist* 16; see also Madison, *Notes of Debates*, 74.

54. *Federalist* 17.

55. *Federalist* 27; see also *Federalist* 17, 34.

56. Madison, *Notes of Debates*, 244.

57. Hence Hamilton's argument that the "extensive inquiry and observation" of merchants makes them the natural patrons of manufacturers and tradesmen; *Federalist* 35.

58. In 1729, for example, Franklin argued that the government should manage the money supply in the interest of general economic prosperity; see Franklin, *Writings*, 119–135.

59. *Federalist* 10.

60. *Papers of James Madison*, 9:76.

61. *Writings of James Madison*, 6:86.

62. *Federalist* 57.

63. *Federalist* 8.

64. Franklin argued for the usefulness of a "Publick Religion," particularly given "the Advantage of a religious Character among private Persons"; see Franklin, *Writings*, 336.

65. Hamilton called Shays a desperate debtor in *Federalist* 6, probably alluding to *Leviathan*, chap. 11.

66. A belief in "particular Providence," Franklin held, is necessary to "weak and ignorant Men and Women, and . . . inexperienced and inconsiderate Youth of both Sexes"; see Franklin, *Writings*, 748.

67. Nathan Tarcov, *Locke's Education for Liberty* (Chicago: University of Chicago Press, 1984).

68. Locke and his school, Daniel Calhoun writes, addressed "the crucial problem of technique"; see Calhoun, *The Intelligence of a People* (Princeton, N.J.: Princeton University Press, 1973), 154.

69. Locke, *Some Thoughts Concerning Education,* par. 66, 73, 87; Tarcov, *Locke's Education*, 82, 114.

70. In fact, Locke held that education is responsible for nine-tenths of character; see Tarcov, *Locke's Education*, 82. For Locke's argument on play and study, see his *Some Thoughts Concerning Education,* par. 128.

71. Locke, *Some Thoughts Concerning Education,* par. 33–35, 38, 44.

72. Ibid., par. 40, 78, 111–213; Locke also warns against excessive strictness, since beyond a certain point, it only stimulates desire (par. 20).

73. Ibid., par. 45, 126; Tarcov, *Locke's Education*, 86, 90, 176–177.

74. Locke, *Some Thoughts Concerning Education,* par. 4, 7, 13, 34, 216; Locke's view that nature assigns responsibility to both parents (see his *Two Treatises of Government*, 2, par. 53) will sound better to modern ears.

75. Locke, *Some Thoughts Concerning Education,* par. 78, 84, 87, 104, 106–108, 112.

76. Calhoun, *Intelligence of a People*, 143, 154; Locke, *Some Thoughts Concerning Education*, par. 43, 44.

77. Locke, *Some Thoughts Concerning Education,* par. 56, 58, 62, 143, 200; Tarcov, *Locke's Education,* 101–141.

78. Locke, *Some Thoughts Concerning Education,* par. 109; Tarcov, *Locke's Education,* 141.

79. Franklin, *Autobiography,* 77.

80. Ibid., 80; letter to Lord Kames, May 3, 1760, in Franklin, *Writings,* 766.

81. Franklin, *Autobiography,* 91–103; Franklin also developed a "Moral or Prudential Algebra," in his Letter to Joseph Priestley, September 19, 1772, in Franklin, *Writings,* 877–878.

82. Franklin, Letter to Lord Kames, May 3, 1760, in Franklin, *Writings,* 765; see also Franklin, *Autobiography,* 100.

83. Franklin, *Autobiography,* 64.

84. Ibid., 13, 24, 81, 83.

85. Ibid., 81, 83; Letter to Joseph Priestley, June 7, 1782, in Franklin, *Writings,* 1047–1048.

86. Franklin, *Autobiography,* 18, 147–148.

87. As Ralph Lerner points out, when Franklin appeals to Pope's authority to support this argument, he underlines the point by improving on Pope's poetry. See Lerner, "Benjamin Franklin: Spectator," in *The Thinking Revolutionary* (Ithaca, N.Y.: Cornell University Press, 1987), 51, 53.

88. Franklin, *Autobiography,* 173–174; Aristotle, *Politics,* 1253a8–1253a18.

89. Franklin, *Autobiography,* 89; Franklin, *Writings,* 748.

90. Franklin, *Autobiography,* 89.

91. Ibid., 135–136

92. Ibid., 103.

93. Ibid., 87, 102.

94. Ibid., 4, 113; Paul W. Conner, *Poor Richard's Politics: Benjamin Franklin and His New American Order* (New York: Oxford University Press, 1965).

95. Franklin, *Autobiography,* 92.

96. Ibid., 105.

97. Michael Ignatieff, *The Needs of Strangers* (New York: Viking, 1985).

98. Harvey C. Mansfield, Jr., *Taming the Prince* (New York: Free Press, 1989), esp. 1–20.

99. Tocqueville, *Democracy in America,* vol. 1, bk. 2, chap. 7.

100. Jacques Ellul, *The Technological Society* (New York: Knopf, 1964).

101. Lewis Lapham, "Notebook: Supply-Side Ethics," *Harper's,* May 1985, 11. Of course, Tocqueville anticipated this; see his *Democracy in America,* vol. 2, bk. 2, chap. 2.

102. Judith Wallerstein, "The Impact of Divorce on Children," *Child Psychiatry* 3 (1980): 459–462.

103. Tocqueville, *Democracy in America,* vol. 2, bk. 2, chap. 2.

104. Ibid., vol. 2, bk. 2, chap. 13, vol. 2, bk. 3, chap. 13; Ignatieff, *Needs of Strangers,* 83–103; Russell Jacoby, *Social Amnesia* (Boston: Beacon, 1975).

105. Marvin Zetterbaum, "Self and Subjectivity in Political Theory," *Review of Politics* 44 (1982): 59–82.

106. Sheldon S. Wolin, "Democracy in the Discourse of Postmodernism," *Social Research* 57 (1990): 5–30.

107. Wolin, *Politics and Vision*, 352–434; Dwight Waldo, *The Administrative State* (New York: Ronald, 1946); Calhoun, for example, calls attention to the growth of professional licensing and testing, in his *Intelligence of a People*, 319–320.

108. John Kenneth Galbraith, *The New Industrial State* (Boston: Houghton Mifflin, 1967), and Galbraith, "Coolidge, Carter, Bush, Reagan," *New York Times*, December 12, 1988, A16.

109. Robert Coles, "The Politics of Ressentiment," *New Republic*, August 2, 1982, 32–34.

110. Tocqueville, *Democracy in America*, vol. 1, bk. 2, chap. 4, vol. 2, bk. 2, chap. 7.

111. Robert Karen, "Becoming Attached," *Atlantic*, February 1990, 35–39.

112. Tocqueville, *Democracy in America*, vol. 2, bk. 1, chap. 10, 11. In the text of chap. 11, Tocqueville comments that Raphael's aspiration to "surpass nature" made him less concerned with rigorous accuracy. In a footnote, however, he argues that Raphael's drawings display a superior "fidelity to nature" and "profound scientific knowledge."

6. In Good Faith

1. George Gilder, *Wealth and Poverty* (New York: Basic Books, 1981), 6–7, 28; Leslie Fiedler, "The Birth of God and the Death of Man," *Salmagundi* 21 (1973): 3–26. Also Robert Bellah, *The Broken Covenant* (New York: Seabury, 1975); Irving Kristol, *Two Cheers for Capitalism* (New York: New American Library, 1979), esp. 243, 246, 253; and such critics of "liberation" as Herbert Hendin, *The Age of Sensation* (New York: Norton, 1975).

2. Peter L. Berger, *Pyramids of Sacrifice* (New York: Basic Books, 1974), 198–214; John H. Schaar, *Legitimacy in the Modern State* (New Brunswick, N.J.: Transaction, 1981).

3. We do, of course, speak of the advantages of religion in general, but no one believes religion in general. It is precisely because particular religious doctrines conflict, with each other and with nonreligious ideas, about the meaning of the just and the unjust that they must be seen as public doctrines.

4. Louis Hartz, *The Liberal Tradition in America* (New York: Harcourt Brace, 1955).

5. Thomas Hobbes, *Leviathan*, ed. C. B. MacPherson (Baltimore, Md.: Penguin, 1968), 173, 177, on the advantages of religion, and 627–715 ("Of the Kingdome of Darknesse") for its dangers. A contemporary statement of the perils of religious faith is Morris R. Cohen's "The Dark Side of Religion," in Cohen, *The Faith of a Liberal* (New York: Holt, 1946), 337–361.

6. John 3:12; see also Eric Voegelin, *Anamnesis* (Notre Dame, Ind.: Notre Dame University Press, 1978), 32–33.

7. John Locke, *Second Treatise on Civil Government*, sec. 149.

8. *Fiducia*, on the Continent, is the obligation of one person to another. See W. Friedmann, *Legal Theory* (London: Stevens, 1953), 357.

9. I refer, of course, to the famous opening sections of *The Crisis*.

10. 2 Corinthians 5:7.

11. Hobbes, *Leviathan*, 85, 98, 167–168.

12. 1 Thessalonians 5:21; see also Miguel de Unamuno, *The Agony of Christianity* (Princeton, N.J.: Princeton University Press, 1974), 10.

13. Max Planck, *The New Science* (New York: Meridian, 1959), 45–51, 316.

14. Genesis 18:20–33, 19:19–22.

15. Hebrews 11:1; John 9:39–41.

16. Machiavelli, *The Prince*, chap. 18.

17. Phillip Rieff, "Aesthetic Functions in Modern Politics," *World Politics* 5 (1953): 478–502.

18. Paul Shorey is right to observe that *pistis* is not Christian faith, but that does not mean it is not part of a broader definition of faith. (Shorey's comment is found in the Loeb Edition of Plato's *Republic,* bks. 6–10 [Cambridge, Mass.: Harvard University Press, 1935], 6:117.) *Pistis* is translated as faith (among other meanings) by F. E. Peters, *Greek Philosophical Terms* (New York: New York University Press, 1967), 160.

19. Plato *Republic* 511e, 534a, 597b; see also Planck, *New Science,* 30–36, 83, and Eugene Miller, "Positivism, Historicism, and Political Inquiry," *American Political Science Review* 66 (1972): 796–817.

20. Planck, *New Science,* 299.

21. Plato *Republic* 519b.

22. Ibid., 603a; Anton C. Pegis, ed., *Basic Writings of St. Thomas Aquinas* (New York: Random House, 1945), 1:13, 15, 115, 119; Voegelin, *Anamnesis,* 29, 103.

23. Plato *Republic* 601e.

24. Ibid., 601d, 602a.

25. Oliver Wendell Holmes, Jr., *The Common Law* (Boston: Little, Brown, 1923), 132–137.

26. For example, it is particularly heinous, in the common view, to conduct an extramarital affair in one's own house and worse still to do so in the conjugal bed. By contrast, "conventional falsehoods," as Planck comments, are acceptable precisely because they are conventional, part of the common order of things; see Planck, *New Science,* 256.

27. Ecclesiasticus 3:18; Matthew 23:12

28. Mark 4:26–30; Matthew 17:20; Luke 13:18–20, 17:6.

29. Matthew 8:9–10; Luke 7:1–10.

30. 1 Corinthians 13:2; similarly James 2:26, "as the body without the spirit is dead, so faith without works is dead also." Faith is likened to mere material potentiality: it can exist, but without enlivening value, if it is without goodness in work. There is a second way in which traitors derive power from the whole. The services of an obscure functionary in a great regime may be more valuable that those of the ruler in a small state. In the same way, treachery is made infamous by the virtue of the regime it betrays.

31. Jonah 4:1–3.

32. Robert Neville, *God, the Creator* (Chicago: University of Chicago Press, 1968), 236.

33. Acts 8:13–24; see also Romans 1:17–22.

34. Augustine, *De Doctrina Christiana,* 1:28; Peter Dennis Bathory, *Political Theory as Public Confession* (New Brunswick, N.J.: Transaction, 1981), 65–68, 81–95.

35. Plato *Apology* 25c–26a.
36. 2 Corinthians 5:17.
37. Romans 4:5.
38. Romans 5:1–5, esp. 5:2.
39. Augustine, *Epistle,* 137, cited in Bathory, *Political Theory,* 27.
40. Planck, *New Science,* 75, 123–151.
41. Augustine, *Confessions,* bk. 10, chap. 43.
42. Eric Voegelin, *The Ecumenic Age* (Baton Rouge: Louisiana State University Press, 1974), 226, 233, 270.
43. We refer to friends as "faithful" and "faithless," but that usage is even more archaic in sound than the language of marital fidelity.
44. Genesis 2:24.
45. There are many useful comments on this point in Kingsley Davis, "Jealousy and Sexual Property," in *Psychoanalysis and the Social Sciences,* ed. Geza Roheim (New York: International Universities Press, 1947), 313–336.
46. Mark 10:2–12; the qualification in Matthew 19:9 reads like a compromise with civil prudence, if not a gloss.
47. Matthew 19:11.
48. Edward J. Bloustein, "Group Privacy," *Rutgers-Camden Law Journal* 8 (1977): 228–229.
49. Friedrich Meinecke, *Machiavellianism,* trans. D. Scott (New York: Prager, 1965), 32.
50. Plato *Republic* 333e–334b.
51. Machiavelli, *The Prince,* chap. 18; Machiavelli, *Discourses,* bk. 1, chap. 37; Machiavelli, *Florentine Histories,* bk. 4, chap. 14.
52. Machiavelli, *The Prince,* chap. 15.
53. Ewart K. Lewis, "Natural Law and Expediency in Medieval Political Thought," *Ethics* 50 (1940): 144–163.
54. Grotius, for example, understood the need to attend to the bestial side of man, but he wrote that there is a "danger of imitating wild beasts too much," with the risk that one will forget his humanity. See Grotius, *Law of War and Peace,* trans. F. W. Kelsey (Oxford: Clarendon Press, 1925), bk. 3, 12.
55. Machiavelli, *Discourses,* bk. 1, chap. 26.
56. Ibid., bk. 3, chap. 5, bk.1, chap. 9.
57. Machiavelli, *The Prince,* chap. 8.
58. Machiavelli, *Discourses,* bk. 1, chap. 9.
59. Ibid., bk. 1, chap. 37.
60. Machiavelli, *The Prince,* chap. 15; Machiavelli, *Discourses,* bk. 2, chap. 21; Harvey C. Mansfield, Jr., *Machiavelli's New Modes and Orders* (Ithaca, N.Y.: Cornell University Press, 1979), 254–255.
61. Machiavelli, *Discourses,* bk. 1, chap. 12; Machiavelli, *Florentine Histories,* bk.1, chaps. 2 and 3; Machiavelli, *The Art of War,* ed. Neal Wood (Indianapolis, Ind.: Bobbs-Merrill, 1965), 79; Mansfield, *Machiavelli's New Modes,* 69–79. I owe a great deal to James Rhodes, "The Kingdom of God and Politics," a paper presented to the Conference of Religion and Politics, Rutgers University, November 21, 1981, esp. 10–11.
62. Rhodes, "Kingdom of God and Politics," 54–57.

63. Machiavelli, *Discourses*, bk. 1, chap. 46, bk. 2, chaps. 2, 14, and 16.
64. Locke, *Essays Concerning Human Understanding,* ed. P. Nidditch (Oxford: Clarendon Press, 1975), 6, 10. I do not mean to deny that Hobbes, in a crucial sense, may be best understood as a creator: see Norman Jacobson, *Pride and Solace* (Berkeley: University of California Press, 1978), 51–92.
65. Justice Marshall in *Dartmouth Collage v. Woodward*, 4 Wh. 636 (1819).
66. Hobbes, *Leviathan*, 239–241, 216.
67. Ibid., 203–204.
68. Ibid., 205; see also 204–206.
69. Ibid., 205–206.
70. Ibid., 207.
71. Ibid., 233–234, 264, 268–269, 370–372, 375.
72. F. W. Maitland, "The Unincorporate Body," in *Frederick William Maitland: A Reader,* ed. V. T. Delany (New York: Oceana, 1957), 137, and see 130–142.
73. Locke, *Second Treatise on Civil Government*, sec. 142–149.
74. *U.S. v. Percheman*, 7 Pet. 87 (1833).
75. *Ogden v. Saunders* 12 Wh. 213, 354–355 (1827); see Robert K. Faulkner, *The Jurisprudence of John Marshall* (Princeton, N.J.: Princeton University Press, 1968), 137–140.
76. Pope, *Essay on Man*, Epistle 3.
77. Jacques Ellul, *The Technological Society* (New York: Knopf, 1964). See also John H. Schaar, "Jacques Ellul: Between Babylon and the New Jerusalem," *Democracy* 2 (Fall 1982): 102–118.
78. Alexis de Tocqueville, *Democracy in America* (New York: Schocken, 1961), 2:118–120.
79. Christopher Lasch, *The Culture of Narcissism* (New York: Norton, 1978).
80. *Griswold v. Connecticut*, 381 U.S. 479 (1965).
81. *Eisenstadt v. Baird*, 405 U.S. 438 (1972).
82. *Roe v. Wade*, 410 U.S. 113, 152–153 (1973).
83. *Planned Parenthood of Central Missouri v. Danforth*, 428 U.S. 52 (1976).
84. Daniel Bell, *The Cultural Contradictions of Capitalism* (New York: Basic Books, 1976); John Hallowell, *The Moral Foundations of Democracy* (Chicago: University of Chicago Press, 1954), 71.
85. David Truman, *The Governmental Process* (New York: Knopf, 1951), 50–51.
86. This, surely, is implicit in Lasswell's formula, which reduces "rationalizations in terms of the public interest" to displaced individual private motives. See Lasswell, "Psychopathology and Politics," in *Political Writings of Harold D. Lasswell* (Glencoe, Ill.: Free Press, 1951).
87. Arnold Rosgow, *The Dying of the Light* (New York: Putnam's, 1975).
88. See my essay "On Equality as the Moral Foundation for Community," in *The Moral Foundations of the American Republic*, ed. Robert Horwitz (Charlottesville: University Press of Virginia, 1977), 183–213. That essay has been republished as chapter 8 in this volume.
89. Deuteronomy 15:7; Proverbs 23:6.
90. St. Thomas Aquinas, *Commentaries on Aristotle's Ethics*, bk. 8, chap. 7.
91. Matthew 20:1–15.

92. Plato *Republic* 518e. See also G. K. Chesterton's splendid essay "What Is America?" in his *What I Saw in America* (New York: Da Capo, 1968), 1–18.

7. The Discipline of Freedom

1. Abraham Lincoln, "Address at Sanitary Fair," in *Collected Works of Abraham Lincoln,* ed. Roy Basler (New Brunswick, N.J.: Rutgers University Press, 1953), 7:301.

2. That Lincoln refers to a "definition" of freedom indicates that he is concerned with the framers' theory of liberty, their understanding of words and in speech, and not the practical decision to compromise with slavery. In his address, Lincoln went on to describe two popular definitions of liberty, one allowing "each man to do as he pleases with himself, and the product of his labor," the second permitting "some to do as they please with other men, and the product of other men's labor"; see Lincoln, *Collected Works,* 7:301–302. Although Lincoln's preference is obvious, both of these doctrines are familiar and hence are included in Lincoln's criticism of previous definitions of freedom. The parties associated with the two views are only "called" by the "names" of liberty and tyranny: the popular definitions, in other words, are conventional, limiting practice but falling short of the standard of theory, partisan rather than philosophic. As Lincoln's phrasing makes clear, both of the popular views rest on the principle that freedom is doing as one pleases. Moreover, he was too shrewd not to recognize that the first definition easily slides over to the second, since doing as I please with myself and my products can result in my establishing ascendancy over you. In addition, Baltimore's adherence to the party of liberty was due to the success of Union arms (see the draft of the first paragraph, omitted from the final version of Lincoln's speech, 7:303). The triumph of the party of liberty, in practice, depended on the Union's ability to do as it pleased with the rebel states and their sympathizers. In either of its popular forms, "doing as one pleases" fell short of Lincoln's standard for a "good definition of liberty." According to Harry Jaffa, Lincoln understood the "enjoyment of freedom" to be "conditional upon one's ordering of one's life and the life of one's community in accordance with the principle of the moral order." See Jaffa, "Is Political Freedom Grounded in Natural Law?" paper presented to the Claremont Institute Conference on "A New Order of the Ages," February 1984.

3. Plato *Symposium* 202b6–202e6.

4. Locke, for example, defined the identity of a man as "nothing but a participation of the same continued Life . . . like that of other Animals in one fitly organized Body"; Locke, *Essay on Human Understanding,* bk. 2, chap, 27, sec. 6. Similarly, the desire for self-preservation, part of the nature man shares with the "inferior animals," is the "first and strongest desire God planted in men," a "fundamental, sacred and unalterable law." It is prior to revelation, reason, or any "verbal donation," and reason must assure man that by "pursuing the natural inclination to preserve his being, he followed the will of his Maker"; Locke, *Two Treatises of Government,* bk. 1, sec. 86–87, bk. 2, sec. 149. In other words, the body with its senses and inclinations has priority in the interpretation of revelation and the understanding of nature; Locke, *Essays on Human Understanding,* bk. 1, chap. 3. Those among the American founders who spoke of natural obligation or sociability

characteristically referred to a moral "sense" or "instinct," that is, a part of bodily nature. As this suggests, even when they sought to uphold classical or religious ideas of virtue and morality, the framers almost always cast their arguments in modern terms. In the debates of the late eighteenth century, for example, Locke is cited more than any other author; see Donald Lutz, "The Relative Influence of European Writers on Late Eighteenth Century American Political Thought," *American Political Science Review* 78 (1984): 193, and see also Gary Schmitt and Robert Webking, "Revolutionaries, Antifederalists, and Federalists," *Political Science Reviewer* 9 (1979): 195–229. Whatever the framers' intent, this modern way of speaking and teaching undermined traditional doctrine.

5. Alexander Hamilton, "A Full Vindication" (1774), in *The Works of Alexander Hamilton,* ed. H. C. Lodge (New York: Putnam's, 1903), 1:12. In "The Farmer Refuted" (1775), Hamilton does call "absurd and impious" Hobbes's doctrine that there is no moral obligation in the state of nature; *Works of Alexander Hamilton,* 1:61–62. But, in the first place, Hamilton is answering the Farmer's charge that Hamilton's principles, as enunciated in the "Full Vindication," are open to the imputation of Hobbesism, especially since Hamilton maintained that we are "bound by no laws to which we have not consented"; Samuel Seabury, *Letters of a Westchester Farmer* (White Plains, N.Y.: Westchester County Historical Society, 1930), 109, 111. Second, Hamilton contends that Hobbes's error lies not in a misreading of human nature in particular but in Hobbes's lack of belief in an "intelligent, superintending principle who is the governor, and will be the final judge of the universe." Hamilton goes on: "To grant that there is a Supreme Intelligence who rules the world, and has established laws to regulate the actions of his creatures, and still assert that man, in a state of nature, may be considered as perfectly free from all restrains of *law* and *government,* appears, to a common understanding, altogether irreconcilable"; *Works of Alexander Hamilton,* 1:62. But this "common understanding" is only partially correct. God may have "established laws" for his creatures by giving them inward instincts, passions, and motives, leaving them free from outward restraints. To obey such a law of nature, man must either (1) be free from the restraints of law and government, in the ordinary sense of those terms, or (2) be subject to laws and governments that are conformed to his inward nature. To obey the divinely ordained law of nature, in this view, is to let human nature take its course. Hamilton subscribes to this view or something very like it. Repeatedly, he refers to the law of nature as the source of the *rights* of mankind; he makes only passing reference to natural duties: "The Supreme Being gave existence to man, together with the means of preserving and beautifying that existence. He endowed him with rational facilities, by the help and duty of which to discern and pursue such things as were consistent with his duty and interest; and invested him with an inviolable right to personal liberty and personal safety"; *Works of Alexander Hamilton,* 1:63. In this light of natural endowments, duty, balanced by interest, yields priority to—and may even be derived from—the preservation and beautification of existence. Moreover, if our rights to liberty and safety are truly *inviolable,* they must, in case of conflict, be preferred to our duties. Hamilton did consider blood kinship as a natural bond and source of authority. This is an important difference between Hamilton and Locke— see, for example, Locke, *Essay on Human Understanding,* bk. 1, chap. 3, sec. 12, or "The Reasonableness of Christianity," in *The Works of John Locke* (London, 1812),

7:143—although Hamilton's principle attempts to derive obligation from the body. With this exception, Hamilton argues that since the law of nature gives "every man a right to his personal liberty," it "can . . . confer no obligation to obedience" in a state of nature; no man had any *moral* power to deprive another of his life, limbs, property, or liberty, nor the least authority to command or exact obedience from him, except that which arose from the ties of consanguinity; *Works of Alexander Hamilton,* 1:63; cf. Locke, *Treatises,* bk. 2, sec. 54. This negative doctrine—the absence of a right to harm or rule—does not entail any positive bond between human beings, not even a duty to respect the life, liberty, and property of others. The absence of "any *moral* power . . . to command or exact obedience" excludes any right to make obligatory claims *on* others (and it is the weak, after all, who are likely to stand in need of "*moral* power"). To be sure, in the "Full Vindication," Hamilton declared that it is a "dictate of humanity to contribute to the support of our fellow creatures and more especially those who are allied to us by ties of blood, interest and mutual protection." But this "dictate" is clearly *not* a duty. Quite the contrary—it is on this point that Hamilton insists that: "humanity does not require us to sacrifice our own security and welfare to the convenience of others. Self-preservation is the first principle of our nature. When our lives and properties are at stake, it would be foolish and unnatural to refrain from such measures as might preserve them because they would be detrimental to others"; *Works of Alexander Hamilton,* 1:112, 15, cf. Locke, *Treatises,* bk. 1, sec. 6. "The *supreme law* of every society," Hamilton wrote, is "*its own happiness*"; *Works of Alexander Hamilton,* 1:66 (emphasis in original). Since civil society is created to secure natural right, this supreme self-interestedness must be a characteristic of individuals as well as polities. In the large analysis, for Hamilton as for Locke, "there is an innate natural right, while there is no innate natural duty"; see Leo Strauss, *Natural Right and History* (Chicago: University of Chicago Press, 1953), 226–227.

6. *The Writings of Samuel Adams,* ed. H. Cushing (New York: Putnam's, 1908), 2:151 (emphasis in original).

7. Thomas Hobbes, *Leviathan,* pt. 1, chap. 13.

8. *Works of Alexander Hamilton,* 1:5–6.

9. For example, Isaiah Berlin, *Four Essays on Liberty* (London: Oxford University Press, 1969).

10. Hence the appropriateness of Benjamin Hichborn's radically democratic and unusual definition of civil liberty as a "power in the people at large" rather than a matter of individual rights; Hichborn, "Oration Delivered at Boston, March 5, 1777," cited in Gerald Stourzh, *Alexander Hamilton and the Idea of Republican Government* (Stanford, Calif.: Stanford University Press, 1970), 56.

11. *Works of Alexander Hamilton,* 2:52.

12. Bertrand de Jouvenel, *On Power* (New York: Viking, 1949).

13. "The autonomous forces of society," Hans Morgenthau wrote, have "engendered new accumulations of power as dangerous to the freedom of the individual as the power of government"; Hans Morgenthau, "The Dilemmas of Freedom," *American Political Science Review* 2 (1957): 721.

14. None of this denies, of course, that vast numbers of Americans live in virtually permanent privation, made more painful by its proximity to affluence.

15. The quotation is from Madison, *Federalist* 10; see also Adam Smith, *Lectures on Jurisprudence* (Oxford: Oxford University Press, 1979), A333, and John Dewey, *The Public and Its Problems* (New York: Holt, 1927), 96–99.

16. Ralph Lerner, "Commerce and Character: The Anglo-American as New Model Man," *William and Mary Quarterly* 36 (1979): 3–26.

17. My indignation decreases, of course, to the extent that I regard being bumped as a normal hazard of flying.

18. This explanation of the farm problems has been offered, among others, by Wayne Angell, one of President Reagan's appointees to the Federal Reserve Board; Alan Murray, "Supply-Siders Cheer Reagan's Two Nominations to Fed Board, but Volcker Seems Unperturbed," *Wall Street Journal,* October 17, 1985, 62. The trade policies of other regimes also contribute. Given this, it is obtuse and more than a little cruel to claim that American farmers brought their fate on themselves by excessive borrowing.

19. Robert Coles, "The Politics of Ressentiment," *New Republic,* August 2, 1982, 32–34.

20. Even Herbert Spencer, the great social Darwinist, observed that increasing mass, complexity, and range of activity in civil life necessarily entails an increased role for the "great nervous centers," despite the cost to individualism; Herbert Spencer, *Principles of Biology* (New York: Appleton, 1874), vol. 2, sec. 374.

21. Michael Ignatieff, *The Needs of Strangers* (New York: Viking, 1985), 10.

22. Jennifer Hochschild, *What's Fair: American Beliefs about Distributive Justice* (Cambridge, Mass.: Harvard University Press, 1981); by reporting American devotion to the idea, I do not mean to endorse it. For one thing, the doctrine defines equality in terms of treatment (at a starting point) rather than seeing equality as a quality of spirit and a political goal. See John H. Schaar, "Equality of Opportunity and Beyond," in *Equality,* ed. J. Roland Pennock and John Chapman (New York: Atherton, 1967), 228–249.

23. Harvey C. Mansfield, Jr., "The Forms and Formalities of Liberty," *Public Interest* 70 (Winter 1983): 127.

24. John H. Schaar, "The Question of Justice," *Raritan Review* 3 (1983): 122; Michael Harrington, *The New American Poverty* (New York: Holt, Rinehart and Winston, 1984).

25. Ignatieff, *Needs of Strangers,* 27–53; the quotation is from *King Lear,* act 3, scene 4.

26. Hannah Arendt, "Revolution and the Public Happiness," *Commentary* 30 (1960): 413–427; on the culture of work at the time of the founding, see Edmund Morgan, "The Puritan Ethic and the American Revolution," *William and Mary Quarterly* 24 (1967): 7, and H. Trevor Colbourn, *The Lamp of Experience* (Chapel Hill: University of North Carolina Press, 1965), 4, 76–77, 180.

27. The American dream, in its contemporary form, is probably exemplified by the twenty-one factory workers who shared New York's Lotto prize in August 1985; *New York Times,* August 23, 1985, sec. ff, 1. On borrowing, see Richard L. Stern, "Tomorrow Will Take Care of Itself," *Forbes,* September 16, 1985, 38–40.

28. Robert Kuttner, "Jobs," *Dissent* 31 (Winter 1984): 30–41.

29. Schaar, "Question of Justice," 1.

30. *Federalist* 73; James Madison, *Notes of Debates in the Federal Convention of 1787,* ed. Adrienne Koch (Athens: Ohio University Press, 1966), 402; see also *Federalist* 79.

31. *Holden v. Hardy,* 169 U.S. 366 (1898); *West Coast Hotel v. Parrish,* 300 U.S. 379 (1937).

32. *Lincoln Federal Savings Union v. Northwestern Iron and Metal Co.,* 355 U.S. 525 (1949).

33. "Labor at socially inadequate wages," after all, could stand as a definition of peonage.

34. *Louisville, Cincinnati, and Charleston Railroad v. Letson,* 2 Nov. 47 (1844); *Santa Clara County v. Southern Pacific Railroad,* 118 U.S. 394 (1886); see also Justice John Campbell's dissent in *Marshall v. Baltimore and Ohio Railroad,* 16 Nov. 314 (1853).

35. Frank Michelman, "Property as a Constitutional Right," *Washington and Lee Law Review* 38 (1981): 1097; see also Bruce Ackerman, *Private Property and the Constitution* (New Haven, Conn.: Yale University Press, 1977).

36. *Goldberg v. Kelly,* 397 U.S. 254 (1970).

37. *Elrod v. Burns,* 427 U.S. 347 (1976); *Branti v. Finkel,* 445 U.S. 507 (1980).

38. *Firefighters v. Stotts,* 104 S.Ct. 2576 (1984); see also *California Brewers Assn. v. Bryant,* 444 U.S. 598 (1980), and *American Tobacco Co. v. Patterson,* 456 U.S. 63 (1982).

39. Franz Neumann, "The Concept of Political Freedom," in Neumann, *The Democratic and the Authoritarian State* (Glencoe, Ill.: Free Press, 1957), 160–200.

40. Alexis de Tocqueville, *Democracy in America* (New York: Schocken, 1961), 1:304–312; see also James Bryce, *The American Commonwealth* (New York: Commonwealth, 1908), 2:358–368.

41. *Federalist* 49.

42. Spinoza, *Tractatus Theologico-Politicus,* chap. 20; cf. *Federalist* 1: "In politics as in religion, it is equally absurd to attempt at making proselytes with fire and sword. Heresies in either can rarely be cured by persecution."

43. Tocqueville, *Democracy in America,* 1:310–311.

44. Ibid., 2:161–162; Ignatieff, *Needs of Strangers,* 83–103.

45. Tocqueville, *Democracy in America,* 2:120.

46. The pace of change and the decline of community also encourage shamelessness, as Lewis Lapham observes: "The emotion of shame probably needs a small theater in which to make its effects. A man can feel shame before an audience of his peers, within the narrow precincts of a neighborhood, profession, army unit, social set, city room, congregation, or football team. The scale and dynamism of American democracy grants the ceaselessly renewable option of moving one's conscience into a more congenial street." See Lapham, "Notebook: Supply-Side Ethics," *Harper's,* May 1985, 11.

47. Bertrand de Jouvenel, *Sovereignty* (Chicago: University of Chicago Press, 1957), 254.

48. Tocqueville, *Democracy in America,* 2:164–165.

49. Howard White, "Comment on Morgenthau's 'Dilemmas of Freedom,'" *American Political Science Review* 51 (1957): 731, 733; Todd Gitlin, *Inside Prime Time* (New York: Pantheon, 1983).

50. Solomon Asch, *Social Psychology* (Englewood Cliffs, N.J.: Prentice Hall, 1952), chap. 16. "The reality of the world," Arendt wrote, "is guaranteed by the presence of others"; see Arendt, *The Human Condition* (Garden City, N.Y.: Doubleday, 1959), 178.

51. David Riesman, Nathan Glazer, and Reuel Denney, *The Lonely Crowd* (New Haven, Conn.: Yale University Press, 1950); modern philosophers sometimes raise this to the level of principle. R. M. Hare writes that "if we can convince (someone) that everyone else can see a cat there, he will have to admit that there is a cat there or be accused of misusing the language"; Hare, *Freedom and Reason* (Oxford: Clarendon Press, 1963), 1–2. Hare attempts, without great success, to distinguish ethical arguments from this rule (110); in practice, it is clear that no such exception applies.

52. For a similar view, see Larry Preston, "Individual and Political Freedom," *Polity* 15 (1982): 79–86.

53. *Miranda v. Arizona*, 384 U.S. 436 (1966); *Gideon v. Wainwright*, 372 U.S. 335 (1963).

54. In my own view, as will become clear, the "just powers" of government derive from the justice of the regime, a matter to which consent is no more than a relevant consideration, whereas the standard of political freedom is having a say—to the extent, sharing in rule—rather than giving consent.

55. Walter Dean Burnham, "The Changing Shape of the American Political Universe," *American Political Science Review* 59 (1965): 7–28.

56. James Ceaser, *Reforming the Reforms* (Cambridge, Mass.: Ballinger, 1982).

57. Benjamin Barber, *Strong Democracy* (Berkeley: University of California Press, 1984); after all, despite Reagan's victory, most voters expressed disapproval of a number of his most important policies.

58. Of course, moderation in practice can conceal the most immoderate opinions, which are always liable to make themselves felt.

59. Seymour Martin Lipset and William Schneider, *The Confidence Gap* (New York: Free Press, 1983).

60. Tocqueville, *Democracy in America*, 2:128–133, 1:216–226.

61. Clark Kerr, "Managing the Managers: The Distribution of Power in American Industrial Society," in *What America Stands For*, ed. J. L. Kertzer and M. A. Fitzsimmons (Notre Dame, Ind.: Notre Dame University Press, 1959), 89–98; Grant McConnell, *Private Power and American Democracy* (New York: Knopf, 1966).

62. John G. Cawelti, *Adventure, Mystery and Romance* (Chicago: University of Chicago Press, 1976).

63. The startling impiety of this creed is clear from the context of Paine's remark; *The Complete Writings of Thomas Paine*, ed. Phillip Foner (New York: Citadel, 1969), 1:45.

64. Robert Eden, *Political Leadership and Nihilism* (Tampa: University of South Florida Press, 1983).

65. Loyalty to party, to take one humble example, makes us less dependent on leaders; see George Reedy, "The Presidency in the Era of Mass Communications," in *Modern Presidents and the Presidency*, ed. Marc K. Landy (Lexington, Mass.: Heath, 1985), 40. And more exalted illustrations come easily to mind (Psalms 146:3–4).

66. Robert Bellah, Richard Madsen, William M. Sullivan, Ann Swidler, and

Steven M. Tipton, *Habits of the Heart: Individualism and Commitment in American Life* (Berkeley: University of California Press, 1985); David R. Carlin makes a similar point, while appreciating the virtues of the framers' doctrines, in his essay "Negative Liberty," *Commonweal*, September 6, 1985, 455.

67. For example, David Truman, *The Governmental Process* (New York: Knopf, 1951).

68. For a recent example of this sort of argument, see Bruce Ackerman, *Social Justice in the Liberal State* (New Haven, Conn.: Yale University Press, 1980), 368–369.

69. Liberal values, Michael Sandel writes, "can hardly be defended by the claim that no values can be defended"; Sandel, "Morality and the Liberal Idea," *New Republic*, May 7, 1984, 15. See also Edward Purcell, *The Crisis of Democratic Theory* (Lexington: University of Kentucky Press, 1973).

70. Morgenthau, "Dilemmas of Freedom," 720.

71. White, "Comment," 730.

72. Robert Nozick, *Anarchy, State and Utopia* (New York: Basic Books, 1974), ix. Benjamin Barber calls this position "premoral without being nonmoral"; Barber, *Strong Democracy*, 31; see also Sandel, "Morality and the Liberal Idea," 16.

73. John Rawls, *A Theory of Justice* (Cambridge, Mass.: Harvard University Press, 1971), 541–548; for a similar argument, see Ackerman, *Social Justice in the Liberal State*, 54, 57, 373–374. According to Rawls, there is also an inherent limit to the size of legitimate government, which modern regimes may be approaching. Since our most pressing wants are satisfied first, Rawls argues, as civilization advances only less urgent wants remain. "Beyond a certain point, it becomes and remains irrational from the standpoint of the original position to acknowledge a lesser liberty for the sake of greater material amenities" (542). The framers, however, would have reminded Rawls that one unsatisfied desire—our desire to preserve ourselves—hardly ranks as an "amenity."

74. Rawls, *Theory of Justice*, 509.

75. William Galston, "Defending Liberalism," *American Political Science Review* 76 (1982): 521–629.

76. Nozick, *Anarchy, State and Utopia*, 33.

77. John Rawls, "A Well Ordered Society," in *Philosophy, Politics and Society*, 5th ser., ed. Peter Laslett and James Fishkin (New Haven, Conn.: Yale University Press, 1979), 7, 15–16; Rawls, *Theory of Justice*, 72–74, 104.

78. Rawls, *Theory of Justice*, 463, 515, 519.

79. William Galston, "Moral Personality and Liberty Theory," *Political Theory* 10 (1982): 492–519. In a similar argument years earlier, John Dewey began an essay on "The Nature of Freedom" by defining freedom as a mind pursuing "purposes which are intrinsically worthwhile." Soon, however, Dewey defined this class of things good in themselves as ends, originating with "natural impulses and desires," which are deliberately chosen with knowledge of their consequences. Liberty is positive, a "freedom which is power," especially the power to "frame purposes" and to design means by which "chosen ends" may be pursued. Dewey, *Experience and Education* (New York: Collier, 1969), 61–67. Dewey's argument, in other words, emphasized farsighted and rational planning—a limitation in method—but his "intrinsically worthwhile" purposes prove, at bottom, to be *any* purposes, originating in genuine impulses and desires, that are freely and deliberately chosen.

80. Marvin Zetterbaum, "Self and Subjectivity in Political Theory," *Review of Politics* 44 (1982): 59–82. For a defense of the modern view, see Marshall Berman, *The Politics of Authenticity* (New York: Atheneum, 1980). At the 1985 meetings of the American Psychological Association, Stanley Krippner of the Saybrook Institute told a panel on "The Concept of Human Potential in the United States and the U.S.S.R." that the Soviet concept of the "hidden reserves of personality" is similar to the American idea of "human potentials." He cited the work of a Russian scientist who allegedly improved the work of his students by telling them, under hypnosis, that they were historical figures—physics students, for example, were told that they were Einstein. See *Los Angeles Times*, August 26, 1985, sec. 5, 8. It does not seem to have mattered to Krippner that his Soviet colleague achieved these results by implanting in his students the idea that they were someone else. Krippner and his Soviet counterpart appear to share the conviction that identity, to a considerable extent, is an artifact and that the most important "human potential" is that of creating or making the self.

81. Tocqueville, *Democracy in America*, 2:118, 257; Russell Jacoby, *Social Amnesia* (Boston: Beacon, 1975).

82. Joseph Veroff, Elizabeth Louvan, and Richard Kulka, *The Inner American* (New York: Basic Books, 1981), 147–151. In the 1950s, Riesman described sex as a "last frontier"; Reisman, *Lonely Crowd*, 145–148. Today, Lewis Lapham writes, "Adultery . . . has become so minor an accomplishment as to be hardly worth mentioning in dispatches"; Lapham, "Notebook: Supply-Side Ethics," 10.

83. James D. Hunter, *American Evangelicalism* (New Brunswick, N.J.: Rutgers University Press, 1983), 91–101.

84. "Je pourrais tres facilement imaginer une societe de termites dont chacun croirait libre." "L'avenir de la Culture," *Bulletin SEDEIS* 847, March 10, 1963.

85. For example, see Larry Preston, "Freedom and Authority," *American Political Science Review* 77 (1983): 670.

86. Albert Camus, *Resistance, Rebellion and Death,* trans. Justin O'Brien (New York: Knopf, 1961), 128.

87. Robert Coles, "Civility and Psychology," *Daedalus* 109 (Summer 1980): 140.

88. In *Cohen v. California,* 403 U.S. 15 (1971), Harlan argued that "one man's obscenity is another man's lyric."

89. Friedrich Nietzsche, *Thus Spake Zarathustra*, chap. 14.

90. Moreover, since one motive for speaking is the desire to be approved and admired, one's speech is apt to be as excellent as the audience it is intended to impress. In that respect, an excellent audience sets us free.

91. Dissenting in *Whitney v. California,* 274 U.S. 376 (1927).

92. Alexander Meiklejohn, *Political Freedom* (New York: Harper & Row, 1960).

93. Plato *Apology* 17d–18a.

94. Barber, *Strong Democracy*, 173–178; "The Greek *polis*," Hannah Arendt wrote, "was precisely that 'form of government' which provided men with a space of appearances where they could act, with a kind of theatre where freedom could appear"; Arendt, "What Is Freedom?" in her *Between Past and Future* (Cleveland: World, 1965), 154.

95. *Buckley v. Valeo,* 424 U.S. 1 (1976).

96. Other Western countries ban it altogether with no loss to democracy or freedom.

97. In the case of an overlap—when I am so identified with my philosophic positions, for example, that I experience any argument against it as a personal affront—a free regime must ordinarily take the side of public argument against personal feelings. For us, given the First Amendment, this is especially true. For the general proposition, see Ronald Dworkin, *Taking Rights Seriously* (Cambridge, Mass.: Harvard University Press, 1978), 272.

98. *Chaplinsky v. New Hampshire*, 315 U.S. 568 (1942); the Court's recent reticence is indicated in *Gooding v. Wilson*, 405 U.S. 518 (1972).

99. Alexander Meiklejohn, *Free Speech and Its Relation to Self-Government* (New York: Harper, 1948); Leo Strauss, *Persecution and the Art of Writing* (Glencoe, Ill.: Free Press, 1952), indicates the possibilities in far more confining situations.

100. Tocqueville, *Democracy in America*, 1:33–34.

101. Even in 1956, Harold Nicolson observed that American manners were "nervously" changing; Nicolson, *Good Behaviour* (Garden City, N.Y.: Doubleday, 1956), 15.

102. To argue that a "classification" using race is "suspect"—or that one involving sex is "semisuspect"—involves the assertion that such language may not be used, without exceptional justification, by public institutions or in the law. Through civil rights statues, this affects a variety of private institutions as well. For example, see *Craig v. Boren*, 429 U.S. 190 (1976); *Runyon v. McCrary*, 427 U.S. 160 (1976). See also Morroe Berger, *Equality by Statute* (Garden City, N.Y.: Doubleday, 1968), 116–117, and Catherine MacKinnon, *The Sexual Harassment of Working Women* (New Haven, Conn.: Yale University Press), 1979.

103. Hadley Arkes, *The Philosopher and the City* (Princeton, N.J.: Princeton University Press, 1981), 23–91; Harry Kalven, *The Negro and the First Amendment* (Chicago: University of Chicago Press, 1965); Donald Downs, *Nazis in Skokie: Freedom, Community, and the First Amendment* (South Bend, Ind.: University of Notre Dame Press, 1985). Joel Grossman would limit public intervention to cases in which the threatened group faces a "likelihood of actual harm." By any reasonable definition, however, "actual harm" includes more than damage to one's body or property, to say nothing of the injury done to public speech and public life; see Grossman, "The First Amendment and the New Anti-pornography Statutes," *News for Teachers of Political Science* 45 (Spring 1985): 20.

104. *Beauharnais v. Illinois*, 343 U.S. 250 (1952); in an important sense, this is part of the intent of programs for affirmative action.

105. Mansfield, "Forms and Formalities," 129–130; Schaar, "Question of Justice," 127–128.

106. *Federalist* 49; as Stourzh indicates, this helps account for the reliance, in the *Federalist*, on theorists the framers associated with the study of the *forms* of government (i.e., Montesquieu) as opposed to thinkers who were concerned with *principles* (i.e., Locke); see Stourzh, *Alexander Hamilton*, 6.

107. Rawls's defense of the "priority" of liberty essentially follows the framers' argument; Rawls, *Theory of Justice*, 243–251.

108. Aristotle *Politics* 1276b10–12.

109. Aristotle *Politics* 1310a28–38, 1317a40–b17.

110. Gerald MacCallum, "Negative and Positive Freedom," *Philosophic Review* 76 (1967): 314; Rawls, *Theory of Justice*, 202.

111. Stanley Benn and W. L. Weinstein, "Being Free to Act and Being a Free Man," *Mind* 80 (1971): 197. De Jouvenel, *Sovereignty*, 249; Charles Taylor, "What's Wrong with Negative Freedom," in *The Idea of Freedom*, ed. Alan Ryan (Oxford: Oxford University Press, 1979), 175–193, esp. 183. It ought to be clear that, given the diversity of subjects, any notion of liberty must also involve an element of inequality or, to put it more precisely, of differences between us.

112. C. B. MacPherson, for example, defines freedom as the "absence of humanly imposed impediments," including those institutions that deny us equal access to "the means of life and the means of labor"; MacPherson, *Democratic Theory* (London: Oxford University Press, 1973), 96.

113. The desire for power, de Jouvenel writes, "is not the story of liberty but of human imperialism"; de Jouvenel, *Sovereignty*, 259. See also Helmeth Plessner, "The Emancipation Power," *Social Research* 31 (1974): 155–174.

114. W. J. Schelling, *Samtliche Werke*, ed. K. F. A. Schelling (Augsburg, Germany: Cottaa, 1860), 1:179, 304, 336, 7:351. For Schelling, this implied that we must see nature as something that is "becoming"—that the "essence of nature" is, in fact, only being approached *through* freedom (7:348, 362). See also Geoffrey Clive, *The Romantic Enlightenment* (New York: Meridian, 1960).

115. The framers recognized this, whatever the other shortcomings of their argument, when they referred to rights as "inalienable." In these terms, a phrase like "the freedom to establish National Socialism" reflects, at best, a truncated idea of liberty.

116. Arendt, "What Is Freedom?" 168.

117. *The Favorite Works of Mark Twain* (Garden City, N.Y.: Garden City Publishing, 1939), 1129–1135.

118. This is no esoteric teaching. In the Disney movie *The Black Cauldron*, the half-human Gurgi, who ordinarily flies from trouble or danger, emerges as the hero because, in the end, he is willing to sacrifice his life to save his friend. Gurgi has no warrior's honor; he is moved by humbler motives, but he is still free. This freedom, however, stops short of full self-rule. Gurgi chooses to be ruled, like a body disciplined to accept its limitations.

119. Epictetus *Discourses* bk. 4, lines 75, 81, 83, 89; the extreme versions of this doctrine hold that any desire or affection restricts our liberty, but radical asceticism sets a standard that, because it is fundamentally inhuman, also leads toward the effort to master human nature, aiming at a kind of tyranny in the soul. Orwell recognized this imperious element in Gandhi's teaching; see *The Complete Essays, Journalism, and Letters of George Orwell*, ed. Sonia Orwell and Ian Angus (New York: Harcourt, Brace and World, 1968), 4:463–470.

120. Michael Platt, "Leo Strauss: Three Quarrels, Three Questions," *Newsletter, Dept. of Political Science, University of Dallas* 2, no. 2 (Winter 1978): 5–6.

8. On Equality as the Moral Foundation for Community

1. G. K. Chesterton, *What I Saw in America* (New York: Dodd, Mead, 1922), 17.

2. Aristotle, *Nicomachean Ethics,* trans. H. Rackham (London: Penguin,

1956), 145–147; see also Rudolf Ekstein, "Psychoanalysis and Education for the Facilitation of Positive Human Qualities," *Journal of Social Issues* 28 (1972): 80.

3. Alexis de Tocqueville, *Democracy in America,* trans. H. Reeve (New York: Schocken, 1961), 1:61–65, 292–294. (For an excellent contemporary treatment, see Benjamin R. Barber, "Command Performance," *Harper's Magazine,* April 1975, 51–56.) Herman Melville, *Moby Dick* (New York: Modern Library, n.d.), 244.

4. Erik Allardt, "A Theory of Solidarity and Legitimacy Conflicts," in *The Dynamics of Modern Society,* ed. W. J. Goode (New York: Atherton, 1966), 169–178.

5. Thomas Hobbes, *Leviathan,* ed. C. B. Macpherson (Baltimore, Md.: Penguin, 1968), 151–152.

6. John H. Schaar, "Equality of Opportunity and Beyond," in *Equality,* ed. J. Roland Pennock and John W. Chapman (New York: Atherton, 1967), 232.

7. Tocqueville, *Democracy in America,* 1:lxvii.

8. Sigmund Freud, *Works,* standard edition (London: Hogarth, 1971), 18:108.

9. William Frankena, "The Concept of Social Justice," in *Social Justice,* ed. R. Brandt (Englewood Cliffs, N.J.: Prentice Hall, 1962), 19; Bernard Williams, "The Idea of Equality," in *Philosophy, Politics, and Society,* ed. Peter Laslett and W. G. Runciman (Oxford: Blackwell, 1962), 112, 114.

10. John H. Schaar, "Some Ways of Thinking about Equality," *Journal of Politics* 26 (1964): 881.

11. Ibid., 876.

12. Ralph Ellison, *Invisible Man* (New York: New American Library, 1952); see also Ellison's "The World and the Jug," in his *Shadow and Act* (New York: New American Library, 1964), 115–147.

13. Leo Strauss, *Natural Right and History* (Chicago: University of Chicago Press, 1952), 137; Schaar, "Equality of Opportunity and Beyond," 230–231.

14. Rudolf Ekstein, "Reflections on and Translation of Federn's *The Fatherless Society,*" *Bulletin of the Reiss-Davis Clinic* 8 (1971): 2–33; John H. Schaar, *Escape from Authority* (New York: Basic Books, 1961).

15. Hugh Bedau, "Equalitarianism and the Idea of Equality," in *Equality,* ed. J. Roland Pennock and John W. Chapman (New York: Atherton, 1967), 11, 12.

16. For example, Plato *Republic* 375d, and Plato *Laches* 196e; heavily ironic, Socrates' comments also have a serious side.

17. From "The Black Cottage," in *The Poetry of Robert Frost,* ed. Edward Connery Lathem (New York: Holt, Rinehart, 1930).

18. Aristotle *Politics* 1284a, 1301b; Aristotle *Ethics* 1131b, 1158b.

19. Aristotle *Politics* 1295b.

20. Plato *Laws* 739b6–c2, 739d9–e3.

21. Aristotle *Politics* 1266b, 1257b.

22. Ibid., 1283b; Plato *Laws* 757a–c.

23. Aristotle *Politics* 1267b, 1292a.

24. Thucydides, *The Peloponnesian War,* trans. J. Finley (New York: Modern Library, 1951), 103–104.

25. Plato *Laws* 739c2–d4.

26. Thucydides, *Peloponnesian War,* 48–49; see also A. G. Woodhead, *Thucydides on the Nature of Power* (Cambridge, Mass.: Harvard University Press, 1970), 33.

27. Plato *Laws* 626d, 633d, 644b.

28. Ibid., 738e.

29. Plato *Statesman* 262d; see also Plato *Laches* 186d.

30. Plato *Protagoras* 337d–e.

31. Aristotle *Rhetoric* 1373b18; on Plato's views, the *Meno* is a case in itself; see also Plato *Laches* 186b.

32. Plato *Republic* 451a–457b.

33. Friedrich Nietzsche, *The Birth of Tragedy,* in his *The Birth of Tragedy and the Genealogy of Morals,* trans. F. Golffing (Garden City, N.Y.: Doubleday, 1956), 23.

34. Hobbes, *Leviathan,* 183–184.

35. See Leo Strauss, *The Political Philosophy of Hobbes* (Chicago: University of Chicago Press, 1962).

36. Hobbes, *Leviathan,* 186, 201–217.

37. In a seeming concession to religious sentiment, Locke noted that the "Lord and Master of them all" may by "manifest declaration of his will" confer "undoubted dominion and sovereignty" on someone in the state of nature (Locke, *Two Treatises of Government,* bk. 2, sec. 4), and there are many indications that Locke regarded such preeminence of force as having been the actual spur to civilization.

38. Ibid., sec. 54; Sanford Lakoff, *Equality in Political Philosophy* (Cambridge, Mass.: Harvard University Press, 1964), 98–99.

39. Locke, *Two Treatises,* bk. 2, sec. 96.

40. Aristotle *Politics* 1301b, 1317b; Plato *Laws* 757e.

41. Montesquieu, *The Spirit of the Laws,* trans. T. Nugent (New York: Hafner, 1949), 3–5.

42. Ibid., 20–22, 40–42, 109, 111.

43. Ibid., 41–42, 112.

44. Ibid., 46, 96, 316, 317.

45. Ibid., 126, 127, 133–148.

46. Robert Ginsberg, "The Declaration as Rhetoric," in *A Casebook on the Declaration of Independence,* ed. Robert Ginsberg (New York: Crowell, 1967), 219–244.

47. Robert Ginsberg, "Equality and Justice in the Declaration of Independence," *Journal of Social Philosophy* 6, no. 1 (1975): 8.

48. Martin Diamond, "Democracy and *The Federalist:* A Reconsideration of the Framers' Intent," *American Political Science Review* 53 (1957): 52–68.

49. James Wilson, *Works,* ed. R. G. McCloskey (Cambridge, Mass.: Harvard University Press, 1967), 1:241–242; Thomas Paine, *Common Sense and Other Political Writings,* ed. Nelson Adkins (New York: Liberal Arts, 1953), 5, 82, 163.

50. Paine, *Common Sense,* 10, 83, 169.

51. Wilson, *Works,* 1:234; Paine, *Common Sense,* 4–5.

52. *Federalist* 49; Paine, *Common Sense,* 5.

53. Paine noted, for example, that property would always be unequal; he only argued for the primacy of the person, regarding property as a social and not a natural right. See Paine, *Common Sense,* 166.

54. Ibid., 21–25.

55. *Federalist* 10; Schaar, "Some Ways of Thinking about Equality," 886–887.

56. *Federalist* 9; Paine, *Common Sense,* 128–130, 170; Bernard Bailyn, *The Ideological Origins of the American Revolution* (Cambridge, Mass.: Harvard University Press, Belknap Press, 1967), 288–301.

57. James Madison, *Notes on Debates in the Federal Convention of 1787,* ed. Adrienne Koch (Athens: Ohio University Press, 1966), 194.

58. Hannah Arendt, *On Revolution* (New York: Viking, 1963), 132–133; Schaar, "Some Ways of Thinking about Equality," 88–91.

59. Gordon S. Wood, "The Democratization of the Mind in the American Revolution," in *The Moral Foundations of the American Republic,* 3rd ed., ed. Robert H. Horwitz (Charlottesville, Va.: University Press of Virginia, 1986), 109–135.

60. *The Works of John Adams, with a Life of the Author,* ed. Charles Francis Adams, 10 vols. (Boston: Little, Brown, 1850–1856), 7:462, 9:569–571; *The Diary and Autobiography of John Adams,* ed. L. Butterfield (Cambridge, Mass.: Harvard University Press, 1962), 3:326–327, 333, 359.

61. John Livingston, "Alexander Hamilton and the American Tradition," *Midwest Journal of Political Science* 1 (1957): 174, 175.

62. *The Life and Selected Writings of Thomas Jefferson,* ed. Adrienne Koch and William Peden (New York: Modern Library, 1944), 531–532, 682, 685.

63. Arendt, *On Revolution,* 195; Daniel Boorstin, *The Lost World of Thomas Jefferson* (Boston: Beacon, 1960), 59–60, 62, 71.

64. Boorstin, *Lost World of Jefferson,* 81–98, Jefferson, *Life and Selected Writings,* 508, 140–141, 310, 395–407, 430–431, 638–639.

65. Jefferson, *Life and Selected Writings,* 412.

66. Ibid., 389–390, 630.

67. Ibid., 437, 632–633, 660–662, 670, 676.

68. Ibid., 263, 265, 440, 604; Boorstin, *Lost World of Jefferson,* 224.

69. Boorstin, *Lost World of Jefferson,* 201–202; Jefferson, *Life and Selected Writings,* 724.

70. Tocqueville, *Democracy in America,* 2:120.

71. Jacques Maritain, *Ransoming the Time* (New York: Scribner's, 1941), 14–18; see also Freud, *Works,* 14:293, 307, 13:60, 156, 18:134–135.

9. Ambiguities and Ironies

1. "Fervent Analyst Suggests Realignment of Values," *Eugene Register-Guard,* October 23, 1963, B1.

2. "Kirk, McWilliams Call for Return to Traditional Ethic," *Minnesota Daily,* February 19, 1963, 1.

3. *The Complete Writings of Thomas Paine,* ed. Phillip S. Foner (New York: Citadel, 1969), 1:45.

4. Ambrose Bierce, *The Devil's Dictionary* (New York: World, 1941), 54–55.

5. John Rawls, *A Theory of Justice* (Cambridge, Mass.: Harvard University Press, 1971), 12, 19, 136–142.

6. Karl Marx and Friedrich Engels, *The Communist Manifesto,* trans. Samuel Moore (New York: Penguin, 1967), 82–86.

7. Ibid., 83–84.

8. Russell Kirk, *The Conservative Mind* (Chicago: Regnery, 1953), 7–8.

9. *The Works of Edmund Burke* (New York: Little, Brown, 1854), 3:352–354.

10. Ibid., 3:392.

11. Harvey C. Mansfield, Jr., *Statesmanship and Party Government* (Chicago: University of Chicago Press, 1965), 201–223.

12. *Works of Edmund Burke,* 3:331.

13. Thomas Jefferson, Letter to Lafayette, November 4, 1823, in *Life and Selected Writings of Thomas Jefferson,* ed. Adrienne Koch and William Peden (New York: Modern Library, 1944), 712.

14. Samuel Huntington, "Conservatism as an Ideology," *American Political Science Review* 51, no. 2 (June 1957): 454–473.

15. Selden Peabody Delaney, "Radicalism or Liberalism?" *North American Review* 217 (May 1923): 616–627.

16. G. K. Chesterton, *Orthodoxy* (New York: Dodd, Mead, 1908), 82.

17. Louis Hartz, *The Liberal Tradition in America* (New York: Harcourt Brace, 1955); Clinton Rossiter, *Conservatism in America* (New York: Knopf, 1955).

18. *Works of Edmund Burke,* 2:123.

19. Alexis de Tocqueville, *Democracy in America* (New York: Knopf, 1945), 2:101.

20. *Works of Edmund Burke,* 3:255.

21. I draw both of Adams's comments, among other things, from Norman Jacobson, "The Politics of Irony," in *Principles of the Constitutional Order,* ed. Robert Utley (Lanham, Md.: University Press of America, 1989), 153, 158.

22. Harvey C. Mansfield, Jr., *America's Constitutional Soul* (Baltimore, Md.: Johns Hopkins University Press, 1991), 77.

23. Ibid., 193–208.

24. Sheldon S. Wolin, "Contract and Birthright," in Wolin, *The Presence of the Past* (Baltimore, Md.: Johns Hopkins University Press, 1989), 137–150.

25. John H. Schaar, *Legitimacy and the Modern State* (New Brunswick, N.J.: Transaction, 1981), 150.

26. Michael Kammen, *People of Paradox* (New York: Knopf, 1972).

27. For example, see J. Allen Smith, *The Spirit of American Government* (New York: Macmillan, 1912), 27–39.

28. *Federalist* 51.

29. Charles G. Haines, *The Making of the Constitution* (Cambridge, Mass.: Harvard University Press, 1937), 392.

30. *Federalist* 63.

31. Michael Lienesch, "The Constitutional Tradition: History, Political Action and Progress in American Political Thought, 1787–1793," *Journal of Politics* 42 (1980): 2–30.

32. Joyce Appleby, *Capitalism and a New Social Order: The Republican Vision of the 1790s* (New York: New York University Press, 1984), 15–17.

33. *The Papers of Alexander Hamilton,* ed. Harold C. Syrett (New York: Columbia University Press, 1961–1979), 1:400–417.

34. Anne Norton, *Alternative America* (Chicago: University of Chicago Press, 1986).

35. James Madison, *Notes of Debates in the Federal Constitution of 1787,* ed. Adrienne Koch (Athens: Ohio University Press, 1966), 419–421.

36. Joshua Miller, *The Rise and Fall of Democracy in Early America* (University Park: Pennsylvania State University Press, 1991), 81–104.

37. "Essay by a Farmer in the *Baltimore Gazette,* March 21, 1788," in *The Complete Anti-Federalist,* ed. Herbert Storing (Chicago: University of Chicago Press, 1981), 5:38.

38. Tocqueville, *Democracy in America,* 1:43–44.

39. Thomas Jefferson, *Notes on the State of Virginia,* ed. William Peden (Chapel Hill: University of North Carolina Press, 1955), 161.

40. "Letter to the *Virginia Independent Chronicle,* June 25, 1788," in Storing, *Complete Anti-Federalist,* 5:273.

41. Mary Ann Glendon, *Rights Talk: On the Impoverishment of Political Discourse* (New York: Free Press, 1991).

42. Tocqueville, *Democracy in America,* 2:122.

43. Leo Strauss, *Natural Right and History* (Chicago: University of Chicago Press, 1953), 245.

44. Glenn Collins, "Tough Leader Wields the Ax at Scott," *New York Times,* August 15, 1994, D1.

45. Thomas Hobbes, *Leviathan,* pt. 1, chap. 10.

46. Joseph Cropsey, *Political Philosophy and the Issues of Politics* (Chicago: University of Chicago Press, 1977), 29.

47. Elizabeth Fox-Genovese, "From Separate Spheres to Dangerous Streets: Postmodern Feminism and the Problem of Order," *Social Research* 60 (1993): 253–254.

48. Christopher Lasch, "Traditional Values: Left, Right, and Wrong," *Harper's,* September 1986, 14.

49. E. J. Dionne Jr., *Why American Hate Politics* (New York: Simon & Schuster, 1991), 157–169.

50. Robert Nozick, *Anarchy, State, and Utopia* (New York: Basic Books, 1974).

51. Mansfield, *America's Constitutional Soul,* 77, 82–83.

52. Reinhold Niebuhr, "Liberalism, Illusions, and Realities," *New Republic,* July 4, 1955, 11–13.

53. "Promises, covenants, and oaths, which are the bonds of human society," Locke wrote, "can have no hold upon an atheist." Locke, *Letter Concerning Toleration,* ed. Patrick Romanell (New York: Bobbs-Merrill, 1955), 52.

54. William Galston, "Public Morality and Religion in the Liberal State," *PS* 19 (1986): 822–824.

55. John Dewey, *Individualism Old and New* (New York: Minton and Balch, 1930).

56. Herbert Croly, *The Promise of American Life* (New York: Macmillan, 1911), 29, 37–46.

57. H. L. Mencken, *Prejudices: Second Series* (New York: Knopf, 1920), 121–123.

58. John Dewey, *Liberalism and Social Action* (New York: Putnam's, 1935), 58–62, 75–76.

59. Eric Goldman, *Rendezvous with Destiny* (New York: Knopf, 1952).

60. Allan Bloom, *The Closing of the American Mind* (New York: Simon & Schuster, 1987), 25, 202–204, 225–226, 228–229.

61. Charles Anderson, "Pragmatism and Liberalism, Rationalism and Irrationalism: A Response to Richard Rorty," *Polity* 23 (1991): 360–363.

62. Thomas Jefferson, Letter to John Adams, October 28, 1813, in Jefferson, *Life and Selected Writings,* 633.

63. Robert Reich, "The Secession of the Successful," *New York Times Magazine*, January 20, 1991, 16–17.

64. Robert N. Bellah, Richard Madsen, William M. Sullivan, Ann Swidler, and Steven M. Tipton, *Habits of the Heart: Individualism and Commitment in American Life* (Berkeley: University of California Press, 1982).

65. George Kateb, *The Inner Ocean* (Ithaca, N.Y.: Cornell University Press, 1992).

66. Rawls, *Theory of Justice*, 509, 541–548.

67. Marvin Zetterbaum, "Self and Subjectivity in Political Theory," *Review of Politics* 44 (1982): 59–82.

68. William Corlett, *Community without Unity* (Durham, N.C.: Duke University Press, 1989), 118–141.

69. Sheldon S. Wolin, "Democracy, Difference, and Recognition," *Political Theory* 21 (1993): 466, 481.

70. Bernard Avishai, "The Pursuit of Happiness and Other 'Preferences,'" *Dissent* 31 (1984): 482–484.

71. Leslie Kaufman, "Life beyond God," *New York Times Magazine*, October 16, 1994, 46–51.

72. Henry David Thoreau, "Life without Principle," in *Works of Henry David Thoreau*, ed. Henry Seidel Canby (New York: Houghton Mifflin, 1946), 813.

73. Michael Sandel, "The Procedural Republic and the Unencumbered Self," in *The Self and the Political Order*, ed. Tracy Strong (New York: New York University Press, 1992), 92.

10. Political Parties as Civic Associations

1. The Twenty-fourth Amendment alludes to parties, since it forbids poll taxes in primary elections, but parties are nowhere discussed explicitly.

2. See the development in constitutional law from *Newberry v. United States*, 256 U.S. 232 (1921) and *Grovey v. Townsend*, 295 U.S. 45 (1935) to *United States v. Classic*, 313 U.S. 299 (1941), *Smith v. Allwright*, 321 U.S. 649 (1944), and *Terry v. Adams*, 345 U.S. 506 (1953).

3. Louis Hartz, *The Liberal Tradition in America* (New York: Harcourt Brace, 1955).

4. On the impact of modernism, see Daniel Bell, *The Cultural Contradictions of Capitalism* (New York: Basic Books, 1976).

5. William Riordon, *Plunkitt of Tammany Hall* (New York: Dutton, 1963), 13. Democrats have more often been spokesmen for the private order, but there is no dearth of Republican examples: see Matthew Josephson, *The Politicos* (New York: Harcourt Brace, 1938).

6. G. K. Chesterton, *What I Saw in America* (New York: Da Capo, 1968), 1.

7. Alexis de Tocqueville, *Democracy in America* (New York: Schocken, 1961), 1:52–99; Mancur Olson, *The Logic of Collective Action* (Cambridge, Mass.: Harvard University Press, 1965).

8. Plato, *Laws*, trans. R. G. Bury (Cambridge, Mass.: Harvard University Press, 1952), 1:361 (bk. 5, 738e); on the political impact of stability, see Robert Alford and Eugene C. Lee, "Voting Turnout in American Cities," *American Political Science Review* 62 (1968): 796–813.

9. See Bertrand de Jouvenel, "The Chairman's Problem," *American Political Science Review* 60 (1961): 368–372.

10. See my discussion in *The Idea of Fraternity in America* (Berkeley: University of California Press, 1973), 185–193.

11. Richard Hofstadter, *The Idea of a Party System* (Berkeley: University of California Press, 1969), 1–73.

12. Ibid., 115, 170–212; *Letters and Selected Writings of Thomas Jefferson,* ed. Adrienne Koch and William Peden (New York: Modern Library, 1944), 460.

13. Jefferson, *Letters and Selected Writings,* 715; Hofstadter, *Idea of a Party System,* 27.

14. Ronald Formisano, "Deferential-Participant Politics: The Early Republic's Political Culture, 1789–1840," *American Political Science Review* 68 (1974): 173–187.

15. Jefferson, *Letters and Selected Writings,* 661.

16. James Ceaser, "Political Parties and Presidential Ambition," *Journal of Politics* 40 (1978): 725, 728.

17. Robert V. Remini, *Martin Van Buren and the Making of the Democratic Party* (New York: Columbia University Press, 1959), 132; George Bancroft, *Martin Van Buren* (New York: Harper & Bros., 1889), 122.

18. George Bancroft, *Oration Delivered before the Democracy of Springfield and Neighboring Towns,* July 4, 1836 (Springfield, Mass.: George and Charles Merriam, 1836), 7, see also 8.

19. George Bancroft, *History of the United States,* ed. Russel. B. Nye (Chicago: University of Chicago Press, 1966), 24.

20. Bancroft, *Oration,* 4; Ceaser, "Political Parties," 726; Remini, *Martin Van Buren,* 35.

21. Hobbes, *Leviathan,* chap. 19.

22. Ceaser, "Political Parties," 727; Remini, *Martin Van Buren,* 8; Bancroft, *Martin Van Buren,* 68–69.

23. For contemporary examples of the argument, see Sigmund Neumann, *Modern Political Parties* (Chicago: University of Chicago Press, 1956), 296; V. O. Key, *Political Parties and Pressure Groups* (New York: Crowell, 1958), 242.

24. Ceaser, "Political Parties," 730.

25. Bancroft, *Martin Van Buren,* 93.

26. Ibid., 110–111.

27. Ibid., 115, 128.

28. Tocqueville, *Democracy in America,* 2:120.

29. Phillips Cutright and Peter Henry Rossi, "Grass Roots Politicians and the Vote," *American Sociological Review* 23 (1958): 171–179; Jeremy Boissevain, "Patronage in Sicily," *Man* 1 (1966): 18–31; C. Wright Mills, *The Power Elite* (Oxford: Oxford University Press, 1956), 298–324.

30. On the duality and danger of partisan fraternity, see Boissevain, "Patronage in Sicily"; Harold Ickes, *The Autobiography of a Curmudgeon* (New York: Reynal and Hitchcock, 1943), 133; Lionel Pearson, *Popular Ethics in Ancient Greece* (Stanford, Calif.: Stanford University Press, 1962), 136–161.

31. Among recent comments, see M. Margaret Conway and Frank Feigert, "Motivation, Incentive Systems and Political Party Organization," *American*

Political Science Review 62 (1968): 1169–1183; Peter Gluck, "Incentives and the Maintenance of Political Styles in Different Locales," *Western Political Quarterly* 25 (1972): 753–760.

32. Remini, *Martin Van Buren,* 165.

33. Robert Kelley, *The Cultural Pattern in American Politics* (New York: Knopf, 1979), 130–131, 266; Key, *Political Parties,* 347, 360, 363.

34. Ronald Formisano, *The Birth of Mass Political Parties: Michigan, 1827–1861* (Princeton, N.J.: Princeton University Press, 1971), 22, 57–58, 70, 87.

35. Perry Goldman, "Political Virtue in the Age of Jackson," *Political Science Quarterly* 87 (1972): 46–62.

36. Joel Silbey, *The Shrine of Party: Congressional Voting Behavior, 1841–1852* (Pittsburgh, Pa.: University of Pittsburgh Press, 1967).

37. Riordon, *Plunkitt,* 13; James A. Farley, *Behind the Ballots* (New York: Harcourt Brace, 1933), 237; Roy Peel, *Political Clubs of New York City* (New York: Putnam's, 1935), 245–246; Robert Merton, *Social Theory and Social Structure* (Glencoe, Ill.: Free Press, 1957), 71–82; Dennis B. Hale, "James Michael Curley: Leadership and the Uses of Legend," in *Political Leadership,* ed. Dennis Bathory (New York: Longmans, 1978), 131–146. The term "master cue" is taken from Frank Sorauf, *Party Politics in America* (Boston: Little, Brown, 1976), 15.

38. Gerald M. Pomper, "The Decline of Party in American Elections," *Political Science Quarterly* 92 (1977): 21–41.

39. The case has been made by many critics. For one example, see my essay "American Pluralism: The Old Order Passeth," in *The Americans, 1976,* ed. Irving Kristol and Paul Weaver (Lexington, Mass.: Heath, 1976), 293–320.

40. Otto Kirchheimer, "The Party in Mass Society," *World Politics* 10 (1958): 289–294.

41. Jack Dennis, "Support for the Party System by the Mass Public," *American Political Science Review* 60 (1966): 600–615; E. Converse and G. Dupleix, "Politicization of the Electorate in France and the United States," *Public Opinion Quarterly* 26 (1962): 1–23.

42. M. Kent Jennings and Richard Niemi, "The Transmission of Political Values from Parent to Child," *American Political Science Review* 62 (1968): 169–184.

43. Richard Hofstadter, *The Age of Reform* (New York: Knopf, 1955).

44. E. E. Schattschneider, *Party Government* (New York: Farrar and Rinehart, 1942), 39–44, 58.

45. Clarence A. Berdahle, "Party Membership in the United States," *American Political Science Review* 36 (1942): 16–50, 241–262.

46. Schattschneider, *Party Government,* 55, 56, 60, 64.

47. David Brady, "A Research Note on the Impact of Intraparty Competition on Congressional Voting in a Competitive Era," *American Political Science Review* 67 (1973): 153–156.

48. David Butler and Donald Stokes, *Political Change in Britain* (New York: St. Martin's, 1969), 41–42.

49. John H. Schaar and Wilson C. McWilliams, "Uncle Sam Vanishes," *New University Thought* 1 (1961): 61–68.

50. Kelley, *Cultural Pattern;* Formisano, *Birth of Mass Political Parties,* 81–90, 93, 166, 179–182.

51. Key, *Political Parties,* 233; Sorauf, *Party Politics in America,* 107; Schatt-schneider, *Party Government,* 61.

52. Leon Epstein, *Political Parties in Western Democracies* (New York: Praeger, 1967), 210.

53. Austin Ranney, "Changing the Rules of the Nominating Game," in *Choosing the President,* ed. James David Barber (Englewood Cliffs, N.J.: Prentice Hall, 1973), 73–74; see also William J. Crotty, *Political Reform and the American Experiment* (New York: Crowell, 1977).

54. Robert S. Hirschfield, Bert Swenson, and Blanche Blank, "A Profile of Political Activists in Manhattan," *Western Political Quarterly* 15 (1962): 489–506; Edward Constantini, "Intraparty Attitude Conflict: Democratic Leadership in California," *Western Political Quarterly* 16 (1963): 956–972.

55. Karl Mannheim, *Ideology and Utopia* (New York: Harcourt Brace, 1955).

56. James Wilson, *The Amateur Democrat* (Chicago: University of Chicago Press, 1966), 165.

11. Democracy and Mystery

1. Nathaniel Hawthorne, *The Marble Faun* (Boston: Houghton Mifflin, 1880), viii.

2. Feodor Dostoevsky, *The Brothers Karamazov* (New York: Harper & Bros., 1960), 280–284.

3. Nevada has at least some claim to what is perhaps the most profound and devious of American mysteries, Mark Twain's "A Double-Barreled Detective Story," since Twain's portrait of a mining camp (in the Esmeralda region of California) draws on the experience of his Comstock years. Twain brings Sherlock Holmes to the camp, and in the attempt to solve a local crime, Holmes's scientific, and mensurative, rationalism comes a humiliating second best to the perceptions of a man who has the instincts of a bloodhound, most notably a superior sense of smell.

4. So that, as Sir Thomas Browne argued, to pursue truth is ultimately to lose oneself in a mystery; Browne, *Religio Medici* (Oxford: J. Vincent, 1831), 17.

5. Dostoevsky, *Brothers Karamazov,* 284.

6. Commenting on the "silent generation" of the 1950s, the late Paul de Brul once observed that "no man is so silent as when he is about to throw up."

7. Michael Ignatieff, *The Needs of Strangers* (New York: Viking, 1985).

8. Leo Strauss, *On Tyranny* (Ithaca, N.Y.: Cornell University Press, 1963), 223–224.

9. Though Truman often acted from inner conviction, one of his most admirable qualities was his ability to subordinate purely personal beliefs to the necessities of political action. See Richard Neustadt, "Truman in Action," in *Modern Presidents and the Presidency,* ed. Marc K. Landy (Lexington, Mass.: D. C. Heath, 1985), 3–7.

10. Harvey C. Mansfield, Jr., "Democracy and the Great Books," *New Republic,* April 4, 1988, 36.

11. Herbert J. Storing, ed., *The Complete Anti-Federalist* (Chicago: University of Chicago Press, 1981), vol. 2, sec. 9, par. 47.

12. Ibid., vol. 5, sec. 13, par. 2, 10, 7.

13. Ibid., vol. 3, sec. 12, par. 7–9.

14. Ibid., vol. 5, sec. 1, par. 92–93.

15. Ibid., vol. 2, sec. 6, par. 14, vol. 4, sec. 16, par. 1.

16. Charles S. Hyneman and Donald S. Lutz, eds., *American Political Writing during the Founding Era* (Indianapolis, Ind.: Liberty Press, 1983), 1:682–683.

17. Romans 11:25, 33.

18. Romans 11:26–32.

19. Ephesians 3:9.

20. Machiavelli, *The Prince*, chap. 15; Descartes, *Ouevres et Lettres*, ed. A. Bridoux (Paris: Gallimard, 1953), 127–128, 885.

21. Augustine, *The City of God*, bk. 11, chap. 26.

22. Descartes, *Ouevres et Lettres*, 168.

23. The protection of the "diversity in the faculties of men," Madison wrote, is the "first object of government"; *Federalist* 10. See also Friedrich Nietzsche, *Thus Spake Zarathustra*, chap. 15.

24. Benedict Spinoza, *Political Treatise*, in *The Chief Works of Benedict Spinoza*, trans. R. H. M. Elwes (New York: Dover, 1951), vol. 1, chap. 10, sec. 7.

25. Madison refers to representation as a "great mechanical power," which permits a large republic; Europe has discovered this power, but America has the opportunity to display its "full efficacy"; *Federalist* 14. On functional rationality, see Karl Mannheim, *Man and Society in an Age of Reconstruction* (New York: Harcourt Brace, 1951), 51–60.

26. Locke, *Second Treatise of Government*, sec. 54.

27. "The *Value* or WORTH of a man, is as of all other things, his Price; that is to say, so much as would be given for the use of his Power: and is not absolute, but a thing dependant on the need and judgement of another"; Hobbes, *Leviathan*, chap. 10.

28. Alexis de Tocqueville, *Democracy in America* (New York: Schocken, 1961), 2:120.

29. Raymond Chandler, *The Simple Art of Murder* (New York: Ballantine, 1972), 20–21.

12. National Character and National Soul

1. For example, see Nicholas Lemann, *The Big Test: The Secret History of American Meritocracy* (New York: Farrar, Straus, 1999), 8.

2. Bentley also favored the epithet "idea ghosts." See Bentley, *The Process of Government* (Bloomington, Ind.: Principia, 1949), esp. 165–172.

3. It is easy to forget, these days, how much Gabriel Almond and Sidney Verba's *The Civic Culture* (Princeton, N.J.: Princeton University Press, 1963) expanded the horizons of political science. There are writers who do speak about character, as Shelby Steele does in *The Content of Our Character* (New York: HarperCollins, 1991), although Steele, of course, is quoting Dr. King.

4. Plato *Apology* 17d–18a; John Patrick Diggins, *The Lost Soul of American Politics* (Chicago: University of Chicago Press, 1986).

5. Jess Stein, ed., *The Random House Dictionary of the English Language* (New York: Random House, 1971), 247.

6. Theodor Reik, *Listening with the Third Ear* (New York: Farrar, Straus, 1949); Reik, *The Secret Self* (New York: Farrar, Straus and Young, 1953).

7. André Siegfried, *Nations Have Souls* (New York: Putnam's, 1952).

8. Plato *Apology* 24d2–25b5.

9. Ibid., 25b5–7.

10. *Federalist* 55.

11. Benjamin Franklin, *Writings,* ed. J. A.Lemay (New York: Library of America, 1987), 748, see also 336.

12. John Locke, *Letter Concerning Toleration,* ed. James H. Tully (Indianapolis, Ind.: Bobbs-Merrill, 1952), 52.

13. *The Legal Papers of John Adams,* ed. L. Kinvin Wroth and Hillel B. Zobel (Cambridge, Mass.: Harvard University Press, 1965), 3:254, see also 244–245.

14. John Locke, *The Reasonableness of Christianity,* ed. I. T. Ramsey (Stanford, Calif.: Stanford University Press, 1958), 64.

15. Alexis de Tocqueville, *Democracy in America,* ed. Henry Reeve (New York: Knopf, 1980), 1:43.

16. Reinhold Niebuhr, *The Irony of American History* (New York: Scribner's, 1954); Michael Kammen, *People of Paradox* (New York: Knopf, 1972); Rogers Smith, *Civic Ideals: Conflicting Visions of Citizenship in U.S. History* (New Haven, Conn.: Yale University Press, 1997).

17. Perry Miller, *The American Character* (Santa Barbara, Calif.: Center for the Study of Democratic Institutions, 1962); Miller, *Errand into the Wilderness* (Cambridge, Mass.: Harvard University Press, 1956), viii–ix, 2, 15.

18. Perry Miller, *The Responsibility of Mind in a Civilization of Machines,* ed. John Crowell and Stanford Searls (Amherst: University of Massachusetts Press, 1979).

19. Oliver Wendell Holmes, *The Professor at the Breakfast Table* (Boston: Houghton Mifflin, 1891), 101.

20. Ralph Barton Perry, *Characteristically American* (New York: Knopf, 1949), 9–16.

21. Ibid., 159.

22. Robert Booth Fowler, *Unconventional Partners: Religion and Liberal Culture in the United States* (Grand Rapids, Mich.: Eerdmans, 1989).

23. Tocqueville, *Democracy in America,* 1:299, 304–305, 2:98–99, 127–130; see Robert N. Bellah, Richard Madsen, William M. Sullivan, Ann Swidler, and Steven M. Tipton, *Habits of the Heart* (Berkeley: University of California Press, 1985).

24. Tocqueville, *Democracy in America,* 2:121–125.

25. Ibid., 2:124.

26. Ibid., 1:310, 2:20–26, 134–135, 148.

27. James Davison Hunter, *Culture Wars* (New York: Basic Books, 1991).

28. Pat Robertson, *The New Millennium* (Dallas, Tex.: Word, 1990), 86.

29. Richard Morin, "Can We Believe in Polls about God?" *Washington Post National Weekly,* June 1, 1998, 30.

30. The Rutgers survey was conducted by my colleague Kerry Haynie.

31. Laurence H. Tribe, "Second Thoughts on Cloning," *New York Times,* December 5, 1997, A31; by contrast, see David Bromwich, "Experience Can't Be Cloned," *New York Times,* January 11, 1998, WK 10.

32. Richard Rorty, *Achieving Our Country* (Cambridge, Mass.: Harvard University Press, 1998), 24.

33. William Galston, "Home of the Tolerant," *Public Interest*, no. 133 (Fall 1998): 116–120.

34. Richard Morin and David Broder, "Worried about Morals, but Reluctant to Judge," *Washington Post National Weekly*, September 21, 1998, 10–11.

35. Alan Wolfe, *One Nation, After All* (New York: Viking, 1998).

36. Harvey C. Mansfield, Jr., "Change and Bill Clinton," *Times Literary Supplement*, no. 4676 (November 13, 1992): 14.

37. David Levering Lewis, "Response to Hochschild and Williams," *Good Society* 8 (Winter 1998): 38.

38. Rorty, *Achieving Our Country*.

39. Bertrand de Jouvenel, *Sovereignty: An Inquiry into the Political Good* (Indianapolis, Ind.: Liberty Fund, 1997), 300, 317.

40. Tocqueville, *Democracy in America*, 2:136–139.

41. Robert H. Frank and Phillip J. Cook, *The Winner-Take-All Society* (New York: Martin Kessler/Free Press, 1995).

42. Kristin Downey Grimsley, "Leaner and Definitely Meaner," *Washington Post National Weekly*, July 20–27, 1998, 21; Clay Chandler, "A Market Tide That Isn't Lifting Everybody," *Washington Post National Weekly*, April 13, 1998, 18.

43. On the general point, see Robert Putnam, "The Strange Death of Civic America," *American Prospect* 24 (Winter 1996): 34–38.

44. Michael Paul Rogin, "'JFK': The Movie," *American Historical Review* 97 (1992): 502–505.

45. W. Lance Bennett, "The Uncivic Culture: Communications, Identity and the Rise of Lifestyle Politics," *PS* 31 (1998): 758; Theodore J. Lowi, "Think Globally, Lose Locally," *Boston Review* 23, no. 2 (April–May 1998): 4–10; Ronald Inglehart, *Modernization and Postmodernization* (Princeton, N.J.: Princeton University Press, 1997), 295–323.

46. G. K. Chesterton, *What I Saw in America* (New York: Dodd, Mead, 1922), 16.

47. John Paul II, "Fides et Ratio," excerpted in *New York Times*, October 16, 1998, A10.

BIBLIOGRAPHY

The Published Writings of
Wilson Carey McWilliams

Papers and Essays

"The Idea of Responsibility in American Politics." In *Readings in Community Involvement*, ed. R. P. Robinson. Philadelphia: USNSA, 1962, 76–98.

"The Souls of Black Folk." *The Activist* 2, no. 3 (Spring 1962): 18–21.

"Reinhold Niebuhr: New Orthodoxy for Old Liberalism." *American Political Science Review* 56, no. 4 (December 1962): 874–885. Reprinted in *Perspectives on Political Philosophy*, vol. 3, *Marx through Marcuse*, ed. James V. Downton, Jr., and David K. Hart. Hinsdale, Ill.: Dryden Press, 1973, 336–353.

"The Constitutional Doctrine of Mr. Justice Frankfurter." *Political Science* (Wellington, New Zealand) 15 (1963): 34–43.

"The Marks of a Profession." *Chapel and College* (Spring 1963): 9–18.

"On Black Power." *The Activist* 7, no. 1 (Fall 1966): 13–15.

"On Time and History." *Yale Review* 56 (Fall 1966): 91–103. Reprinted by the Japan-America Forum in *A Monthly Journal with Articles of Binational Interest* 13, no. 12 (December 1967).

"The New Face of History: International Politics in the Post-modern Era." *1968 Conference on Contemporary Issues*. Springfield, Mo.: Drury University, 1968, 39–47.

"The CDC" and "The Beats." In *California Dream*, ed. Dennis Hale and Jonathan Eisen. New York: Macmillan, 1969, 74–76, 293–295.

"Democracy, Publics and Protest: The Problem of Foreign Policy." *Journal of International Affairs* 23, no. 2 (1969): 189–209. Reprinted in *Crisis and Continuity in World Politics: Readings in International Relations*, ed. George A. Lanyi and Wilson Carey McWilliams. New York: Random House, 1973.

"Honesty and Political Authority." In *The Right to Know, to Withold and to Lie*, ed. William J. Barnds. New York: Council on Religion and International Affairs, 1969, 50–62.

"Political Development and Foreign Policy." In *Foreign Policy and the Developing Nation*, ed. Richard Butwell. Lexington: University of Kentucky Press, 1969, 11–39.

"Civil Disobedience and Contemporary Constitutionalism: The American Case." *Comparative Politics* 1, no. 2 (January 1969): 211–227.

"Political Arts and Political Sciences." In *Power and Community: Dissenting Essays in Political Science*, ed. Philip Green and Sanford Levinson. New York: Random House, 1970, 357–382.

"On Violence and Legitimacy." *Yale Law Journal* 79, no. 4 (March 1970): 623–646.

"On Political Illegitimacy." *Public Policy* 19, no. 3 (Summer 1971): 429–456.

"The American Constitutions." In *The Performance of American Government: Checks and Misuses,* ed. Gerald Pomper. New York: Free Press, 1972, 1–45.

"Fraternity and Nature: A Response to Philip Abbott." *Political Theory* 2, no. 3 (August 1974): 321–329.

"Natty Bumppo and the Godfather." *Colorado Quarterly* 24, no. 2 (Fall 1975): 133–144.

"American Pluralism: The Old Order Passeth." In *The Americans, 1976: An Inquiry into Fundamental Concepts of Man Underlying Various U.S. Institutions,* ed. Irving Kristol and Paul Weaver. Lexington, Mass.: Lexington Books, 1976, 293–320.

"The Meaning of the Election." In *The Election of 1976,* ed. Gerald M. Pomper and Marlene M. Pomper. New York: Longman, 1977, 147–162.

"Lyndon Johnson and the Politics of Mass Society." In *Leadership in America: Consensus, Corruption, and Charisma,* ed. Peter Dennis Bathory. New York: Longman, 1978, 177–194.

"Democracy and the Citizen: Community, Dignity, and the Crisis of Contemporary Politics in America." In *How Democratic Is the Constitution?* ed. Robert A. Goldwin and William A. Schambra. Washington, D.C.: American Enterprise Institute Press, 1980, 79–101.

"Parties as Civic Associations." In *Party Renewal in America,* ed. Gerald R. Pomper. Westport, Conn.: Praeger, 1980, 51–68.

"Liberty and Equality in Contemporary America." Presented as part of The Colleges' Summer Program on Social Transformation, July 28, 1980, and published in *Alternatives: A Publication Series Sponsored by the Colleges, State University of New York at Buffalo,* 1–38.

"The Meaning of the Election." In *The Election of 1980: Reports and Interpretations,* ed. Marlene Michels Pomper. Chatham, N.J.: Chatham House Publishers, 1981, 170–188.

"America's Cultural Dilemma." CRIA Symposium, "The U.S. and South Korea: Values in Conflict." *Worldview* 24, no. 10 (October 1981): 15–19.

"The Machiavellian as Moralist." *Democracy* 2 (1982): 97–106.

"In Good Faith: On the Foundations of American Politics." *Humanities in Society* 6 (1983): 19–40.

"Liberty, Equality and the Problem of Community." In *Liberty and Equality under the Constitution,* ed. John Agresto. Washington, D.C.: American Historical Association and American Political Science Association, 1983, 111–134.

"Equality and Citizenship: The Rights of Man and the Rights of Women." *Discourses* (a monthly publication sponsored by the Institute for Political Philosophy and Policy Analysis, Department of Political Science, Loyola University of Chicago), April 1983.

"Politics." *American Quarterly* 35, no. 1–2 (Spring–Summer 1983): 19–38.

"The Bible in the American Political Tradition." In *Religion and Politics,* ed. Myron J. Aronoff. New Brunswick, N.J.: Transaction, 1984, 11–45.

"George Orwell and Ideology." *Freedom at Issue* 77 (March–April 1984): 23–28.

"The Arts and the American Political Tradition." In *Art, Ideology, and Politics*, ed. Judith H. Balfe and Margaret Wyzomirski. New York: Praeger, 1985, 15–39.

"Lyndon B. Johnson: Last of the Great Presidents." In *Modern Presidents and the Presidency*, ed. Marc Landy. Lexington, Mass.: Lexington Books, 1985, 163–181.

"The Meaning of the Election." In *The Election of 1984: Reports and Interpretations*, ed. Marlene Michels Pomper. Chatham, N.J.: Chatham House Publishers, 1985, 157–184.

"On Equality as the Moral Foundation for Community." In *The Moral Foundations of the American Republic*, 3rd ed., ed. Robert H. Horwitz. Charlottesville: University Press of Virginia, 1986, 183–213.

"Religion and the American Founding." *Princeton Seminary Bulletin* 8, no. 3 (1987): 46–56. Reprinted in *An Unsettled Arena: Religion and the Bill of Rights*, ed. Ronald C. White and Albright G. Zimmerman. Grand Rapids, Mich.: William B. Eerdmans Publishing, 1990, 20–36.

"Civil Religion in the Age of Reason: Thomas Paine on Liberalism, Redemption and Revolution." *Social Research* 54, no. 3 (Autumn 1987): 447–490.

"The Discipline of Freedom." In *To Secure the Blessings of Liberty: First Principles of the Constitution*, ed. Sarah Baumgartner Thurow. Lanham, Md.: University Press of America, 1988, 31–63.

"American Culture and the Foundations of American Politics." Paper presented at the "U.S.-Japan Relations and the American Black Community" conference held at the Christian Theological Seminary, Indianapolis, Ind., December 8–9, 1988.

"Democracy and Mystery: On Civic Education in America." *Halcyon: A Journal of the Humanities* 11 (1989): 43–56.

"The Meaning of the Election." In *The Election of 1988*, ed. Gerald M. Pomper. Chatham, N.J.: Chatham House Publishers, 1989, 177–206.

"The Anti-Federalists, Representation, and Party." *Northwestern University Law Review* 84, no. 1 (Fall 1989): 12–38.

"Pudd'nhead Wilson on Democratic Governance." In *Mark Twain's Pudd'nhead Wilson: Race, Conflict and Culture*, ed. Susan Gillman and Forrest G. Robinson. Durham, N.C.: Duke University Press, 1990, 177–189.

"Comments on Schneck's Reading of Tocqueville's Democracy." *Polity* 25, no. 2 (Winter 1992): 299–306.

"Tocqueville and Responsible Parties: Individualism, Partisanship and Citizenship in America." In *Challenges to Party Government*, ed. John K. White and Jerome M. Mileur. Carbondale: Southern Illinois University Press, 1992, 190–211.

"The Meaning of the Election." In *The Election of 1992: Reports and Interpretations*, ed. Gerald M. Pomper. Chatham, N.J.: Chatham House Publishers, 1993, 190–218.

"Science and Freedom: America as the Technological Republic." In *Technology in the Western Political Tradition*, ed. Arthur Melzer, Jerry Weinberger, and Richard Zinman. Ithaca, N.Y.: Cornell University Press, 1993, 85–108.

"Ambiguities and Ironies: Conservatism and Liberalism in the American Political Tradition." In *Moral Values in Liberalism and Conservatism*, ed. W. Lawson Taitte. Richardson: University of Texas at Dallas Press, 1995, 175–212.

"Two-Tier Politics and the Problem of Public Policy." In *The New Politics of Public*

Policy, ed. Marc K. Landy and Martin A. Levin. Baltimore, Md.: Johns Hopkins University Press, 1995, 268–276.

"Poetry, Politics and the Comic Spirit." *PS: Political Science and Politics* 28, no. 2 (June 1995): 197–200.

"The Meaning of the Election." In *The Election of 1996: Reports and Interpretations*, ed. Gerald M. Pomper. Chatham, N.J.: Chatham House Publishers, 1997, 241–272.

"Democratic Multiculturalism." In *Multiculturalism and American Democracy*, ed. Arthur Melzer, Jerry Weinberger, and Richard Zinman. Lawrence: University Press of Kansas, 1998, 120–129.

"Leo Strauss and the Dignity of American Political Thought." *Review of Politics* 60, no. 2 (Spring 1998): 231–246.

"Standing at Armageddon: Morality and Religion in Progressive Thought." In *Progressivism and the New Democracy*, ed. Sidney M. Milkis and Jerome M. Mileur. Amherst: University of Massachusetts Press, 1999, 103–125.

"On Rogers Smith's Civic Ideals." *Studies in American Political Development* 13, no. 1 (Spring 1999): 216–229.

"Community and Its Discontents: Politics and Etzioni's 'The New Golden Rule.'" In *Autonomy and Order: A Communitarian Anthology*, ed. Edward Lehman. Lanham, Md.: Rowman & Littlefield, 2000, 111–123.

"Television and Political Speech. The Medium Exalts Spectacle and Slights Words." *Media Studies Journal* 14, no. 1 (Winter 2000): 110–115.

"Faith and Morals: Religion in American Democracy." *The Good Society: A PEGS Journal* 10, no. 1 (2001): 17–20.

"The Meaning of the Election." In *The Election of 2000: Reports and Interpretations*, ed. Gerald M. Pomper. Washington, D.C.: CQ Press, 2001, 177–201.

"The Search for a Public Philosophy." In *The Politics of Ideas: Intellectual Challenges Facing the American Political Parties*, ed. John Kenneth White and John Clifford Green. Albany: State University of New York Press, 2001, 11–28.

"Two-Tier Politics Revisited." In *Seeking the Center: Politics and Policy-Making at the New Century*, ed. Martin A. Levin, Marc K. Landy, and Martin Shapiro. Washington, D.C.: Georgetown University Press, 2001, 381–400.

"Toward Genuine Self-Government." *Academic Questions* 15, no. 1 (Winter 2001–2002): 50–56.

"National Character and National Soul." *Willamette Journal of the Liberal Arts* 12 (Summer 2002): 25–40.

"Jouvenel on Politics and Political Science in America." *Political Science Reviewer* 32 (2003): 76–92.

"The President and His Powers: Commentary." In *The Collected Works of William Howard Taft*, vol. 6, *The President and His Powers and the United States and Peace*, ed. Wilson Carey McWilliams and Frank X. Gerrity, general ed. David H. Burton. Athens: Ohio University Press, 2003, 1–9.

"Critical Rebound: Why America Needs a Catholic Recovery." *Boston College Magazine* 63, no. 3 (Summer 2003): 53–55.

"Descendants of Machiavelli." *Society* 41, no. 4 (May–June 2004): 63–65.

"'Go Tell It on the Mountain': James Baldwin and the Politics of Faith." In *Democracy's Literature*, ed. Patrick J. Deneen and Joseph Romance. Lanham, Md.: Rowman & Littlefield, 2005, 153–170.

"Great Societies and Great Empires: Lyndon Johnson and Vietnam." In *The Great Society and the High Tide of Liberalism*, ed. Sidney M. Milkis and Jerome M. Mileur. Amherst: University of Massachusetts Press, 2005, 214–232.

"The Meaning of the Election: Ownership and Citizenship in American Life." In *The Elections of 2004*, ed. Michael Nelson. Washington, D.C.: CQ Press, 2005, 187–213.

"Minstrels, Kings and Citizens: Mark Twain's Political Thought." In *Democracy and Excellence: Concord or Conflict?* ed. Joseph Romance and Niel Riemer. Westport, Conn.: Praeger, 2005, 43–56.

"Divine Right: Mark Twain's *Joan of Arc*." *Review of Politics* 69 (2007): 329–352.

"Power after Power: Reflections on Liberalism in Politics and Vision." *Theory & Event* 10, no. 1 (2007).

"Henry Adams and the 'Burden of History': Intimations of Fraternity amidst the Ravages of Nature Conquered." In *A Political Companion to Henry Adams*, ed. Natalie Fuehrer Taylor. Lexington: University Press of Kentucky, 2010, 246–256.

"Mark Twain's 'A Connecticut Yankee': The Prince and the Public." Elmira Mark Twain Papers, n.d. Elmira College, Elmira, N.Y.

Journalism and Occasional Articles

"The Need for Student Political Parties." *Student Government Bulletin, United States National Student Association* 2, no. 1 (Spring 1962): 5–6.

"The Dilemma of Atomic Power," with Editor's Postscript: "Toward a Realistic Realism." Monograph published for the National Student Councils of the YMCA and YWCA, ed. Harvey Cox. New York: Association Press, 1963.

"A Non-aggression Pact?" *Commonweal*, November 8, 1963, 191–195.

"The Poor White South and the Civil Rights Crisis." *The Activist* 4, no. 2 (1964): 68–74.

"The Nationalists: Winston and Malcolm." *Motive* 25, no. 8 (May 1965): 30–32.

"The Drama in Southeast Asia." *Political* 1, no. 1 (July 1965): 40–44.

"Poverty: Public Enemy Number One." *Saturday Review*, December 10, 1966, 48–58.

"Ending the Cold War: Vietnam Need Not Slow the Thaw." *Commonweal*, January 6, 1967, 363–365.

"Will China Intervene? The Stakes in Vietnam." *Commonweal*, February 17, 1967, 553–555.

"Obviously Naïve? C.I.A. and the Students." *Commonweal*, March 3, 1967, 613–614.

"California: Notes of a Native Son." *The Activist* 20 (Fall 1967): 3–5. Reprinted in *California Dream*, ed. Dennis Hale and Jonathan Eisen. New York: Macmillan, 1969.

"Toward a Politics of Imagination." *Motive*, May 1968, 6–14.

"Wallace: America's Self-fulfilling Prophecy." *Motive*, November 1968, 5–10.

"The Same Two Nations." *Commonweal*, November 29, 1968, 307–310.

"The Liberal's Lament: 'How Could They Do This to Me?'" *The Activist* 22 (Fall 1968): 11–14.

"Military Assistance, Yes; Unconditioned Involvement, No." *Commonweal*, March 21, 1969, 12–13.

"Intervention: A Two-Way Street." *Worldview* 12, no. 4 (April 1969): 14–18.

"On Choosing to Be Involved." *Current*, August 1969, 56–59.

"The End of a Love Affair? The Army and Secularized America." *Worldview* 14, no. 5 (May 1971): 4–7.

"Nixon a Sinistra: The Path to Peking." *Commonweal*, August 6, 1971, 397–398.

"Concurring and Dissenting Opinions: On Pornography." *Public Interest* 22 (Winter 1971): 25–44.

"A Bill to Pay?" *Commonweal*, March 31, 1972, 79–80.

"Mr. Nixon in Peace and War." *Commonweal*, November 23, 1973, 206–209.

"Excursus I: The New Mandarins Revisited." *Worldview* 18, no. 6 (January 1975): 7.

"The Politics of Assassination. Can Assassination Ever Be an Appropriate Technique of Foreign Policy?" *Commonweal*, July 18, 1975, 265–267.

"Excursus V: Open Season for Madness." *Worldview* 18, no. 11 (November 1975): 9–10.

"Symposium: 'What Now?'" *Alternatives* 1 (Spring 1976): 2–10.

"Excursus III: Conscription and Public Service." *Worldview* 19, no. 6 (June 1976): 29–30.

"The Power of a Good Lecture." *Change* 6, no. 8 (July 1976): 68–69.

"Down with the Primaries: Extremely Costly, Time-Consuming, and Dependent on the Mass Media." *Commonweal*, July 2, 1976, 427–428.

"California: A Remembrance of Things Present." *California Monthly* 87, no. 4 (March 1977): 12–13.

"The Sadat Initiative." *Commonweal*, December 23, 1977, 806–808.

"Excursus IV: The Crown of St. Stephen, the Panama Canal, and Other Sacred Objects." *Worldview* 21, no. 1–2 (January–February 1978): 33–36.

"Excursus I: The Humphrey Not Everybody Loved." *Worldview* 21, no. 3 (March 1978): 27.

"The Politics of Agenda Building." *Alternatives* 6 (Spring 1978): 1–4.

"Contending with God, Fidelity, and Freedom." *Worldview* 23, no. 3 (March 1980): 30–31.

"The City and the Race." *Worldview* 23, no. 6 (June 1980): 2.

"Muskie, the Allies, and Iran." *Worldview* 23, no. 7 (July 1980): 2.

"Public Speech and Public Men." *Worldview* 23, no. 8 (August 1980): 2.

"National Greatness and Other Fallacies." *Worldview* 23, no. 9 (September 1980): 2.

"The Cardinal, the Liberals, and the Moral Majority." *Worldview* 23, no. 11 (November 1980): 2.

"Shogun, the Mikado and Modern America." *Worldview* 23, no. 12 (December 1980): 2.

"Poland and El Salvador." *Worldview* 24, no. 5 (May 1981): 2.

"Reagan Republicanism." *Commonweal*, May 8, 1981, 273–275.

"Reign of Terror." *Worldview* 24, no. 7 (July 1981): 2.

"On Human Rights and Good Fortune." *Worldview* 24, no. 8 (August 1981): 2.

"The Craft of History." *Worldview* 24, no. 9 (September 1981): 2.

"Laws and Liberties." *Worldview* 24, no. 10 (October 1981): 2.

"Arms and the Man." *Worldview* 24, no. 11 (November 1981): 2.

"The Captain and the King." *Worldview* 24, no. 12 (December 1981): 2.

"Fidelity and Solidarity." *Worldview* 25, no. 2 (February 1982): 2.

"Remove Abortion from Federal Agenda." *Fort Worth Star-Telegram*, February 22, 1982, 7A.

"Independence and Affluence." *Worldview* 25, no. 5 (May 1982): 2.

"Paying the Price." *Worldview* 25, no. 6 (June 1982): 2.

"On Making the Pledge." *Worldview* 25, no. 8 (August 1982): 2.

"Peace and the Demand for Justice." *Worldview* 25, no. 9 (September 1982): 2.

"Liberating Theology." *Worldview* 25, no. 10 (October 1982): 2.

"A Tale of Two Worlds." *Worldview* 25, no. 12 (December 1982): 2.

"Half Past Reagan." *Worldview* 26, no. 1 (January 1983): 2.

"Orwell in '84." *Worldview* 26, no. 2 (February 1983): 2.

"The Wearing of the Orange." *Worldview* 26, no. 3 (March 1983): 2.

"Gandhi's Truth." *Worldview* 26, no. 4 (April 1983): 2.

"Unwelcome Visitors and Valued Guests." *Worldview* 26, no. 5 (May 1983): 2.

"Just Wars and Civilian Life." *Worldview* 26, no. 6 (June 1983): 2.

"The Silly Season in Foreign Policy." *Worldview* 26, no. 7 (July 1983): 2.

"The British Election and the Politics of Dignity." *Worldview* 26, no. 8 (August 1983): 2.

"Gunboats and Euphemisms." *Worldview* 26, no. 9 (September 1983): 2.

"The State and the Soul." *Worldview* 26, no. 10 (October 1983): 2.

"KAL 007: Non Possumus." *Worldview* 26, no. 11 (November 1983): 2.

"The Democrats' Dilemma." *Worldview* 27, no. 2 (February 1984): 2.

"The State of the President." *Worldview* 27, no. 3 (March 1984): 2.

"Lebanon and Common Sense." *Worldview* 27, no. 4 (April 1984): 2.

"Mr. Reagan and Miss Manners." *Worldview* 27, no. 6 (June 1984): 2.

"The Political Olympics." *Worldview* 27, no. 7 (July 1984): 2.

"Endowing Democracy." *Worldview* 27, no. 8 (August 1984): 2.

"Mrs. Gandhi: Legacy of a Nationalist." *Worldview* 27, no. 12 (December 1984): 2.

"The New Activism." *Worldview* 28, no. 7 (July 1985): 2.

"The Anti-Federalists vs. . . . " *Humanities* 8, no. 2 (March–April 1987): 12–17.

"The Undergraduate Learner: Challenges for the Year 2000." New Jersey Board of Higher Education Twentieth Anniversary Lecture, New Jersey State Museum, October 27, 1987.

"What Will Jackson Do? The Paradoxes of Success." *Commonweal*, September 23, 1988, 486–488.

"A Republic of Couch Potatoes: The Media Shrivel the Electorate." *Commonweal*, March 10, 1989, 138–140.

"We the People Have Had Enough: Why Americans Are Indifferent to Politics." *Today in Hunterdon*, November 1–14, 1990, 1–5.

"Bush's Dilemma: Brinkmanship and Butter." *Today in Hunterdon*, December 13–26, 1990, 1–3.

"What Clinton Should Do: Let Democrats Be Democrats." *Commonweal*, July 17, 1992, 4–5.

"Clinton's New Political Geography: Renewing the Language of Equality." *Commonweal*, April 23, 1993, 14–18.

"Summer '94: The State of Politics—Slouching toward November." *Commonweal*, August 19, 1994, 15–17.

"Clear the Decks: Campaign '94—The Political Storm Ahead." *Commonweal*, October 21, 1994, 11–12.

"Can Republicans Govern? Not the Way They Campaigned." *Commonweal*, December 2, 1994, 6–8.

"Primarily, It's a Failure." *Sunday Star-Ledger*, March 3, 1996, Perspectives section, 1–4.

"Republicans vs. the Republic: Can the Idea of Government Survive the GOP Primaries?" *In These Times*, March 18, 1996, 26–27.

"The Republican Candidate: Dole, Like Clinton, out of the Loop." *Commonweal*, April 19, 1996, 11–12.

"Losing—the Hard Way: Dole's Old-Time Protestant Virtues Speak to an America That's Now Long Gone." *In These Times*, June 10, 1996, 22–39.

"Clinton's Re-election: The 'X' Factor." *Commonweal*, October 11, 1996, 8–9.

"The Electoral College: Pro." *Home News and Tribune* (East Brunswick, N.J.), October 20, 1996.

"Congress in the Balance: Empty Campaign Rhetoric Notwithstanding, Much Is at Stake in This Year's Elections." *In These Times*, October 28, 1996, 20–24.

"The Disenchanted Majority Speaks." *Currents: Newsday's Sunday Journal of Policy, Politics and Ideas*, November 10, 1996, A47.

"What We Voted For: Ambivalence, Anxiety, and Gridlock." *Commonweal*, December 6, 1996, 8–9.

"Ties That Almost Bind." *Commonweal*, August 15, 1997, 24–25.

"How to Rein in White House Roguery." *Currents: Newsday's Sunday Journal of Policy, Politics and Ideas*, October 12, 1997, B5.

"The Real Trial of the Century." *Commonweal*, January 30, 1998, 20–21.

"The Presidency at Risk: We Need a Grown-Up." *Commonweal*, July 17, 1998, 11–12.

"For Clinton and the Public: A Need to Focus on Rebuilding." *Newsday*, August 19, 1998, A41–A43. Reprinted in *Cape Cod Times*, August 23, 1998, G1–G5.

"Fallout from the Clinton Capers: A Bleak Outlook for the Democrats." *Commonweal*, October 9, 1998, 11–12.

"Gingrich Out, Democrats Not Quite In." *Commonweal*, November 20, 1998, 9–10.

"Who Got Impeached? Assessing the Political Damage." *Commonweal*, February 26, 1999, 12–14.

"Bill Bradley's Magic: It's Not Just Hoop Dreams." *Commonweal*, October 22, 1999, 9–10.

"Putting America's Meritocracy to the Test." *Newsday*, November 21, 1999, B6–15.

"Parties Lose Big in NH Primary." *Newsday*, February 6, 2000, B1–15.

"Primary Lessons: What McCain Taught Us." *Commonweal*, March 24, 2000, 9–10.

"The Great Triangulator." *Commonweal*, April 21, 2000, 26–27.

"Campaign 2000: Most Voters Remain Indifferent." *Commonweal*, September 22, 2000, 10–11.

"Politics after September 11: Domestic and Foreign Affairs at Odds." *Commonweal*, December 7, 2001, 13–14.

"One Nation, Including God." *Commonweal*, February 22, 2002, 21–11.

"The Reign of Terror and the Rule of Law." *Rutgers, The State University of New Jersey, Faculty of Arts and Sciences, New Brunswick* 9 (Summer 2002), 7.

"Shell Game: Bush's Domestic Agenda." *Commonweal*, February 28, 2003, 10–11.

"Commander in Waiting." *Commonweal*, October 10, 2003, 8–9.

"Campaign 2004." *Commonweal*, October 8, 2004, 10–11.

"Anti-Semitism and *A Mask for Privilege*." *Society* 42, no. 3 (March–April 2005): 48–51.

Book Reviews

"Sadness in Appalachia: *Night Comes to the Cumberland: A Biography of a Depressed Area* by Harry C. Caudill." *Dissent* 9, no. 3 (Summer 1964): 366–367.

"*What the French Learned the First Time Around: The Battle of Dienbienphu* by Jules Roy." *Commonweal*, April 16, 1965, 119–120.

"Dullness on the Right: Devitalizing the American Dream—*Reclaiming the American Dream* by Richard Cournuelle." *The Activist* 6, no. 1 (May 1965): 35–36.

"*Forge of Democracy: The House of Representatives* by Neil MacNeil; *New Perspectives on the House of Representatives*, ed. by Robert L. Peabody and Nelson W. Polsby." *Midwest Journal of Political Science* 9, no. 2 (May 1965): 200–202.

"*How We Bungled Our Way in Vietnam: A Diplomatic Tragedy* by Victor Bator; *The New Face of War* by Malcolm W. Browne; *The Making of a Quagmire* by David Halberstam." *Commonweal*, July 23, 1965, 537–538.

"Some Lessons of World War II—*Hostile Allies: FDR and De Gaulle* by Milton Viorst; *The Murder of Admiral Darlan* by Peter Tompkins." *Commonweal*, October 8, 1965, 28–30.

"A Throw-Back to Nineteenth Century Romanticism—*Castroism: Theory and Practice* by Theodore Draper." *Commonweal*, October 29, 1965, 126–128.

"*The Accidental Century* by Michael Harrington; *Coming of Age in America* by Edgar Z. Friedenberg; *Statesmanship and Party Government* by Harvey Mansfield, Jr.; *Martin Chuzzlewit* by Charles Dickens." *Commonweal*, December 3, 1965, 286–287.

"The Search for a Unified Portrait: *The Three Lives of Charles de Gaulle* by David Schoenbrun." *Commonweal*, March 4, 1966, 643–645.

"National Interest and International Ideology: *Power and Impotence* by Edmund Stillman and William Pfaff." *Commonweal*, July 8, 1966, 442.

"*Functionalism and World Politics* by James P. Sewell." *American Political Science Review* 60, no. 3 (September 1966): 760–761.

"*The Gentle Reformers* by Geoffrey Blodgett." *Western Political Quarterly* 19, no. 3 (September 1966): 541–543.

"*Three Faces of Fascism* by Ernst Nolte." *Chicago Jewish Forum* 25, no. 2 (Winter 1966–1967): 155.

"*The Arrogance of Power* by Senator J. William Fulbright." *Commonweal*, March 17, 1967, 685–686.

"*Paul de Lagarde: A Study of Radical Conservatism in Germany* by Robert W. Lougee." *Chicago Jewish Forum* 26, no. 2 (Winter 1967–1968): 157–158.

"*Infidel in the Temple* by Matthew Josephson." *Commonweal*, January 19, 1968, 476–477.

"A World of Its Own: *The Rise of Ronald Reagan* by William Boyarsky; *Dancing*

Bear: An Inside Look at California Politics by Gladwin Hill." *New York Times Book Review*, May 19, 1968, 10.

"Conservatives for Change: *The Goldwater Coalition: Republican Strategies in 1964* by John H. Kessel; *Actions Speak Louder* by J. Daniel Mahoney; *The Future of Conservatism: From Taft to Reagan and Beyond* by M. Stanton Evans." *New York Times Book Review*, October 20, 1968, 3.

"George Kennan—The Myth Contained: *Memoirs: 1925–1950* by George F. Kennan." *Commonweal*, November 29, 1968, 25–28.

"*The Arms of Krupp* by William Manchester." *Commonweal*, February 7, 1969, 598–599.

"Heretic on the Left: *The Unperfect Society* by Milovan Djilas." *New Republic*, May 17, 1969, 22–24.

"Has Liberalism Come Apart at the Seams? No, Says Arthur Schlesinger: *The Crisis of Confidence: Ideas, Power, and Violence in America* by Arthur M. Schlesinger Jr." *New York Times Book Review*, June 22, 1969, 6.

"Voices of the 'Establishment.'" *New York Times Book Review*, September 14, 1969, 38–42.

"Political Violence: *The Behavioral Process* by H. L. Nieburg." *New York Times Book Review*, October 26, 1969, 3.

"Revisionism: *The Politics of War: The World and United States Foreign Policy, 1943–45* by Gabriel Kolko; *Empire and Revolution: A Radical Interpretation of Contemporary History* by David Horowitz." *Commentary* 48, no. 6 (December 1969): 104–107.

"*The End of Liberalism* by Theodore Lowi; *The Politics of War* by Gabriel Kolko; *Men in Groups* by Lionel Tiger; *The Age of Rock* by Jonathan Eisen." *Commonweal*, December 5, 1969, 315–316.

"*Present at Creation* by Dean Acheson." *Commonweal*, December 26, 1969, 384–385.

"*Justice: The Crisis of Law, Order, and Freedom in America* by Richard Harris." *New York Times Book Review*, March 22, 1970, 7–34.

"*On Violence* by Hannah Arendt." *Commonweal*, May 8, 1970, 196–197.

"*The Real Majority* by Richard M. Scrammon and Ben J. Wattenberg; *The Troubled American* by Richard Lemon; *The Conscience of a Majority* by Barry Goldwater." *New York Times Book Review*, October 18, 1970, 58–59.

"*Henry A. Wallace of Iowa: The Agrarian Years* by Edward L. and Frederick H. Schapsmeier; *Prophet in Politics: Henry A. Wallace and the War Years* by Edward L. and Frederick H. Schapsmeier." *New York Times Book Review*, April 11, 1971, 5.

"*The Perverted Priorities of American Politics* by Duane Lockard." *Commonweal*, September 24, 1971, 504–505.

"*The Great Commoner: Bryan—A Political Biography of William Jennings Bryan* by Louis W. Koenig." *Commentary* 52, no. 5 (November 1971): 94–96.

"When Irish Eyes Are Smarting: *Ireland since the Famine, 1850 to the Present* by F. S. Lyons; *Government without Consensus: An Irish Perspective* by Richard Rose; *The Secret Army: The IRA, 1916–1970* by J. Bowyer Bell." *Society* 9, no. 5 (March 1972): 43–45.

"*American Communism in Crisis 1943–1957* by Joseph R. Starobin." *New York Times Book Review*, April 16, 1972, 2.

"*Meany* by Joesph C. Goulden." *New York Times Book Review*, October 22, 1972, 2.

"*Mr. Republican: A Biography of Robert A. Taft* by James T. Patterson." *New York Times Book Review*, November 19, 1972, 3–32.

"*Harry S. Truman* by Margaret Truman." *New York Times Book Review*, December 24, 1972, 1–15.

"Let Who Will Be Wise: *Educability and Group Differences* by Arthur R. Jensen; *The Intelligence of a People* by Daniel Calhoun; *Genetic Diversity and Human Equality* by Theodosius Dobzhansky; *I.Q. in the Meritocracy* by R. J. Hernstein; *The Fallacy of I.Q.*, ed. by Carl Senna." *Washington Post Book World*, December 2, 1973, 1–2.

"Arthur Schlesinger and the Presidential Mystique: *The Imperial Presidency* by Arthur Schlesinger, Jr." *Chronicle of Higher Education Review*, December 3, 1973, 17.

"*The Mythology of the Secret Societies* by J. M. Roberts." Supplement to *JAAR*, June 1975, 406–408.

"The Contradictions of Daniel Bell: His New Book Is a Critique of America's Dominant Patterns of Thought—*The Cultural Contradictions of Capitalism* by Daniel Bell." *Chronicle of Higher Education Review*, April 19, 1976, 15–16.

"*The Gun and the Olive Branch* by David Hirst; *Honor the Promise* by Robert F. Drinan." *Commonweal*, July 21, 1978, 474–475.

"Weapons and Virtues: Book Reviewed—*National Defense* by James Fallows." *Democracy* (July 1982): 97–106.

"*The Needs of Strangers* by Michael Ignatieff; *Exodus and Revolution* by Michael Walzer." *Commonweal*, June 21, 1985, 378–379.

"*The Old Christian Right: The Protestant Far Right from the Great Depression to the Cold War* by Leo P. Ribuffo." *Society* 22, no. 6 (September–October 1985): 76–77.

"A Glorious Discontent: *Reinhold Niebuhr: A Biography* by Richard Wightman Fox." *Freedom at Issue* 92–93 (November–December 1986): 21–22.

"*The Grand Failure: The Birth and Death of Communism in the Twentieth Century* by Zbigniew Brzezinski." *Commonweal*, May 19, 1989, 309–310.

"*Pledging Allegiance: The Last Campaign of the Cold War* by Sidney Blumenthal." *Commonweal*, February 22, 1991, 139–140.

"*The True and Only Heaven: Progress and Its Critics* by Christopher Lasch." *Commonweal*, April 19, 1991, 264–265.

"*Why Americans Hate Politics* by E. J. Dionne, Jr." *Commonweal*, May 17, 1991, 331–332.

"*The End of Equality* by Mickey Kaus." *Commonweal*, October 23, 1991, 20–21.

"*Poverty and Compassion: The Moral Imagination of the Late Victorians* by Gertrude Himmelfarb." *Commonweal*, February 14, 1992, 24–25.

"Democracy and Power in America: *The Democratic Wish: Popular Participation and the Limits of American Government* by James A. Morone." *Review of Politics* 54, no. 2 (Spring 1992): 29–32.

"*Mystic Chords of Memory* by Michael Kammen." *Commonweal*, April 10, 1992, 20–21.

"*America's Constitutional Soul* by Harvey C. Mansfield, Jr." *Political Theory* 20, no. 3 (August 1992): 518–523.

"*The Debate on the Constitution: Federalist and Antifederalist Speeches, Articles and Letters during the Struggle over Ratification*, ed. Bernard Bailyn." *Commonweal*, December 17, 1993.

"*The Constitution in the Courts: Law or Politics?* by Michael J. Perry." *Commonweal*, July 15, 1994, 27–29.

"The Populist Persuasion: *An American History* by Michael Kazin." *Commonweal*, June 2, 1995, 24–25.

"Night of the Living Progressives" (a review of *They Only Look Dead* by E. J. Dionne, Jr.). *In These Times*, March 4, 1996, 34–35.

"True Believer" (a review of *Reason to Believe* by Mario Cuomo). *In These Times*, March 18, 1996, 35–36.

"*The End of the Republican Era* by Theodore J. Lowi." *Review of Politics* 58, no. 3 (Summer 1996): 597–601.

"Humanity and Nobility: *The Humanity of Thucydides* by Clifford Orwin." *American Scholar*, Summer 1996, 465–467.

"*The One and the Many: America's Struggle for the Common Good* by Martin E. Marty; *The New Golden Rule: Community and Morality in Democratic Society* by Amitai Etzioni." *Commonweal*, August 15, 1997, 24–25.

"*Big Trouble* by J. Anthony Lukas." *Commonweal*, January 30, 1998, 20–21.

"Pretty and Pink: *Tricky Dick and the Pink Lady: Richard Nixon vs. Helen Gahagan Douglas—Sexual Politics and the Red Scare, 1950* by Greg Mitchell." *In These Times*, March 22, 1998, 24.

"*Dead Center: Clinton-Gore Leadership and the Perils of Moderation* by James MacGregor Burns and Georgia J. Sorenson." *Commonweal*, April 21, 2000, 26–27.

"*American Pharaoh: Richard J. Daley—His Battle for Chicago and the Nation* by Adam Cohen and Elizabeth Taylor." *San Francisco Chronicle*, July 16, 2000.

"Let It Bleed: A Writer Examines the Liberal Legacy of His Forefathers—*Blood of the Liberals* by George Packer." *San Francisco Chronicle Literary Guide*, August 27–September 2, 2000, 1–6.

"*Down and Dirty: The Plot to Steal the Presidency* by Jake Tapper." *Washington Post Book World*, April 29–May 5, 2001, 4.

"To the Extreme" (review of *Before the Storm: Barry Goldwater and the Unmaking of the American Consensus* by Rick Perlstein). *In These Times*, July 23, 2001, 22–23.

"Up from Postmodernism: *Postmodernism Rightly Understood: The Return to Realism in American Thought* by Peter Augustine Lawler." *Intercollegiate Review* 37, no. 1 (Fall 2001): 45–48.

"*On Two Wings: Humble Faith and Common Sense at the American Founding* by Michael Novak." *Commonweal*, February 22, 2002, 21–22.

"Against the Tide: *Crashing the Party: How to Tell the Truth and Still Run for President* by Ralph Nader; *Spoiling for a Fight: Third Party Politics in America* by Micah L. Sifry." *Washington Post Book World*, February 24–March 2, 2002, 8.

"*War without End: Cultural Conflict and the Struggle for America's Political Future* by Robert Shogan." *Commonweal*, October 25, 2002, 24–25.

"*We Report, and We Decide: What Liberal Media? The Truth about Bias and the News* by Eric Alterman." *Commonweal*, May 9, 2003, 34–35.

"That Old-Time Religion: *Theology in America: Christian Thought from the Age of the Puritans to the Civil War* by E. Brooks Holifield." *Claremont Review of Books* 4, no. 3 (Summer 2004): 33–34.

Coauthored Articles and Papers

"Uncle Sam Vanishes." *New University Thought* 50 (Summer 1961): 61–68, with John Schaar.

"Student Leaders and Campus Apathy." *The Nation* 193, no. 8 (September 16, 1961): 155–157, with Steven Roberts.

"The Migrant Worker and the Technological Revolution." *Intercollegian* 81, no. 5 (March 1964): 4–8, with Jonathan Eisen.

"Pan-Africanism and the Dilemmas of National Development." *Phylon* 23 (Spring 1964): 44–64, with Jonathon Wise Polier. Reprinted in *Crisis and Continuity in World Politics: Readings in International Relations*, ed. George A. Lanyi and Wilson Carey McWilliams. New York: Random House, 1966.

"Uncle Sam's Stepchildren." *The Activist* 5, no. 1 (January 1965): 7–10, with John Schaar.

"The Vietnam Protest: Are the Liberals Listening?" *Commonweal*, December 17, 1965, 333–336, with Dennis Hale.

"Spain and Vietnam. Comparing Two Civil Wars." *Commonweal*, September 16, 1966, 575–578, with Dennis Hale.

"John Steinbeck, Writer." *Commonweal*, May 9, 1969, 229–230, with Nancy R. McWilliams.

"The Year of the Losers: Liberalism Has Failed to Provide the 'New Politics' Which America Demands and Desperately Needs—A Politics of Dignity." *Commonweal*, November 27, 1970, 214–216, with Henry Plotkin and William Stevenson.

"Military Honor after Mylai." *Worldview* 15, no. 1 (January 1972): 39–46, with Henry Plotkin.

"The Private World of Political Science Journals." *Change* 6, no. 7 (September 1974): 53–55, with Alan M. Cohen.

"The Historic Reputation of American Business." *Journal of Contemporary Business* 5, no. 4 (Fall 1976): 1–18, with Henry A. Plotkin.

"Political Theory and People's Right to Know." In *Government Secrecy in Democracy*, ed. Itzhak Galnoor. New York: Harper Colophon Books, 1977, 3–21, with Dennis Bathory.

"Political Leadership in Contemporary America: A Theoretical Analysis." *Asian Perspective: A Biannual Journal of Regional and International Affairs* 4, no. 1 (Spring–Summer 1980): 31–53, with Dennis Bathory.

"On Political Edification, Eloquence and Memory." *PS* 17, no. 2 (Spring 1984): 203–210, with Marc K. Landy.

"Civic Education in an Uncivil Culture." *Society*, March–April 1985, 52–55, with Marc Landy.

"Freedom, Civic Virtue, and the Failure of Our Constitution." *Freedom at Issue* 84 (May–June 1985): 12–16, with Dennis Hale and Marc Landy.

"The Idea of Representation and Its Critics in the Liberal Tradition." *Extensions,* Fall 1985, 3–13, with conference participants Ross M. Lence, Harvey C. Mansfield, and Gordon Wood and conference codirectors Don Maletz (moderator) and Ron Peters. Reprinted in *Humanities Interview* 3, no. 4 (Winter 1985): 1–12.

"The Constitutional Convention and the Founding Principles." In *Principles of Constitutional Order: The Ratification Debates*, ed. Robert L. Utley, Jr., and Patricia B. Gray. Lanham, Md.: University Press of America, 1989, 11–32, with Dennis Hale.

"The 1988 Election and the Decline of Citizenship." *Political Chronicle* 2, no. 1 (1990): 1–9, with J. Clifford Fox.

"Pluralism and the Education of the Spirit." In *Debating Moral Education: Rethinking the Role of the Modern University*, ed. J. Peter Euben and Elizabeth Kiss. Durham, N.C.: Duke University Press, 2009, 125–139, with Susan J. McWilliams.

Books

The Idea of Fraternity in America. Berkeley: University of California Press, 1973.

The Politics of Disappointment: American Elections 1976–1994. Chatham, N.J.: Chatham House Publishers, 1995.

Beyond the Politics of Disappointment: American Elections 1980–1998. New York: Seven Bridges Press, 1999.

The Democratic Soul: A Wilson Carey McWilliams Reader, ed. Patrick J. Deneen and Susan J. McWilliams. Lexington: University Press of Kentucky, 2011.

Edited and Coedited Books

Garrisons and Government: Politics and the Military in New States. New York: Chandler, 1967.

Crisis and Continuity in World Politics: Readings in International Relations, coedited with George A. Lanyi. New York: Random House, 1966, 2nd ed. 1973.

The Federalists, the Anti-Federalists and the American Political Tradition, coedited with Michael T. Gibbons. Westport, Conn.: Greenwood Press, 1992.

The Active Society Revisited. Lanham, Md.: Rowman & Littlefield, 2005.

Textbook

American Government, with Ross K. Baker and Gerald R. Pomper. New York: Macmillan, 1983.

Introductions and Afterwords

"Introduction." *Garrisons and Government: Politics and the Military in New States*, ed. Wilson Carey McWilliams. New York: Chandler, 1967, 1–41.

"Foreword." *The Nature of Politics: Selected Essays of Bertrand de Jouvenel*, ed. Dennis Hale and Marc Landy. New York: Schocken Books, 1987, vii–xi.

"Afterword." *Ratifying the Constituion*, ed. Michael Allen Gillespie and Michael Lienesch. Lawrence: University Press of Kansas, 1989, 391–400.

"Introduction." *The Glasnost Reader*, ed. Jonathan Eisen. New York: New American Library, 1990, xiii–xvii.

"Introduction." *The Constitution of the People: Reflections on Citizens and Civil Society*, ed. Robert E. Calvert. Lawrence: University Press of Kansas, 1991, 1–17.

"Foreword." *A Soviet Postmortem: Philosophical Roots of the "Grand Failure,"* by Sigmund Krancberg. Lanham, Md.: Rowman & Littlefield, 1994, xi–xv.

"Introduction: Carey McWilliams and Anti-Semitism." *A Mask for Privilege,* by Carey McWilliams. New Brunswick, N.J.: Transaction, 1999, ix–xxii.

"Preface." *Fool's Paradise: A Carey McWilliams Reader*. Berkeley, Calif.: Clapperstick Institute, 2001, ix–xvii.

"Preface." *Democracy and the Claims of Nature: Critical Perspectives for a New Century*, ed. Ben A. Minteer and Bob Pepperman Taylor. Lanham, Md.: Rowman & Littlefield, 2002, vii–viii.

"Introduction." *The Active Society Revisited*, ed. Wilson Carey McWilliams. Lanham, Md.: Rowman & Littlefield, 2005, 1–12.

Encyclopedia Entries

"Calhoun," "Fraternity," "Hamilton." In *Blackwell Encyclopedia of Political Thought*, ed. David Miller. New York: Oxford University Press, 1987, 54–55, 162–163, 191–192.

"Cleveland, Grover," "Malory, Sir Thomas," "Machiavelli," "Politics, Mark Twain's Involvement in." In *The Mark Twain Encyclopedia*, ed. J. R. LeMaster and James D. Wilson. New York: Garland Publishing, 1993, 164–165, 479–480, 483–484, 586–589.

"Adams, John," "Antifederalists," and "Federalists." In *The Encyclopedia of Democracy*, ed. Seymour M. Lipset. Washington, D.C.: Congressional Quarterly, 1995, 11–12, 69–70, 482–485.

INDEX

Abbott, Lyman, 52
abortion, 124, 139, 151, 187
Ackerman, Bruce, 276n35, 278n68, 278n73
Adair, Douglas, 264n21
Adams, Henry, 169, 265n24
Adams, John
  conservatism and, 169, 182, 186
  on equality, 169–170
  on public life, 169
  on self-preservation, 223
Adams, Samuel, 44, 128
administrative state, 105, 268n107
adultery, 269n26, 279n82. *See also* marriage
affirmative action, 134, 280n104
"Agrippa" (Anti-Federalist), 20, 252n36, 254n50
Ahlstrom, Sydney, 234n6, 241n119
Alford, Robert, 287n8
Allardt, Erik, 150–151
Almond, Gabriel, 291n3
ambition
  American framers on, 18, 75, 92, 97, 16
  Anti-Federalists on, 216, 256n72
  capitalism and, 188
  equality and, 126
  in small states, 14, 24, 216
American character, 169, 196, 220, 224–229. *See also* character
American dream, 275n27
American founders. *See* Anti-Federalists; Federalists; framers of the Constitution
American framers. *See* Anti-Federalists; Federalists; framers of the Constitution
American Tobacco Co. v. Patterson, 276n38
Ames, Fisher, 251n14
Anderson, Charles, 286n61
Anderson, Quentin, 241n121
Angell, Wayne, 275n18
Anti-Federalists
  Bill of Rights and, 72, 77, 186, 253n43
  on citizenship, 20, 22, 77, 81, 185
  on civic education, 20, 78–79, 86, 186, 215–216, 223, 246n50, 254n56
  on civic virtue, 20, 22, 78, 86, 254n54
  on commerce, 185, 256n72
  on community, 20, 79–81, 86, 185, 253n40

on the Constitution, 20, 22–23, 75, 77, 81, 84, 185, 216, 255n61, 258n83, 259n95
on democracy, 20, 23, 78, 83, 185
on dignity, 79, 82
diversity among, 20
on education, 186, 215, 223, 254n56
on elections, 22, 79, 86, 256n73, 258n85, 260n98
on equality, 20, 80, 215–216, 261n109
on the executive, 85
Federalists and, 20–21, 23, 75, 77, 223
on government, 20, 78–79, 254n51, 258n83
on human nature, 78, 186, 253n40, 254n51, 255n58, 261n109
on innovation, 185
on juries, 185, 253n44, 259n92, 260n101
on justice, 77
on large republics, 79–80, 82, 84, 186, 216, 256n65, 259n95
on liberty, 20, 76–78, 185, 246n60, 254n54, 258n83
on locality, 20–23, 72, 79–82, 185, 216, 252n26, 256n67, 257n81, 259n92
on manners, 23, 256n65
on monarchy, 254n54
on mystery, 216
on morality, 20, 78, 223, 246n50, 254n55
on parties, 83–86, 261n109
on political friendship, 80, 83, 85, 257n79
on politics, 20, 22, 76–77, 216
on reason, 215, 253n40
on religion, 20, 75, 77, 216, 223, 255n56
on representation, 21, 72, 75, 77, 79–86, 185, 248n5, 252n26, 257n74, 257n75, 257n76, 257n77, 257n79, 258n81, 258n85, 259n88, 260n104
rhetoric of, 20, 22, 76, 233n50, 253n43
on rights, 20, 76, 185, 215, 223, 246n60
on speech, 83
on stability, 185, 255n61
on standing armies, 253n49, 254n54, 258n83
Tocqueville and, 24, 186
on virtue, 75, 78, 81, 215, 254n54, 254n55

311

friendship
  citizenship and, 27, 196, 231n12
  civic education and, 196
  in contemporary America, 27, 104, 213
  democracy and, 28, 231n12
  dependence and, 158
  dignity and, 213
  equality and, 158
  faith and, 270n43
  freedom and, 136, 147
  locality and, 171
  parties and, 25, 205
  politics and, 12, 147, 196
  representation and, 80, 83, 85, 86,
    257n79
Frost, Robert, 155–156
frugality
  democracy and, 165–166
  liberty and, 65
  Montesquieu on, 165–166
  Niles on, 65
Frye, Northrop, 234n1

Galbraith, John Kenneth, 268n108
Galston, William, 278n75, 278n79,
  286n54, 293n33
Gandhi, Mohandas Karamchand
  (Mahatma), 281n119
Gehlen, Arnold, 141
Gehringer, R. E., 232n19
Gibbons v. Ogden, 23
Gideon v. Wainwright, 277n53
Gilbert and Sullivan, 215
Gilder, George, 107
Ginsberg, Robert, 166, 244n22
Glendon, Mary Ann, 286n41
globalism, 229
Gluck, Peter, 289n31
Godfather, The, 247n88
Goldberg v. Kelly, 276n36
Goldman, Eric, 53, 242n146, 286n59
Goldman, Perry M., 262n125, 289n35
Goldman, Solomon, 235n18
Gondoliers, The, 215
Gooding v. Wilson, 280n98
Gordon, Thomas, 249n6
Goudzwaard, Bob, 242n148
Grand Inquisitor, 211–212
Grant, Ruth, 243n11
Great Depression, 199, 205
Grimsley, Kristin Downey, 229
Griswold v. Connecticut, 124

Grossman, Joel, 280n103
Grotius, Hugo, 270n54
Grovey v. Townsend, 287n2

Haines, Charles G., 285n29
Hale, Dennis B., 289n37
Hallaman, Arthur, 242n148
Hallowell, John, 237n53, 271n84
Hamilton, Alexander
  on ancient republics, 96, 250n13
  on commerce, 93, 98, 132, 170, 184,
    266n57
  on consent, 128
  Constitution and, 20
  on employment, 132
  on equality, 170
  on the executive, 84–85, 261n120,
    262n121
  on human nature, 249n6, 250n10,
    254n55, 273n5
  on large republics, 19, 75, 251n13,
    256n65
  on liberty, 19, 128, 132, 170
    274n5
  on manufacture, 266n57
  on natural rights, 273n5
  public life and, 169
  on representation, 75
  scientific and technological thought of,
    93
  on size of state, 19
  on virtue, 75
  on wealth, 170
Hammond, Phillip E., 39
Hare, R. M., 277n51
Harlan, John, 142, 279n88
Haroutunian, Joseph, 244n31
Harrington, James, 247n76
Harrington, Michael, 275n24
Hartz, Louis, 181–182, 234n2, 268n4,
  287n3
Hatch, Nathan, 240n110, 245n47
Hawthorne, Nathaniel
  "Celestial Railroad, The," 46
  Marble Faun, The, 290n1
  Scarlet Letter, The, 30
  on scientific and technological thought,
    46–47
  on scripture, 32
Hayden, Tom, 214
Haynie, Kerry, 292n30
Hegel, Georg W. F., 232n25

Index

pursuit of truth and, 217, 290n4
science and, 218–219
technology and, 219

National Labor Relations Board v. Jones and Laughlin Steel Corporation, 233n65
nature. *See* human nature
Needham, Robin, 234n10, 237n48
Neumann, Franz, 276n39
Neumann, Sigmund, 288n23
Neustadt, Richard, 290n9
Neville, Robert, 114
Newberry v. United States, 287n2
"new science of politics," 18, 23, 40, 161, 183–184, 218
Nicgorski, Walter, 231n2
Nicolson, Harold, 280n101
Niebuhr, H. Richard, 238n72, 240n108, 241n132
Niebuhr, Reinhold, 37, 286n52, 292n16
Niemi, Richard, 289n42
Nietzsche, Friedrich, 141, 191, 291n23
Niles, Nathaniel
    Bellamy's influence on, 245n48, 245n49
    biography of, 245n47
    on civic education, 63, 65
    on community, 63
    on government, 66
    Harrington's influence on, 247n76
    on liberalism, 63, 66–67
    on liberty, 63–66, 69, 245n54, 246n66, 246n69
    on love, 64
    on majority rule, 246n70
    on politics, 65, 67, 246n64
    on religion, 63
    on sacrifice, 64
    on secularism, 64
    on slavery, 66
Niles, Samuel, 245n47
Nixon, Richard, 177, 213
Norton, Anne, 285n34
Nozick, Robert, 140, 188–189

obedience
    of the body, 15
    citizenship and, 197
    freedom and, 45
    large republics and, 14, 19
obligation
    American framers on, 15–16, 167, 171, 190, 223, 272n4, 273n5

in the biblical tradition, 53, 119
citizenship and, 60, 229
in contemporary America, 135, 137, 151, 187, 229
equality and, 230
faith and, 109
freedom and, 13
individualism and, 135
in liberal political thought, 58, 121–123, 219, 224, 250n12
love and, 135
parties and, 204, 207
rights and, 230
trust and, 108, 122
O'Brien v. Brown, 262n129
Ogden v. Saunders, 271n75
Olson, Mancur, 232n17, 287n7
Oppenheim, A. L., 237n46
Oppenheim, Lassa, 237n65
organizational power
    in contemporary America, 129, 137
    inequalities of, 26
    large-scale, 26, 129, 133, 137, 219
    technology and, 151
Orwell, George, 281n119

Paine, Thomas
    on democracy, 168
    on equality, 167
    on human nature, 57, 167–168
    on independence, 57
    on mastery, 43, 138, 177–178, 239n88
    on property, 283n53
    religion and, 41–43, 57, 109, 239n88, 277n63
    on representation, 168
Pangle, Thomas, 239n79, 248n6
partiality, 12–13, 33, 46, 73, 147, 197, 232n25
parties
    American framers and, 84–85, 103, 181, 199–200
    in American law, 195
    in American political thought, 199–205
    caucuses and, 209
    civic education and, 25, 196, 199, 202, 204–207
    civic virtue and, 25, 202, 204–205
    Constitution and, 195
    in contemporary America, 27–28, 86, 204–210
    Democratic party, in America, 208

Warren, Mercy Otis
 on civic virtue, 254n55, 261n109
 on commerce, 256n72
 on elections, 258n85
 on equality, 261n109
 on parties, 83, 261n109
Warren, Robert Penn, 242n149
"A Watchman" (Anti-Federalist), 75
Watergate, 213
wealth
 American framers on, 60, 82, 93–95, 97,
  170–171
 Anti-Federalists on, 259n95, 261n109
 conservatism and, 187
 in contemporary America, 26, 103,
  131–132, 189, 191–192
 democracy and, 14
 elections and, 22, 259n95
 equality and, 60
 individualism and, 35
 inequalities of, 26, 103, 189, 191–192
 large republics and, 82, 259n95
 in liberal political thought, 165
 lure of sudden riches and, 131–132,
  275n27
 and organizational power, 26–27
 religion and, 90
 small state and, 14
 work and, 131–132
Webking, Robert, 273n4
Webster, Noah, 249n8
Weinstein, W. L., 281n111
Wellhausen, Julius, 31
West, John G., 247n97

West, Samuel, 56–57
West Coast Hotel v. Parrish, 276n31
Whigs
 Jefferson on, 181
 Niles on, 67
 Van Buren and, 201–202
 Wilson, Woodrow, on, 262n122
White, Howard, 139
Whitman, Walt, 148, 228
Whitney v. California, 279n91
Williams, Bernard, 152–153
Wilson, James, 74–75, 96, 167, 184,
  248n6, 251n13, 266n52
Wilson, James Q., 290n56
Wilson, Woodrow, 262n122, 262n124,
  262n126
Winthrop, Delba, 11
Winthrop, John, 59–60, 224
Wise, John, 62
Witherspoon, John, 245n51
Wolfe, Alan, 242n3, 293n35
Wolin, Sheldon, 243n9, 244n26, 264n23,
  267n106, 268n107, 285n24, 287n69
Wood, Gordon, 44, 169
work. *See* employment; labor
Wright, Nathalia, 234n5

Yarbrough, Jean, 248n3
Young, Alfred F., 20

Zeno, 151
Zetterbaum, Marvin, 267n105, 279n80,
  287n67
Zuckert, Michael, 55–61